Heidegger, Art, and Postmodernity

Heidegger, Art, and Postmodernity offers a radical new interpretation of Heidegger's later philosophy, developing his argument that art can help lead humanity beyond the nihilistic ontotheology of the modern age. Providing pathbreaking readings of Heidegger's "The Origin of the Work of Art" and his notoriously difficult *Contributions to Philosophy (From Enowning)*, this book explains precisely what postmodernity meant for Heidegger, the greatest philosophical critic of modernity, and what it could still mean for us today. Exploring these issues, Iain D. Thomson examines several postmodern works of art, including music, literature, painting, and even comic books, from a post-Heideggerian perspective. Clearly written and accessible, this book will help readers gain a deeper understanding of Heidegger and his relation to postmodern theory, popular culture, and art.

Iain D. Thomson is Professor of Philosophy at the University of New Mexico, where he also serves as Director of Graduate Studies. He is the author of *Heidegger on Ontotheology: Technology and the Politics of Education* (Cambridge, 2005), and his articles have appeared in numerous scholarly journals, essay collections, and reference works.

T0364201

Heidegger, Art, and Postmodernity

IAIN D. THOMSON

University of New Mexico

CAMBRIDGE
UNIVERSITY PRESS

CAMBRIDGE UNIVERSITY PRESS
Cambridge, New York, Melbourne, Madrid, Cape Town,
Singapore, São Paulo, Delhi, Tokyo, Mexico City

Cambridge University Press
32 Avenue of the Americas, New York, NY 10013-2473, USA

www.cambridge.org
Information on this title: www.cambridge.org/9780521172493

First published 2011
Reprinted 2011

A catalog record for this publication is available from the British Library.

Library of Congress Cataloging in Publication Data

Thomson, Iain D. (Iain Donald), 1968–
   Heidegger, art, and postmodernity / Iain D. Thomson.
      p.   cm.
   Includes bibliographical references (p.   ) and index.
   ISBN 978-1-107-00150-3 (hardback) – ISBN 978-0-521-17249-3 (pbk.)
   1. Heidegger, Martin, 1889–1976.   2. Arts – Philosophy.   3. Postmodernism.
   I. Title.
   B3279.H49T478   2011
   193–dc22   2010040285

ISBN 978-1-107-00150-3 Hardback
ISBN 978-0-521-17249-3 Paperback

For Mungo, an artist who still amazes after more than forty years;
and for Kirsten, whose love discloses life's beauty every day.

At times of despair, we must learn to see with new eyes.

Desmond Tutu, *Believe*

It is enough to say that we understand in a *different* way, *if we understand at all*.

Hans-Georg Gadamer, *Truth and Method*

It would be necessary, in sum, to choose between art and death.

Jacques Derrida, *Copy, Archive, Signature*

Contents

Illustrations

Acknowledgments

More than a decade teaching hermeneutic phenomenology in the high desert has taught me that a sense of real community is a rare and precious thing, especially for those of us caught between the established philosophical territories – *coyotes*, as we say in New Mexico, that is, border-crossers, smugglers, tricksters – "too continental" for the narrowly analytic, "too analytic" for the ideologically continental. Stealing across the desert, coyotes sometimes run afoul of the philosophical border patrol (self-appointed, self-righteous, and aggressively exclusionary toward those who dare to cross their arbitrary lines in the sand), but that is the price we pay to discover the stark freedom of the new expanse and the joy of finding our own paths. Those of us who do not feel entirely at home on either side of the continental-analytic divide, moreover, may take some comfort from the thought that the best way to move beyond such outdated territorial divisions is simply to populate the borderlands, thereby helping to create something more livable for the future. That task is no pipe dream, but (as I suggested at the end of *Heidegger on Ontotheology*) it can only be accomplished by communities of *individuals* (birds not of a feather who nevertheless flock together – from time to time). I feel truly fortunate to have received generous help from more unique and irreplaceable individuals (and the living communities they compose) than I can hope to thank here. Their thoughts made this book much better, so the problems that remain I happily claim as my own.

Heidegger, Art, and Postmodernity is composed in large part of significantly revised and expanded materials first presented and published elsewhere, and I heartily thank all those whose thoughtful responses helped improve the work along the way, as well as those who originally published my work and allowed me to make use of it here. Chapter 1 began as a lecture delivered first to the Philosophy Department at Colorado College in their J. Glenn Gray colloquium series (7 February 2008), and then to the International Society for Phenomenological Studies (19 July 2008), and will be included in an abbreviated form in Daniel Dahlstrom, ed., *Interpreting Heidegger: New Essays*. For their helpful comments and criticisms on this chapter, I am especially grateful to Anne-Margaret Baxley, Kelly Becker, William Blattner, Ian Bogost, William Bracken, Taylor Carman, David Cerbone, Benjamin Crowe, Steven Crowell, Daniel Dahlstrom, Hubert Dreyfus, Manfred Frings, Rick Furtak, John Haugeland, Stephan Käufer, Jonathan Lee, Paul Livingston, Béatrice Longuenesse, Joachim Oberst, Robert Pippin, John Riker, Joseph Schear, Joeri Schrivers, Thomas Sheehan, Charles Siewert, Carolyn Thomas, and Mark Wrathall.

Chapter 2 was originally presented as the Gale Memorial Lecture to the Department of Art and Art History at the University of New Mexico (17 November 2008), Chapter 3 to the International Society for Phenomenological Studies, in Asilomar, California (21 July 2009). A shorter version of both was published as the entry on "Heidegger's Aesthetics" in Edward N. Zalta, ed., *The Stanford Encyclopedia of Philosophy*. (That piece contains links to some other art images that I could not afford to include here.) For helpful responses to these chapters, I would like to thank Kelly Becker, David Craven, Benjamin Crowe, Steven Crowell, Hubert Dreyfus, Jesús Adrián Escudero, Manfred Frings, Rick Furtak, Charles Guignon, Allison Hagerman, Brent Kalar, Jonathan Lear, Joachim Oberst, Mark Okrent, Tao Raspoli, Matthew Ratcliffe, James Reid, Joseph Rouse, Carl Sachs, Joseph Schear, Matthew Shockey, Gino Signoracci, Robert Stolorow, Tina Tahir, Mungo Thomson, Mark Wrathall, several anonymous referees, as well as the other participants of the inaugural meeting of the Southwest Seminar in Continental Philosophy, who heard parts of Chapter 3 here in Albuquerque, New Mexico (28 May 2010).

Thanks again to Mark Wrathall for the enthusiastic invitation to write the essay that formed the basis of Chapter 4, as well as for his many valuable suggestions about U2; an earlier version was published (under the same title) in *U2 and Philosophy: How to Decipher an Atomic Band*, Mark A. Wrathall, editor; © 2006 Carus Publishing. Here thanks also go to Anne Margaret Baxley, Francisco Gallegos, Sara Amber Rawls, and Christian Wood for sharing their insights. Chapter 6, the work of oldest vintage here, was originally written in the mid-1990s (and included in my 1999 dissertation); an early version was presented to the 21st annual "Heidegger Symposium" at the University of North Texas in Denton (20 April 2001) and published as "The Philosophical Fugue: Understanding the Structure and Goal of Heidegger's *Beiträge*," *Journal of the British Society for Phenomenology* 34: 57–73, Wolfe Mays, editor; © 2003 British Society for Phenomenology. I would especially like to thank Keith Wayne Brown, Taylor Carman, Gerald Doppelt, Hubert Dreyfus, Michael Eldred, Manfred Frings, Ted Kisiel, Edward Lee, Ken Maly, Wayne Martin, Rajesh Sampath, Ananda Spike-Turner, and Tracy Strong for thoughtful responses.

Chapter 5 was first presented to a Philosophy Department Colloquium at the University of New Mexico (25 April 2003) and later delivered to the International Society for Phenomenological Studies (26 July 2010). It first appeared as "Deconstructing the Hero" in *Comics as Philosophy*, Jeff McLaughlin, editor; © 2005 University Press of Mississippi. Special thanks to Anne Margaret Baxley, Kelly Becker, William Blattner, Bill Bracken, David Carr, David Cerbone, Steven Crowell, Hubert Dreyfus, Kevin Hill, Brent Kalar, Stephan Käufer, Mark Lance, Leslie MacAvoy, Irene McMullin, Joe Schear, Kirsten Thomson, Mungo Thomson, Kate Withy, Gideon Yafee, and Chris Young for insights and critique, and especially to Jeff McLaughlin for encouraging me to write it in the first place. Chapter 7 was originally presented at the French Parliament of Philosophers' international colloquium on "Heidegger: The Danger and the Promise" at the University of Strasbourg, France (4 December 2004), and was published with a different introduction as "Understanding Technology Ontotheologically, or: The Danger and the Promise of Heidegger, an American Perspective," in *New Waves in Philosophy of Technology*, Jan-Kyrre Berg Olsen, Evan Selinger, and Søren Riis, editors. In addition to the editors, I would like to thank Anne Margaret Baxley, Kelly Becker, Joseph Cohen, Jacques Derrida, Hubert Dreyfus, Peter Gordon, Don Ihde, Carlos Sanchez, Gianni Vattimo, Samuel Weber, Mark Wrathall, and Holger Zaborowski for their critique and encouragement.

I am also grateful for the support of my colleagues at UNM. In addition to those already mentioned, thanks especially to Andy Burgess, John Bussanich, Brenda Claiborne, Mary Domski, Felipe Gonzales, Russell Goodman, Barbara Hannan, Richard Hayes, Adrian Johnston, Paul Schmidt, John Taber, and Hector Torres. I feel proud to belong to such a diverse, rigorous, and friendly philosophical community. I also owe debts of gratitude to the College of Arts and Science at UNM and to the National Endowment for the Humanities for generous research support. I hope the many wonderful students in my Heidegger seminars will forgive being thanked collectively: I have learned more with and from you than I can possibly recount here. I find myself deeply grateful once again to my editors and referees at Cambridge University Press for their enthusiasm for and care of my book. In these strange days of glut and its blight ("the wasteland grows"), I hope we can find ways to transcend the enframing of books together.

Finally, to all my teachers, students, friends, family, and countless other philosophical interlocutors, named and unnamed: I could not have done this without you. As Heidegger saw, thinking *is* thanking, our best way of responding to what we are given. So, until we can think together in person again, please let this book serve as my humble *thanks*.

Abbreviations Used for Works by Heidegger
(Translations frequently modified)

BC   *Basic Concepts.* G. E. Aylesworth, trans. Bloomington: Indiana University Press, 1993.

BQP   *Basic Questions of Philosophy: Selected "Problems" of "Logic."* R. Rojcewicz and A. Schuwer, trans. Bloomington: Indiana University Press, 1994.

BT   *Being and Time.* J. Macquarrie and E. Robinson, trans. New York: Harper & Row, 1962.

CP   *Contributions to Philosophy (From Enowning).* P. Emad and K. Maly, trans. Bloomington: Indiana University Press, 1999.

CPC   *Country Path Conversations.* B. Davis, trans. Bloomington: Indiana University Press, 2010.

EP   *The End of Philosophy.* J. Stambaugh, trans. New York: Harper & Row, 1973.

DT   *Discourse on Thinking.* J. Anderson and E. Freund, trans. New York: Harper & Row, 1966.

EHP   *Elucidations of Hölderlin's Poetry.* K. Hoeller, trans. New York: Humanity Books, 2000.

ET   *The Essence of Truth.* T. Sadler, trans. London: Continuum, 2002.

FCM   *The Fundamental Concepts of Metaphysics: World, Finitude, Solitude.* W. McNeill and N. Walker, trans. Bloomington: Indiana University Press, 1995.

FS   *Four Seminars.* A. Mitchell and François Raffoul, trans. Bloomington: Indiana University Press, 2003.

G   *Gelassenheit.* Pfulligen: Neske, 1959.

GA1   *Gesamtausgabe,* Vol. 1: *Frühe Schriften.* F.-W. von Herrmann, ed. Frankfurt: V. Klostermann, 1978.

GA3   *Gesamtausgabe,* Vol. 3: *Kant und das Problem der Metaphysik.* F.-W. von Herrmann, ed. Frankfurt: V. Klostermann, 1991.

GA4   *Gesamtausgabe*, Vol. 4: *Erläuterungen zu Hölderlins Dichtung.*
           F.-W. von Herrmann, ed. Frankfurt: V. Klostermann,
           1981.
GA5   *Gesamtausgabe*, Vol. 5: *Holzwege.* F.-W. von Herrmann, ed.
           Frankfurt: V. Klostermann, 1977.
GA7   *Gesamtausgabe* Vol. 7: *Vorträge und Aufsätze.* F.-W. von
           Herrmann, ed. Frankfurt: V. Klostermann, 2000.
GA8   *Gesamtausgabe* Vol. 8: *Was Heißt Denken?* P.-L. Coriando, ed.
           Frankfurt: V. Klostermann, 2002.
GA9   *Gesamtausgabe* Vol. 9: *Wegmarken.* F.-W. von Herrmann, ed.
           Frankfurt: V. Klostermann, 1976.
GA11   *Gesamtausgabe* Vol. 11: *Identiät und Differenz.* F.-W. von
           Herrmann, ed. Frankfurt: V. Klostermann, 2006.
GA13   *Gesamtausgabe* Vol. 13: *Aus der Erfahrung des Denkens,*
           1910–1976. H. Heidegger, ed. Frankfurt: V. Klostermann,
           1983.
GA14   *Gesamtausgabe* Vol. 14: *Zur Sache des Denkens.* F.-W. von
           Herrmann, ed. Frankfurt: V. Klostermann, 2007.
GA15   *Gesamtausgabe*, Vol. 15: *Seminare.* C. Ochwadt, ed. Frankfurt:
           V. Klostermann, 1986.
GA16   *Gesamtausgabe* Vol. 16: *Reden und andere Zeugnisse eines
           Lebensweges, 1910–1976.* H. Heidegger, ed. Frankfurt:
           V. Klostermann, 2000.
GA20   *Gesamtausgabe*, Vol. 20: *Prolegomena zur Geschichte des Zeitbegriffs.*
           P. Jaeger, ed. Frankfurt: V. Klostermann, 1979.
GA29–30   *Gesamtausgabe*, Vol. 29–30: *Die Grundbegriffe der Metaphysik:
           Welt, Endlichkeit, Einsamkeit.* F.-W. von Herrmann, ed.
           Frankfurt: V. Klostermann, 1983.
GA34   *Gesamtausgabe*, Vol. 34: *Vom Wesen der Wahrheit.* H. Mörchen,
           ed. Frankfurt: V. Klostermann, 1988.
GA38   *Gesamtausgabe*, Vol. 38: *Logik als die Frage nach dem Wesen der
           Sprache.* G. Seubold, ed., Frankfurt: V. Klostermann,
           1998.
GA39   *Gesamtausgabe*, Vol. 39: *Hölderlins Hymnen "Germanien" und
           "Der Rhein."* S. Ziegler, ed., Frankfurt: V. Klostermann,
           1980.
GA40   *Gesamtausgabe*, Vol. 40. *Einführung in die Metaphysik.* P. Jaeger,
           ed. Frankfurt: V. Klostermann, 1983.
GA43   *Gesamtausgabe*, Vol. 43. *Nietzsche: Der Wille zue Macht als Kunst.*
           B. Heimbüchel, ed. Frankfurt: V. Klostermann, 1985.
GA45   *Gesamtausgabe*, Vol. 45. *Grundfragen der Philosophie: Ausgewählte
           "Probleme" der "Logik."* F.-W. von Herrmann, ed.
           Frankfurt: V. Klostermann, 1984.

GA50   *Gesamtausgabe*, Vol. 50: *Nietzsches Metaphysik*. P. Jaeger, ed. Frankfurt: V. Klostermann, 1990.

GA51   *Gesamtausgabe*, Vol. 51: *Grundbegriffe*. P. Jaeger, ed. Frankfurt: V. Klostermann, 1981.

GA65   *Gesamtausgabe*, Vol. 65: *Beiträge zur Philosophie (Vom Ereignis)*. F.-W. von Herrmann, ed. Frankfurt: V. Klostermann, 1989.

GA66   *Gesamtausgabe*, Vol. 66: *Besinnung*. F.-W. von Herrmann, ed. Frankfurt: V. Klostermann, 1997.

GA67   *Gesamtausgabe*, Vol. 67: *Metaphysik und Nihilismus*. H.-J. Friedrich, ed. Frankfurt: V. Klostermann, 1999.

GA69   *Gesamtausgabe*, Vol. 69: *Die Geschichte des Seyns*. P. Trawny, ed. Frankfurt: V. Klostermann, 1998.

GA75   *Gesamtausgabe*, Vol. 75: *Zu Hölderlin – Greichenlandreisen*. C. Ochwadt, ed. Frankfurt: V. Klostermann, 2000.

GA77   *Gesamtausgabe*, Vol. 77: *Feldweg-Gespräch*. I. Schüßler, ed. Frankfurt: V. Klostermann, 1995.

GA79   *Gesamtausgabe*, Vol. 79: *Bremer und Freiburger Vorträge*. P. Jaeger, ed. Frankfurt: V. Klostermann, 1994.

GA90   *Gesamtausgabe*, Vol. 90: *Zu Ernst Jünger*. P. Trawny, ed. Frankfurt: V. Klostermann, 2004.

HB   "Selected Letters from the Heidegger-Blochmann Correspondence." F. Edler, trans. *Graduate Faculty Philosophy Journal* 14–15 (1992): 559–77.

HBC   Heidegger, Martin, and Blochmann, Elizabeth. *Martin Heidegger-Elizabeth Blochmann, Briefwechsel 1918–1969*. J. W. Storck, ed. Marbach: Deutsche Literaturarchiv, 1989.

HCT   *History of the Concept of Time*. T. Kisiel, trans. Bloomington: Indiana University Press, 1985.

HHI   *Hölderlin's Hymn "The Ister."* W. McNeill and J. Davis, trans. Bloomington: Indiana University Press, 1996.

HR   *The Heidegger Reader*. G. Figal, ed. J. Veither, trans. Bloomington: Indiana University Press, 2009.

ID   *Identity and Difference*. J. Stambaugh, trans. New York: Harper & Row, 1969.

IM   *Introduction to Metaphysics*. G. Fried and R. Polt, trans. New Haven, CT: Yale University Press, 2000.

KPM   *Kant and the Problem of Metaphysics*. R. Taft, trans. Bloomington: Indiana University Press, 1997.

LQ   *Logic as the Question Concerning the Essence of Language*. W. T. Gregory and Y. Unna, trans. Albany: State University of New York Press, 2009.

M   *Mindfulness*. P. Emad and T. Kalary, trans. London: Continuum, 2006.

N1   *Nietzsche: The Will to Power as Art.* David Farrell Krell, ed. and
        trans. New York: Harper & Row, 1979.

N3   *Nietzsche: The Will to Power as Knowledge and as Metaphysics.* David
        Farrell Krell, ed. J. Stambaugh, D. F. Krell, and F. Capuzzi,
        trans. New York: Harper & Row, 1987.

N4   *Nietzsche: Nihilism.* David Farrell Krell, ed. F. Capuzzi, trans. New
        York: Harper & Row, 1982.

NII   *Nietzsche.* Pfullingen: G. Neske, 1961, vol. II.

OBT   *Off the Beaten Track.* J. Young and K. Haynes, eds. and trans.
        Cambridge: Cambridge University Press, 2002.

P   *Pathmarks.* William McNeill, ed. Cambridge: Cambridge
        University Press, 1998.

PLT   *Poetry, Language, Thought.* A. Hofstadter, trans. New York:
        Harper & Row, 1971.

Q&A   *Martin Heidegger and National Socialism: Questions and Answers.*
        Günther Neske and Emil Kettering, eds. L. Harries, trans.
        New York: Paragon House, 1990.

QCT   *The Question Concerning Technology.* W. Lovitt, trans. New York:
        Harper & Row, 1977.

SZ   *Sein und Zeit.* Tübingen: M. Niemeyer, 1993.

T&B   *On Time and Being.* J. Stambaugh, trans. New York: Harper &
        Row, 1972.

TTL   "Traditional Language and Technological Language." W. T.
        Gregory, trans. *Journal of Philosophical Research* XXIII (1998):
        129–45.

UK1   "Vom Ursprung des Kunstwerks: Erste Ausarbeitung." *Heidegger
        Studies* 5 (1989): 1–22.

USTS   *Überlieferte Sprache und Technische Sprache.* H. Heidegger, ed.
        St. Gallen: Erker-Verag, 1989.

WCT   *What Is Called Thinking?* J. G. Gray, trans. New York: Harper &
        Row, 1968.

A Note on the Notes (Redux)

My fondness for footnotes can be cast in a postmodern light, as demonstrating another way in which our modern desire for completeness shatters our modern striving for unity – and so suggests the impossibility of both. The juxtaposition of text and notes generates an undeniable tension, one not easily resolved. I hope this tension proves productive, so I have elected not to repress the notes by consigning them to the back of the book. Footnote people like me find endlessly flipping to the end for endnotes tiresome. For those who find detailed footnotes too distracting from the flow of the text, my perhaps obvious suggestion is: *Please do not feel compelled to read every note as you go.* If you have an unanswered question about a sentence, paragraph, or section that ends with a note (or simply want to consult the secondary references), then you should read that note. With any luck your question will be answered there (and if it is not, then you will see that in fact I do not have *enough* notes). Otherwise, I invite you to read through the remaining notes at your leisure. Some supplemental and specialized argument gets done in the notes, and some *Holzwege* – other paths and views – can be found there as well.[1]

---

[1] On the full meaning of "*Holzwege*," a crucial Heideggerian term of art, see Chapter 3, section 1.3.

Introduction

Heidegger, Art, and Postmodernity

Martin Heidegger (1889–1976) was probably the most influential philosopher of the twentieth century; certainly he remains the most controversial. This enduring controversy stems not only from Heidegger's undeniably horrendous politics, legendarily difficult prose, and profoundly challenging views, but also from the fact that a list of the major thinkers inspired by the works he wrote after *Being and Time* (1927) reads like the required table of contents for any good anthology of "contemporary continental philosophy": Giorgio Agamben, Alain Badiou, Jean Baudrillard, Maurice Blanchot, Stanley Cavell, Gilles Deleuze, Jacques Derrida, Hubert Dreyfus, Michel Foucault, Luce Irigaray, Jacques Lacan, Emmanuel Levinas, Jean-François Lyotard, Herbert Marcuse, Jacques Rancière, Richard Rorty, Charles Taylor, Gianni Vattimo, and Slavoj Žižek. For all these "postmodernists" (the heading under which this diverse group is often lumped together), Heidegger's later philosophy served as a formative influence as well as a primary point of departure. Yet, despite his immense influence, Heidegger's own philosophical attempt to articulate a postmodern understanding of being – and so help usher in a postmodern age – remains shrouded in darkness and confusion along with the other views at the heart of his later thought.[1] That is a situation this book hopes to help remedy.

Heidegger, Art, and Postmodernity serves as a happy shorthand for what I think of as this book's full title: *Heidegger Beyond Ontotheology: Art and the Possibilities of a Meaningful Postmodernity*. As that more unwieldy title more clearly suggests, this book constitutes something of a sequel to my *Heidegger*

---

[1] Pioneering investigations of this topic include Fred Dallmayr, "Democracy and Postmodernism"; Leslie Paul Thiele, *Timely Meditations: Martin Heidegger and Postmodern Politics*; and Gregory Bruce Smith, *Nietzsche, Heidegger, and the Transition to Postmodernity*. These praiseworthy works approach their topic from a more political than philosophical perspective and, despite their insightfulness, they do not uncover the ontotheological roots of Heidegger's critique of modernity and so cannot convey the full specificity of his philosophical vision of postmodernity.

on Ontotheology: Technology and the Politics of Education. There I showed how understanding the details of the later Heidegger's philosophical critique of metaphysics as "ontotheology" allows us to greatly improve our grasp of his controversial critique of technology, his appalling misadventure with Nazism, his prescient critique of the university, and his important suggestions for the future of higher education. *Heidegger on Ontotheology* showed, in other words, that *ontotheology* works like a skeleton key to Heidegger's notoriously difficult later thinking, a conceptual key that unlocks the door to the underlying structure of his later work and so allows us to understand it as much more philosophically coherent, unified, and defensible than is usually supposed. The underlying unity of Heidegger's later thinking can be seen clearly, I argued, in the fact that his diverse philosophical efforts all serve the same philosophical goal of trying to help us recognize, undermine, and transcend the nihilistic, "technological" ontotheology that continues to shape our late-modern age. Yet, if Heidegger's mature thinking is dedicated entirely to helping us uproot and transcend the ontotheological core of the late-modern age, then this immediately raises a number of pressing questions: How does Heidegger motivate the philosophical transition beyond modernity for which he calls? What specifically does he think such a genuine "postmodernity" would entail? Why does he think we late-moderns should seek such a postmodernity, and how does he think we might actually get there from here? Finally, how does Heidegger's own philosophical conception of postmodernity relate to and differ from what more typically passes under the cover of that much used and abused label?

Heidegger, Art, and Postmodernity provides answers to these important questions – and several others besides. Here I explain Heidegger's philosophical critique of our "technological" late-modernity, clarify his view that art can help lead us beyond the nihilism of the modern age, think through several "postmodern" works from a post-Heideggerian vantage point, and conclude by examining the continuing danger and promise of Heidegger's thinking in a sympathetic yet critical way. It is my hope that this book will appeal not only to those concerned to understand the profound philosophical vision at the heart of Heidegger's later work, but also to those who are more broadly interested in contemporary theorizing about art and popular culture, about which this book contains several detailed discussions. Although these discussions often focus on works rather different from the ones Heidegger himself discussed, *Heidegger, Art, and Postmodernity* continues to pursue the Heideggerian conviction that thinking through art can help guide us into the future. This book is not another vague and starry-eyed celebration of the postmodern, however, but a philosophical exploration of what exactly "postmodernity" means *for Heidegger* (undoubtedly the greatest philosophical critic of modernity), as well as a partial attempt to elaborate and defend a set of post-Heideggerian views about what a genuinely meaningful postmodernity could still be for us.

Building on the perspective developed in my earlier book, *Heidegger, Art, and Postmodernity* begins by showing that when we understand what Heidegger really means by ontotheology, then we can also see that his critical broadsides against modernity – and his complementary calls for a genuinely *postmodern* understanding of being – are not nearly as philosophically indiscriminate, empty, or unmotivated as they otherwise appear to be. The first two chapters thus show how Heidegger's philosophical critiques of the modern age follow from – and so can only really be understood in terms of – his conception of the history of Western metaphysics as a series of ontotheologically structured ways of understanding the being of entities, that is, different ways of understanding what and how entities *are*. Chapter 1 provides an overview of Heidegger's still too often misunderstood view of Western metaphysics as ontotheology, clarifying the crucial details and exploring the larger significance of this key concept of his later thought. Building on this ontotheological background, Chapter 2 turns to focus on Heidegger's critique of the modern tradition of philosophical aesthetics in particular, because it is this tradition, Heidegger suggests, that obstructs our view of the clearest path leading beyond modernity. Together, the first two chapters show how the two epochs of modernity relate to and differ from one another as crucial permutations in "the history of being," Heidegger's name for Western humanity's changing sense of what it means for something to *be* at all. Chapter 3 then develops the positive philosophical vision at the core of Heidegger's later thought by presenting a new interpretation of his minor masterpiece, "The Origin of the Work of Art." Here I show that recognizing Heidegger's ambiguous use of the "nothing" in his phenomenological interpretation of Vincent van Gogh's painting *A Paiv of Shoes* (1886) allows us to reconstruct, for the first time, the specific phenomenological insights responsible for Heidegger's conviction that thinking through art can help show us the way to a genuinely postmodern understanding of being. This central chapter of my book thus shows concretely just what postmodernity really meant for Heidegger – and what it might still mean for us today.

To explore this question of the meaning of postmodernity today, Chapters 4 and 5 take Heidegger's thinking as the point of departure for two attempts to think through distinctive works of "postmodern" art. These works are drawn from our contemporary popular culture and reflect the implicitly contested understanding of being within it. The goal of these two post-Heideggerian discussions of postmodern art, then, is to help raise, clarify, and begin to come to terms with a few of the important questions already pressing in on our late-modern age from some of its possible "postmodern" futures. Chapter 4 opens the discussion by exploring the dominant meanings the term "postmodernity" currently possesses, seeking to clarify both their relationship to and their differences from Heidegger's philosophical vision of a postmodern understanding of being. Chapter 5 then discusses one of these differences in particular, casting a critical eye over the postmodern deconstruction of the hero. By critically exploring some of the serious philosophical issues that these popular "postmodern" works raise about the nature of our contemporary age, these two chapters of (what is sometimes called) "applied Heidegger" seek to address a few of those questions every generation must face concerning what we should preserve from the past to carry with us into the future, and what we should try to leave behind.

It will be obvious, however, that I make no attempt to apply Heidegger's understanding of art to the many different aesthetic genres in any comprehensive or systematic way.[2] If my own philosophical attempts to draw out the central lessons from Heidegger's understanding of art remain relatively modest, this is perhaps in keeping with the artistic subject matter this book ranges over: Works such as Jonathan Swift's popular satire, *Gulliver's Travels*; Vincent van Gogh's much beloved painting of *A Pair of Shoes* (1886); a single hit song by the rock band U2 ("Even Better than the Real Thing"); and Alan Moore and Dave Gibbons's comic book miniseries, *Watchmen* (a genre-transforming work currently taught in universities around the world as a "masterpiece of postmodern literature"). One could say that my hermeneutic analyses focus on "low" more often than "high" art, were that not to invoke a problematic distinction that most postmodern movements begin by rejecting, preferring instead to follow in Heidegger's footsteps by bringing the most advanced theoretical tools to bear on the popular works that quietly yet pervasively shape our historical self-understanding.[3] Heidegger famously thought that we need to learn to read Nietzsche's seemingly most "literary" work, *Thus Spoke Zarathustra*, "in the same rigorous way we read one of Aristotle's treatises" (WCT 70/ GA8 75). I go one step further here by extending Heidegger's dictum even

---

[2] At best, that would mean repeating the work already carried out by Julian Young in his important book on *Heidegger's Philosophy of Art*. At worst, it would mean committing the kind of category mistake Robert Bernasconi diagnoses in "Heidegger's Displacement of the Concept of Art," in which one tries to assimilate or apply Heidegger's thinking about art to the very categories of the aesthetic tradition that, as we will see, he was in fact seeking to transcend from within.

[3] On the postmodern rejection of the distinction between fine and commercial art (most obvious in Andy Warhol's work), see Frederick Jameson, *Postmodernism, or, the Cultural Logic of Late Capitalism*, 2. The present book, however, can be understood as a sustained rebuttal of Jameson's Marxian assertion that "Heidegger's 'field path' is, after all, irredeemably and irrevocably destroyed by late capital" (34–5), a claim Jameson can maintain so confidently only by *literalizing* Heidegger's philosophical metaphor. Indeed, the remarkable contrast between Jameson's insightful interpretations of multifarious cultural phenomena, on the one hand, and his superficial understanding of the philosophers he invokes, on the other, makes his book the inverted image of another influential work from the same period (albeit from the other side of "the culture wars"), viz., Allan Bloom's *The Closing of the American Mind*, which combines an impressive grasp of modern philosophy with an incredibly shallow understanding of contemporary culture.

to that "lowliest" of the low genres, the comic book, and, in so doing, I suggest that we only ever truly *read* insofar as we practice the kind of slow and rigorous hermeneutics that Nietzsche, Heidegger, and Wittgenstein all taught. (This remains true, I think, even if the philosophical imperative to "Take your Time!" is lost on those oxymoronic "speed-readers" who set the daily values of the cultural marketplace.)[4] As we will see, Heidegger's view of art suggests that no one can predict ahead of time where the great works of art will emerge, those artworks capable of pervasively reshaping an historical age's self-understanding. Today's high art is often yesterday's low art (much "classical" music and Shakespeare, for instance, began as the popular works of their day), so it is only reasonable to suppose that some of today's low art will become tomorrow's high art – perhaps even some of the works discussed here.[5] Rather than worry too much about the inevitable controversies concerning canonization, however, I shall simply try to suggest that the important insights and lessons these seemingly humble works can still teach us about the possibilities of postmodernity make their philosophical study well worth our while.

My final chapters conclude by returning the focus to Heidegger's own thinking of postmodernity, seeking to dispel some more of the darkness and confusion surrounding the views at the core of his later thought. Chapter 6 helps explain Heidegger's postmodern call for an "other beginning" to Western history by clarifying the structure and goal of his notoriously difficult work, *Contributions to Philosophy (From Enowning)*. My thesis is that this esoteric work in fact records Heidegger's experimental attempt to develop a philosophical version of the musical art of the fugue, an innovative (but not entirely successful) experiment he devised in order to help articulate his postmodern ambitions. Chapter 7 brings the book to a close by exploring the danger and promise of Heidegger's thinking. Recognizing the complexity of that thinking, I continue to reject the superficial demand to either condemn or exonerate Heidegger's work whole-cloth, preferring to remain critical of what deserves our criticism and sympathetic about what merits our sympathy. (It is strange that something so obvious could still be so controversial.) At the same time, however, I also suggest that what remains dangerous and promising in Heidegger cannot be entirely separated but, instead, need to be thought in relation to one another. In this spirit of critical sympathy (the approach Heidegger himself called for as "hearing with thoughtful reticence" [FCM v/GA29–30 v]), I once again seek to clarify and so advance Heidegger's pivotal hope for

---

[4] "The greeting of philosophers to one another should be: 'Take your time!'" Wittgenstein, *Culture and Value*, 80.

[5] That U2 has become too "popular" to remain "hip" thus works in their favor here. Personally, however, I would be much more inclined to bet on *Watchmen* to make it into the canon, especially given the central role comics have come to play in the ongoing cultural shift, as one generation takes over the reigns from another.

an "other beginning" to Western history, this time by elucidating his deeply mysterious vision of a phenomenological gestalt switch capable of instantly transforming the greatest danger of late-modern technologization into the promise of a new, postmodern understanding of being. Finally, a brief concluding section makes a case "Against Conclusions" by gathering together and reflecting on some of the book's central insights into Heidegger, art, and the possibilities of a genuine postmodernity that remain open to us today.

1

Understanding Ontotheology,
or "The History that We Are"

> The significant problems we face cannot be solved by the same level of think-
> ing that created them.
>
> Albert Einstein (popular bumper sticker)

> It is one of life's ironies in our times that so many of us require more knowl-
> edge, even to find our way home, than we really care to have.
>
> J. Glenn Gray, *The Promise of Wisdom*

What does Heidegger mean by *ontotheology*, and why should we care? We will
see that Heidegger understands ontotheology as the two-chambered heart
of Western metaphysics, "the history that we are" (N3 20/GA47 28). As I
showed in *Heidegger on Ontotheology: Technology and the Politics of Education*,
Heidegger's deconstruction of the metaphysical tradition leads him to
the view that metaphysics does not just concern philosophers isolated in
their ivory towers; on the contrary, "Metaphysics grounds an age." As he
explains: "Metaphysics grounds an age in that, through a specific interpretation of what is ..., it gives the age the ground of its essential form"
(QCT 115/GA5 75). Here Heidegger advances the thesis I call *ontological
holism*. Put simply: Everything *is*, so by changing our understanding of
what "is-ness" itself is, metaphysics can change our understanding of everything. In other words, metaphysics molds our very sense of what it means
for something – anything – to *be*. Because everything intelligible "is" in
some sense, Heidegger holds that: "Western humanity, in all its comportment toward entities, and that means also toward itself, is in every respect
sustained and guided by metaphysics" (N4 205/GA6.2 309). By shaping
and reshaping our understanding of what "is-ness" is, metaphysics plays
a foundational role in establishing and maintaining our very sense of the
intelligibility of all things, ourselves included.[1]

---

[1] See *Heidegger on Ontotheology: Technology and the Politics of Education*, Ch. 1; 20 note 16.

Heidegger's view that "metaphysics grounds an age" (*"ein Zeitalter,"* literally "an age of time," in the singular) presupposes two further theses, which I call *ontological historicity* and *epochality*. Ontological historicity, in a nutshell, is the thesis that our basic sense of reality *changes* with time. As Heidegger put it, "what one takes to be 'the real' is something that comes to be only on the basis of the essential history of being itself" (N4 232/NII 376). *Ontological epochality* just further specifies that Western humanity's changing sense of reality congeals into a series of relatively distinct and unified historical "epochs." Ontological holism teaches that metaphysics can change our sense of everything simply by changing our understanding of what "is-ness" is, but "light dawns gradually over the whole" (as Wittgenstein observed near the end of his life), and Western humanity's sense of what-is changes slowly and infrequently enough that individual human beings tend not to notice the change.[2] Many of us even experience a troubling sense of vertigo when first faced with the contention that humanity's basic experience of reality is historically variable, the kind of vertigo we might feel when first noticing that the ground we live and build our homes on is slowly shifting. Nonetheless, Heidegger's deconstruction of metaphysics makes a convincing case for ontological holism, historicity, and epochality by uncovering a succession of different ways in which Western humanity has understood what entities are. In the "history of being," these different "understandings of being" each "ground" and "guide" their respective ages.

Heidegger's deconstruction of the metaphysical tradition suggests that ontological historicity – our changing sense of what-is – congeals into five distinct but overlapping ontohistorical "epochs" in the "history of being," which we could call the *pre-Socratic, Platonic, medieval, modern,* and *late-modern epochs.* Foucault adopts Heidegger's epochs in his investigation of the different occidental *epistemes* or "regimes of truth," as does Levinas when he writes more poetically of different "mutations in the light of the world."[3]

---

[2] See Wittgenstein, *On Certainty*, 21. We tend not to notice this fundamental change, not only because of our "blindness to the immediate" (this paradoxical "distance of the near" is the first law of phenomenology, as we will see), but also because, in Heidegger's influential view (a kind of "punctuated equilibrium" theory), history – in the deepest "ontohistorical" (*seinsgeschichtlich*) sense – does not "happen" within epochs so much as between them, when a new ontotheological "truth event" or understanding of what and how entities *are* takes hold and spreads, consolidating past insights and catalyzing an historical transformation of our very sense of intelligibility. I shall suggest that these new understandings of being do not fall from the heavens (*à la* Badiou) but instead happen when a new way of understanding being that has been taking shape at the margins of an historical age (e.g., in works of art) suddenly becomes all encompassing, giving rise to a new understanding of being that pulls everything into its gravitational field. (See Alain Badiou's *Ethics: An Essay on the Understanding of Evil* and, for a telling critique of Badiou's view, see Adrian Johnston, *Badiou, Žižek, and Political Transformations: The Cadence of Change*.)

[3] See Foucault, *The Order of Things*, and Levinas, *Humanism of the Other*, 59.

I find it illuminating to think of these epochs as historical *constellations of intelligibility*. Heidegger himself calls them "epochs" because, as readers of Husserl know, *epochê* is the Greek word for "holding back," "bracketing off," or as Derrida liked to say, "putting in parentheses," and Heidegger saw that each of the epochal understandings of the being of entities "holds back" the floodwaters of ontological historicity for a time – the "time" of an *epoch*.[4] Each of the five different historical epochs is unified by its shared sense of what is and what matters, but each of these epochs is grounded in a *different* way of understanding what and how entities *are*.

How, then, is it possible for each epoch to *share* a sense of what is and what matters, and yet for this shared sense of the intelligibility of things to be *different* for each epoch? By what "mechanism," as it were, is Western humanity's shared sense of the being of entities transformed and maintained? This question brings us directly to the two-chambered heart of Heidegger's view of metaphysics. For, an *ontotheology* is what puts the parentheses around an epoch, temporarily shielding a particular sense of what is and what matters from the corrosive sands of time. In Heidegger's terms, ontotheologies "sustain" and "guide" their epochs by establishing an historical understanding of the being of entities; ontotheologies supply the aforementioned "ground" from which an age takes its "essential form" (QCT 115/GA5 75). In other words, an ontotheology provides a temporarily unshakable understanding of *what* and *how* entities *are*, and thereby doubly anchors an epochal constellation of intelligibility. To say that "Metaphysics grounds an age" is thus to say that the shared sense of intelligibility unifying an epoch derives, in the last analysis, from an *ontotheology*.[5]

---

[4] In the metaphysical tradition, Heidegger maintains, the question of the being *of entities* stands in for (and so eclipses) the deeper question of "being as such." Being as such "conceals itself in any given phase of metaphysics, [and] such keeping to itself determines each epoch of the history of being as the *epochê* of being itself" (N4 239/NII 383). (See also the explanation of T&B 9/GA14 8–9 in *Heidegger on Ontotheology*, 19–20.) This is why Heidegger often maintains that our next, "postmodern" understanding of being will not usher in another *epoch*; it will not lead to another metaphysical (i.e., ontotheologically-grounded) age. For, by understanding the being of entities in terms of being as such (i.e., as conceptually inexhaustible), the postmodern (and post-metaphysical) understanding of being will not "hold back" the floodwaters of ontological historicity; it will not temporarily dam time with another ontotheology and so ground another historical constellation of intelligibility. Instead, Heidegger believes that the radically pluralistic, postmodern age will be the "last" age (hence his talk of "the last God," which we will examine in Chapter 6), in so far as it constitutes a permanent openness to other possible interpretations, and so to the future.

[5] This suggests that the philosopher who understands how exactly metaphysics "grounds" and "guides" an age should also be able to discern the general direction in which it is moving historically. At first blush, the claim of any connection between philosophy and prophecy sounds dangerously hubristic (especially in light of Heidegger's own history). Nonetheless, we can see how metaphysics facilitates a kind of general historical prognostication once we grasp the relation between our own late-modern ontotheology and

I realize that, at first, "ontotheology" can sound like a dauntingly unfamiliar word. As an index of this unfamiliarity, "ontotheology" and its cognates have yet to make it into the official *Oxford English Dictionary*.[6] Shortly after *Heidegger on Ontotheology* was published, my intrepid teenage cousins pressed me on what "that big word" in my title meant. We happened to be at a public pool so, inspired by the moment, I suggested that if they thought of all reality as a beach ball, then they could think of ontotheology as the attempt to grasp the beach ball from the inside and the outside at the same time. (As a first approximation of Heidegger's views, I am still not too unhappy with this analogy, but I shall present more precise and suggestive images later.) What is crucial is that ontotheologies allow the metaphysical tradition to temporarily establish what it means for an entity to *be*, and that they do so by answering the question of what it means for something to be *in two different ways at the same time*.[7] We could say that metaphysics' ways of understanding what it means to be resemble what advertisers call "two-for-ones"; the "great metaphysicians" implicitly answer the question of reality's ultimate foundation twice-over by understanding the being of entities ontologically *and* theologically.

Indeed, for an ontotheology to work, it must "doubly ground" its age's sense of reality by comprehending the intelligible order in terms of both its innermost core and its outermost form or ultimate expression. Because these dual ontotheological foundations are what allow metaphysics to provide a temporarily stable basis for the intelligible order, Heidegger's notorious antipathy to "metaphysics" obscures the fact that, in his view, it is the two-chambered, ontotheological heart of metaphysics that unifies and secures our successive historical epochs. A series of metaphysical ontotheologies doubly anchor our successive constellations of historical intelligibility, securing the intelligible order (for the time of an "epoch") by grasping reality from both ends of the conceptual scale simultaneously: Both *ontologically* (from the inside-out) and *theologically* (from the outside-in). In this way, metaphysics secures our understanding of reality

the current global movement toward increasing technologization. Understanding this connection will help us to appreciate why Heidegger continues to inspire philosophical resistance to the *Zeitgeist* of global technologization.

[6] "Ontotheology" is listed in the "draft revision" of the on-line version of the OED (dated June 2004), but it is defined there only in (1) Kant's sense (explained below) and (2) as: "A branch or system of theology in which God is regarded as a being, esp. the supreme being." We will see that this latter construal of ontotheology, although common, mistakenly reduces the genus to one of its species.

In order to secure its understanding of the being of entities, metaphysics seeks to establish "the truth concerning the totality of entities as such." This phrase is meant by Heidegger to be "positively ambiguous" between the ontological and theological ways of understanding the being of entities, connoting not ontology *or* theological but *both*. (I explain this point in detail in *Heidegger on Ontotheology*, 11–23.)

floor-to-ceiling, microscopically and telescopically, or, in a word (albeit a big one), *ontotheologically*.[8]

1. BACK TO BASICS

Briefly recounting a few decisive moments from the history of Western metaphysics should help clarify and motivate what can sound initially like an implausibly idiosyncratic view. What I shall suggest is that, ever since Western philosophy began with Thales and Anaximander, our metaphysical tradition has indeed sought to establish both the *fundamental* and the *ultimate* conceptual parameters of intelligibility by ontologically grounding and theologically founding – and thereby legitimating – our changing historical sense of what is.[9]

When, at the birth of Western metaphysics, Thales and Anaximander search for the foundation of reality, they understand this *archê* or "ground" in two very different ways. For Thales, the "ground" of reality is "water"; water is the "one element" out of which everything else is composed. As the most basic constitutive component of what-is, water is the fundamental ground that provides the terms in which to understand what everything is. Thales, in Heidegger's terminology, understands the being of entities *ontologically*. Now, sitting atop our historical perch, many find it easy to laugh at Thales' seemingly simplistic claim that "water" is the *archê* or fundamental ground of reality. Philosophers sometimes try to motivate Thales's view by pointing out that the seeds from which things grow are moist, or that many different kinds of things tend to dissolve in water, but such retrospective rationalizations make the great sage look like a rudimentary empirical scientist at best. It is much more important to appreciate just what an amazing leap of thought it was for humanity simply to postulate that the

---

[8] That this word has eight syllables has not gone unnoticed or unpunished. Amusingly, technology seems to be taking its revenge on my critique of it *via* Amazon.com's "statistical analyses" of a book's "readability." Relying only on the crude measures of syllables per word and words per sentence, Amazon's computers have calculated that my first book is virtually *impossible* to read, since reading it requires no less than "27.5 years of formal education." (I did not take quite that long in school myself – which means I cannot read my own book – an intriguingly "postmodern" implication!) Of course, these same blunt "readability" calculations conclude that James Joyce's *Ulysses* can be read by sixth graders. Although students continue to prove such facile calculations false, it remains ironic that a book criticizing technology's preemptive delegitimation of genuine alternatives should itself be preemptively delegitimated by that technology, processed by a literally illiterate machine and presented as unreadable to human beings. Let me return to this critique of technology, however, only after presenting its ontotheological foundations, without which it cannot really be understood.

[9] Because Western philosophy is coeval with the metaphysical tradition whose ontotheological structure Heidegger deconstructs, he will renounce the title "philosophy" as a description of his own later "thinking."

seemingly endless diversity of material entities are all fundamentally composed of the same kind of stuff. Thales's great idea was that there is a final
ground somewhere beneath our feet, so to speak, and thus a kind of being
that *everything* shares in common. This was the *ontological* intuition, and it is
a postulate that our metaphysicians have never abandoned – even as these
metaphysicians dropped the "meta" from their title (disowning, with false
modesty, its extra-empirical implications). Contemporary metaphysicians
still seek to uncover reality's final building blocks, the elementary constitu-
ents of matter; they just prefer to call the ontological endeavor they have
inherited from Thales's "physics."

For Thales's student Anaximander, by contrast, the *archê* or "ground"
of reality is *apeiron*, the "indefinite, unlimited, or infinite." That is,
Anaximander understands the ultimate ground of what-is in terms of that
source from which all entities derive and by appeal to which they can be
justified – or, as in Anaximander's case, *condemned*, judged undeserving of
finite existence. According to Anaximander's beautiful but tragic vision
of reality, the existence of discrete entities is inherently unjust. For, the very
existence of individual entities as finite and limited represents an implicit
violation of the infinite and unlimited source, *apeiron*, from which all things
derive or emerge only by differentiating themselves, thereby committing
a kind of original sin for which each individual entity must eventually pay
penance by being destroyed. Thus "justice" decrees it, for only through
their destruction may finite entities be reunited with their infinite source,
merged once again with the indefinite from which definite entities originally emerged. Here Anaximander thinks himself to the very limits of the
intelligible order so as to grasp the source from which all things derive, and
he understands the being of what-is in terms of this outermost condition on
the possibility of the meaning of the cosmos. Because he takes up this "view
from nowhere" or God's-eye perspective on all that is, a perspective that
enables him to vindicate the meaningfulness of the cosmic order as a whole,
Anaximander, in Heidegger's terms, understands the being of entities *theologically*. Many today like to think that they have nothing in common with
"theology," but, in Heidegger's terms, the theological intuition is simply the
idea that somewhere above us – somewhere *out there*, as it were – there is an
ultimate source from which all things finally derive, a source by appeal to
which the meaning of the cosmos as a whole can be finally explained. Our
contemporary metaphysicians continue to follow this theological intuition
whether they think of this ultimate source of all being as a creator God or as
an infinitely hot and dense "singularity" existing at the beginning of cosmic
time (some 13.7 billion years ago). Theologians and astrophysicists alike
remain heirs to the Anaximandrian approach.[10]

---

[10]   The persistence of this ontotheological inheritance – even in scientism itself – can be witnessed in Richard Dawkins's hubristic prediction that physics combined with Darwinism

The birth of Western philosophy is thus the birth of two radically different ways of understanding the "ground" of what-is: Thales's ontological understanding of water as the fundamental element of being and Anaximander's theological understanding of *apeiron* as the ultimate source of being. It took a thinker as great as Plato to implicitly appropriate these two different ways of understanding the being of what is – the ontological *and* the theological – and combine them into a single, *ontotheological* view, almost as if he were performing a kind of retroactive Siamese twinning on what began as separate but related conceptual children.[11] Plato gives the philosophical tradition its first ontotheology when he presents the forms both as the common element unifying all the different instantiations of a thing and also as the highest, most perfect, or exemplary embodiment of that kind of thing. For example, Plato's *Symposium* presents the form of beauty as the unifying element shared in common by the many different kinds of beautiful things; that is, the form of beauty is what explains why beautiful bodies, beautiful artworks, beautiful state constitutions, and so on, are all *beautiful* – namely, they are all imperfect instantiations of the perfect form of beauty. At the same time, as this suggests, the *Symposium* also presents the form of beauty as the most beautiful of all that is beautiful, as the most perfect expression and so the ultimate standard of beauty. Plato thereby suggests that the form of beauty is a beauty so perfect that nothing in this imperfect world can ever measure up to it. Thus, following in Anaximander's footsteps, Plato's theological conception of the forms makes sense of the intelligible order as a whole only by postulating a supersensory realm, degrading our finite world of mortal experience by comparison. (Nietzsche suggests that Christianity took over this nihilistic way of conceiving mortal existence in the middle ages and thereby made it central to Western humanity's self-conception, as we will see in the next section.)

will "furnish a totally satisfying naturalistic explanation for the existence of the universe and everything that's in it, including ourselves." Ironically, this famous author of *The God Delusion* "optimistically" predicts "that the physicists of our species will complete Einstein's dream and discover the final theory of everything before superior creatures, evolved on another world, make contact with us and tell us the answer." What is this hope that superior beings will descend from the heavens to confirm our theories but another form of the theological superstition that *God will prove us right in the end?* Dawkins's implicit admission that we need a kind of higher being to confirm one ontotheology as finally correct suggests the same old regress, moreover, because we would then need even smarter aliens to tell us if the first aliens were right that we were right, and so on, leading us right back to the ontotheological understanding of God as the regress-halting, *highest* entity. (See Dawkins, "The Final Scientific Enlightenment," 27.)

[11] To extend the metaphor, this ontotheological Siamese twinning increases rather than decreases the viability of the conceptual offspring thus conjoined, so perhaps Plato spliced his ontotheological hybrid together as a defensive formation against the haunting threat of his teacher Socrates, that famous son of a midwife who – in his incessant search for an answer to the ontological question, "What *is* it?" (piety, friendship, justice, etc.) – euthanized every conceptual child he himself ever delivered.

Let us cut to the chase. Plato's student Aristotle makes the ontotheological duality implicit in Plato's doctrine of the forms explicit when he
distinguishes between "primary and secondary substance," differentiating
the "thatness" of entities from their "whatness." This, moreover, is the very
distinction that medieval scholastics would treat as the difference between
existentia and *essentia*. This ontotheological distinction between "existence"
and "essence" subsequently became so deeply ingrained in our Western
philosophical tradition that Heidegger can convincingly claim that even
the proudly "godless" Nietzsche conceives of "the *existentia* of the totality
of entities as such *theologically* as the eternal return of the same," just as
Nietzsche's "ontology of entities as such thinks *essentia* as will to power"
(N4 210/NII 348/GA6.2 314). As one can see most clearly in that undeniably beautiful passage that has become famous as the last entry of the
infamous "book," *The Will to Power*, Nietzsche too seeks to grasp all of reality both *ontologically*, from the inside-out, as will-to-power, and *theologically*,
from the outside-in, as eternal recurrence.[12] Nietzsche thus gives us, in
Heidegger's terms, an ontotheology of will-to-power eternally recurring.

In Heidegger's "history of being," Plato is the first ontotheologist, and
Nietzsche is the last, because Nietzsche teaches the futility of metaphysics'

---

[12] Nietzsche himself was clearly troubled by the tension between his naturalistic understanding of will to power and his cosmological understanding of eternal recurrence; his notebooks and letters show that he was tremendously frustrated by his inability to provide a
consistent naturalistic explanation capable of validating his seemingly supernatural Sils-
Maria experience (which Klossowski suggests was actually an early psychotic break; see
his "Nietzsche's Experience of the Eternal Return"), an experience that left him utterly
convinced of the truth of eternal recurrence. Thus Nietzsche returns repeatedly in his
notebooks to the thought that, given finite matter and space and infinite time, all possible combinations of events must already have occurred – and recurred. (A version of
this argument can already be found in *Thus Spoke Zarathustra*, 299.) Indeed, I think it
clear that Nietzsche himself (unlike most of his subsequent interpreters, who turn away
from the view because of its lack of empirical plausibility) remained convinced to the end
that there must be a plausible way to bring will-to-power and eternal recurrence together,
even if he could not fully see how. If this is right, however, then despite the undeniable
reductiveness of Heidegger's reading, he remains faithful to Nietzsche's deepest inner
conviction by joining will-power and eternal recurrence as the two extreme poles of the
"unthought" ontotheology toward which Nietzsche's thinking points – thereby fulfill-
ing Nietzsche's struggle to put into words the "secret" even *Zarathustra* can only whisper,
silently, into the ear of life at the culmination of *Thus Spoke Zarathustra*. (Heidegger quotes
from Nietzsche's notebooks the passage that gives away *Zarathustra's* climactic secret –
apparently the secret was too important for Nietzsche to trust his audience to figure it out
for themselves: "Zarathustra, *out of the superman's happiness* [i.e., the superabundance of
will-to-power Zarathustra feels when the doctrine of eternal recurrence allows him to overcome his nihilism-inducing inability to "will backward" or affirm the past], *tells the secret
that everything recurs*" [WCT 106/GA8 109].) This is not to absolve Heidegger's Nietzsche
interpretation of its undeniable hermeneutic violence (evident in its great selectiveness,
e.g.), but only to suggest that it is not some external imposition on the unwilling matter
of Nietzsche's thought. On the contrary, the core of Heidegger's Nietzsche interpretation
can be understood (the way Heidegger himself understood it) as a faithful attempt to

foundationalist project and yet nevertheless succeeds in supplying humanity with an ontotheology – albeit one that "grounds" reality as a whole only
by dissolving it into the endless involutions of eternally recurring will-
to-power in its "sovereign becoming."[13] The metaphysical tradition thus
culminates and exhausts itself in Nietzsche, whose ontotheology, Heidegger
believes, lays the ground for "the metaphysics of the atomic age." In fact,
Heidegger's entire understanding of metaphysics as ontotheology *turns* on
his understanding of Nietzsche's ontotheology, in two senses: Heidegger
holds Nietzsche's ontotheology responsible for that increasingly global
technologization of our very sense of reality in which we currently remain
caught, and yet Heidegger also thinks that the only way to transcend the
nihilistic, "technological" ontotheology we have inherited from Nietzsche
is to think its "unthought," that is, to develop or think through Nietzsche's
ontotheology to the point that it "transcends" itself, *turning* into another
way of understanding the being of what-is.

2. THINKING THROUGH NIETZSCHE'S UNTHOUGHT ONTOTHEOLOGY

In order to understand Heidegger's crucial interpretation of Nietzsche's
ontotheology, let us ask a more basic question: How are ontology and theology *joined* in an ontotheology? What kind of conceptual bonds hold the
ontological and theological ways of understanding the being of entities
together? For Heidegger, ontology and theology are held together in a
kind of chiasmus: Ontology leads to theology and theology feeds back into
ontology. Put more precisely, an ontology, as an understanding of *what*

"think after" and so express the "innermost thinking will" Nietzsche explicitly gave voice
to only in his notebooks – most beautifully, in what has come down to us as the final apho-
rism (#1067) of *The Will to Power*, the notoriously problematic posthumous text assembled
by Nietzsche's sister and his friend "Peter Gast" (Heinrich Köselitz, the "guest" Nietzsche
charged with keeping his faith), a text Heidegger read in his youth, "in the exciting years
between 1910 and 1914" (GA1 56). In fact, Heidegger was already criticizing the book's
pro-eugenicist vision in 1909, and by the time he began his famous *Nietzsche* lectures in
1936, the book's serious editorial problems had become obvious to him, since in 1935
he joined the commission charged with putting together a scholarly edition of *Nietzsche*'s
works and so had Nietzsche's original notebooks before him and could see with his own
eyes all the heavy-handed black-pencil work of the previous editors. Nietzsche's sister's
resistance to any corrected edition reportedly helped prompt Heidegger to resign from
the commission. (See Nietzsche, *The Will to Power*, 549–50 [#1067]; a virtually identical version of the famous passage can be found in Nietzsche, *Writings from the Late Notebooks*, 38–9;
Heidegger on Ontotheology, 148 note 4; and Hans Sluga, "Heidegger's Nietzsche," 102.)

13 See *Heidegger on Ontotheology*, 20–3. As Charles Taylor insightfully observes, our late-modern
sense of self now hovers in a groundless void, unable to secure the temporal origins of the
species or the spatial limits of the universe. (See Taylor's chapter on "The Dark Abyss of
Time" in *The Secular Age*, 322–51; and my "Taylor, Heidegger, Nietzsche: Transcendence
and the Problem of Otherworldly Nihilism.")

entities are, generates a theology, an understanding of that "highest" (or "supreme," *höchste*) entity that embodies this kind of being most perfectly. Conversely, a theology, as a conception of this highest entity, feeds back into ontology by impacting our understanding of the being of what-is as a whole – typically, by shaping our understanding of whether or not the being of this whole is justified or meaningful. This ontology-theology feedback loop is clearly visible in Nietzsche's ontotheological conception of being as will-to-power, eternally recurring. For, Nietzsche's ontological conception of what entities are essentially – namely, will-to-power – leads to his conception of eternal recurrence as the most perfect embodiment and ultimate expression of will-to-power. And conversely, Nietzsche's theological conception of the eternal recurrence of the cosmic order allows him to understand the being of what-is as justified (or at least justifiable), as meaningful rather than nihilistic.

To see this, remember that for Nietzsche, what-is is *essentially* will-to-power. In Nietzsche's neo-Darwinian view, will-to-power is the "essence" of life, the inner force generating that continual self-overcoming of existing life forms that works to keep life itself alive. Eternal recurrence, moreover, is the way that the totality of all that is exists when viewed from a God's-eye perspective; "the eternal return of the same" is Nietzsche's name for his speculative understanding of the endless repetition of the cosmic cycle: big bang, universe, big crunch; big bang, universe, big crunch; and so on *ad infinitum*.[14] Ontology leads to theology, then, because will-to-power is the force driving the cycle of cosmic recurrence, leading the universe to unfold as a kind of magnificent perpetual motion machine of endless growth and decay. Viewed from the greatest possible distance (that "view from nowhere" Nietzsche sometimes calls the "super-historical perspective"), will-to-power is *as* the eternal return of the same. That is, Nietzsche's ontology generates his theology because will-to-power ultimately unfolds as eternal recurrence.

[14] In his early lectures on *The Pre-Platonic Philosophers*, Nietzsche discerns versions of eternal recurrence in Anaximander, Heraclitus, Xenophanes, and the Pythagoreans, but it is the Pythagorean version that most closely resembles Nietzsche's cosmological doctrine of the eternal return of the same. Still, the Empedoclean conception of cosmic time as forever oscillating back and forth between the poles of unity and complexity (in which the swing of the cosmic pendulum is driven by the competing motivations of attraction and repulsion) helps Nietzsche conceive of how an overall cycle of growth and decay might take place within each of the "tremendous years of recurrence." For Nietzsche himself, of course, time does not actually move backward; the growth of forms jι ιl.ι ιlιιll ιlιειι declines within each "grιιnιl jι.ιι" υf ιῪιῪιιιɾeɲce. It is also clear from these early lectures that Nietzsche developed his "aesthetic justification" of existence ("only as an aesthetic phenomenon is existence and the world eternally *justified*," Nietzsche famously writes in *The Birth of Tragedy*, 33) by borrowing Heraclitus's "sublime metaphor" of eternity as the innocent "play of the child (or that of the artist)," joyfully building castles in the sand and then exuberantly destroying them (as I show in "Interpretation as Self-Creation: Nietzsche on the Pre-Platonics").

According to Nietzsche, moreover, the eternal return of the same is also the *highest* conceivable mode of existence.[15] For, the universe conceived in its eternal recurrence is both the closest that the endless stream of becoming ever comes to *being* and also the means we need in order to be able to affirm all of existence by affirming just one moment of our lives. For, if all events are interconnected in an unbroken circle of cause and effect, then "future" events circle around to help cause "past" ones, and to affirm *any* moment of your life is thus to affirm not only your whole life but also the entire cosmic cycle, without which that moment could not have existed. In this way, the theological understanding of being feeds back into the ontological; with eternal recurrence Nietzsche reaffirms, as it were, the connection we observed in Anaximander and Plato between the theological understanding of the whole of what-is and the question of whether the being of this whole is meaningful. Nietzsche too provides a "cosmodicy," albeit a godless cosmic theodicy that seeks to vindicate the meaningfulness of what-is as a whole by appeal to eternal recurrence.

Of course (as mentioned earlier), it was Nietzsche himself who saw that Plato's theological conception of the forms as perfect exemplars led to the "nihilism" or meaninglessness of "devaluing" the finite achievements attainable by mortals by comparing them to unattainable "otherworldly" ideals. (Nietzsche extends the same charge to the Christian understanding of heaven as an afterlife for the eternal soul, an afterlife compared to which this life is merely a "vale of tears," hence his famous description of Christianity as "Platonism for the masses.") Nietzsche challenges us with his powerful call for *amor fati* to embrace eternal recurrence in order to justify our finite lives non-nihilistically – that is, solely on their own terms, without redeeming them in some afterlife or otherwise judging them by unfulfillable, "otherworldly" standards.[16] Nonetheless, Heidegger suggests, Nietzsche fell into the same theological trap he discerned in Plato, because

---

[15] Most crucial, from Heidegger's perspective, are the words expressed in Notebook 7 (from the end of 1886 to the Spring of 1887), where Nietzsche writes: "To imprint upon becoming the character of being – that is the highest *will to power*"; and, one sentence later, "That *everything recurs* is the most extreme *approximation of a world of becoming to one of being*: [this is the] *pinnacle of contemplation.*" (Nietzsche, *Writings from the Late Notebooks*, 138.) Heidegger's reading of Nietzsche turns on this "pinnacle," this point where Nietzsche himself joins eternal recurrence to will-to-power as its highest expression, i.e., as the closest becoming comes to being and as the key to affirming existence. (See below and Chapter 7.) It is also revealing to recall Nietzsche's famous description of his 1881 "Sils-Maria experience" of the truth of eternal recurrence as "beyond humanity and time" (a description he wrote across the top of the notebook page that recorded this Sils-Maria experience), as well as his portrayal of eternal recurrence (in *Ecce Homo*) as "the highest formula for affirmation that can ever be attained." (On the uses of the "superhistorical perspective" and its dangers, see Nietzsche's second *Untimely Meditation*, "On the Advantage and Disadvantage of History for Life.")

[16] For a detailed argument for this point, see my "Taylor, Heidegger, Nietzsche: Transcendence and the Problem of Otherworldly Nihilism."

Nietzsche held that human existence can be justified only by affirming the doctrine of eternal recurrence, the truth of which Nietzsche secretly admitted was ultimately "unknowable."[17]

Heidegger agrees that eternal recurrence is unknowable. For Heidegger, "the essential knowing of the thinker [always] begins by knowing something unknowable" (N3 5–6/NI 477). Despite its "factual" unknowability, Heidegger insists that "Nietzsche's thought of the eternal recurrence of the same" is anything but "a mystical fantasy." Quite the contrary: Owing to the theses of ontological holism, historicity, and epochality discussed earlier, Heidegger believes that "Nietzsche is the name for an age of the world" (GA50 84). What this means, we can now see, is that Nietzsche supplies the ontotheological scaffolding of own epoch; Nietzsche's understanding of being as eternally recurring will-to-power undergirds and suspends our own historical constellation of intelligibility. This is why Heidegger rather mysteriously prophesies that, in "the coming age, ... the essence of modern technology – the constantly [*ständig*] rotating recurrence of the same – will come to light" (WCT 109/GA8 112). Such gnomic remarks, properly understood, show us that *Heidegger's famous critique of our technological late modernity in fact follows from his understanding of ontotheology.*[18] Indeed, although no one seems to have recognized this connection before, it is clear that Heidegger holds the Nietzschean ontotheology of eternally recurring will-to-power ultimately responsible for the increasingly global *technologization* of our world.

3. TRANSCENDING OUR TECHNOLOGICAL ONTOTHEOLOGY

To see this, one has to know that the constellation of intelligibility characteristic of our own late-modern epoch is what Heidegger famously calls "enframing" (*Gestell*). In Heidegger's view, many of the deepest problems plaguing our "technological" age of enframing emerge from or are exacerbated by the particular Nietzschean ontotheology in which this technological enframing is rooted.[19] In effect, Nietzsche's ontotheology implicitly

---

[17] Near the climax of *Thus Spoke Zarathustra* (339), when Zarathustra whispers the "secret" of eternal recurrence into the ear of life, she tellingly replies: "You *know* that, O Zarathustra? Nobody knows that."

[18] This is one of the central theses of *Heidegger on Ontotheology*. Here Heidegger uses "*ständig*" to suggest that the ontotheology of eternally recurring will to power is ultimately responsible for "enframing," the technological mode of revealing that reduces every thing to mere "*Bestand*," i.e., intrinsically-meaningless "resources" standing by for optimization. On Heidegger's reading, eternal recurrence is ironically fulfilled in enframing's ontological homogenization, "the endless etcetera of what is most desolately transitory" (CP 287/GA65 409).

[19] When Heidegger refers to "the source of these destructive phenomena in their essence" (N4 221/NII 363), he is thinking of Nietzsche's ontotheology of eternally recurring will to power as an historical understanding of the being of entities that dissolves being itself

provides the lenses through which we see the world and ourselves, leading us to pre-understand the being of all things as eternally recurring
will-to-power, that is, as mere forces coming together and breaking apart
with no end beyond this continual self-overcoming. Insofar as our sense
of reality is shaped by this "technological" understanding of the being of
entities, we increasingly come to treat all entities, ourselves included, as
intrinsically meaningless "resources" (*Bestand*) standing by merely to be
optimized, enhanced, and ordered for maximally flexible use.[20] As I have
argued elsewhere, environmental devastation, our growing obsession with
biogenetic optimization, the increasing reduction of higher education to
empty optimization imperatives, and the nihilistic erosion of all intrinsic
meaning are just some of the most problematic symptoms of the underlying ontotheology "enframing" our sense of reality.[21] These problems are as
serious as they are deeply entrenched in the metaphysical substructure of
our historical self-understanding.

Fortunately, Heidegger's work also helps suggest a treatment, and
so a mission for any thinking that would be truly "postmodern." We
need to become aware of the subtle and often unnoticed impact of our

into *nothing* but becoming and thereby occludes the condition if its own possibility. Yet, this
"essence of nihilism contains nothing negative" (ibid.), because this strange "noth-ing"
or "nihilating" needs to be understood as the way being itself shows up when viewed
through the lenses of Nietzsche's ontotheology. In the active "noth-ing" or "nihilating" by
which being's "presencing" can be felt, being paradoxically "comes across" in its very "staying away." The "fulfilled peak" of Western nihilism is Nietzsche's reduction of being to
nothing (by dissolving being into becoming), but this peak "looks down both slopes" (as
Derrida recognized); for, to understand this "noth-ing" as the way we experience being
from within our Nietzschean ontotheology is already to be turning or pivoting phenomenologically beyond nihilism. I explain Heidegger's difficult but crucial idea of a salvific
turn from understanding being as nothing to experiencing this dynamic nothing as the
presencing of being in Chapters 3 and 7.

[20] What Heidegger teaches us (and this is one of the important things Feenberg helped me
see) is that the view, shared by both Marxism and liberalism, of technology as a neutral tool
that can be used for either constructive or destructive purposes is far too simplistic. In fact,
technology reinforces a particular historical drift, owing to the ontotheology it expresses,
and Heidegger's great merit is to have helped us discern the underlying historical direction
in which we are still moving as our sense of reality becomes increasingly *technologized*. One
need think not only of Latour's automatic door-closer, of speed-bumps, or of the spreading
panopticon of traffic and other security cameras – devices the evolution of which threatens
to render autonomy obsolete by making punishment automatic and instantaneous. We
can instead think of how seemingly more neutral phenomena like email and the Internet
encourage an accelerated rate of exchange, make the distant near and the near distant,
and foment irresponsibility and brusque hostility through their facelessness. These and
other technologies can be used, to be sure, to combat *technologization* (i.e., enframing), but
to use them so (i.e., to use our technology without being used by it), we must first learn to
recognize and resist their tendency to serve empty optimization. (See Feenberg's *Critical
Theory of Technology* and my *Heidegger on Ontotheology*, Ch. 2.)

[21] See my "Ontology and Ethics at the Intersection of Phenomenology and Environmental
Philosophy."

late-modern, technological ontotheology so that we can learn to resist and transcend it. Throughout this book, we will thus explore Heidegger's different but complementary suggestions about how we might transcend our late-modern, technological ontotheology and so inaugurate a postmodern understanding of being. The key to all these transitions, Heidegger suggests, is learning to practice the phenomenological comportment he calls "dwelling" (or "releasement to things"). To put it much too briefly (but by way of anticipation), to learn to *dwell* is to become attuned to the phenomenological "presencing" (*Anwesen*) whereby "being as such" manifests itself. "Being as such" is one of the later Heidegger's names for that conceptually inexhaustible dimension of intelligibility that all metaphysics' different ontotheological ways of understanding the being of entities *partly capture* but never *exhaust*, the recognition of which can help lead us beyond our current ontotheology.[22]

As we will see (in Chapter 3), Heidegger thinks we can best learn this comportment from a phenomenological encounter with great art, the very essence of which is poetry. The later Heidegger's well-known turn to poetry thus derives not from some antiphilosophical exaltation of the literary, let alone of the "irrational," but instead from what he thinks poets can teach us about those enduringly meaningful experiences that make our finite lives

---

[22] I emphasize "partly capture" here because Heidegger consistently describes "being as such" as a dynamic and inexhaustible ontological "abundance" or "excessiveness" that both "gives itself and refuses itself simultaneously" (P 255/GA9 335), i.e., that *both* informs *and* partly escapes all our attempts to fix it in place once and for all. Unfortunately, an increasingly common misreading of the later Heidegger simply conflates his "being as such" with Levinas's "alterity," and so misconceives being as something in principle ineffable, rather than as effable but also as "*inexhaustibly* given to human beings to think" (CCP 156, my emphasis/GA77 239). For a phenomenologist like Heidegger, pure ineffability or alterity is a paradoxical (if not simply contradictory) concept, because it is a concept for which there can be no convincing phenomenological evidence. Merely for something to be intelligible to us, we have to have *some* sense of it, in which case it will not be "infinitely other" or completely ineffable. As Heidegger pointedly writes: "But has it really been established that the absolutely nameless is given [to us]? For us much is often ineffable, but only because its name has not yet come to us." (CPC 77/GA77 119) Heidegger is thus particularly interested in those events of poetic "naming, in which the nameable, the name, and named bring each other into their own together [*sich zumal... ereignen*]" (ibid.). For, in such events of poetic sense-making, what the poet's names disclose ("the named") also help illuminate what they do not ("the nameable," that is, the *not yet* named), giving us some light by which we can "surmise" (CPC 96/GA77 148) and so continue to make sense of what might otherwise seem "unnameable." As Bret Davis nicely suggests, Heidegger's notion of "surmising" (*Vermuten*) means "a mindful and courageous attempt to follow a hunch or pursue an inkling. Surmising is thus ... a dedication to following presentiments, to presaging pathways of thought that are opened up by intimations of being" (see CPC 96–7, note 56). (We will flesh this idea out in more concrete phenomenological terms when we explain Heidegger's postmodern understanding of art in Chapter 3.)

most worth living.[23] For, Heidegger's hope for a truly "postmodern" understanding of being follows from his conviction that if we can learn from the great poets and artists to become comportmentally attuned to the dynamic phenomenological presencing that both precedes and exceeds all conceptualization, then we too can come to understand and experience entities as being richer in meaning than we are capable of doing justice to conceptually, rather than taking them as intrinsically meaningless resources awaiting optimization. Such experiences can become microcosms of, as well as inspiration for, the revolution beyond our underlying ontotheology that we need in order to transcend the nihilism of late-modern enframing and set our world on a different, more meaningful path. In other words, Heidegger's later thinking as a whole is dedicated to the *postmodern* goal of helping us learn to transcend our late-modern, technological ontotheology and its devastating nihilistic effects, in our lives, our sense of self and other, and our world at large.[24]

Perhaps the best way to approach the drastically different ways of comporting ourselves toward things that Heidegger contrasts – namely, the active receptivity of poetic dwelling, on the one hand, and the obtuse domination of technological enframing, on the other – is to think about the difference between these poetic and technological modes of revealing in the terms Heidegger traces back to the ancient Greek distinction between *poiêsis* and *technê*. Just think, on the one hand, of a poetic shepherding into being that respects the natural potentialities of the matters with which it works, just as Michelangelo (who, let us recall, worked in a marble quarry) legendarily claimed he simply set his "David" free from a particularly rich piece of marble (after studying it for a month); or, less hyperbolically, as a skillful woodworker notices the inherent qualities of particular pieces of wood – attending to subtleties of shape and grain, different shades of color, weight, and hardness – while deciding what might be built from that wood (or whether to build from it at all). Then contrast, on the other hand, a technological making that imposes a predetermined form on matter without paying heed to any intrinsic potentialities, the way an industrial factory indiscriminately grinds wood into woodchips in order to paste them back together into straight particle board, which can then be used flexibly and efficiently to construct a maximal variety of useful objects.[25]

---

[23] Even in 1934, Heidegger tellingly rails against the "comical and already almost ridiculous spectacle that precisely the many mediocrities who take the field today and formerly against rationalism and intellectualism blindly get stuck and founder in it" (LQE 7/GA38 8).

[24] See *Heidegger on Ontotheology*, Ch. 4.

[25] Admittedly, this crucial difference is difficult to define philosophically without falling back into ontotheology (e.g., by grounding the contrast in intrinsic *properties*), but one need not rely on what some criticize as historically outdated examples in order to bring this still widely shared intuition into focus. Instead, one could think of the difference

While many late-moderns continue to believe (with Nietzsche) that all meaning comes from us (as the result of our various "value positings"), Heidegger is committed to the more phenomenologically accurate view that, at least with respect to that which most matters to us – the paradigm case being *love* – what we most care about is in fact not entirely up to us, not simply within our power to control, and this is a crucial part of what makes it so important. Indeed, one of the primary phenomenological lessons that Heidegger drew from art, as we will see, is that when things are approached with openness and respect, they push back against us, making subtle but undeniable claims on us, and we need to learn to acknowledge and respond creatively to these claims if we do not want to deny the source of genuine meaning in the world. For, only meanings that are at least partly independent of us and so not entirely within our control – not simply up to us to bestow and rescind at will – can provide us with the kind of touchstones around which we can build meaningful lives and loves.

Heidegger sometimes calls such an enduringly meaningful encounter an "event of enowning" (*Ereignis*). In such momentous events, we find ourselves coming into our own (as world-disclosers) precisely by creatively enabling things to come into their own, just as Michelangelo came into his own as a sculptor by creatively responding to the veins and fissures in that particular piece of marble so as to bring forth his "David"; or as a woodworker comes into her own as a woodworker by responding creatively to the subtle weight, color, and grain of an individual piece of wood in order to make something out of it (or to leave it be); or as a teacher comes into his or her own as a teacher by learning to recognize and cultivate the particular talents and capacities of each individual student, thereby enabling our students to come into their own; or as parents and children come into their own together when parents learn from children to be open to what is seeking to emerge "unbidden" in their lives, thereby helping our

---

between web page design just a few years ago and the standardized web palette instantly available to users of Facebook and MySpace, which encourage these users to imagine they can best express themselves by selecting from an array of predefined options, rather than by struggling to understand what they really want to say so that, in the process, they create a style of their own that fittingly expresses their views. Or one can think about the difference between an educational approach that helps students identify and cultivate their own unique talents and intrinsic skills and capacities in order to help them meet their generation's emerging needs (and, in so doing, simultaneously encourages teachers to come into their own as teachers), as opposed to an approach that treats students merely as raw materials, "human resources," and seeks to remake them so that they can pursue whatever society currently deems to be the most "valuable" career path. (I develop these suggestions in detail in *Heidegger on Ontotheology*, Chs. 2 and 4.) Here it helps to think about how one responds to the resistances one encounters in each case: Does one seek to flatten out and overcome them or, instead, to cultivate that which resists one's will and so help bring it to its own fruition? (I owe this important point to a discussion with Bill Blattner. See also his insightful and pellucid work, *Heidegger's Being and Time: A Reader's Guide*.)

children to discover and develop their own gifts rather than willfully trying to shape them into some preconceived mold (a profound lesson we learn most unmistakably from children who are "differently abled," as Michael Sandel recognizes). In all such cases, a poetic openness to what pushes back against our pre-existing plans and designs helps disclose a texture of inherent meanings, affordances, significations, and solicitations, a texture Heidegger teaches us to discover "all around us" (CCP 147/GA77 227) – not only in nature, our workshops, classrooms, and homes but even in our lives as a whole.[26] For, we truly learn to "make something" out of our lives not when we try to impose an artificial shape on them but, rather, when we learn to discern and develop creatively that which "pushes back" in all the ways mentioned here, and many more.

If intelligibility can be thought of as composed of "texts" that we continually read and interpret (as Derrida's famous *aperçu*, "there is nothing outside the text," suggests), then we can hear Heidegger as reminding us that we need to learn to recognize and respond to the *texture* of these ubiquitous texts. This texture of meanings independent of our wills can be more or less subtle, but by dissolving all being into becoming, the current of Nietzschean technologization tends to sweep right past this texture and can even threaten to wash it away, as in the case of particle board and, much more "dangerously," Heidegger suggests, in the technological reengineering of human beings. Nonetheless, Heidegger remains hopeful that once we learn to discern this technological current, we can also learn to cultivate a "free relation to technology" in which it becomes possible to use even technological devices themselves to resist *technologization*, the nihilistic obviation of any meaning independent of the will. In fact, we are already doing this, for example, when we use a camera, microscope, telescope, or even glasses to help bring out something meaningful that we might not otherwise have seen, when we use a synthesizer or computer to compose a new kind of music that helps us develop and share our sense of what is

---

[26] Put otherwise, Heidegger seeks to teach us "to listen out into the undetermined" for a "coming [which] essentially occurs all around us and at all times" (CCP 147/GA77 226–7). I shall explain what this means in terms of his phenomenology of art in Chapter 3. For an insightful exposition of (what I think of as) the Heideggerian lessons of parenting, see Sandel, *The Case Against Perfection*. For more on the broader existential lesson of this approach, see Hubert Dreyfus and Sean Kelly, *All Things Shining*. Kenneth Maly describes the tripartite "enowning" at the heart of the phenomenon of *Ereignis* in terms that cleave closely to Heidegger's own: "Things emerge into their own, into what is own to them; humans come into their own as they respond to the owning dynamic in being as emergence; being as emergence enowns Dasein – all these dynamics belong to the matter said in 'enowning'" (Maly, *Heidegger's Possibility: Language, Emergence – Saying Be-ing*, 174). As Maly suggests, there is a third dimension of enowning in which being too comes into its own; that happens, I shall suggest, when Dasein and the being of entities come into their own together in such a way that being itself is disclosed in its essential plenitude or polysemy – and this, as we will see, is the crucial *postmodern* moment.

most significant to us, or even when we use a word processor to help bring out what is really there in the texts that matter to us and the philosophical issues that most concern us.

To put the larger point that emerges here in philosophical terms, what the later Heidegger suggests is a fundamental *ontological pluralism* (or *plural realism*). We need to be sensitive enough to meanings independent of the will to be able to "cut reality at the joints," but because those joints provide us with more of a multiply suggestive outline than a final design (as we will see in detail in Chapter 3), there will in most cases be more than one way of disclosing the genuine hints we are offered.[27] This means, for example, that, just as a talented artisan can make more than one thing from a single piece of wood, so there was also more than one form slumbering in the grain of the marble from which Michelangelo "released" his David. And, for the same reasons, there will usually be more than one right answer to the existential question of what we should each do with our lives. (That helps explain the persistent recurrence of the question, since it can never be settled once and for all, as well as why those looking for the one right answer never seem finally to find it.)[28] Indeed, like the neo-Aristotelian view of "open resoluteness" (*Ent-schlossenheit*) that Heidegger developed in *Being and Time*, his later view of the active receptivity of "releasement" (*Gelassenheit*) suggests a kind of ethical and aesthetic *phronêsis* or practical wisdom. The guiding idea here is that, rather than getting hung up looking for the one right answer – and, when we finally despair of finding it, rebounding back to the relativistic view that no answer is better than any other (or concluding nihilistically that intrinsic meanings are an obsolete myth, thereby ignoring the multiple suggestions nature offers us, or overwriting these hints with our own preconceived ideas rather than seeking to develop them creatively) – we should instead cultivate the recognition that in most situations there will be more than one right answer to questions of what to do or how best to go on.

The hermeneutic principle to follow – in ethics as well as aesthetics – is that there is more than one inherent meaning to be found in things. For, if being is conceptually inexhaustible, capable of yielding meaning again and again, then the intrinsic meanings of things must be plural (or essentially polysemic), however paradoxical such a doctrine of ontological pluralism might now seem, given our current obsession with formal systems capable of securing monosemic exactitude. Indeed, as we will see,

---

[27] As Chapter 3 will show, Heidegger suggests in "The Origin of the Work of Art" that intelligibility contains a complex texture of edges, lines, and breaks, and that this "rift-structure" forms an open-ended "basic design" or "outline sketch" (PLT 63/GA5 51) to which we need to learn to be creatively receptive in order to bring at least one of the potentially inexhaustible forms slumbering in the earth into the light of the world.

[28] I make the case for this view in "Heidegger's Perfectionist Philosophy of Education in *Being and Time*."

to understand the being of the entities we encounter in a *postmodern* way is to no longer preconceive everything we experience as *modern* objects to be controlled or as *late-modern* resources to be optimized, but instead to learn to discern and creatively develop the independent meanings, solicitations, and affordances of things, staying open to the multiple suggestions that things offer us and dedicating ourselves to bringing forth such hints creatively and responsibly into the world. That is what I mean by Heidegger's *plural realism*, which (as we will see) comes through in his postmodern call for us to cultivate a comportment receptive to poetic polysemy. I hope that this all-too-brief overview provides some preliminary sense of what is at stake in Heidegger's thinking of the genuine possibilities of postmodernity, a matter I shall seek to bring out more fully in the rest of the book by approaching it from several different but complementary perspectives.

4. IMAGES OF ONTOTHEOLOGY

Let me thus introduce the more precise images for ontotheology promised earlier, images that can help us head-off some common misunderstandings of Heidegger's view. Jonathan Swift's wonderful satire, *Gulliver's Travels*, begins with Lemuel Gulliver recounting his famous experiences among the miniscule Lilliputians, where Gulliver lives like a mountain among men. Then, in his second adventure, Gulliver describes the inverted experience of life among the gargantuan Brobdingnagians (even their name is big), who tower above Gulliver just as he once towered above the tiny Lilliputians. It is easy to imagine Gulliver's sense of perspective being thoroughly relativized by these successive experiences of immensity and minuteness, and Gulliver's third adventure begins (not coincidentally, I would suggest) with him set adrift at sea, a state from which he is rescued and then hoisted aboard a great floating island called Laputa. Gulliver's fundamental bearings thus get reestablished, paradoxically, by a land that hovers in mid-air – a seeming impossibility nicely captured in René Magritte's rather ominous painting, *La Château des Pyrénées* [*"The Castle of the Pyrenees"*] (1959).[29] (See Figure 1.)

The male inhabitants who rule the floating island of Laputa are deeply autistic. Swift writes that "the minds of these people are so taken up with intense speculations that they neither can speak nor attend to the discourses of others"; they require servants to tap them on the mouth or the ear when it is their turn to talk or to listen. These Laputans remain so lost in thought that, like their philosophical forebear, Thales (whom

---

[29] The impression that Magritte's "La Château des Pyrénées" seems inspired by Swift's portrait of Laputa is reinforced by one of two early sketches of the painting (held, along with the painting itself, in the Israel Museum, Jerusalem), which shows the giant rock floating ominously *above* a large dwelling, as if threatening to crush it. See http://www.imj.org.il/imagine/item.asp?table=comb&itemNum=243183 (accessed 12 January 2008).

FIGURE 1. René Magritte, *La Château des Pyrénées*, 1959, Israel Museum, Jerusalem, Israel. © 2010 C. Herscovici, London/Artists Rights Society (ARS), NY. Reproduced by permission from Art Resource, NY, and ARS. Photo credit: Banque d'Images, ADAGP/Art Resource, NY.

Swift knowingly caricatures), when they leave their homes they are in constant "danger of falling down every precipice."[30] Although the Laputans'

---

[30] In *The Promise of Wisdom*, J. Glenn Gray remarks that "theoretical wisdom ... does not, as the Greeks poetically put it, 'teach a man how to find his way home.'" Although their poets

theoretical obsessions leave them nearly incapacitated in practical matters, they nevertheless govern the country below them by applying to all practical problems a speculative philosophy the twin foci of which are pure mathematics and astronomy. The distance between these everyday problems and the Laputans' soaring speculations generate absurd and destructive "solutions," but the Laputans back up their speculative philosophy with brute force, literally crushing rebellions by landing their giant island on any city that refuses their rule. Even the Laputans' physiognomy reflects their twin philosophical fixations on mathematics and astronomy; "one of their eyes [is] turned inward, and the other [looks] directly up to the zenith."[31]

Thinking of Swift's striking image of the Laputans' dual gaze – a gaze directed simultaneously inward and outward, with one eye looking for truth deep within while the other searches for it beyond the heavens – we have to ask: Is this not a nearly perfect analogy for the ontotheological obsessions of the metaphysical tradition? Swift's image is pushed even closer toward perfection, for our purposes, by the fact these Laputans, whose ontotheological

sometimes liked to make fun of them, I think the Greek philosophers understood better than we do that the ultimate practical virtues are extremely difficult to attain without theoretical wisdom to help guide the way. Gray suggests as much with his droll observation that: "It is one of life's ironies in our times that so many of us require more knowledge, even to find our way home, than we really care to have." Gray's insight (the pithy epigram I have taken as my epigraph) can itself be heard ironically, as pointing out that our lives are maintained by technological devices the mechanics of which most of us no longer even want to understand. But it can also be taken unironically, as suggesting that if we human beings are ever going to become at home in our contemporary world, then we need to understand not just the mechanics of technological devices but also the underlying "principles" driving global technologization. The theoretical wisdom we need to guide us derives, then, not just from the metaphysical quest for unshakeable ontotheological foundations (the quest that generated the growing technologization of the earth), but also from thoughtful insight into the limits and dangers of the ontotheological foundations of our own age. For, without insight into the way the Nietzschean ontotheology continues to generate and reinforce our growing sense of ontological homelessness, we are unlikely to find a way to become at home in our world. Gray nicely underscores the importance of this ontological odyssey when he concludes his book by claiming that "the search for an education is man's age-old search to become at home in the world." Gray even seems to agree with Heidegger that the path to such homecoming is through that "reflective thinking" that yields "equanimity," a rather Heideggerian virtue (cf. *Gelassenheit*) that Gray defines, with evocative simplicity, as "the fruit of self-possession and discipline in the pursuit of more comprehensive experience." Indeed, as Martin Woessner recognizes, "Heidegger is referred to only twice in *The Promise of Wisdom*, but his influence suffuses the whole project." (See Gray, *The Promise of Wisdom: An Introduction to Philosophy of Education*, 24, 203, 271, 275; Woessner. "J. Glenn Gray: Philosopher, Translator (of Heidegger), and Warrior," 498.)

[31] Swift, *Gulliver's Travels*, Part Three, Chapter II, 170–1. Kierkegaard similarly imagines "a novel in which the main character would be a man who had obtained a pair of glasses, one lens of which reduced images as powerfully as an oxyhydrogen microscope, and the other magnifies on the same scale." (See Rick Anthony Furtak, *Wisdom in Love: Kierkegaard and the Ancient Quest for Emotional Integrity*, 203 note 14.)

gaze blinds them to the immediate and leads them to destroy the world they rule, live on a solid island paradoxically floating in mid-air. From a Heideggerian perspective, *they are us*, living on an ungrounded ground that is supported by dual insights into the innermost core of reality and its ultimate expression. The Laputans *look like* ontotheologists, in short, and the floating island of Laputa is a nearly perfect image for Heidegger's understanding of the way in which metaphysics' dual ontotheological understandings of the being of entities leave our unified constellations of intelligibility, our shared sense of what is and what matters, suspended epistemically, floating somewhere between the unshakeable foundation we continue to yearn for and the yawning abyss we still fear.

The strange suspension of this solid ground allows me to speak to a worry that might have occurred to you earlier: Why think that the history of being takes the shape of a series of overlapping but relatively distinct "epochs"? The answer is that ontotheologies join the dual points at which humanity's microscopic and telescopic conceptual spadework turns; that is, these ontotheologies establish for their time both the innermost element out of which (the being of) everything else is composed and the outermost perspective from which (the being of) reality as a whole can be grasped. The fact that these ontotheological foundations are neither absolute nor arbitrary but instead represent the historically variable limits of human knowledge explains why the history of being takes the form of a series of unified epochs rather than either a single monolithic epoch or an unbroken flux. Swift thus gives us a suggestive image of ontological epochality and historicity: Our ontotheologies supply our epochal constellations of intelligibility with the firmest ground possible historically, and yet our firm ground nevertheless seems to hover in thin air, like Laputa, when viewed from a sufficient distance.

Other worries arise for the post-Heideggerian reader of *Gulliver's Travels* when Swift has Gulliver speculate about the etymology of "Laputa." Gulliver rejects the stock derivation according to which the floating island's name means *governing from on high* (from *Lap*, "high," plus *untah*, "governor"), a straightforward etymology Gulliver ironically dismisses as "too strained." Instead, Gulliver offers "to the learned" his own etymological conjecture that Laputa derives from *Lap*, "the dancing of sunbeams in the sea," plus *outed*, "a wing."[32] Gulliver's outlandish poetic

[32] Swift, *Gulliver's Travels*, 173–4. The main worry I have in mind is not, as readers might expect, Heidegger's own occasional etymological debates, examples of which I have dealt with in detail elsewhere (more sympathetically in *Heidegger on Ontotheology* and more critically in "On the Advantages and Disadvantages of Reading Heidegger Backwards: White's *Time and Death*," 103–120). My moderate conclusion would be that Heidegger's use of etymology is more defensible than commonly thought but less reliable than the Heideggerian faithful like to believe, and must thus be examined on a case by case basis.

speculations obscure the fact that, for Swift himself, Laputa is obviously a simple contraction of the Spanish words meaning "the prostitute," *la Puta*. What this suggests, perhaps, is that Swift's own sympathies do not lie with Heidegger's idealistic view that metaphysics, despite its ivory-tower autism, does indeed rule the world. Swift's own view seems closer to an historical materialist critique of such a high-flown conception of philosophy, a critique that suggests that even the most seemingly disconnected speculations of metaphysics can ultimately be reduced to a covert apologia for the economic order. At any rate, Swift helps raise the question: Is philosophy ultimately just a high-minded prostitute for the economy? Or at the very least, doesn't Heidegger credit the great metaphysicians with an unjustifiably exalted role in establishing and maintaining intelligibility, thereby ignoring the broader and deeper historical and material forces that shape the world out of which even the great metaphysicians think their lofty thoughts?[33]

Heidegger is careful to stress that the epochal transformations catalyzed by ontotheologists like Nietzsche are not the creations of some Promethean philosopher's private imagination. As he puts it: "Nietzsche neither made nor chose his way himself, no more than any other thinker ever did. He

---

[33] For a more detailed response to this question, see *Heidegger on Ontotheology*, Ch.2. Crowe advances a similar criticism of this "implausibly inflated view of the real influence of philosophers," but Crowe motivates the criticism with a different and interesting worry: How could metaphysicians reshape a culture in which "literacy was the achievement of a small minority"? When one thinks about *ontological holism* – which, as the name suggests, holds that all meaning is *interconnected* (hence *holism*) and also turns on an understanding of the meaning of *being* (hence *ontological*) – this objection becomes less pressing. For, there is no reason why the interconnected networks of intelligibility that constitute Dasein's world should be transmitted solely within *written* language (or even writing *and speech*). As Heidegger already recognized in *Being and Time*, discourse goes deeper than our explicit use of language. My account of ontotheology seeks to explain Heidegger's (admittedly underelaborated) view of the mechanism by which the "deep framework" of a culture gets refocused, transformed, and disseminated by metaphysicians, who are thus not simply "invisibly shaped" by some mysterious process that they passively serve (even though they often take important cues to what being is from poets and other artists, as Crowe, following Dreyfus, rightly points out). In Heidegger's view, the great metaphysicians help universalize and disseminate a new understanding of what is and what matters (one often first disclosed by works of art, as we will see next chapter), thereby shaping the future in the same way they themselves have been shaped by the past. (This is precisely what Heidegger thinks makes them "great.") Heidegger's insights into ontotheology thus allow him to appropriate Nietzsche's insights that "the world revolves ... *invisibly* ... around the inventors of new values" and that the thoughts that change the world "arrive on the wings of a dove," i.e., quietly, "far from the marketplace and from fame." Of course, even if Heidegger were wrong about the historical influence of ancient ontotheologies, his critique of technologization turns on his reading of Nietzsche's ontotheology, which is why I have mostly been concerned to explain and defend the core of this crucial reading. (See Benjamin D. Crowe, *Heidegger's Phenomenology of Religion: Realism and Cultural Criticism*, 27 note 11; Nietzsche, *Thus Spoke Zarathustra*, 164.)

is *sent* on his way." (WCT 46/GA8 50) Heidegger's idea that historical transformations are "sent" by being is usually given a mystical or quietistic interpretation, but I think it is better heard as a *realistic* acknowledgment of our situatedness within (and, hence, the importance of our *receptivity* to) ontohistorical currents that shape us much more than we shape them. In fact, the later Heidegger came to believe that spitting into the wind of the history of being is pointless, and that we can change this history only by pushing it forward, developing it to the point where it turns into something else.[34]

Heidegger should have been more clear, nonetheless, that the ontotheologies that catalyze epochal shifts in our history often do so by generalizing discoveries from subdomains ("positive science" or "regional ontologies") of our knowledge. Ontotheologies can rapidly accelerate preexisting historical trends by moving them from the periphery to the center of our culture's historical self-understanding. In Nietzsche's case, for example, Adam Smith had already described the way an "invisible hand" optimizes economic growth when the forces of supply and demand are unfettered and allowed to fight it out, just as Darwin had suggested that competition over scarce resources generates an escalating evolutionary arms-race between living things, an endless struggle that serves the continued growth of life itself. Nietzsche, long sympathetic to the Greek's Olympian enthronement of the agonistic principle that *competition is good*, can be understood as having ontologized and so universalized the cutting-edge insights of economics and biology, thereby celebrating will-to-power as the fundamental law of being in general and so extrapolating it to its ultimate expression in the endless cosmic boom-and-bust cycle of eternal recurrence.

We must, of course, acknowledge that Heidegger's interpretation of Nietzsche is reductive and (as he frequently admitted) "violent." Heidegger's

---

[34] As I show in "On the Advantages and Disadvantages of Reading Heidegger Backwards," to "err" in Heidegger's distinctive sense is not (*pace* White) to swim against the tide of the history of being but, on the contrary, to be carried along by this tide so as to develop the understanding of being implicitly guiding one's own historical epoch. Thus Heidegger believed that his own middle-period thinking from the early 1930s had "erred" by inadvertently extending Nietzsche's ontotheology instead of contesting and transcending it, as his later work seeks to do. Yet, this does not mean Heidegger believed that this "errancy" of thought was simply a mistake. The idea underlying Heidegger's notoriously unapologetic "He who thinks greatly errs greatly," on the contrary, is that *the only way out of an historical understanding of being is to think it through to its end and so pass beyond it.* As Heidegger puts it: "Errancy is that within which a particular understanding of being [*Seyn*] must err, which erring alone truly traverses the clearing of refusal – traverses in accord with the clearing of what is lighted up." (M 229/GA66 259) Errancy does not mean swimming upstream ontohistorically, then, but rather following the current all the way to its end, where it turns into something else, as Heidegger thought his own extreme Nietzscheanism in the 1930s developed Nietzsche's technological ontotheology to exhaustion and, in so doing, opened a path leading beyond it. I develop this view in detail in the chapters that follow.

single-minded focus on Nietzsche's "unthought" ontotheology, while extremely revealing, leads him to ignore many other significant aspects of Nietzsche's thought. Although Heidegger proudly opposed the partisan distortions of "Nietzscheanism" (HR 203/GA90 255), it is undeniable that Heidegger – in his lifelong confrontation with Nietzsche's thought (which can be traced back to Heidegger's very first publication in 1909) – took Nietzsche seriously and even, in a certain sense, sympathetically.[35] To put it starkly, Heidegger is the only other major philosopher who believed that Nietzsche's thinking really was as important as Nietzsche himself believed. Nietzsche was a philosopher, let us not forget, who gave his autobiography section titles like "Why I am a Destiny," and who claimed that his thought predicted "the history of the next two centuries."[36] In his own way, Heidegger agreed, proclaiming that: "Nietzsche is the name for an age of the world" (GA50 84).

In fact, it is difficult to emphasize sufficiently just how profoundly ambiguous a figure Heidegger's Nietzsche really is. In the end, Heidegger thinks of Nietzsche as "a transition, pointing before and behind, … and therefore everywhere ambiguous," a great thinker who recognized "that it was his own thought that would first have to bring about a devastation in whose midst, in another day and from other sources, oases would rise here and there and springs well up" (WCT 51/GA8 54). A great thinker's "unthought" is that point toward which their thinking is moving, not so much their unconscious – although "the thinker can never say that which is most his own" (EP 77–8/NII 484) – as their internal avant-garde. This unthought is the great thinker's understanding to being, an unformulated understanding that quietly stands behind or before all a great thinker's other thoughts, driving them and calling them forth. Questioning means thinking after or toward (*nachdenken*) this unthought point that (in ontohistorical terms) reaches the furthest ahead in another thinker's thought. In plain English, questioning is an endeavor to pick up and push forward that which thinks the furthest ahead in a predecessor's thinking – and so help move history. Heidegger attempts to think Nietzsche's "unthought" ontotheology because it is this ontotheology that supplies our late-modern constellation of intelligibility with its fundamental and ultimate conceptual parameters (its understanding of being as nothing but will-to-power eternally recurring), and Heidegger believed that only by thinking through and beyond this nihilistic reduction of being to nothing

---

[35] Heidegger's deeply ambivalent, lifelong altercation with Nietzsche begins in his very first publication, "*Allerseelenstimmungen*" ("Moods and Voices of All Souls," from 1909). In this dark and imaginative work of philosophically informed religious fiction, the climactic moment comes from the then-twenty-year-old Heidegger's portrayal of the unexpected religious conversion of a young Nietzschean atheist. (See Denker, Gander, and Zaborowski, eds., *Heidegger – Jahrbuch 1: Heidegger und die Anfänge seines Denkens*, 18–21.)

[36] See Nietzsche, *Ecce Homo: How to Become What You Are.*

but intrinsically meaningless "resources" can we hope to transcend the nihilistic undercurrents of the age and begin to understand being in a genuinely *postmodern* way.

Heidegger's attempt to think Nietzsche's unthought is thus an effort not to refute his thinking but instead to develop it beyond where Nietzsche left it by making explicit the point toward which it was heading ontohistorically. Heidegger's "altercation" (*Auseinandersetzung*) with Nietzsche sought this Nietzsche beyond Nietzsche in two senses: First, the Nietzsche whose unthought ontotheology helped catalyze the ongoing technologization of reality in which we remain caught; but also, second (and even further ahead), the Nietzsche who struggled valiantly to help inspire a way beyond the nihilistic age he both predicted and inadvertently ushered in. Thus, in the same crucial notebook entry in which Nietzsche joins will-to-power and eternal recurrence as "the pinnacle of contemplation," Nietzsche also observes that we have reached the historical "tipping point" into nihilism, imagining his philosophers of the future as "amphibians" capable of crawling out of the old sea of meaning and surviving on the desert-dry landscape of nihilism. Urging "bravery" and "patience," Nietzsche calls for us to balance between worlds – "no 'going back,' no ardent rush forward," he advises – and his final word is "plenitude." This, I think, is the postmodern Nietzsche who anticipates Heidegger, the Nietzsche of youth and creativity, of abundance and excess, and we should acknowledge this Nietzsche even as we share Heidegger's suspicions, learned the hard way, of the late-modern Nietzsche whose own *magnum opus* came to teach the world "the *superman*," the notorious doctrine that "humanity is something that should be *superseded*." Rather than defend the Nietzsche of optimization, the Nietzsche of "breeding and selection," the Nietzsche who eagerly anticipated "the task of rearing a master race," who called for the emergence of a "higher type" of human being who would embrace the "deadly truth" that life is will-to-power and so set out to reshape human beings the way artists sculpt clay, let us instead celebrate the other Nietzsche who leads beyond the pro-eugenicist, late-modern Nietzsche whom Heidegger was right, I think, to subject to such relentless and sometimes acerbic criticism.[37]

---

[37] See Nietzsche, *Writings from the Late Notebooks*, 71. We will examine *Thus Spoke Zarathustra*'s notorious doctrine of "the *superhuman*: Humanity is something that should be *superseded*" in Chapter 5. Heidegger's Nietzsche interpretation cannot simply be dismissed on textual grounds (because evidence for it can be drawn from published works like *Zarathustra* as well as from Nietzsche's unpublished *Nachlaß*). Nor can it be ruled out on principle, even by a radically perspectivalist or "postmodern" reading, which would seek to disabuse us of any "myth of unity" in Nietzsche's work, thereby trying to undercut the systematic interpretations defended by Heidegger and, more recently, by such leading Nietzsche scholars as John Richardson, Laurence Lampert, R. Kevin Hill, Bernard Reginster, and Julian Young. (See Richardson's *Nietzsche's System*; Lampert's *Nietzsche's Teaching: An Interpretation of* Thus Spoke Zarathustra; Hill's *Nietzsche's Critiques: The Kantian Foundations of His Thought*; Reginster's *The Affirmation of Life: Nietzsche on Overcoming Nihilism*; and Young's

5. CONCLUSIONS: ON THE USE AND ABUSE
OF ONTOTHEOLOGY FOR RELIGION

Let me address one final misunderstanding. Many readers seem to think that by *ontotheology* Heidegger simply means any view that treats God as the self-caused cause of creation, the ultimate anchor meant to halt the regress in an otherwise unending chain of cause and effect. As should now be clear, however, this is only one part of Heidegger's larger view of metaphysics as ontotheology – an undeniably interesting part, and one which has helped inspire that return to religion currently underway in contemporary continental circles, but a single part nevertheless. We should thus be careful not to reduce Heidegger's complex view of ontotheology to one of its component parts. For, by treating this theological part as if it were the ontotheological whole, one eclipses that larger and more important whole from view – obscuring the way Heidegger's understanding of ontotheology explains his famous critique of late-modern technologization, for example, and the way it reveals his later attempt to help us think our way into a postmodern age to be much more philosophically coherent and persuasive than is usually recognized (as I shall suggest in the chapters that follow). It remains worthwhile, nonetheless, to see how an appreciation of this ontotheological whole allows us to better understand that theological part to which it is too often reduced.

Nietzsche's Philosophy of Religion.) Not surprisingly, it is Derrida who pushes this postmodern reading of Nietzsche to its limit, notoriously suggesting that "there is no such thing either as the truth of Nietzsche, or of Nietzsche's texts," a claim he argues for by parodying Heidegger's method. Drawing on a fragment from Nietzsche's unpublished *Nachlaß*, the seemingly irrelevant "I have forgotten my umbrella," Derrida makes this fragment the basis of his own alternative reading of Nietzsche. "I have forgotten my umbrella" becomes (through some rather tortured arguments I shall not try to reconstruct) a reminder not to forget Nietzsche's "hermaphroditic" style, a style that both proposes interpretations and recedes from them. Derrida's conclusion is that Nietzsche's work, like his forgotten umbrella, remains "at once" both "open and closed" – that is, always "indefinitely open" to another reading, and yet closed to any *totalizing* reading that would preemptively foreclose all future readings. (See Derrida, *Spurs: Nietzsche's Styles*, 103, 137.) As we will see, Heidegger himself suggests that this is true of any great text, which is why Derrida claims that what is at stake in Heidegger's interpretation of Nietzsche is nothing less than "the question of interpretation itself" (73). In the end, I think the right conclusion to draw both from the leading Nietzsche scholars and the postmodern "new Nietzscheans" is not that Heidegger's interpretation is false but, instead, that it is far from having exhausted the meaning of Nietzsche's thinking (which did indeed anticipate some of Heidegger's central ideas). Heidegger reveals something deep and important that is genuinely there in Nietzsche's work, just not the whole story (which means that Heidegger's reading can be dismissed only in its occasional pretensions to completion). This is why *Heidegger on Ontotheology* consistently refers to Heidegger's Nietzsche interpretation as "reductive yet revealing"; I show why it is revealing, and Heidegger's Nietzschean critics suggest different ways in which it is reductive, but we should deny neither.

Remember that Kant coined the term *ontotheology* in order to designate that "transcendental" approach to theology exemplified by Saint Anselm's famous "ontological proof" for the existence of God. Such a theological approach believes, as Kant put it, that the existence of God can be derived from "mere concepts, without the help of any experience whatsoever."[38] What Kant calls *ontotheology*, in other words, is the idea that the existence of God can be proved simply by analyzing the concept "God." This "ontological proof," put simply, holds, first, that the concept "God" should be analyzed as "that being greater than whom none can be conceived" and, second, that this "greatest possible being" must exist *for strictly logical reasons*, because a perfect god who exists would be "greater" than one who does not.[39] The problem with the ontological proof, in Kant's view, is that adding to a conceptual description of some being *that this being exists* actually adds no further *content* to that conceptual description. Thus Kant argues that if I completely list all the predicates describing the coin in my pocket – it is circular, silver-colored, metallic, imprinted with images, hatched all the way around the edge, and so on – and then I add as the last item on my list that the coin in my pocket *exists*, that last step will have added no further content to my concept of the coin in my pocket.

What is most interesting about this old debate, from our perspective, is that Heidegger never simply accepted the claim on which Kant's rejection of the ontological proof rests – namely, that (in Kant's terms) "existence is not a real predicate."[40] Heidegger points out that a *real* predicate means a predicate belonging to "a *res*, a substance, to the substantive content of a thing" (P 341/GA9 451). Heidegger thus reinterprets Kant's thesis to mean "that being itself can never be explained by *what* any given being is" (P 342/GA9 452). In Heidegger's view, what metaphysics has taught us to call "existence" does not itself simply possess some determinate content; rather, "it" remains the source of all the possible contentful descriptions we have yet to discover and enumerate. We could thus say that what for Kant is not a real predicate is for Heidegger the source of all the predicates yet to be disclosed. The very idea of a complete description or an exhaustive conceptual analysis of any entity, even one as commonplace as the coin

---

[38] See Immanuel Kant, *Critique of Pure Reason*, A632/B660, 525.

[39] Perhaps the easiest way to see the point is the Cartesian one. Compare the two leading candidates for the title of greatest possible being. Both are conceived of as possessing all the conceptually-maximized, divine attributes (omniscience, omnipotence, and so on), but only the second is conceived of, in addition, as actually *existing*. Which of these two candidates would be the *greatest* entity? It seems obvious that the perfect being who actually exists possesses something the other perfect being lacks, namely, existence. But if so, then that being "than whom none greater can be conceived" – that is, God – must actually exist. (Given the well-documented problems with this ontological proof for the existence of God, it is noteworthy that as strict a logical mind as the young Bertrand Russell initially found it compelling; see *The Autobiography of Bertrand Russell*.)

[40] See Kant, *Critique of Pure Reason*, A598/B626, 504.

in my pocket, is not something Heidegger would accept, precisely because the being of an entity remains conceptually inexhaustible. That, as we will see, is what Heidegger thinks the great artists and poets teach us, *pace* the great metaphysicians. For, even if we spent months seeking to completely describe a quotidian entity like the coin in my pocket, enumerating a list of predicates several pages long, a sufficiently insightful poet would still be able to notice something about the coin that we had missed and, what is more, this poet could put a name on that contentful quality that renders it visible to us, allowing us to see it and to see that we had overlooked it.

Still, poets are more painfully aware than anyone of the fact that the words they use to disclose and communicate these heretofore unglimpsed aspects of reality fail to fully express and communicate their poetic insights. A thoughtful insight into poetry itself can thus help teach us to experience "being as such" as what both elicits and resists poetic naming. We can learn to see – over the shoulder of the poet, as it were – the way poets themselves experience this conceptually inexhaustible dimension of our reality as a kind of preconceptual givenness and extra-conceptual excess that precedes and exceeds the poetic act of concept formation. Heidegger thus believes that thinking carefully through poetry can help attune us to that dimension of our experience of being in which he places his hope for the future. For, the future itself comes from the poetic naming-into-being of still unglimpsed aspects of our experience, as well as from the thoughtful rediscovery of aspects of being we were once aware of but whose full meaning has been lost to us through disuse or worn away through overuse.[41] (We will flesh out this view as we explore Heidegger's phenomenology of art in the next two chapters.)

What conclusion, then, is suggested by Heidegger's critique of Kant on ontotheology? For Heidegger, the real problem with the ontological proof is not that it might be invalid but, rather, that it reflects and reinforces a phenomenologically misguided and historically disastrous approach to thinking about humanity's relation to "the divine."[42] The problem with conceiving of God ontotheologically – whether ontotheology is taken in the sense Kant criticizes, as an attempt to provide a purely conceptual proof of God's existence, or in the sense Heidegger criticizes, which includes any understanding of God as a self-caused cause or as the outermost entity in the causal chain of creation – is that such attempts to secure our relation to God conceptually in fact work to disconnect Western humanity from

---

[41] See, e.g., Heidegger, "Homecoming/To Kindred Ones" (1943), EHP 23–49/GA4 9–31. Here I take myself to be supplementing the insightful view articulated by Hubert Dreyfus in "Heidegger on the connection between nihilism, art, technology, and politics."

[42] One objection to the ontological proof, especially relevant from our perspective, is that "the greatest possible being" is not intrinsic to the concept of God as such but is only an influential way in which the Judeo-Christian tradition has sought to conceive of the ontotheological creator God.

the real and immediate relation to the divine experienced by ancients and mystics alike, an experience that, Heidegger believes, still remains open to us today (whether or not we consider ourselves "believers").

It is here that Heidegger's critique of metaphysics as ontotheology importantly includes his critique of this metaphysical understanding of God as a self-caused cause. His famous criticism is that this "God of the metaphysicians" is not the God of religious faith, that is, not the God before whom humanity has historically knelt in prayer or danced in ecstatic celebration. Hence, near the end of his difficult but important lecture on "The Ontotheological Constitution of Metaphysics" (1957), Heidegger criticizes philosophy's narrowly rational and so religiously deflated understanding of God as the "*Causa sui*," the primal, self-caused cause of the universe:

This is the right name for the god of philosophy. Man can neither pray nor sacrifice to this god. Before the *Causa sui*, man can neither fall to his knees in awe nor can he play music and dance before this god. / The godless thinking which must abandon the god of philosophy, god as *Causa sui*, is thus perhaps closer to the divine God. (ID 72/GA11 77)

For the early, Christian Heidegger, the "God of faith" meant "the crucified God," Christ, a Pauline faith in whom opens up a radically transformed experience of temporality as eschatological (as culminating in an end of time for humanity on earth), and hence as linear rather than as cyclical and continuously self-resurrecting. (Easter, written atop the pagan rites of Spring, allows Christianity to absorb and reappropriate rebirth, taking it out of the recurring cycles of nature and transposing it into the purported resurrection of the human soul in an afterlife.)[43] As we will see in Chapter 7, the later, post-Christian Heidegger's mysterious hints about gods and God refer to the departed gods of Greece and the as-yet unnamed (and so unarrived) God whom Hölderlin evokes in his poetry and prose, situating our technological age of divine "destitution" in the time "between" the gods who have fled and the God who is yet to come.[44]

For reasons I shall explain in Chapter 6, I find myself increasingly inclined to conclude that "being as such" – that is, "be-ing" in its *difference* from the metaphysically conceived understanding of the being of entities – *is* the later Heidegger's unnamed name for this God to come, "the last or ultimate God" whom he evokes ("against the Christian" [CP 283/ GA65 403]) at the climax of his *Contributions to Philosophy (From Enowning)*. Heidegger's post-Christian "last God" is a phenomenologized (and so

---

43 See, e.g., Heidegger, "Phenomenology and Theology," *Pathmarks*, 44. Nietzsche's thinking of eternal recurrence seeks to restore rebirth to nature (as, ultimately, the endless cycle of the cosmos itself), which is one of the reasons he ends *Ecce Homo* by setting "*Dionysus against the Crucified.*"

44 On the "Last God" in Heidegger's *Contributions to Philosophy (From Enowning)*, see Chapter 6; on the riches inherent in the poverty of this "destitution," see Chapter 7.

secularized) rethinking of Meister Eckhart's "Godhead" (that is, a finally unnamable source of all our different conceptions of god), one whose name the later Heidegger will tellingly write only under erasure in his "fourfold," and thereby pluralize (no longer speaking of God but, instead, of gods).[45] Here it is crucial to remember that this fourfold of "earth and the heavens, mortals and divinities" emerged from the later Heidegger's "cross-wise striking-through" of being in 1955.[46] Through this fourfold, the later Heidegger's hidden and unnamed postmodern Godhead, being as such, reveals itself as an in principle multiplicity, an ontological pluralism beyond ontotheology – and irreducible even to polytheism. For, after rejecting the labels "monotheism," "pantheism," and "atheism" as metaphysically overloaded concepts, Heidegger dismisses "all types of 'theism' as the confused legacy of 'Judeo-Christian 'apologetics.'" Heidegger also thinks it is a mistake to try to quantify the divine because he associates our obsession with quantification (which ends up replacing quality with quantity) with the very nihilistic technological ontotheology that he hopes to help us transcend, in part by redescribing – in secular, phenomenological terms – the kind of enduringly meaningful experiences traditionally described as encounters with the "divine." Nonetheless, Heidegger's phenomenological redescription of "the gods" can still be tentatively characterized as *polytheistic*, in keeping with his contention that: "The multitude of gods cannot be quantified.... The last God is not the end but rather the other beginning of immeasurable possibilities for our history" (CP 289/ GA65 411). As I have suggested (and shall try to show in what follows), this initially esoteric doctrine of ineliminable *ontological pluralism* stands at the center of Heidegger's hope for a postmodern understanding of being as an inexhaustible source of those genuine meanings that remain at least partly independent of the will.[47]

---

[45] See Reiner Schürmann, *Wandering Joy: Meister Eckhart's Mystical Philosophy*; see also Benjamin Crowe, *Heidegger's Phenomenology of Religion*, 122–34.

[46] See Heidegger, "On the Question of Being" (1955), P 291–322/GA9 385–426.

[47] "The Last God" begins with this epigraph: "The entirely other against that which has been, especially against the Christian" (CP 283/GA65 403). In the "incalculable moment" of the "turning" into this other beginning (when we suddenly recognize that what we experienced as nothing but constant becoming was instead the way that the presencing of being as such makes itself felt within our Nietzschean ontotheology), being "is like the nothing" (CP 292/GA65 415). Indeed, Heidegger writes: "All these decisions, which seem to be so many and varied, are gathered into one thing only: whether being definitively withdraws or whether this withdrawal as refusal becomes the first truth and the other beginning of history." (CP 63/GA65 91) In this experience (of, in Heidegger's language, the "nihilating" of the nothing as the concealed "presencing" of being), Heidegger writes in *Contributions*, "god ... appears ... solely in the space of 'being' itself" (CP 293, my emphasis/ GA65 416). Heidegger always explicitly disavows any equation of being with God, leading Derrida to write, misleadingly, of Heidegger's "negative theology" (see Derrida, "How to Avoid Speaking: Denials," in *Psyche: Inventions of the Other*, and "Sauf le nom" in *On the Name*). These very denials suggest to me that for Heidegger God is not the source of

Ontotheological approaches to religion were historically disastrous, then, precisely because they eclipse what Western humanity originally experienced as a direct attunement to holistically (but not necessarily peacefully) interconnected aspects of a reality larger and more powerful than ourselves – as, for example, the polytheistic Greeks were struck by Apollo in the sudden epiphany, experienced Athena when just the right judgment came to them, were seized by Ares when overtaken by war-like aggression, and knew Aphrodite in moments of erotic ecstasy.[48] Ontotheological approaches lead us away from such immediately felt experiences of genuine meaning and toward a cognitive demand for a kind of detached intellectual certainty regarding some entity standing outside this world. Such approaches thus work to enforce our alienation from genuinely "holy" experiences – that is, experiences capable of helping to *heal* human beings by reminding us of our place in the larger *whole*. For Heidegger, such restorative encounters help us recall that we are humble, earth-bound "shepherds of being" in all its conceptually inexhaustible, holistic interconnectedness, and not just ontotheologically domineering "lords over entities," insatiably driven to seek mastery over an "objective" world of entities from which we are becoming increasingly alienated by our modern ways of conceptualizing and so experiencing ourselves.

As we will see in the chapters that follow, Heidegger suggests that finding our way into a genuinely "postmodern" understanding – one in which we experience our worlds as inherently meaningful and so can truly find ourselves at-home in them, as belonging there (rather than merely becoming numb to our own alienation) – enjoins us to cultivate a more thoughtful

being (as in ontotheology) but rather the reverse, that being as such remains the source of any experience or thinking of God. Heidegger often disassociates being from God, e.g., by writing that "being is never a determination of God itself; rather, being is that which God needs in order to [be] God and yet remain completely different [*das Seyn ist Jenes, was die Götterung des Gottes braucht, um doch und vollends davon unterscheiden zu bleiben*]" (CP 169/GA65 240). (Here Heidegger employs the neologism *Götterung*, "Godding," in order to evoke the being of God – the way God "is" – without using the word "being" or its inflections.) His point is not that being is God but, instead, that being is (what Meister Eckhart called) the *Godhead* of God; i.e., "God" is only one of the names by which being shows itself, a showing that, even in the richest polytheism, does not exhaust being. For, being always withholds itself for future manifestations – profane as well as sacred – in its very *difference* from that which presently shows itself (even as God). Thus, what Heidegger once called by a succession of names such as "being as such," and which he will in the end no longer name but only evoke through the fourfold, becomes in *Contributions* the "last" or "ultimate" (*Letzte*) God, an unnamed – and never completely nameable – source of all historical intelligibility. I would thus suggest that Heidegger rejects "pantheism" because he himself is a pan-beingist, disavows "monotheism" because he is a polytheist, and repudiates "atheism" because that is what his own religious position will look like to a traditional, monotheistic, Christian ontotheologist.

48 See Hubert L. Dreyfus and Sean Kelly, *All Things Shining: Reading the Western Classics to Find Meaning in a Secular Age.*

awareness of the relation between our most fundamental ways of conceiving of our reality, on the one hand, and the basic experiences that first give rise to these worlds of meaning, on the other. Let us thus turn, in Chapter 2, to Heidegger's critique of those fundamental ways of conceiving ourselves and our relationship to the world that most directly obscure the source from which he thinks a history changing transformation of our understanding of being might yet come. Let us turn, in other words, to the reductive modern understanding of *art* as "aesthetics."

2

Heidegger's Critique of Modern Aesthetics

> Aesthetics is for the artist as ornithology is for the birds.
>
> Barnet Newman (famous witticism)

> The essence of art is not the expression of lived experience.... Nor does this essence consist in the artist depicting reality more accurately and precisely than others, or producing ([that is,] representing) something that gives pleasure to others, that provides enjoyment of a higher or lower type.... But in order to understand what the work of art and poetry are as such, philosophy must first break the habit of grasping the problem of art as one of aesthetics.
>
> Heidegger (ET 47/GA34 63–4)

1. INTRODUCTION: HEIDEGGER – AGAINST AESTHETICS, FOR ART

Heidegger is against the modern tradition of philosophical "aesthetics" because he is for the true "work of art" which, he argues, the aesthetic approach to art eclipses.[1] Heidegger's critique of aesthetics and his advocacy of art thus form a complementary whole, as I shall show in the next two chapters. Here in Chapter 2, section 1 orients the reader by providing a brief overview of Heidegger's philosophical stand *against aesthetics, for art*. Sections 2 and 3 explain Heidegger's philosophical critique of aesthetics, showing why he thinks aesthetics follows from modern "subjectivism" and leads to late-modern "enframing," historical worldviews Heidegger

---

[1] As Bernasconi observes, "there has been relatively little scrutiny of Heidegger's attempt to free the concept of art itself from its status as an aesthetic category" (see Bernasconi, "Heidegger's Displacement of the Concept of Art," 378); that is the gap this chapter seeks to fill. For illuminating discussions of the broader historical context of Heidegger's hermeneutic and phenomenological understanding of art, see the insightful essays by Charles Guignon, "Meaning in the Work of Art: A Hermeneutic Perspective," and Steven Crowell, "Phenomenology and Aesthetics; or, Why Art Matters."

seeks to transcend from within – in large part by way of his phenomenological interpretations of art. In Chapter 3, sections 1 and 2 develop this attempt to transcend modern aesthetics from within, focusing on the way Heidegger seeks to build a phenomenological bridge from a particular ("ontic") work of art by Vincent van Gogh to the ontological truth of art in general. Here we will see how exactly Heidegger thinks art can help lead us into a genuinely meaningful postmodernity. We will then conclude, in Section 3, by explaining how this phenomenological understanding of Heidegger's project allows us to resolve the longstanding controversy surrounding Heidegger's interpretation of Van Gogh.

1.1. "Heidegger's Aesthetics": Beyond the Oxymoron

Perhaps the first thing I should say about "Heidegger's aesthetics" is that Heidegger himself would consider the very topic oxymoronic, a contradiction in terms like the idea of a "square circle," "wooden iron," or a "Christian philosopher" (Heidegger's three favorite examples of oxymorons).[2] Treating Heidegger's own thinking about art as "aesthetics" would strike him as incongruous and inappropriate because he consistently insisted that the "aesthetic" approach has led Western humanity to understand and experience the work of art in a way that occludes its true historical significance. Yet, Heidegger's thinking cannot be sympathetically classified as "anti-aesthetic" either, because he suggests that any such anti-aesthetics would remain blindly entangled in aesthetics in the same way that, for example, atheism remains implicated in the logic of theism (both claiming to know something unknowable) – or indeed as, in his view, any merely oppositional movement remains trapped in the logic of what it opposes (QCT 61/GA5 217; CPC 33/GA77 51). For Heidegger, as we will see, the only way to get beyond aesthetics is to first understand how it shapes us and then seek to pass through and beyond that influence, thereby getting over it as one might "recover" from a serious illness (ID 37/101). Because the aesthetic approach continues to eclipse our access to the role artworks quietly play in forming and informing our historical worlds, Heidegger thinks that only such a post-aesthetic thinking about art can allow us to recognize art's true significance, helping us understand the inconspicuous way in which art works to shape our basic sense of what is and what matters.

From a strictly Heideggerian perspective, then, any attempt to explain "Heidegger's aesthetics" (or "anti-aesthetics") will look either malicious

---

[2] In the early 1920s, Heidegger will repeatedly proclaim that genuine philosophy "is and remains atheism" (HCT 80/GA20 109–10) because true philosophical questioning must follow where the questions themselves lead and so cannot agree ahead of time to abide by any external limits imposed by the Church or other would-be authorities over matters of the mind or spirit. For precisely the same reason, of course, a "Nazi Philosopher" is also an oxymoron, a fact Heidegger unfortunately failed to grasp between 1933 and 1937.

or misconceived, like a deliberate flaunting or else an unwitting display of ignorance concerning the basic tenets of his views on art. Fortunately, our starting point is not really so misconceived.[3] Once we understand why exactly Heidegger criticizes what we could call the *aestheticization* of art, we will thereby have put ourselves on the right track to understanding his own post-aesthetic thinking about the work of art. (We should not confuse the aestheticization Heidegger critiques with "aestheticism," a term standardly taken to refer to the "art for art's sake" movement. For Heidegger, any such attempt to disconnect art from politics, philosophy, and other history-shaping movements misses the full scope of the *work* of art, a misunderstanding made possible by the prior reduction of art to aesthetics.)[4] So, what exactly is supposed to be wrong with the aestheticization of art? What leads Heidegger to critique the modern tradition that understands art in an "aesthetic" way, and why does he believe this aesthetic approach eclipses the true significance of the work of art?

1.2. Heidegger's Understanding of the True Work of Art

To understand Heidegger's critique of aesthetics, it will help first to sketch his positive view of art's true historical role. Heidegger's own understanding of the work of art is resolutely populist but with revolutionary aspirations.[5] He believes that, at its greatest, art "grounds history" by "allowing truth to spring forth" (PLT 77/GA5 65).[6] Building on Heraclitus's view of the pervasive tension of normative conceptual oppositions (good/bad,

---

[3] I should mention that this chapter began when the *Stanford Encyclopedia of Philosophy* commissioned me to write their entry on "Heidegger's Aesthetics."

[4] David Whewell defines "aestheticism" as: "The doctrine that art should be valued for itself alone and not for any purpose or function it may happen to serve," thereby connecting aestheticism to the *l'art pour l'art* movement that emerged in mid-nineteenth century France. (See Whewell, "Aestheticism," 6.) In the first version of "The Origin of the Work of Art," Heidegger explicitly rejects such a view: "Does not the attempt at *separating* out the work from all relation to other things outside of it act precisely contrary to the essence of the *work itself?* To be sure, for the work wants to be disclosed *as a work*" (HR 133/UK1 8).

[5] The revolutionary dimension is even more pronounced in the first version of the essay, in which Heidegger writes that: "Where an 'audience' exists, the work's only relation to that pre-existing audience is to destroy [*zerstört*] it. And the power for this destruction measures the greatness of an artwork." (HR 134/UK1 8) Because the work sets "up *only* its own world" (HR 135, my emphasis/UK1 10), this newly disclosed world "moves into the common reality" of the status quo as its "shattering and refutation" (HR 142/UK1 15) Around the same time, Heidegger also uses this image of exploding from within (or "blasting open") to explain the effect that thinking of the self as fundamentally an engaged being-in-the-world will have on our common conception of consciousness as a self-enclosed subjective sphere (LQ 129/GA38 156).

[6] I have frequently consulted Julian Young's excellent translation of "The Origin of the Work of Art" (see OBT), often adopting the emendations he makes to the better known translation of the essay by Albert Hofstadter (in PLT).

worthy/worthless, noble/base, and the like) that undergird and implicitly structure our sense of ourselves and our worlds, Heidegger imagines the way an ancient Greek temple at Paestum once worked to help unify its historical world by tacitly disclosing a particular sense of what is and what matters:

> It is the temple-work that first joins together and simultaneously gathers around itself the unity of those paths and relations in which birth and death, disaster and blessing, victory and disgrace, endurance and decline obtain the form of destiny for human being.... The temple first gives to things their look and to humanity their outlook on themselves. (PLT 42–3/GA5 27–9)

Great art works in the background of our historical worlds, in other words, by partially embodying and so selectively reinforcing an historical community's implicit sense of *what is and what matters*. In this way, great artworks both (1) "first give to things their look," that is, they help establish an historical community's implicit sense of what things *are*, and they (2) give "to humanity their outlook on themselves," that is, they also help shape an historical community's implicit sense of *what truly matters* in life (and so also what does not), which lives are most (or least) worth living, which actions are "noble" (or "base"), what in the community's traditions most deserves to be preserved (or forgotten), and so on. In this way, an artwork can first open up the historical sense for what is and what matters that an ontotheology will subsequently disseminate.[7]

As this suggests (and as we saw last chapter), Heidegger subscribes to a doctrine of *ontological historicity*. Refining a view first developed by Hegel, Heidegger thinks that humanity's fundamental sense of reality changes over time (sometimes dramatically), and he suggests that the work of art helps explain the emergence of such historical transformations of intelligibility at the most primordial level.[8] Because great art *works* inconspicuously to establish, maintain, and transform humanity's historically variable sense of what is and what matters, Heidegger emphasizes that *"art is the becoming and happening of truth"* (PLT 71/GA5 59). In other words, great artworks first open up the implicit (or "background") ontology and ethics

---

[7] Heidegger describes his understanding of the relation between art and metaphysics in 1946, writing: "the destiny of world is heralded in poetry, without yet becoming manifest as the history of being" (P 258/GA9 339). In other words, art – the essence of which is poetry, i.e., disclosive bringing-into-being (as we will see next chapter) – opens up and so inaugurates an historical sense of what-is and what matters. Such an historico-cultural sense can then subsequently take the firm conceptual shape of a dual, ontotheological understanding of the being of entities and thereby enter into the "history of being" (i.e., the history of epochal understandings of the being of entities, as we saw in Chapter 1).

[8] For Heidegger, the historical transformation of intelligibility (or "history of being") proceeds – *via* what we would now call a "punctuated equilibrium" – through five different Western "epochs" or historical constellations of intelligibility: the pre-Socratic, Platonic, medieval, modern, and late-modern epochs.

through which an historical community comes to understand itself and its world.[9] In keeping with this understanding of art (as what first opens and focuses the historical world that an ontotheology later universalizes and secures), Heidegger rethinks "truth" ontologically as the historically dynamic disclosure of intelligibility in time. As we will see next chapter, this historical unfolding of truth takes place – to use Heidegger's preferred philosophical terms of art – as an "*a-lêtheiac*" struggle to "dis-close" (*a-lêtheia*) that which conceals (*lêthê*) itself, an "essential strife" between two interconnected dimensions of intelligibility (namely, revealing and concealing) that Heidegger calls "world" and "earth" in his most famous essay on art.

In sum, great art *works* by selectively focusing an historical community's tacit sense of what is and what matters and reflecting it back to that community, which thereby comes implicitly to understand itself in the light of this artwork. Artworks thus function as ontological *paradigms*, serving their communities both as "models of" and "models for" reality, which means (as Dreyfus nicely puts it) that artworks can variously "manifest," "articulate," or even "reconfigure" the historical ontologies undergirding their cultural worlds.[10] Heidegger suggests, in other words, that art can accomplish its world-disclosing work on at least three different orders of magnitude: (1) micro-paradigms he will later call "things thinging," which help us become aware of what matters most deeply to us; (2) paradigmatic artworks like Van Gogh's painting and Hölderlin's poetry, which disclose how art itself works; and (3) macro-paradigmatic "great" works of art like the Greek temple and tragic drama (works Heidegger also sometimes calls

---

[9] Heidegger's view of art applies to all great art, including great *poetic* works of art. Thus he writes that in a masterful Greek tragedy like Aeschylus's *Oresteia*, "the struggle of the new gods against the old is being fought. The work of language ... does not speak about this struggle; rather, it transforms the saying of the people so that every essential word fights the battle and puts up for decision what is holy and unholy, what great and what small, what brave and what cowardly, what precious and what fleeting, what master and what slave (cf. Heraclitus, Fragment 53)" (PLT 43/GA5 29). We will return to Aeschylus's *Oresteia* in Chapter 4. It would, however, be irresponsible not to mention the complex political subtext of the obliquely self-referential passages I have quoted, with their abundant use of such Nazi buzzwords as *Kampf* (struggle), derivatives of *führen* (leading), and the opposition of *Sieg* (victory) and *Schmach* (disgrace). As the passage itself suggests (and as I show in *Heidegger on Ontotheology*, ch. 3), Heidegger's general rhetorical strategy is to try to appropriate such political buzzwords by radically reinterpreting them in terms of his own philosophy.

[10] Hubert L. Dreyfus draws on Clifford Geertz (along with Thomas Kuhn and Charles Taylor) to help explain Heidegger in his illuminating essay, "Heidegger's Ontology of Art," 410. As Dreyfus nicely explains (412): "The temple draws the people who act in its light to clarify, unify, and extend the reach of its style, but being a material thing it resists rationalization. And since no interpretation can ever completely capture what the work means, the temple sets up a struggle between earth and world. The result is fruitful in that the conflict of interpretations that ensues generates a culture's history."

"gods"), which succeed in fundamentally transforming an historical community's "understanding of being" (its most basic and ultimate understanding of what is and what matters, which ontotheologies can then work to universalize and secure for an epoch, as we saw last chapter).[11]

It is with this ontologically revolutionary potential of great art in mind that Heidegger writes:

> Whenever [great] art happens – that is, when there is a beginning – a push [or "jolt," *Stoß*] enters history, and history either starts up or starts again. (PLT 77/ GA5 65)

Great art is literally *revolutionary*, in other words, capable of overcoming the inertia of existing traditions by jolting the interconnected ontological and ethical wheels of history into motion. By beginning to open up a new sense of what is and what matters, great art either extends or transforms the ontotheology through which we make sense of the world and our place in it.[12] Given Heidegger's view of the revolutionary role art can thus play in inconspicuously developing or transfiguring the sense of what is and what matters that governs an age, his occasionally ill-tempered critiques of the reduction of art to aesthetics become much easier to understand. In his view, the stakes of our understanding of and approach to art could not be any higher.

2. HEIDEGGER'S PHILOSOPHICAL CRITIQUE OF AESTHETICS

Heidegger believes that the aestheticization of art has gotten us late moderns stuck in the rarefied and abstract view according to which "the enjoyment of art serves [primarily] to satisfy the refined taste of connoisseurs and aesthetes." His complaint is not that we treat food as art but rather the reverse, that we treat art in categories meant to describe the enjoyment of

---

[11] This view was first sketched in my "The Silence of the Limbs: Critiquing Culture from a Heideggerian Understanding of the Work of Art." Heidegger raises an important puzzle for this view, however, when he (implicitly but deliberately) includes Van Gogh's painting as a "great" work of art in "The Origin of the Work of Art," stating that "great art ... is all we are talking about here" (PLT 40/GA5 26). The solution to this puzzle is that the way Van Gogh's painting illuminates what art itself is, as we will see, is supposed to help us transcend modern aesthetics from within. I.e., our encounter with Van Gogh is supposed to exemplify – and so help us learn to understand – what it means to encounter being in a *postmodern* way. For Heidegger, then, Van Gogh's painting is both a paradigmatic and a macroparadigmatic work; for, *it shows us what art is in a way that changes our understanding of what it means for anything to be.* (Although this postmodern understanding of being applies universally, it is not totalizing, thanks to the inherently open-ended, pluralistic way in which it teaches us to understand and so encounter all that is as conceptually inexhaustible, as we will see in Chapter 3.)

[12] Young recognizes "the inseparability of ontology and ethics" as "a thesis fundamental to all phases of Heidegger's thinking" in his seminal work, *Heidegger's Philosophy of Art*, 24.

delicate sensory delights. Hence Heidegger's amusing but harsh judgment that: "For us today, … art belongs in the domain of the pastry chef" (IM 140/GA40 140). We can all learn to appreciate the "finer" things in life (and so come to make increasingly "refined" discriminations of taste). But the fact that our culture blithely celebrates café baristas who compete over the "art" of pouring foamed milk into our cappuccinos suggests that we have lost sight of the role art can play in shaping history at the deepest level, an ontologically revolutionary role compared to which Heidegger finds even the most "artful" gestures of culinary expertise relatively empty.[13]

For the same reason, Heidegger is no more impressed by Kant's high-brow view that the disinterested contemplation of art works to "serve the moral elevation of the mind" (IM 140/GA40 140).[14] Instead, Heidegger is clearly sympathetic to the "complaint" that, as he puts it:

innumerable aesthetic considerations of and investigations into art and the beautiful have achieved nothing, they have not helped anyone gain access to art, and they have contributed virtually nothing to artistic creativity or to a sound appreciation of art. (N1 79/GA43 92)

Heidegger would thus agree with the sentiment behind Barnet Newman's famous quip: "Aesthetics is for the artist as ornithology is for the birds."[15] Still, for Heidegger such complaints, while "certainly right," are really only symptomatic of a much deeper philosophical problem, a problem that stems from the way modern aesthetics is rooted in the subject/object divide at the very core of the modern worldview. In order to reach the core of the problem, then, let us first to take a step back and ask: How exactly does Heidegger understand *aesthetics*?[16]

---

[13] It is telling that in Neill and Ridley's collection, *Arguing About Art: Contemporary Philosophical Debates*, the two chapters the editors present as a debate of the question, "Is our experience of food and drink ever correctly thought of as an aesthetic experience?" (9), in fact both agree that food can be "art." This agreement is not surprising, viewed in the light of Heidegger's critique of the reduction of art to "aesthetic experience," a reduction typically presupposed in contemporary "aesthetics." In "Food as Art," e.g., Tefler offers a partial "definition" of art that fits Heidegger's critical understanding of the aesthetic approach: "if something is a work of art, then its maker or exhibitor intended it to be looked at or listened to with intensity, for its own sake" (14).

[14] Even if this rather esoteric view represents the romantic kernel in Kant's aesthetic thought, it nevertheless presupposes the same subject/object divide that, we will see, Heidegger believes has led the modern aesthetic tradition off track.

[15] See also T. S. Eliot's well-crafted lines (from "The Love Song of J. Alfred Prufrock"): "And I have known the eyes already known them all / The eyes that fix you in a formulated phrase, / And when I am formulated, sprawling on a pin, / When I am pinned and wriggling on the wall, / Then how should I begin…" (*The Wasteland and Other Poems*, 5).

[16] In the scholarly literature, the answer to this question is often drawn from Heidegger's "Six Basic Developments in the History of Aesthetics" (section 13 from the first of Heidegger's famous *Nietzsche* lectures, *The Will to Power as Art*, delivered between 1936 and 1937). The history of aesthetics Heidegger presents here is typically taken as Heidegger's own view,

2.1. How Heidegger Understands Aesthetics

As Heidegger points out, the term "aesthetics" is a modern creation. It was coined by Alexander Baumgarten in the 1750s and then critically appropriated by Kant in his *Critique of Judgment* (published in 1790).[17] Baumgarten formed the term "aesthetics" from the Greek word for "sensation" or "feeling," *aisthêsis* (N1 83/GA43 98). As this indicates, modern "aesthetics" was originally conceived as the science of *aisthêta*, matters perceptible by the senses, as opposed to *noêma*, matters accessible to thought alone, like the truths dealt with in mathematical logic. In fact, modern aesthetics is borne of the aspiration to be "in the field of sensuousness what logic is in the domain of thinking" (N1 83/GA43 98). That is, just as logic (conceived as the science of thought) seeks to understand our relation to the true, so aesthetics (conceived as the science of sensation or feeling) seeks to understand our relation to the beautiful.[18]

To recognize that the central focus of modern aesthetics is beauty is not to deny its traditional interest in the sublime or its late-modern preoccupations with the abject, the obscene, kitsch, and so on. Heidegger's point, rather, is that

aesthetics is that kind of meditation on art in which humanity's state of feeling in relation to the beautiful represented in art is the point of departure and the goal that sets the standard for all its definitions and explanations. (N1 78/GA43 91)

despite the fact that this assumption leads to unresolved puzzles about why Heidegger would then have presented drastically different views in essays written at almost the same time. It is not always easy to separate Heidegger's own view from the Nietzschean position he claims to be explicating (especially in the first of his *Nietzsche* lectures – this becomes much less of a problem by the end of the second lecture series, as Heidegger becomes increasingly disillusioned with Nazism and so more careful to distinguish Nietzsche's views from his own). Nevertheless, Heidegger clearly claims that the history of aesthetics he presents here is in fact drawn *from Nietzsche*, and should be understood as "an attempt to simplify Nietzsche's presentations concerning art to what is essential" (N1 122/GA43 143). Recognizing this makes it less surprising that Heidegger contradicts some of these views when speaking in his own voice elsewhere (as in the lecture delivered the following year, "The Age of the World Picture, explicated below).

[17] In 1937, Heidegger suggests that modern aesthetics stays within the traditional philosophical approach to art. "The name 'aesthetics' for a meditation on art and the beautiful is young and stems from the eighteenth century. But the matter itself so aptly named by this name – that is, the way of inquiring into art and the beautiful on the basis of the state of feeling in enjoyers and producers – is old, just as old as mediation on art and the beautiful in Western thought. *The philosophical meditation on the essence of art and the beautiful already begins as aesthetics.*" (N1 79/GA43 92) Heidegger's more careful view is that aesthetics proper presupposes the modern subject/object divide, but because he holds Plato responsible for inaugurating this divide, he can loosely trace the "aesthetic" way of conceiving art all the way back to Plato and Aristotle, as he does here.

[18] As Heidegger puts it: "What determines thinking, that is, logic, and what thinking comports itself toward, is the true." Analogously: "What determines human feeling, that is, aesthetics, and what feeling comports itself toward, is the beautiful" (N1 78/GA43 90).

In its paradigmatic form (the form "that sets the standard" for all its other "definitions and explanations"), modern "aesthetics is the consideration of humanity's state of feeling in relation to the beautiful" (N1 78/GA43 90). Nor is Heidegger denying that there are numerous disagreements within the modern aesthetic tradition (between Kant and Baumgarten, just to begin with). Instead, his thesis is that even the disagreements in the modern aesthetic tradition take place within the framework of a common approach. It is this shared framework that Heidegger designates when he refers to the "aesthetic" approach to art.

As we would expect, this basic framework undergirds the paradigmatic inquiry of modern aesthetics, the study of beauty through a "consideration of humanity's state of feeling in relation to the beautiful." In all the aesthetic investigations that take their cues from this one, Heidegger observes:

> The artwork is posited as the "object" for a "subject," and this subject-object relation, specifically as a relation of feeling, is definitive for aesthetic consideration. (N1 78/GA43 91)

In other words, modern aesthetics frames its understanding of art by presupposing the subject/object dichotomy: Aesthetics presupposes a fundamental divide between the art "object" and the experiencing "subject," a divide that is subsequently crossed by the commerce of sensation or feeling. Of course, the subject/object dichotomy forms the very basis of the modern worldview, so we would be surprised if modern aesthetics did not presuppose it. So, what specifically does Heidegger object to about the way the aesthetic approach to art presupposes a viewing subject, standing before some art object, enjoying (or not enjoying) his or her sensory experience of this artwork? What is supposed to be the problem with this aesthetic picture of art?

2.2. Heidegger's Critique of the Aesthetic Approach

In a provocatively titled essay delivered in 1938, "The Age of the World Picture," Heidegger provides a succinct formulation of what it means to approach art aesthetically that helps us reach the core of his objection to aesthetics. When "art gets pushed into the horizon of aesthetics," he writes, this

> means [1] that the artwork becomes an object of lived experience [*Gegenstand des Erlebens*], and [2] in this way art comes to count as an expression of human life [*Lebens*]. (QCT 116/GA5 75)

Heidegger is making two connected points here (which I have numbered accordingly). The first is that when art is understood and approached "aesthetically," artworks become *objects* for human subjects to experience in an especially intense, vital, or meaningful way. We can see this if we unpack his typically dense language: As Heidegger frequently points out, in the modern, post-Cartesian world, an "object," *Gegenstand*, is something that "stands opposite" a human subject, something *external* to subjectivity. In order to experience an object, the modern subject must supposedly first get outside the immanent sphere of its own subjectivity so as to encounter this "external" object, and then return back to its subjective sphere bearing the fruits of this encounter. Given the modern subject/object dichotomy, such an adventure beyond subjectivity and back again is required for the experience of any object. But in the case of the art object, Heidegger is pointing out, the adventure beyond subjectivity and back again is a particularly intense, meaningful, or enlivening one: A "lived experience" is an experience that makes us feel "more alive," as Heidegger suggests by emphasizing the etymological connection between *Erleben* and *Lebens*, "lived experience" and "life."

The second point Heidegger is trying to make is that when artworks become objects for subjects to have particularly meaningful experiences of, these artworks themselves also get understood thereby as meaningful expressions of an artistic subject's own life experiences. Heidegger does not ever develop any argument for this point; the thought simply seems to be that once aesthetics understands artworks as objects of which we can have meaningful experiences, it is only logical to conceive of these art objects themselves in an isomorphic way, as meaningful expressions of the lives of the artists who created them. Still, this alleged isomorphism of aesthetic "expression and impression" is not immediately obvious.[19] Think, for example, about the seriously playful "found art" tradition in Surrealism, dada, Fluxus, and their heirs, a tradition in which ordinary objects get seditiously appropriated as "art." (The continuing influence of Marcel Duchamp's "readymade" remains visible in everything from Andy Warhol's meticulously reconstructed *Brillo Boxes* [1964] to Ruben Ochoa's large-scale installations of industrial detritus like broken concrete, rebar, and chain-link fencing, in works such as *Ideal Disjuncture* (2008). Gianni Vattimo therefore suggests that Duchamp's *Fountain* illustrates the way an artwork can disclose a new world, a world in which the fine art tradition comes to celebrate not only the trivial and ordinary but also the vulgar and even the obscene.)[20] This "found art" tradition initially seems like a series

---

[19] Heidegger presupposes the same point again in *What Is Called Thinking* (1951–52). Here he glosses "seeing art aesthetically" by adding: "that is, from the point of view of expression and impression – the work as expression and the impression as experience" (WCT 128/GA8 132).

[20] See Gianni Vattimo, *Art's Claim to Truth*, xv–xvi, 45–7, 105, and 159. Here Santiago Zabala even suggests that Duchamp's *Fountain* is a better illustration of art's revolutionary potential than Heidegger's own example of the Greek temple (xv). Yet, for Heidegger there are clearly different orders of magnitude here. In this regard, Wright nicely captures

of deliberate counter examples to the aesthetic assumption that artworks are meaningful expressions of an artist's own subjectivity.

Even in this tradition, however, the artists' appropriations are never truly random, but invariably require some selection, presentation, and the like, and thus inevitably reopen interpretive questions about the significance these art objects have for the artistic subject who chose them. (Why this particular object? Why present it in just this way?) It is thus not surprising that the founding work of found "anti-art," Duchamp's *Fountain* (1917) – his deliciously seditious installation of a deliberately inverted, humorously signed (by "R. Mutt"), and brilliantly retitled urinal in an art gallery – is typically treated in contemporary aesthetics as an extreme expression of Duchamp's own artistic subjectivity, not as its absence.[21] Here one could also point to the failure of Robert Rauschenberg's attempt to deconstruct the found art ideal of unique and spontaneous artistic invention in his incredible "combines," *Factum I* and *Factum II* (1957), works that, despite Rauschenberg's painstaking efforts to make them identical, instead suggest the stubborn uniqueness of any given artwork.[22] So, even the found art tradition of Duchamp's ready-made and its heirs reinforces Heidegger's point that, *in the basic aesthetic approach to art, art objects are implicitly understood as meaningful expressions*

Heidegger's larger point when she writes that: "The temple celebrates the extraordinary event of Greece's emergence as a history-making force that gives direction to the next two thousand years of Western history." (See Wright, "Heidegger and Hölderlin," 385.) Or, as Dreyfus puts it: "The [Greek] temple and the Presocratic thinkers had to take the style that was already in the language and, for the first time, focus it and hold it up to the people. According to Heidegger, this is the origin (*Ur-sprung*) of our Western culture." (See Dreyfus, "Heidegger's Ontology of Art," 419 note 4.) For a picture of Ochoa's *Ideal Disjuncture*, see <http://www.artslant.com/userimages/3/Ideal_Disjuncture1.jpg> (accessed 18 August 2010).

[21] In his treatment of Schapiro's critique of Heidegger, Michael Kelly raises the same objection to Heidegger's interpretation of Van Gogh, suggesting that Heidegger sets himself a difficult challenge in his "attempt to desubjectivize aesthetics while discussing Van Gogh," an artist who placed his work under the bold signature, "Vincent," and is often taken as "the paradigm case of subjective art." Kelly's interpretation of "the subjectivization of aesthetics" as the tendency "to understand and judge art in terms of the viewer's subjective experience or judgment of it" allows Kelly to bring Heidegger into a productive dialogue with central issues in contemporary aesthetics, but this interpretation overlooks what Heidegger most fundamentally objects to about aesthetics, viz., its relation to "subjectivism." Heidegger's deepest objection to aesthetics is not that our understanding of art is overly constrained by idiosyncratic, "subjective" biases but, as we will see, that aesthetics follows from (and feeds back into) the modern subject's "subjectivistic" compulsion to control the entire objective world – a compulsion that Heidegger argues derives from modern metaphysics and thus from the "history of being," and so requires a response at this deeper level. (See Michael Kelly, *Iconoclasm in Aesthetics*, 49–50.)

[22] For Robert Rauschenberg, "Factum I" and "Factum II" (1957), see <http://www.portlandart.net/archives/Rauschenberg%20Factum%20I%20and%20Factum%20II%201957.bmp> (accessed 12 April 2010).

of artists' lives that are capable of eliciting particularly intense or meaningful experiences in viewing subjects.

In this aesthetic approach, to put it succinctly, *art objects express and intensify subjects' experiences of life.* What Heidegger thus characterizes as the aesthetic approach to art will probably seem so obvious to most people that it can be hard to see what he could possibly find objectionable about it. Art objects express and intensify human subjects' experiences of life; to most people, it might not even be clear what it could mean to understand art in any other way. How should we understand and approach art, if not in terms of the meaningful experiences that a subject might have of some art object, an art object that is itself a meaningful expression of the life of the artist (or artists) who created it? What exactly does Heidegger think is wrong with this "picture" of art?

Despite what one might expect from a phenomenologist like Heidegger, his objection is not that the aesthetic view mischaracterizes the way we late moderns ordinarily experience "art." On the contrary, Heidegger clearly suggests that what he characterizes as "the increasingly aesthetic fundamental position taken toward art as a whole" (N1 88/GA43 103) does accurately describe the experiences of art that take place – when they do take place – in museums, art galleries, and installations; in performance spaces, theaters, and movie houses; in cathedrals, coliseums, and other ruins; in cityscapes as well as landscapes; in concert halls, music clubs, and comic books; even when we listen to our speakers, headphones, ear-buds; and, sometimes (who could credibly deny it?), when we sit in front of our television screens, computer monitors, iPods and iPads, car stereos, and so on. The experiences we have of what rises to the level of "art" in all such settings are typically "aesthetic" experiences, that is, particularly intense or meaningful experiences that make us feel more alive; and, if we think about it, we do tend to approach these art objects as expressions of the lives of the artists who created them. The aesthetic view correctly characterizes our typical experience of "art" in the contemporary world – and for Heidegger that is part of the problem.[23]

2.3. Symptoms of Subjectivism

This returns us to the bigger question we have been pursuing, and which we are now prepared to answer: Why exactly does Heidegger object to our contemporary tendency to understand and approach art in this aesthetic way? In the revealingly titled essay we have been drawing on ("The Age

---

[23] As Heidegger begins to extend his critique of aesthetic subjectivism so as to connect it to "enframing" (i.e., our reductive way of understanding the being of entities in terms of Nietzsche's ontotheology of eternally recurring will-to-power), he will go so far as to claim that "The aesthetic state is the lucidity through which we constantly see." (N1 139/GA43 170)

of the World Picture"), Heidegger explains that "the process by which art gets pushed into the horizon of aesthetics" is neither conceptually neutral nor historically unimportant. On the contrary, the historical process by which Western humanity came to understand art as "aesthetics" is so freighted with significance that it needs to be recognized as "one of the essential phenomena of the contemporary age" (QCT 116/GA5 75). Strikingly, Heidegger goes so far as to assert that our tendency to treat art as aesthetics is just as significant for and revealing of our current historical self-understanding as are the increasing dominance of science and technology, the tendency to conceive of all meaningful human activity in terms of "culture," and the growing absence of any god or gods in our Western world (QCT 116–7/GA5 75–6). This is a surprising and deliberately provocative claim, one apparently meant to provoke us into noticing and thinking through something we ordinarily overlook. For, how can our understanding of art as aesthetics be just as essential to our current historical self-understanding as are the dominance of science, the growing influence of technology, the ubiquitous discussions of culture, and the withdrawal of gods from our history – four seemingly much larger and more momentous historical developments?

These five "essential phenomena" – the historical ascendance of science, technology, aesthetics, and culture, on the one hand, and, on the other, that historical decline of the divine that Heidegger, echoing Schiller, calls the "ungodding" or "degodification" (*Entgötterung*) of the world – these all are "equally essential" (*gleichwesentliche*), Heidegger explains, because these five interlocking phenomena express and so reveal the underlying direction in which the contemporary world is moving historically.[24] In other words, science, technology, aesthetics, culture, and degodification are "equally essential" as five major historical developments that feed into and disclose (what we could think of as) *the current*, that is, the underlying historical direction or *Zeitgeist* of our contemporary world. In the late 1930s, Heidegger's name for the underlying direction in which the age is moving is "subjectivism," a movement that he defines as humanity's ongoing attempt to establish "mastery over the totality of what-is" (QCT 132/GA5 92). *Subjectivism* thus designates humanity's increasingly global quest to achieve complete control over every aspect of our objective reality, to establish ourselves as the being "who gives the measure and provides the guidelines for everything that is" (QCT 134/GA5 94). Heidegger's fundamental objection to the aesthetic approach to art, then, is that this approach follows from and feeds back into *subjectivism*, contemporary humanity's ongoing effort to

---

[24] Schiller's famous poem, "The Gods of Greece," mournfully contrasts the experience of the ancient Greeks, in which "Everything to the initiate's eye / Showed the trace of a God," with our modern experience of "A Nature shorn of the divine [or, less poetically, "a de-godified nature," *die entgötterte Natur*]" (quoted by Taylor, *The Secular Age*, 316–17).

establish "our unlimited power for calculating, planning, and molding [or "breeding," *Züchtung*] all things" (QCT 135/GA5 94).

3. HOW AESTHETICS REFLECTS AND REINFORCES SUBJECTIVISM

In order to understand why Heidegger thinks the aesthetic approach to art reflects and reinforces subjectivism, we need to know why Heidegger characterizes humanity's ongoing attempt to master every aspect of our objective reality as "subjectivism" in the first place.[25] We saw earlier that in the modern, post-Cartesian world, an "object" (*Gegenstand*) is something that "stands opposite" a human *subject*, something that is "external" to the subjective sphere. This subject/object dichotomy seems obvious when one is theorizing from within the modern tradition, in which it has functioned as an axiom since Descartes famously argued that the subject's access to its own thinking possesses an indubitable immediacy not shared by objects, which must thus be conceived of as external to subjectivity.

Yet, as Heidegger argues in *Being and Time* (1927), taking this modern subject/object dichotomy as our point of departure leads us to fundamentally mischaracterize the way we actually encounter the everyday world in which we are usually unreflectively immersed, the world of our practical engagements. By failing to recognize and do justice to the integral entwinement of self and world that is basic to our experiential navigation of our lived environments, modern philosophy effectively splits the subject off from objects and from other subjects. In this way, modern philosophy lays the conceptual groundwork for *subjectivism*, the "worldview" in which an intrinsically meaningless objective realm ("nature") is separated epistemically from isolated, value-bestowing, self-certain subjects, and so needs to be mastered through the relentless epistemological, normative, and practical activities of these subjects. Heidegger suggests that this problem is not merely theoretical, because the subjectivism of the modern worldview functions historically like a self-fulfilling prophecy. Its progressive historical realization generates not only the political freedoms and scientific advances we cherish, but also unwanted downstream consequences such as our escalating environmental crisis and less predictable side-effects like the aestheticization of art.[26]

---

[25] In his broader "history of being," Heidegger traces "subjectivism" back to Plato, whose doctrine of the ideas begins a movement whereby truth is no longer understood solely in terms of the manifestation of entities themselves but, instead, becomes a feature of our own "representational" capacities. In this way, truth becomes primarily a matter of the way we secure our knowledge of entities rather than of the prior way entities disclose themselves to us. (On this "displacement of the locus of truth" from being to human subjectivity, see also *Heidegger on Ontotheology*, 160.)

[26] The modern prejudice that (to put it simply) *all meaning comes from the human subject* reaches its most powerful apotheosis in Nietzsche and Freud. From Heidegger's perspective,

3.1. Undermining the Subject/Object Dichotomy Phenomenologically

So, how does the aestheticization of art follow from subjectivism? (This is easier to see than Heidegger's converse claim – that the aestheticization of art feeds back into and reinforces subjectivism – so we will address it first.) *Being and Time* does not undermine the subject/object dichotomy by trying to advance the incredible thesis that the self really exists in a continuous and unbroken unity with its world. Instead, Heidegger seeks to account for the fact that our fundamental, practical engagement with our worlds can easily break down in ways that generate the perspective the subject/object dichotomy describes. Most of the time, we encounter ourselves as immediately and unreflectively immersed in the world of our concerns rather than as standing over against an "external" world of objects. Just think, for example, of the way you ordinarily encounter a hammer when you are hammering with it, or a pen while you are writing with it, a bike while riding it, a car while driving it, or even, say, a freeway interchange as you drive over it for the umpteenth time.

This all changes, however, when our practical engagement with the world of our concerns breaks down. When the head flies off the hammer and will not go back on (and no other hammering implement is available to complete the task at hand); when the pen we are writing with runs out of ink (and we have no other); when our bike tire goes flat or our car breaks down in the middle of a trip; when we find ourselves standing before an artwork that we cannot make sense of; or, in general, when we are still learning how to do something and encounter some unexpected difficulty that stops us in our tracks – in all such cases what Heidegger calls our ordinary, immediate "hands-on" (*zuhanden*) way of coping with the world of our practical concerns undergoes a "transformation" (*Umschlag*) in which we come to experience ourselves as isolated subjects standing reflectively before a world of external objects, which we thereby come to experience as standing over against us in the mode of something objectively "on hand" (*vorhanden*) (BT 408–9/SZ 357–8).

In other words, Heidegger does not deny the reality of the subject/object relation but, instead, points out that our experience of this subject/object relation *derives from* and so *presupposes* a more fundamental level of experience, a primordial modality of engaged existence in which self and world are united rather than divided. Heidegger believes that modern

however, this phenomenologically mistaken view misses (and subsequently obscures) the fact that meaning emerges at the prior, practical intersection of human beings with their worlds (as well as in our engaged negotiations with one another). In other words, Heidegger is an *ethical realist*, one whose phenomenological investigations led him to recognize that the world is no mute partner but, rather, actively contributes to our most profound sense of what matters. (On this point, see my "Ontology and Ethics at the Intersection of Phenomenology and Environmental Philosophy.")

philosophy's failure to solve the problem of skepticism about the external world shows that those who begin with a subject/object dichotomy will never be able to bridge that divide subsequently (BT 249–50/SZ 205–6). He thus insists that this more primordial level of practically engaged, "hands-on" existence – in which self and world are unified – must be the starting point of any description of ordinary human experience that seeks to do justice to what such experience is really like, a phenomenological dictum Heidegger insists should also govern our attempts to describe our meaningful encounters with works of art.

3.2. Phenomenology Against Aesthetic Subjectivism

Following the phenomenological dictum that we should describe our experience of art in a way that is not distorted by the presuppositions we have inherited from the metaphysical tradition is easier said than done, however, for at least two reasons. First, the subject/object dichotomy is so deeply entrenched in our self-understanding that it has come to implicitly structure the fundamental aesthetic approach (as we have seen). Second, it is not immediately clear where (let alone how) we should look to discover art in a nonaesthetic way. Indeed, it now seems natural for us to think that what makes our experience of art objects significant is that such experiences allow us temporarily to transcend the sphere of our own subjectivity by getting in touch with art objects outside ourselves, because these transcendent experiences can profoundly enrich our subjective experience.

In Heidegger's view, however, this aesthetic perspective gets the story backward. We do not begin confined to our subjective spheres, temporarily leave those spheres behind in order to experience art objects, only to return back to subjectivity once again, enriched by the "booty" we have captured during our adventure in the external world of art objects (BT 89/SZ 62). The reverse is true: Human *existence* originally "stands outside" (*ek-sistere*) itself, integrally involved with the world in terms of which we ordinarily make sense of ourselves.[27] We do occasionally experience ourselves as subjects confronting objects (for example, when we first learn to draw or paint realistically, or when we find ourselves standing befuddled before an art object), but the experience of ourselves as subjects confronting objects is comparatively infrequent and takes place on the background of a more basic experience of ourselves as integrally involved with the

[27] In "The Origin of the Work of Art," Heidegger again presents his phenomenological conception of "existence" as the way to undercut and transcend the modern subject/object dichotomy: "In existence, however, humanity does not first move out of something 'interior' to something 'exterior'; rather, the essence of existence is the out-standing standing within the essential separation [i.e., the essential strife that joins "earth and world"] belonging to the clearing of beings." (PLT 67/GA5 55)

world of our practical concerns, an experience of fundamental self/world intertwinement to which we always return subsequently.[28]

"Proximally and for the most part [or "initially and usually," *zunächt und zumeist*]," as Heidegger likes to say, we do not stand apart from the entities that populate our world, observing them dispassionately – or even passionately, hoping to transcend an isolated subjective sphere that in fact we are usually already beyond. Why, then, should we privilege the detached, subject/object framework that emerges from a breakdown of our engaged experience when we try to approach art philosophically? We should not; trying to approach art while staying within the aesthetic approach is like trying to learn what it is like to ride a bike by staring at a broken bicycle. It is so to privilege the detached perspective of the observer that the participatory perspective gets eclipsed and forgotten. In Heidegger's view, the phenomenologically faulty presuppositions of modern philosophy have misled aesthetics into looking for the work of art in the wrong place, at a derived rather than fundamental level of human interaction with the world, and thus into mistaking an intense subjective experience of an external object for an encounter with the true work of art.

Modern aesthetics presupposes the subject/object dichotomy and then problematically tries to describe the subsequent interaction between two allegedly heterogeneous domains, instead of recognizing and seeking to describe the prior role works of art play in the background of our everyday worldly engagement, in which no such dichotomy can yet be found. Heidegger's post-aesthetic thinking about the work of art instead seeks to describe the usually unnoticed way in which artworks can form and inform our basic historical sense of what is and what matters (as we saw in section 1.2). Heidegger's thinking about the formative role art can play in the background of our self-understanding is "post-aesthetic" in that it seeks to get past the constitutive mistakes of aesthetics, but it might also be characterized as "pre-aesthetic" insofar as the way he tries to go beyond aesthetics is by getting back behind the aesthetic starting point in order to do justice to that more primordial level of existence modern aesthetics overlooks. Indeed, although this initially sounds paradoxical, Heidegger suggests that *the best way to get beyond aesthetic experience is to transcend it from within* (that is, to encounter the way a subject's experience of an aesthetic object can lead beyond or beneath itself), as we will see when we turn to his phenomenological analysis of Van Gogh's painting next chapter.

To sum up, then, because aesthetics tries to describe artworks from the perspective of a subject confronting an external art object, the aesthetic approach begins always-already "too late" (BT 249/SZ 207). Aesthetics looks for art in the wrong place (at a derivative rather than primordial level

---

[28] This is to assume, of course, that we do not suffer a nervous breakdown or else demise first. (See my "Death and Demise in *Being and Time*.")

of human interaction with the world), and what it finds there is not the true work of art. Misled by the presuppositions of modern philosophy, aesthetics overlooks that more originary level of human existence where, Heidegger will argue, great art inconspicuously accomplishes its ontologically revolutionary work.

3.3. From Modern Subjectivism to Late-Modern Enframing in Aesthetics

Before turning our attention to Heidegger's postaesthetic thinking, the last thing we need to do is to clarify his more difficult claim that aesthetics not only follows from but also *feeds back into* subjectivism. What makes this claim difficult to grasp is the specific twist Heidegger gives to it: Put simply, aesthetics feeds back into subjectivism in a way that leads subjectivism beyond itself – and into something even worse than subjectivism. In aesthetics, Heidegger suggests, subjectivism "somersaults beyond itself [*selbst überschlägt*]" into enframing (N1 77/GA43 90). We can see how subjectivism somersaults beyond itself into enframing if we return to Heidegger's definition of subjectivism in "The Age of the World Picture," according to which modern *subjectivism* names our modern attempt to secure "our unlimited power for calculating, planning, and molding [or "breeding," *Züchtung*] all things" (QCT 135/GA5 94). It is not difficult to detect a (lamentably) subtle resistance to the National Socialist worldview and what Heidegger came to understand as its Nietzschean roots in Heidegger's 1938 critique of Western humanity's drive toward the total mastery of the world through "calculating, planning, and breeding." More importantly for our purposes, however, such descriptions of humanity's drive to master the world completely through the coldly rational application of *calculative* reasoning also show that what Heidegger calls "subjectivism" is a conceptual and historical precursor to what he will soon call "enframing" (or *Gestell*).

As we saw in Chapter 1, "enframing" is Heidegger's famous name for the technological understanding of being that underlies and shapes our contemporary age. Just as Descartes inaugurates *modern subjectivism*, so Nietzsche inaugurates *late-modern enframing* by understanding being – the "totality of entities as such" – as "eternally recurring will to power." Heidegger thinks that Nietzsche's "ontotheology" (his way of conceptually grasping the being of what-is from both the inside-out and the outside-in) lays the conceptual groundwork for our own late-modern view that reality is nothing but forces coming-together and breaking-apart with no end other than the self-perpetuation of force itself. By tacitly approaching reality through the lenses of this Nietzschean ontotheology, we increasingly come to understand and so to treat all entities as intrinsically meaningless "resources" (*Bestand*) standing by for efficient and flexible optimization. It is, we have seen, this nihilistic *technologization* of reality that Heidegger's later thinking is dedicated to finding a path beyond.[29] For Heidegger, great art opens just such a path, one that can help guide us beyond enframing's ontological "commandeering of everything into assured availability" (PLT 84/GA5 72), as we will see next chapter.

First, however, we need to understand how subjectivism leads beyond itself into enframing. Put simply, subjectivism becomes enframing when the subject objectifies *itself* – that is, when the human subject, seeking to master and control all aspects of its objective reality, turns that modern impulse to control the world of objects back on itself. If we remember that modern *subjectivism* designates the human subject's quest to achieve total control over all objective aspects of reality, then we can see that late-modern *enframing* emerges historically out of subjectivism as subjectivism increasingly transforms the human subject itself into just another object to be controlled. *Enframing*, we could say, *is subjectivism squared* (or subjectivism applied back to the subject). For, the subjectivist impulse to master reality redoubles itself in enframing, even as enframing's objectification of the subject dissolves the very subject/object division that initially drove the subject's relentless efforts to master the objective world standing over against it.[30]

Subjectivism "somersaults beyond itself" in our late-modern age of "enframing," then, because the impulse to control everything intensifies and accelerates even as it breaks free of its modern moorings and circles back on the subject itself, turning the human subject into just one more object to be mastered and controlled. In this way, the modern subject increasingly becomes just another late-modern "resource" to be efficiently optimized along with everything else. We are thus moving from modern subjectivism to the late-modern enframing of reality insofar as we understand and relate to all things, *ourselves included*, as nothing but intrinsically meaningless resources standing by for endless optimization. Interestingly, Heidegger saw this technological understanding of being embodied in contemporary works of art such as the butterfly interchange on a freeway, which, functioning in the background of our experience like a late-modern temple, quietly reinforces the technological understanding of all reality as "a network of long-distance traffic, spaced in a way calculated for maximum speed" (PLT 152/GA7 155).[31] Of course, this empty optimization

---

[29] As this suggests, Heidegger's later work is dedicated to detecting, resisting, and, ultimately, transcending what he took to be the core of the Nazi ideology (For a justification of this admittedly provocative claim, see *Heidegger on Ontotheology*, ch. 3 and ch. 7.)

[30] For a detailed explanation of this strange fact, see my *Heidegger on Ontotheology*, ch. 1.

[31] Dreyfus calls the freeway interchange a "debased work of art" because he thinks it "imposes such an efficient order on nature that earth is no longer able to resist." Although Heidegger says as much in his middle period (see M 23/GA66 30), I suggest in *Heidegger on Ontotheology* (70–1) that this is too one-sidedly bleak to be Heidegger's mature view, which instead hews more faithfully to the Janus-faced Hölderlinian dictum: "Where the

function is now served even more efficiently and pervasively by the Internet, to which we find ourselves connected by millions of little technological shrines, increasingly comprehensive computational devices made ever faster, more efficient, and portable, devices we already find ourselves almost unable to live without. In the late 1930s, Heidegger understood such technological optimization as an all-encompassing attempt to derive the maximal output from the minimal input, a quantification of quality that threatens to replace quality in the same way that the objectification of the subject threatens to displace subjectivity. Heidegger seems first to have recognized this objectification of the subject in the Nazis' coldly calculating eugenics programs for "breeding" a master race, but (as he predicted) that underlying impulse to objectively master and then optimize the human subject continues unabated in more scientifically plausible and less overtly horrifying forms of contemporary genetic engineering.[32]

Most important for us here, Heidegger also recognized this ongoing objectification of the subject in the seemingly innocuous way that aesthetics "somersaults beyond itself" into neuroscientific attempts to understand and control the material substrate of the mind. For, once aesthetics reduces art to intense subjective experience, such experiences can be studied objectively through the use of EEGs, *f*MRIs, MEGs, and PET scans (and the like), and in fact aesthetic experiences are increasingly being studied in this way. At the University of New Mexico's prestigious MIND Institute, to mention just one telling example, subjects were given "beautiful" images to look at and the resulting neuronal activity in their brains was studied empirically using one of the world's most powerful functional Magnetic Resonance Imaging machines. In this way, as Heidegger predicted in 1937:

Aesthetics becomes a psychology that proceeds in the manner of the natural sciences; that is, states of feeling become self-evident facts to be subjected to experiments, observation, and measurement. (N1 89/GA43 106)

"Here," Heidegger writes, "the final consequences of the aesthetic inquiry into art are thought through to the end" (N1 91/GA43 108). Modern aesthetics reaches its logical conclusion – the "fulfillment or consummation" (*Vollendung*) which completes it and so brings it to its end – when it thus "somersaults beyond itself" into late-modern enframing.[33]

---

danger is, however, there grows / that which saves as well [*Wo aber Gefahr ist, wächst / Das Rettende auch*]." (See Dreyfus, "Heidegger's Ontology of Art," 413; David Brodsley, *L.A. Freeway: An Appreciative Essay*; and Hubert L. Dreyfus, *On the Internet*.)

[32] On Heidegger's prediction, see Chapter 7. For an insightful neo-Heideggerian critique of our ongoing attempts to optimize ourselves technologically, see Michael J. Sandel, *The Case Against Perfection: Ethics in the Age of Genetic Engineering.*

[33] As Heidegger writes in 1937–8: "Art becomes a means for machination's fulfillment in the pervasive construction of entities into the unconditioned, secure availability of the organized." (M 23/GA66 30)

Heidegger's objection to such aesthetic enframing, then, is not just that the work of art is increasingly falling under the influence of enframing – that artworks too are becoming mere resources for the art industry, standing reserves piled in storerooms "like potatoes in a cellar" to be quickly and efficiently "shipped like coal … or logs … from one exhibition to another" (PLT 19/GA5 3). He is even more troubled by the way art, reduced to aesthetics, does not just get enframed but participates in the enframing – for example, when the feeling of beauty is reduced to a purportedly objective brain state to be precisely measured and controlled through cognitive neuroscience – as well as computer science.[34] In another example of this aesthetic "enframing" by which the subject objectifies itself and so seeks to optimize its aesthetic experiences, computer scientists at Penn State now claim to have developed "the first publicly available tool for automatically determining the aesthetic value of an image." Ironically, according to this "Aesthetic Quality Inference Engine (AQUINE)," Van Gogh's treasured painting of *A Pair of Shoes* (1886), so important for Heidegger (for reasons we will explain next chapter), only receives an "aesthetic value" rating of 5.5 out of 100![35]

This almost comically faulty "aesthetic evaluation" suggests the incredible hubris of such attempts to quantify the qualitative by programming genuine artistic judgment – an impossibly ambitious project that will surely fail, in this instance at least, because of the fatal flaws inherent in the doubly problematic concept of an "aesthetic value" on which the project relies. For Heidegger, such "thinking in terms of values is radical killing," literally a "murdering that kills at the roots" (QCT 108/GA5 263), because he is convinced that only the *invaluable* – only that which we would never exchange for anything else, that is, only nonquantifiable qualities – can truly *matter* to us or give genuine *worth* to our lives. Heidegger does not deny that values exist (or that invaluable goods can come into conflict); instead, he denies that what most matters to us can ever be satisfyingly reduced to (or understood in terms of) the "value" that a subject determines for an object (let alone for another human being).[36]

As human "subjects" turn the subjectivist impulse to control the objective world back on ourselves in such neuroscientific and computer science experimentation, aesthetics increasingly becomes just one more approach

---

[34] In the early 1950s, e.g., Heidegger again asks, "while science records the brain currents, what becomes of the tree in bloom? … [W]e shall forfeit everything before we know it, once the sciences of physics, physiology, and psychology, not to forget scientific philosophy, display the panoply of their documents and proofs, to explain to us that what we see and accept is properly not a tree but in reality a void, thinly sprinkled with electric charges here and there that race hither and yon at enormous speeds" (WCT 42–3/GA8 45–6).

[35] See ACQUINE <http://live.psu.edu/story/39575/email> (accessed and tested 15 May 2009).

[36] I develop the argument for these claims further in "Ontology and Ethics."

reinforcing the technological "enframing" of all reality. Heidegger thus reaches a harsh verdict: Aesthetic "experience is the element in which art dies. This dying goes on for so long that it takes several centuries" (PLT 79/GA5 67).[37] Fortunately, Heidegger's prognosis is not as bleak as this apparent death sentence suggests. That art is slowly dying as aesthetics, he later clarifies,

does not mean that art is utterly at an end. That will be the case only if [aesthetic] experience remains the sole element for art. Everything depends on getting out of [aesthetic] experience and into being-here [*Da-sein*], which means reaching an entirely different "element" for the "becoming" of art. (P 50 note b/GA5 67 note b)[38]

In other words, art is dying only as aesthetics, and the death of art as aesthetics makes possible the transformative rebirth of art as something other than a subject's experience of an object.

Indeed, just as modern subjectivism led beyond itself historically into late-modern enframing, so Heidegger believes enframing, in turn, can lead beyond itself into a genuine postmodernity, an age that transcends our late-modern epoch's ongoing technologization of reality and its nihilistic

---

[37] Heidegger acknowledges that many great "works themselves [still] stand and hang in museums and exhibitions," but asks: "[A]re they here in themselves as the works they themselves are, or are they not rather here as objects of the art industry?" Heidegger's point is that "placing artworks in a collection has withdrawn them from their own world" (PLT 40/GA5 26); i.e., many "great works of art" have been uprooted from the worlds of meaning they once focused and preserved in a way that kept the future of those worlds open. Although it might initially sound counterintuitive, then, Heidegger is suggesting that most of the great works we find collected in museums no longer keep their worlds open, and thus no longer *work* as art. As he puts it: "As soon as the thrust into the extraordinary is parried and captured by the sphere of familiarity and connoisseurship," the work of art has ended and "the art business has begun" (PLT 68/GA5 56). In Heidegger's rather polemical and one-sided view: "The whole art industry, even if carried to the extreme and exercised in every way for the sake of the works themselves, extends only to the object-being of the works. But this object-being [of artworks] does not constitute their work-being" (PLT 41/GA5 27). Although (*pace* Heidegger) the art industry cannot thrive without devoting attention to the *work* of art, its typical reduction of artworks to art "objects" is, as we have seen, at the core of the aestheticization of art he opposes. The common objection that Heidegger's own work on Van Gogh, e.g., cannot hope to be heard and still to escape making a contribution to aesthetics and the art industry, moreover, misses the fact that Heidegger seeks to transcend aesthetics from within – as we will see, by hermeneutically "preserving" what he takes to be the true phenomenological significance of Van Gogh's painting. (PLT 68/GA5 55–6). Such hermeneutic preservation neither does nor should, I think, remain entirely heterogeneous to the "the sphere of familiarity and connoisseurship" (as Heidegger too cynically assumes). With respect to the entire world of aesthetics, then, Heidegger is better understood as employing the rhetorical strategy Derrida refers to as a "phoenix motif": "One burns or buries what is *already dead* [or dying] so that life ... will be reborn and regenerated from these ashes." (See Derrida, *The Ear of the Other: Otobiography, Transference, Translation*, 154.)

[38] On the translation of *Dasein* as "being-here" (rather than the more common "being-there"), I have been convinced by Daniel Dahlstrom, *Heidegger's Concept of Truth*, xxiii-xxvi.

erosion of all intrinsic meaning (the very void that we try to fill with all our superficial talk about "values"). This hope for an historical turning toward a genuinely meaningful postmodernity is what motivates Heidegger's phenomenological attempt to describe and so convey a post-aesthetic encounter with art. He expresses this task as follows:

> For aesthetics, art is the display of the beautiful in the sense of the pleasant, the agreeable. [That is, modern aesthetics understands the beautiful as what produces the pleasant or agreeable sensations that bridge the gap between aesthetic subjects and art objects.] And yet, art is the opening [or revelation, *Eröffnung*] of the being of entities. On the basis of a fundamental orientation toward being that has been won back in an originary way, we must gain a new content for the word "art" and for what it attempts to name. (IM 140/GA40 140)

Let us thus turn to this attempt to understand art in a way that will help lead us beyond aesthetics by getting us back in touch phenomenologically with being (or, better, with what the word "being" itself attempts to name).

4. CONCLUSION AND TRANSITION: FROM HEGEL'S END OF ART TO HEIDEGGER'S OTHER BEGINNING

Because of the predicament in which modern aesthetics has left us, Heidegger provisionally accepts the truth of Hegel's famous judgment that:

> Art no longer counts for us as the highest manner in which truth obtains existence for itself.... [I]n its highest determination, vocation, and purpose [*Bestimmung*], art is and remains for us ... a thing of the past. (PLT 80/GA5 68)

Still, Heidegger nurtures the hope that (*pace* Hegel) the distinctive truth manifest in art could once again attain the kind of history-transforming importance Hegel and Heidegger agree it had for the ancient Greeks but has lost in the modern world.

This "highest" truth of art for which Heidegger still hopes, however, is not Hegel's "certainty of the absolute" (GA5 68 note a). That is, Heidegger does not hold out hope for some perfect correspondence between (1) the historically unfolding "concept" Hegel believes is implicit in the development of humanity's intersubjective self-understanding and (2) an objective manifestation of that intersubjective self-understanding in art. Thus, in Hegel's most famous example, the tragic conflict between Antigone and Creon in Sophocles' *Antigone* perfectly embodied the fundamental but as of yet unresolved ethical conflicts – between conscience and law, the family and the state, and so on – which had arisen implicitly in the intersubjective self-understanding of fifth-century Athens. Hegel thinks it is no longer possible for an artwork to perfectly express the tensions implicit in the self-understanding of the age – and thereby call for an historical people to envision a future age in which those tensions would be resolved – because this role was taken over by religion and then by philosophy as our historical self-understanding grew increasingly complex. Heidegger, however, continues to hope for even more, namely, an artwork that *already* embodies the transition between this age and the next and that is thus capable of helping to inaugurate that postmodern age, here and now.

In tacit opposition to Hegel, Heidegger thus suggests that art's highest "[t]ruth is [not "the certainty of the absolute" but] the unconcealedness of entities as entities. Truth is the truth of being" (PLT 81/GA5 69). Heidegger's defining hope for art, in other words, is that works of art could manifest and thereby help usher in a new understanding of the being of entities, a literally "postmodern" understanding of what it means for an entity to be, a new ontology that would no longer understand entities either as modern objects to be controlled or as late-modern resources to be optimized.[39] Heidegger expresses this hope that separates him from Hegel in the form of a question: "The truth of Hegel's judgment has not yet been decided," he writes, because

the question remains: Is art still an essential and a necessary way in which that truth happens which is decisive for our historical existence, or is art this no longer? (PLT 80/GA5 68)

Heidegger's point is that Hegel will no longer be right – the time of great art will no longer be at an end – if contemporary humanity needs an encounter with art in order to learn how to understand the being of entities in a genuinely postmodern way, and if we remain capable of such an encounter.[40]

As this suggests, the ultimate goal of Heidegger's thinking about art is to show what it would mean to move from a modern aesthetic experience of an art object to a genuinely postmodern encounter with a work of art, so that we can thereby learn from art how to transcend modernity from within.[41] Heidegger, moreover, clearly believes this is possible; hence his later claim that when we encounter a true work of art,

[39] Heidegger calls an artwork's manifestation of the truth of being "beauty" (PLT 81/GA5 69), and thus understands *beauty* in a post-aesthetic way, ultimately, as the revelation of a new understanding of being. As he puts it in the early 1950s: "Beauty is a fateful gift of the essence of truth, whereby truth means the unconcealment of the self-concealing. The beautiful is not what pleases, but what falls within that fateful gift of truth which comes into its own when that which is eternally unapparent [or inconspicuous, *Unscheinbare*] and therefore invisible attains its most radiantly apparent appearance." (WCT 19/GA8 21) (On the distinctive sense of "postmodern" that can rightly be applied to Heidegger, see Chapter 4.)

[40] As Hammermeister shows, however, "Heidegger's claim for a fresh start glosses over his affinities for the idealist tradition, especially Schelling." (See Hammermeister, *The German Aesthetic Tradition*, 175.)

[41] John Sallis follows a different path to similar conclusions in *Transfigurements: On the True Sense of Art*, 164.

the presencing [*Anwesen*] of that which appears to our look ... is different than the standing of what stands-opposite [us] in the sense of an object. (PLT 82/GA5 71)

But what exactly is the difference between an aesthetic experience of an art object and an encounter with the true "presencing" of a work of art? And how is the traversing of that difference in our engagement with a particular work of art supposed to teach us to understand being in a post-modern way? Chapter 3 explains Heidegger's fairly complex answers to these difficult but momentous questions.

3

Heidegger's Postmodern Understanding of Art

> The essence of art consists ... in the artist possessing the essential insight for the possible, for bringing the hidden possibilities of what-is into the work and thereby making human beings first able to see what that with which they blindly busy themselves really is.
>
> Heidegger (ET 47/GA34 63–4)

> They will never be able to understand what painting is. They cannot understand that the figure of a laborer – some furrows in a ploughed field, a bit of sand, sea and sky – are serious subjects, so difficult, but at the same time so beautiful, that it is indeed worthwhile to devote one's life to expressing the poetry hidden in them.
>
> Vincent van Gogh (letter to Theo van Gogh, 26 August 1882)

1. INTRODUCTION: THE THREE PILLARS OF HEIDEGGER'S UNDERSTANDING OF ART

"The Origin of the Work of Art" – an essay Heidegger delivered repeatedly between 1935 and 1936, rewriting and expanding it into three lectures (which became the three main sections of the published essay, to which he added a brief "Afterword" near the end of the 1930s and a slightly longer "Addendum" in 1957) – is far and away the most important source for understanding Heidegger's attempt to articulate an alternative to the aesthetic understanding of art, although several other works (contemporaneous as well as later) also provide important clues to his view.[1] In the final

---

[1] Heidegger's famous essay was first published in 1950, along with its undated "Afterword" (which, judging from its terminology, was written around 1938), as the first chapter of *Holzwege*. Its 1956 "Addendum" was first added to the 1960 Reclam edition. For interpretations of the changes that take place between the earliest drafts of Heidegger's famous essay, see Jacques Taminiaux, "The Origin of 'The Origin of the Work of Art'"; and Robert Bernasconi, "The Greatness of the Work of Art." What is clear is that a significant change of emphasis takes place between the earliest and more *nationalistic* version of Heidegger's essay

version of this famous essay, Heidegger meditates on three different works of art in succession: A painting of *A Pair of Shoes* by Vincent van Gogh; a poem entitled "The Roman Fountain" by C. F. Meyer, and an unspecified Greek temple at Paestum (most likely the temple to Hera).

Leading Heidegger scholars such as Hubert Dreyfus and Julian Young rely almost entirely on Heidegger's interpretation of the ancient Greek temple in order to explicate his "Promethean" view of art's historically revolutionary potential, its world-disclosing ability to transform our sense of what is and what matters (the view we examined in Chapter 2, Section 1). Dreyfus and Young suggest that Heidegger's interpretation of Van Gogh is "anomalous" and "largely irrelevant" to this view, despite the fame generated by the controversy that still surrounds Heidegger's treatment of Van Gogh (to which we will return at the end of this chapter).[2] Like almost all other scholars, moreover, Dreyfus and Young simply overlook Heidegger's introduction of Meyer's poem – despite recognizing that for Heidegger (like Plato) "poetry" names the very essence of art (namely, *poiêsis* or "bringing into being"), hence Heidegger's striking claim that: "*All art* [that is, all bringing into being] ... *is essentially poetry*" (PLT 73/GA5 59).[3] We thus have to wonder: Is the only complete poem Heidegger included in the essay that advances this claim that poetry is the essence of art really of no significance itself?

In my view, Heidegger's analysis of each of these three works contributes something important to his overarching attempt to guide readers into a phenomenological encounter with art that is capable of helping us transcend modern aesthetics from within. Put simply, the temple motivates and helps develop the details of that larger project; the poem implicitly contextualizes and explains it; and the painting (and only the painting) directly embodies and exemplifies the transition for which Heidegger calls. In order to see how, let us take these points in order.

Heidegger's imaginative reconstruction of the lost world of the temple helps motivate his quest for a nonaesthetic encounter with art, but not (as

and the much more famous, published version, in which traces of that earlier nationalism still survive (e.g., in the largely undeveloped references to Greek tragedy and to Hölderlin) but can no longer be said to dominate the piece or determine its meaning (*pace* Wright's "Heidegger and Hölderlin"). For an interpretation of the ways in which Heidegger further modified his view after the 1930s, see Young's *Heidegger's Philosophy of Art*.

[2] (See Young, *Heidegger's Philosophy of Art*, 22; cf. Dreyfus, "Heidegger's Ontology of Art," 409.) Young is right that Heidegger's interpretation of Van Gogh is "anomalous" if we hear *anomaly* in a Kuhnian way, as an inexplicable detail that, when properly understood, transforms our entire previous view.

[3] As Plato writes, "everything that is responsible for creating something out of nothing is a kind of poetry; and so all the creations of every craft and profession are themselves a kind of poetry, and everyone who practices a craft is a poet" (*Symposium*, 205b). For some of the other profound and surprising affinities between Plato and Heidegger, see Mark Ralkowski's provocative and insightful book, *Heidegger's Platonism*.

is often said by critics) because he seeks some nostalgic return to the Greek world. Heidegger dismisses such a revival as an impossibility because the ancient temple, just like the medieval cathedral, no longer gathers its historical world around it and thus no longer works as great art, and such "world-withdrawal and world-decay can never be reversed" (PLT 41/GA5 26). Instead, the Greek temple shows that art was once encountered in a way other than as a subject's intense aesthetic experience of an object, and thus suggests that, although those ancient and medieval worlds have been lost irretrievably, other works of art might yet be encountered nonaesthetically in our late-modern world. In other words, Heidegger elaborates his philosophical vision of how the temple worked for a time to unify a coherent and meaningful historical world around itself (by inconspicuously focusing and illuminating its people's sense of what is and what matters) in order to suggest that a nonaesthetic encounter with art might do the same thing once again: A work of art might still help to gather a new historical world around itself by focusing and illuminating an understanding of being that does not reduce entities either to modern objects to be controlled or to late-modern resources to be optimized.

While Heidegger's project is thus undeniably inspired by the past, this inspiration serves his goal of helping us move historically into the future. His guiding hope, we have seen, is that a nonaesthetic encounter with a contemporary artwork will help us learn to understand the being of entities not as modern objects ("subjectivism") or as late-modern resources ("enframing") but in a genuinely postmodern way, thereby inaugurating another historical beginning. So, which work of art does Heidegger think can help us late moderns learn to transcend modern aesthetics from within and thereby discover a path leading beyond modernity? There are, in my view, only two viable candidates to fill this crucial role in "The Origin of the Work of Art": Meyer's poem and Van Gogh's painting.[4]

---

[4] There are, nonetheless, other possibilities. It could be that "The Origin of the Work of Art" merely prepares for this crucial encounter with an artwork capable of ushering in a new understanding of being (as it is often read), an encounter that perhaps *never* arrives (such that Heidegger himself dies waiting for the arrival of a salvific event that never comes, as Wolin and others suggest by misreading Heidegger's *Der Spiegel* interview, "Only a God Can Save Us," as a work of quietistic despair). Or it could be that Heidegger is here simply setting-up his reading of the German Romantic poet Friedrich Hölderlin, whose work Heidegger does most frequently nominate to play such a pivotal role (including in his 1934–5 lectures, see GA39). The latter reading receives some support from the fact that "The Origin of the Work of Art" closes by quoting two lines from Hölderlin's poem, "The Journey": "What dwells near the origin / Leaves that place with reluctance" (PLT 78/ GA5 66). Wright makes the strongest case for hearing these lines as a nationalistic call for Germany to break with the history of the West that began in Greece and begin history again (see her "Heidegger and Hölderlin," 383–6). Wright's genealogical analysis of Heidegger's essay is insightful and revealing, but it misses the emergent view that took shape only in the final version of the essay, where Van Gogh rather than Hölderlin plays the starring role. (By the time Heidegger wrote the final draft of "The Origin of the Work of Art," he is

So, why does Heidegger give such pride of place to Meyer's poem? The answer to this puzzle (which too few readers even notice)[5] is that the poem introduces the broader philosophical context of Heidegger's project by conveying his emerging understanding of *historicity* and *epochality*, the doctrines according to which, respectively, our fundamental sense of reality (1) changes with time and (2) takes the shape of a series of unified

no longer assigning a vanguard role to "Germany" in the dissemination of this postmodern view, as he did in its first draft, following GA39. By "Germany," moreover, Heidegger usually really meant *himself*, as a thinker creatively interpreting Hölderlin's meaning for German history *in terms of his own philosophical views*, and Heidegger's idea that these philosophical insights would be crucial for a postmodern revolution is something he never stopped believing.) Heidegger does conclude his famous essay by proposing Hölderlin's lines as "a test" that is supposed "infallibly" to tell us whether, "in our comportment to art," our existence still stands within art's "origin" or whether we are merely relying on a cultured acquaintance with the past. Hölderlin's suggestive lines are polysemic (and their full significance for Heidegger could be explicated at length, bringing in such facts as Heidegger's recent and very public refusal to leave his home near the Black Forest in order to accept a prestigious chair of philosophy in Berlin, as well as the allusion to the Greek adage, "All beginnings are difficult," which Wright nicely picks up on). Read in the context of the published essay, however, Heidegger's way of ending with Hölderlin's lines primarily suggests that *we can tell that we are genuinely encountering art when we find it as difficult to put its meaning into words as the artist found it to capture that meaning in the work in the first place.* "The Origin of the Work" seeks to lead its audience *performatively* to encounter this "enigma of art" (PLT 79/GA5 67) for ourselves, in order to learn thereby to understand being in a postmodern way. Indeed, this performative dimension is a central and defining feature of all Heidegger's most important later works, each of which (despite their many important interconnections) seeks to be self-contained in this respect. For, each of these essays tries to help its audience see something important – even existentially transformative – for ourselves. Heidegger's famous essay does not indefinitely postpone such an encounter, or even merely prepare for it to happen at some point in the future, in another of his works. Instead, he thinks he has prepared for it to happen in (or, better, through) "The Origin of the Work of Art" itself. As he thus puts it here: "Our efforts concerning the actual working of the work [*die Wirklichkeit des Werkes*] should have prepared the ground for discovering, in this working of the work, art and its essential nature" (PLT 70/GA5 58). As strange as it sounds initially, this means that it is primarily Van Gogh rather than Hölderlin whom Heidegger turns to in his most famous essay on art in order to teach us how to encounter the work of art in a postmodern way.

[5] Since writing this chapter, I have come across a single scholar who does notice this intriguing puzzle; see Karen Gover's nice essay, "The Overlooked Work of Art in 'The Origin of the Work of Art.'" Gover herself goes so far as to present Meyer's poem as the most important artwork in Heidegger's essay. I agree that Meyer's poem is much more significant than previous interpreters have realized, but I shall nevertheless suggest that, once we recognize that *Heidegger's goal is to transcend modern aesthetics from within*, then Van Gogh's painting clearly emerges as the most crucial work of art in his essay. Further evidence for this view can be found in the fact that Heidegger's three examples – the Greek temple, the "Roman Fountain" poem, and Van Gogh's painting – map onto the three main ages in his history of being, viz., the ancient, medieval, and modern, respectively. The poem nicely illustrates that history for Heidegger (I shall suggest), but his attempt to transcend modernity from within takes place primarily through his interpretation of the modern work: Van Gogh's painting of *A Pair of Shoes*.

constellations of intelligibility (as we saw in Chapter 1). For, the ontological "truth" that Meyer's poem embodies – and "sets to work," in Heidegger's creative appropriation of the poem – is that truth itself is essentially historical and, moreover, that this essential history of "the truth of being" forms three successive "epochs," just as the "jet" of water fills the three consecutive "basins" in Meyer's poetic fountain.[6] For Heidegger, to put it more

---

[6] Concerning the "truth set into the work" of the poem, Heidegger asks (rhetorically – rhetorical questions are his preferred means for making bold assertions): "Which truth happens in the work? Can truth *happen* at all and thus *be historical?*" (PLT 38, my emphasis/GA5 23) Because Meyer surely did not intend his poem to mean what Heidegger takes it to mean (viz., that truth is essentially historical, that this history is tri-epochal, and that it is fed by the forgotten spring of being), it is only natural to worry here about the thorny hermeneutic issue of what significance authors' intentions have for the meaning of their work. For Heidegger, works of art have two *equally* important sides: their creation (by an artist) and their preservation (by a community of interpreters). As he puts it: "Just as a work cannot be without being created and thus is essentially in need of creators, so what is created cannot itself come into being without those who preserve it." (PLT 66/GA5 54) *An artwork without an interpretive community remains mute, and an interpretive community without a guiding artwork remains blind.* At the same time, Heidegger suggests that artworks' creators are often unreliable guides to the meaning of their own work. Notoriously, Heidegger was never shy about asserting that he understood a work better than its own creator, whether that creator was a philosopher (whose essential but "unthought" thoughts Heidegger sought to explicate) or an artist (with an insufficient philosophical understanding of his work). E.g., Petzet tells us that, although Paul Klee's work was "of crucial significance for Heidegger," Heidegger was convinced that Klee himself "does not know what is happening" in his own work. Ironically, as if to justify this view, Heidegger quotes from Klee's *Creative Confession* (*Schöpferische Konfession*), where Klee writes: "Art plays an unknowing game with the ultimate things and yet reaches them nonetheless!" Proceeding in his typical way (toward those to whom he is sympathetically inclined), Heidegger seeks to deepen Klee's self-understanding by questioning Klee's own presuppositions in a way that leads to Heidegger's own philosophical views. Heidegger thus takes the first sentence of Klee's *Creative Confession* – viz., "Art does not give the visible but, instead, makes visible" – and asks: "What [makes visible]? The invisible, and from where and in what way [does] the invisible determine [the visible]?" Heidegger's hermeneutic arrogance is legendary, but it stems from the strength of his philosophical views and the fact that, as a trained phenomenologist, he is committed to the idea that our knowledge of authors' intentions can narrow and so distort our appreciation of the meaning of their work (which, if it is a "great" work, will be essentially polysemic, as we will see). At any rate, this commitment to the phenomenological method helps explain Heidegger's contention that the truth of the work shows itself to us most "purely... [p]recisely where the artist and the process and the circumstances surrounding the genesis of the work remain unknown" (PLT 65/GA5 53). Such sentiments occasionally bleed over into a well-known hostility to the biographical. Yet, Heidegger's dramatic view that "the artist remains something inconsequential in comparison with the work, almost like a passageway that destroys itself in the creative process for the emergence of the work" (PLT 40/GA5 26), shows clearly that Heidegger was influenced by the romantic celebration of madness as a sign that the artist has been "touched" by the divine ("Apollo has struck me" [EHP 62/GA4 44], Hölderlin famously wrote), as does Hiedegger's very predilection for such figures as Hölderlin, Nietzsche, and Van Gogh, who all "fell into madness" (WCT 52/GA8 56). (See Petzet, *Encounters and Dialogues with Martin Heidegger,* 147, 149; Seubold, "Heideggers nachgelassene Klee-Notizen," 9, 12.)

precisely, the relations Meyer's poem describes between the fountain's original "jet" and its three successive water basins suggestively illuminate the relations between "being" itself (that is, the inexhaustible ontological source of historical intelligibility) and the three main historical "epochs" in Western humanity's understanding of being (as Heidegger conceived of this "history of being" in 1936), namely, ancient "Greece," "the middle ages," and "the modern age" (PLT 76–7/GA5 64–5).[7]

Thus, for example, just as the original "jet" of water "falls" into the fountain's successive basins in Meyer's poem, so the "overflowing" ontological riches concealed in the ancient world were first diminished in the medieval world. "The Origin of the Work of Art" make the contentious case that this ontological diminution "begins" when concepts central to the ancient Greek understanding of being were translated into Latin without a full experience of what those concepts originally revealed (PLT 23/GA5 8). Hence the obvious appeal for Heidegger of Meyer's lines: "Veiling itself, this [first basin] overflows / Into a second basin's ground" (PLT 37/GA5 23). What remained of these ontological "riches" in the medieval world was then transposed into and reduced further in the modern epoch, which, like the fountain's third basin, stands at the furthest remove from its original source. It thus seems clear that Heidegger includes Meyer's poem because he believes it suggestively illuminates the way the history of being unfolds as a history of decline, a "fall" that results from this history's increasing forgetting of the source from which it *ultimately springs* – the *Ur-sprung* or "origin" of Heidegger's essay's title – in a word: "Being." "Being" (*Sein*) is Heidegger's most famous name for that inexhaustible ontological source from which all historical intelligibility *originates* – by way of the disclosive "naming-into-being" that Heidegger understands as the "poetic" essence of art (as we will see in the next section).

Heidegger thus uses Meyer's poem to allude to the broader philosophical context that helps explain and motivate the new historical beginning he believes art can help us inaugurate. Heidegger's use of this particular poem suggests, moreover, that in order to accomplish this "other beginning," Western humanity needs to learn to tap back into that original, ontological source (the overflowing "jet" of being), and that such a reconnection with the primordial source of historical intelligibility is something art can still teach us. (Although interpreters also overlook this, the quiet but ominous presence of a homophonous "third reich" in Meyer's poem

---

[7] As we saw in part one, it was not until 1938 (in The Age of the World Picture") that Heidegger began clearly to distinguish modern "subjectivism" (the modern subject's quest to completely control the objective world) from late-modern "enframing" (the objectification of that subject whereby everything gets reduced to the status of an intrinsically-meaningless "resource," *Bestand*, standing by to be optimized and efficiently ordered for further use). Heidegger also later distinguishes between two phases in the Ancient world, viz., the pre-Socratic and the Platonic (see *Heidegger on Ontotheology*, ch. 1).

reminds us of the deeply troubling dimension of Heidegger's thinking in the mid-1930s, the fact that his philosophical hopes for the future were for a brief time deeply entwined with his idiosyncratic understanding of the philosophical direction he believed the burgeoning National Socialist "revolution" might yet take.)[8]

While both the temple and the poem thus remain quite important, only Van Gogh's painting directly exemplifies what Heidegger thinks it means to encounter art in a way that allows us to transcend modern aesthetics from within. This means that *Heidegger's interpretation of Van Gogh's painting, far from being irrelevant, is actually the most important part of his essay.* For, it is only

---

[8] It is possible that Heidegger does not envision a new fountain, or even a fourth basin, here in 1936 but, instead, continues to imagine a (more politically problematic) *revitalization* of the third basin, along the lines of his then current faith in the possibility of redirecting the Third Reich philosophically. (On this point, see *Heidegger on Ontotheology*, 120–1.) Given the historical context of Heidegger's essay, the suggestive proximity of the words "reich / Der dritten" ("... riches / the third ...") in lines 5 and 6 of Meyer's poem are certainly troubling in this regard (PLT 37/GA5 23; cf. P 17, where one of these lines is unintentionally elided). This worry cannot be dismissed by pointing to the obvious fact that Meyer's "Roman Fountain" employs the *reich* of "riches" rather than the homophonic *Reich* of "empire," because Heidegger's own understanding of poetry stresses the central importance of poetry's ineliminable polysemy (as we will see in the next two chapters). Indeed, in my view, *it is here that those searching for a hidden allusion to Nazism in Heidegger's essay should look*, rather than to his interpretation of Van Gogh's painting (as Schapiro influentially, but falsely, suggests – as we will see in section 3). That Heidegger chose a poem containing these words at this time is surely no coincidence but, instead, another significant aspect of the otherwise mysterious attraction Meyer's seemingly rather mediocre poem held for him. Notice, however, that this initially alarming allusion, when taken in context, actually suggests Heidegger's view of the spiritual poverty of the Third Reich as it existed in 1935–6, a poverty that for a brief time Heidegger hoped to remedy by helping to lead the Nazi movement philosophically to a "second, deeper awakening" (HB 571). Heidegger megalomaniacally thought Nazism could attain this more profound spiritual "awakening" by being uprooted from Hitler's eugenic vision (which Heidegger consistently rejects as a "biologistic" extension of Nietzschean metaphysics) and grounded, instead, in his own philosophical understanding of the history of being. In general, the political context of Heidegger's essay is too complicated and momentous an issue to address adequately here. I might just add that Heidegger's simultaneous celebration of Van Gogh (an artist Hitler hated, and who became for the Nazis a prime example of "degenerate art") and of a *female* farmer (the very image of a *woman* laborer soon became an anti-fascist trope) shows how far Heidegger already was in 1935–6 from the central tenets of Nazi ideology. In 1937–8, Heidegger will privately express his disgust with the Nazi's aesthetic "productions" celebrating the Aryan superman, in which "e.g., the masculinity of man is produced in giant muscles and genitals, in blank faces tense with brutality" (M 26/GA66 34). (Thanks to David Craven for suggesting the penultimate point. For a careful treatment of the broader political issues raised by Heidegger's thinking of art, see Young, *Heidegger's Philosophy of Art*, as well as the competing view outlined by Wright in "Heidegger and Hölderlin." Contrast the polemical view advanced by Geulen in *The End of Art: Readings in a Rumor after Hegel*, Ch. 6. On the direct connection between Heidegger's philosophy and his politics, see my *Heidegger on Ontotheology*, ch. 3. For more on the "other beginning" Heidegger was then calling for, see Chapter 6.)

from Heidegger's phenomenological interpretation of Van Gogh's artwork that we late moderns can learn how to transcend modern aesthetics from within, thereby learning from art what it means to encounter being in a postmodern way. Since we have already summarized Heidegger's "Promethean" view of the historically revolutionary work accomplished by the ancient Greek temple (in Chapter 2.1), we will expand on the point of his return to Greece only briefly (in the next section), in order to say more about how this return to the past is supposed to help guide us into the future. The rest of this chapter will be dedicated primarily to explaining Heidegger's pivotal understanding of Van Gogh's painting.[9] My ultimate objective will be to show how Heidegger's interpretation of Van Gogh allows him to move phenomenologically from the analysis of a particular, individual ("ontic") work of art to the ontological structure of artwork in general. Along the way, we will examine the main details of the postmodern understanding of being that Heidegger thinks we can learn from a nonaesthetic encounter with the work of art. Once we understand the precise sequence of steps in the phenomenological interpretation whereby Heidegger thinks we can transcend modern aesthetics from within, moreover, we will finally be able to resolve the long-standing controversy surrounding his interpretation of Van Gogh's painting (as we will see in Section 3).

1.1. Back to the Future: Heidegger on the Essence of Art

Heidegger's introduction of "a well-known painting by Van Gogh, who painted such shoes several times" (PLT 33/GA5 18), is notoriously abrupt and puzzling to many readers. The path that leads Heidegger to Van Gogh's painting should not be too surprising, however, because it is the same path we followed last chapter. Looking back at "The Origin of the Work of Art" two years later (in 1938), Heidegger will write that:

The question of the origin of the work of art does not aim to set out a timelessly valid determination of the essence of artwork which could also serve as the guiding thread for an historically retrospective clarification of the history of art. The question is most intimately connected with the task of overcoming aesthetics,

---

[9] Understanding Heidegger's phenomenological interpretation of Van Gogh allows us to recognize that the less culturally monolithic understanding of art that Dreyfus and Young rightly discern in Heidegger's later writings can already be found in a nascent form in his phenomenological interpretation of Van Gogh, alongside the more culturally unified view suggested by Heidegger's thoughts on the ancient Greek temple. In the earliest version of the essay, each "people" (*Volk*) would have its own "singular" understanding of the being of entities (HR 147/UK1 20). The crucial difference that emerges in the later, published version is that the postmodern understanding of being that Heidegger suggests Van Gogh can help us inaugurate historically would understand the being of entities in terms of being as such, i.e., not in a single, monolithic way but, instead, as essentially inexhaustible and thus necessarily polysemic (as we will see in Section 2.3).

which also means overcoming a certain conception of entities as what are objectively representable. (CP 354/GA65 503)[10]

We have seen that because aesthetics tries to describe artworks as objects that express and intensify human subjects' experiences of life, the aesthetic approach begins "always-already" too late. Modern aesthetics presupposes the perspective of a subject confronting an external art object and thereby misses the way art works inconspicuously in the background of human existence to shape and transform our basic sense of what is and what matters.

Heidegger expands his critique to include "representation" here because representations are what modern philosophy typically uses to try to bridge the divide Descartes opened between subjects and objects. The objective world allegedly "external" to subjectivity gets duplicated in miniature, as it were, and "re-presented" to the mind – as in the famous Cartesian picture of consciousness as an internal "theater of representations." Of course, Heidegger does not deny that representations sometimes mediate our experience of the world. What he denies is that representations go "all the way down," that they plumb the depths of existence. Instead, representations presuppose a level of existence they cannot fully recapture. Remember that Heidegger's fundamental phenomenological critique of the modern theoretical picture is that it overlooks and then cannot subsequently do justice to the more basic level of engaged existence, a practical coping with equipment in which no subject/object dichotomy has yet opened up because self and world remain integrally entwined and mutually determining.[11] This primordial level of engaged existence, we will see,

---

[10] In this quotation from his middle period, Heidegger calls for an "overcoming" (*Überwindung*) of modern aesthetics, but he will soon reject the idea of overcoming modern metaphysics directly (for the reason that any such attempt to move directly "anti–" inevitably remains entangled in the logic of that which it opposes), instead calling for a "twisting-free" (*Verwindung*) of modern metaphysics, i.e., a kind of passing through and getting beyond, as one might "get over" or recover from a serious illness.

[11] According to the theoretical picture at the core of modern philosophy, we have no unmediated acquaintance with reality; instead, we only ever experience the objective world as it is re-presented in our own consciousness. From the perspective of phenomenology, this doubling of the world in "representation" looks like a mischaracterization of ordinary existence, in which we typically encounter people and trees, e.g., not representations of people and trees. Of course, we do explicitly encounter representations in certain types of break-down cases, for example, when our only access to a painting is through various representations of it and, as we study them, we become aware of subtle differences between these different representations of the same work; or when our only chance to see our family is by way of a low-resolution videoconference, in which problems with the sound or picture make it difficult to ignore the medium of our interaction. In such break-down cases, we become aware of representations coming between us and the world precisely because we experience them as a poor substitute for the thing they represent. Interestingly, thinking about such media of perception (especially the empirical study of optics) originally helped Descartes motivate the rather strange idea that representations of which we are unaware pervasively mediate our experience of the world.

is what Heidegger thinks Van Gogh's painting allows us to encounter and understand in a way no mere aesthetic representation ever could. In so doing, Heidegger thinks, Van Gogh's painting allows us to encounter the very essence of art.

On the basis of passages like the one quoted above, however, some interpreters claim that "The Origin of the Work of Art" does not seek to "uncover the essence of art," but that is quite misleading.[12] As Heidegger says, his essay does not seek to set out one "timelessly valid determination" of the essence of art which would apply retrospectively to the entire history of art, but that is only because he does not understand essences the way they have been understood from Plato to Kripke, namely, as "timelessly valid determinations" of what something is.[13] In fact, "The Origin of the Work of Art" does attempt to uncover and communicate art's historical "essence," by which Heidegger means that structure that allows art to reveal itself in different ways as it unfolds in the human understanding

(On Heidegger's radical challenge to this view, see the major works by Guignon, *Heidegger and the Problem of Knowledge*; Richardson, *Existential Epistemology: A Heideggerian Critique of the Cartesian Project*; F. A. Olafson, *Heidegger and the Philosophy of Mind*; and H. L. Dreyfus, *Being-in-the-World: A Commentary on Heidegger's* Being and Time, *Division I*.) Heidegger's theory of the transformation from the "hands on" (*zuhanden*) the "on hand" (*vorhanden*), discussed in the previous chapter, helps explain why it is that when our practical engagement with the world of our involvements breaks down or runs into unexpected difficulties, we then often find ourselves explicitly deliberating, making plans, articulating our beliefs and desires, trying out various interpretations, and the like.

[12] (K. Hammermeister advances this claim in *The German Aesthetic Tradition*, 238 note 8; cf. Bartky, "Heidegger's Philosophy of Art.") The specific question of whether Heidegger believes art has an essence (he does) leads to the larger question of whether, given Heidegger's understanding of this essence (in terms of the *alêtheiac* tension of emerging and withdrawing that gives rise to *all* historical intelligibility), he can properly be said to have a "philosophy of art" as such. Pöggeler famously argues that Heidegger does not have a "philosophy of art" at all, because Heidegger does not think of art distinctively *as* art but only in terms of the role art plays disclosing being in time. (See Pöggeler, *Philosophie und Politik bei Heidegger*.) Pöggeler's criticism, however, begs the question against Heidegger's phenomenological understanding of art. For, as Steven Crowell explains, "the phenomenologist does not reflect on experience in order to describe it in its particularity but to uncover the 'essential' or *a priori* structures that inform it" ("Phenomenology and Aesthetics; or, Why Art Matters"). In *Heideggers Philosophie der Kunst*, F.-W. von Herrmann thus responds to Pöggeler simply by elaborating the philosophy of art that von Herrmann, like Young, rightly finds in Heidegger's later work (although we will see that it can already be discerned in his phenomenological reading of Van Gogh). (On the disagreement between Pöggeler and von Herrmann, see also Günter Seubold, *Kunst als Ereignis: Heideggers Weg zu einer nicht mehr metaphysischen Kunst*, 11–71.)

[13] Plato's metaphysical understanding of the "eternal forms" already lays the ground for Kripke's influential definition of an essence as an invariant property that can be "rigidly designated" across all possible worlds. (See Kripke, *Naming and Necessity*. For more on Heidegger's historical understanding of essences, which is closer to Hegel than to Plato, but lacks Hegel's teleological commitments, see my *Heidegger on Ontotheology*, 52–61.)

across time. What is so confusing for many readers, however, is that this historical essence of art is not some substance underlying the different forms of art or even a fixed property that would enable us to distinguish art from nonart but, instead, an insubstantial and ever-changing "essential strife" that is built into the structure of all intelligibility (that is, the structure whereby entities become intelligible as entities), as we will see.[14]

Rather than obliging Heidegger to elaborate an entire art history, the normative demands of his critical project only require him to focus on two crucial moments in Western humanity's changing historical understanding of art – a kind of before and after, as it were, which allows him to contrast the fullness of what has been possible with the narrowness of what is currently actual. Indeed, Heidegger is primarily concerned to show, first, how the ancient Greeks encountered art in a nonaesthetic way (and so enshrined it in their temples), and second, how art is typically understood and experienced by us late moderns, who remain caught in the grip of modern aesthetics and so under the influence of "modern subjectivism" (PLT 76/GA5 63). As subjectivism's unlimited ambition to establish "mastery over the totality of what-is" (QCT 132/GA5 92) works to objectify even modernity's vaunted subject, moreover, it increasingly transforms modern subjectivism into late-modern "enframing" (as we saw last chapter).

In "The Origin of the Work of Art," Heidegger suggests that modern subjectivism and late-modern enframing can be understood as symptoms of Western humanity's continuing inability to accept our defining existential finitude. The limitless ambition of our subjectivist quest to master all reality conceptually is a kind of manic refusal to own up to, make peace with, and find non-nihilistic ways to affirm a tragic truth that Heidegger gleans from the ancients:

> Much of what is cannot be brought under the rule of humanity. Only a little becomes known. What is known remains approximate; what is mastered remains unstable. What-is is never something [entirely] man-made or even only a representation, as it can all too easily appear. (PLT 53/GA5 39)

Heidegger takes off here from the second choral ode in Sophocles' *Antigone* (which he discusses at length in 1935's *Introduction to Metaphysics*). For Sophocles' Theban elders, the one thing humanity cannot master is

---

[14] For Heidegger, the essence of art is also the essential tension whereby being becomes intelligible in time. This essential tension conditions the becoming-intelligible of all things, Heidegger suggests, even the technological works of art that efface and deny this struggle like the freeway interchange noted earlier. For this reason, such works can be subjected to immanent critiques that show that they deny, efface, or contradict their own conditions of possibility.

death. For Heidegger, thinking about death opens us up to the terrifyingly "awesome" insight that the known rests on the unknown, the mastered on the unmastered, like a small ship floating on a deep and stormy "sea" (IM 159, 164/GA40 159, 162).[15] We like to believe that humanity is well on its way to mastering the universe, but art teaches us that we will never exhaust the possibilities inherent in what we like to call "reality."

Yet, rather than leading us into despair over our essential human finitude (the fact that we will never master the totality of what-is), art helps us learn to embrace our defining finitude by reminding us of its other side, namely, the fact that intelligibility will never exhaust its source. For, it remains possible for being to continue to become newly intelligible only if it cannot ever become fully intelligible. Art thus teaches us to embrace the insight that meanings will never be exhausted as precisely what makes it possible for us to continue to discover new meanings. In this way art helps us see that human finitude is not something we should despair over or seek to deny though compensatory subjectivistic fantasies. Of course, the claim that we should give up thinking we could ever know everything does not entail that we should give up trying to know new things – quite the contrary. If the heroic is what helps us affirm and thereby transform the tragic (as we will see in Chapter 5), then Heidegger's thinking about art is implicitly heroic. For, art teaches us to embrace the initially tragic insight that being will never be completely revealed in time as the very thing that makes it possible for human beings to continue to understand what-is in new and potentially more meaningful ways.

In sum, the point of Heidegger's juxtaposition of modern spleen and ancient ideal is not to call for the impossible revival of the lost Greek past but, rather, to help motivate a new, post-aesthetic understanding of what art could still mean for us, now and in the future. If, instead of trying to obtain a kind of cognitive mastery over art through aesthetics – or using aesthetics to extend our late-modern understanding of all that is as intrinsically meaningless resources standing by to be optimized – we simply allow ourselves to encounter what is happening within a great work of art, then Heidegger thinks we will be able to recognize the "essential strife" in which a true work of art paradoxically "rests" and finds its "repose" (PLT 48–9/GA5 34–5). When we encounter this "movement" that paradoxically rests in the masterful "composure" of a great artwork, moreover,

---

[15] Heidegger's more specific point here is that the way things show themselves to us is not determined solely by us: Human beings do not get to decide the fundamental conceptual parameters through which we make sense of reality and ourselves. Instead, the great poets and thinkers receptively shape the lenses through which we see the world and ourselves by creatively responding to the ways things show or suggest themselves. Even for the great poets and thinkers, then, the way that entities reveal their being is never entirely within human control or simply a product our own representational capacities.

what we discover therein is an "instability" that underlies the entire intelligible order, an ontological tension (between revealing and concealing, emerging and withdrawing) that can never be permanently stabilized and so remains even in what is "mastered."[16] Indeed, what is truly mastered artistically, Heidegger suggests, is what somehow captures, preserves, and communicates this tension in the structure of intelligibility, allowing us to encounter and understand this essential tension in a way that can help us learn to transcend the limits of our modern and late-modern ways of understanding what and how beings are.

1.2. Heidegger's Phenomenological Approach to Art

To encounter the paradoxical movement at rest within a great artwork (the mysterious movement that, as Hammermeister nicely suggests, enables art to move us in turn), Heidegger believes we need only follow the phenomenological dictum that we should "simply describe" our experience of the

---

[16] Heidegger describes the paradoxical movement at rest in a great work of art as "the constantly self-exceeding composure of the work's movement" (PLT 50/GA5 36). The fundamental ontological instability that can be discovered in the inconspicuous movement of a great artwork is precisely what "The Origin of the Work of Art" describes as the "essential strife" between "earth" and "world." For Heidegger, the preservation of this inconspicuous movement at rest in a work (e.g., in the paintings of Van Gogh, Cézanne, and Klee) is a sign of the highest artistic mastery, for it allows such compositions to convey rather than conceal the conditions of their own generation. In 1934, Heidegger succinctly describes this paradoxical movement at rest as "the harnessed frenzy [or bound rush, *der gebändigte Rausch*] of creative works" (LQ 140/GA 38 169). Heidegger's nice formulation strongly suggests that his thinking of the essential tension of earth and world was deeply influenced by the early Nietzsche's understanding of art in terms of the struggle between Apollo and Dionysus (because *Rausch* also means drunkenness), but it also points toward the crucial difference, which is the difference between Nietzschean succession and Heideggerian simultaneity. In Nietzsche's (self-described) "aesthetic metaphysics," the fundamental conflict between Dionysian and the Apollonian forces similarly drives the unfolding of history; yet, the underlying Dionysian flux gives rise to an Apollonian form that stills that flux temporarily, thereby generating an alternating cycle of opposites in which "wherever the Dionysian broke through, the Apollonian was suspended and annulled," and vice versa. For Heidegger, by contrast, the artwork does not still or annul the tension but rather captures it in its "bound frenzy." If, for Nietzsche, we could thus think of rigidly disciplined martial formations or athletic movement stilled in a sculpture (or religious rapture given a stable form in the tragic chorus), I would say that for Heidegger we should think instead of Odysseus bound to the mast while *still struggling* to break free. As Young nicely shows, Heidegger traces Nietzsche's Dionysus/Apollo opposition back to Hölderlin's distinction between Greek "fire from heaven" and German "clarity of presentation" (which Heidegger discusses at length in 1942's HHI), but Young goes too far when he suggests that Hölderlin's view is "identical" with Heidegger's thinking of the earth/world tension. (See Nietzsche, *The Birth of Tragedy and Other Writings*, 27, 30; Young, *Heidegger's Philosophy of Art*, 40–1. See also Dennis Schmidt, *On Germans and Other Greeks*.)

work of art "without any philosophical theory" (PLT 32/GA5 18).[17] The phenomenological approach to art instructs us to

restrain from all usual doing and prizing, knowing and looking, in order to linger within the truth that is happening in the work. Only the restraint of this lingering allows what is created to first be the work that it is. (PLT 66/GA5 54)[18]

Yet, simply "to let a being be the way it is [*wie es ist*]" turns out to be "the most difficult of tasks" (PLT 31/GA5 16). For, insofar as the concepts we use to make sense of our experience remain uninterrogated as to their built-in interpretive biases, we tend not even to notice when inappropriate conceptual categories lead us to a distorted or inadequate apprehension of the phenomenon at issue.

Phenomenology's ideal of pure description thus requires us to struggle vigilantly against our usual tendency to force the square peg of recalcitrant experience into the round hole of ready-made conceptual categories. (For example, we typically presuppose that things at rest cannot move, so we are inclined to dismiss any inkling of movement in an artwork as some sort of idiosyncratic, subjective projection on our parts, whereas Heidegger will show phenomenologically that such movement is in fact an essential part of any true encounter with great art.) In order truly to be open to the way things show themselves to us, then, we have "to keep at a distance all preconceptions and interfering misconceptions [*Vor- und Übergriffe*]" concerning what and how things *are*. Rather than giving us license simply to do what comes "naturally," then, Husserl's famed phenomenological dictum – "Back to the things themselves!" – enjoins us to struggle to discern and neutralize the usually unnoticed metaphysical presuppositions (such as the modern assumption of a fundamental subject/object dichotomy) that, although they remain "derivative" of more basic experiences that they cannot explain, nevertheless continue to pass themselves off as "self-evident" and so lead modern aesthetics off track (PLT 31/GA5 16).

It is not a coincidence that Van Gogh's painting is the first example of an actual work of art that Heidegger mentions in "The Origin of the Work

---

[17] Picking up on Heidegger's paradoxical description of the movement resting in a great artwork, Hammermeister boldly proposes that: "Only because the work of art moves can it move us. Yet there is nothing restless about the work of art either. ...[The artwork] must be thought of as simultaneously moving and at rest." Mining a parallel vein, Karsten Harries rightly sees that: "To be open to the earth is inevitably to be affected, moved, claimed. Heidegger's talk of the earth thus gestures also toward the affective base without which all our talk of values or divinities in ultimately groundless. ... The step beyond nihilism is possible only as a recovery of the earth." (See Hammermeister, *The German Aesthetic Tradition*, 183; Harries, "Heidegger's Confrontation with Aesthetics," 376.)

[18] Heidegger continues: "This letting the work be a work is what we call preservation [*Bewahrung*] of the work" (PLT 66/GA5 54). Such "preservation" designates the safeguarding of a work's *alētheiac* truth by the individual or community of those who keep the meaning of the work alive in their lives, without whom the work cannot do any work.

of Art," and the context, when examined closely, is revealing. Heidegger is introducing the concept of a "thing," a seemingly obvious idea the complex history of which he then goes on to explicate in great detail (PLT 20–30/ GA5 5–16), thereby undermining its initial appearance of obviousness.[19] By showing that none of the three standard metaphysical conceptions of a thing – which conceive of a thing variously as "the bearer of traits, as the unity of a sensory manifold, and as formed matter" (PLT 30/GA5 15) – manages to capture fully our sense of what things are, Heidegger is able to make the crucial suggestion that there is something about a thing that eludes all our attempts to capture and express it conceptually:

The inconspicuous thing withdraws itself from thought most stubbornly. Or can it be that this self-refusal of the mere thing, this self-contained refusal to be pushed around, belongs precisely to the essential nature of things? (PLT 31–2/GA5 17)

By suggesting that an ineliminable elusiveness – an independence from human designs – is in fact *essential* to what things are, Heidegger is motivating his own concept of the "earth" as what both informs and resists conceptualization.[20] At the same time, he is also illustrating his

---

[19] Heidegger recounts the genealogy whereby (1) the *ancient* concept of a thing as a unity of *hypokeimenon* and *symbebêkos* first gets reduced (when the Greek is translated into Latin) to the *medieval* "substance and accidents," and then to the *modern* "primary and secondary properties." He also briefly discusses (2) Kant's conception of a thing as the "unity of a sensory manifold" as well as (3) Aristotle's understanding of a thing as "formed matter" (see PLT 20–30/GA5 5–16). "The Origin of the Work of Art" suggests that the first two conceptions render the essence of the thing phenomenologically inaccessible (the first by placing the core of the thing too far away from the body and its sensory capacities, the second by bringing it too close). For Heidegger, this recognition of the thing's inaccessibility is only half right; there will always be aspects of a thing that elude our encounter with it, but there is no single aspect of that stands forever beyond our reach, in principle inaccessible, as if located in some transcendent realm outside space and time. In other words, *Heidegger phenomenologizes the noumenal*: What does not completely show itself to us conditions our experience of what does show itself (and vice versa), but its not completely showing itself to us does show up to us, either implicitly (such that our seeing the chair, e.g., as having other sides that we do not see is what gives it the three-dimensional appearance we take for granted) or, in great art, explicitly (where we actually see, e.g., that there is something we do not see at the heart of what we do see, and this initially paradoxical disclosure of what both conditions and withdraws from our experience is precisely what Heidegger calls "earth"). As for the third conception of the thing (as formed matter), Heidegger suggests that this influential conception needs to be understood as a metaphysically rigidified (and so overly narrow) descendent of the phenomenon he is seeking to discover in the essay, viz., the joining of "world and earth." The form/matter dichotomy derives from approaching things in a comportment of *technê* (rather than *poiêsis*), with a preexisting form in mind that one merely imposes on things (rather than creatively disclosing the possibilities inherent in the way "the material" [*der Stoff*] of the thing "resists" [and even "opposes," *Widerstand*] such pregiven designs [PLT 46/GA5 32]).

[20] This crucial phenomenological insight that there is something essential to things that remains "stubbornly" recalcitrant to human control seems to be what motivates Heidegger to make the transition from evoking the "nothing" to elaborating the "earth."

phenomenological dictum that our common-sense view of things – although it appears "natural" and "self-evident" – is often freighted with unnoticed metaphysical presuppositions that can eclipse and so prevent a full encounter with the phenomena we face. By revealing the limitations of Western philosophy's metaphysical conceptions of what "things" are, Heidegger gives a concrete demonstration of his critical-phenomenological view (obviously influenced by Nietzsche) that: "What seems natural to us is presumably just the familiarity of a long-established custom which has forgotten the unfamiliarity from which it arose" (PLT 24/GA5 9).

The fact that Heidegger's first mention of Van Gogh is framed by these two ways of undermining our usual sense of the obviousness of things should lead us to suspect that he is introducing a seemingly obvious idea that he will subsequently use phenomenology to try to call into question, excavate beneath, and so go beyond. Once we recognize the context, it is not difficult to detect the irony in Heidegger's initial suggestion that "artworks are familiar to everyone" already since they "obviously" populate our world just like all the other objects "on hand":

One [*Man*] finds works of architecture and sculpture erected in public places, in churches, and in private dwellings.... Works obviously are on hand [*vorhanden*, i.e., objectively present] like any other thing. The picture hangs on the wall like a rifle or a hat. A painting, for example the one by Van Gogh that represents a pair of farmer's shoes, travels from one exhibit to another. Works are shipped like coal from the Ruhr and logs from the Black Forest. (PLT 19/GA5 3)

The last line points toward the way aesthetics serves enframing (as we saw last chapter). Indeed, Heidegger clearly means to suggest that the very obviousness of the public knowledge he appeals to ironically here – which assumes that artworks are *objects* and that they *represent* things – conceals the more "original" truths about art which he seeks to uncover in "The Origin of the Work of Art."[21]

That the initial familiarity of the anonymous "everyone" (*jedermann*) with art objects and representational paintings turns out to be a superficial acquaintance that covers over the true depths of the matter at issue should not be surprising. Almost a decade earlier, when *Being and Time* famously sought to disclose the ubiquitous and thus usually unnoticed ways in which the anonymous "one [*das Man*] unfolds its true dictatorship," Heidegger had already observed that "we read, see, and judge literature and art the way *one* sees and judges." So, for example, "everyone knows" that Da Vinci's "Mona Lisa" is a great work of art; we think we "know" this even if the painting has never spoken to us personally at all, or if we have only heard that

---

[21] We also have good reason to be skeptical of this description because for Heidegger (as Taylor Carman nicely explains), "just as a useful thing is not a mere object with functional properties added on, neither is a work of art simply a useful thing with aesthetic qualities in addition." (See Carman, "Heidegger, Martin: Survey of Thought," 373.)

"they say" the enigmatic hint of a smile on her face is supposed to suggest the numinous presence of God, or the wry smirk of a secret lover – or if we have heard (more recently) that the sublime elusiveness of her smile can finally be "explained" by neuroscientific findings about the way our brains process different spatial frequencies.[22] Yet through this kind of "leveling down" to a publicly accessible, take-home message,

> everything primordial gets glossed over as something long familiar. Everything gained by a struggle becomes just something to be manipulated. Every mystery loses its power. (BT 164–5/SZ 126–7)

"The Origin [*Ursprung*] of the Work of Art" will suggest, conversely, that by struggling with the mysteries of a work like Van Gogh's *A Pair of Shoes*, we can gain an insight into art's most "primordial" (or "original," *Ursprüngliche*) level of truth – the very level from which such widespread insights initially emerged.

Unfortunately, as this suggests, it is quite difficult to present the deepest truths that emerge from the kind of personal struggle existential phenomenology demands without thereby inadvertently supplying the public with another leveled-down formula to bandy about, a familiar catchphrase (like "language is the house of being") that quickly becomes a superficial substitute for the insight it bespeaks. The problem, expressed metaphorically, is that receiving a souvenir from someone else's journey makes a poor substitute for taking that voyage for oneself. Heidegger's recognition of this difficulty helps explain why he seeks to *show* at least as much as to *say* what he takes to be art's deepest truths in "The Origin of the Work of Art." Indeed, what is easily recognized as the later Heidegger's distinctive, "poetic" style comes from the fact that, after *Being and Time*, he is no longer content simply to construct arguments in relatively straightforward philosophical prose, but also begins to try to lead his audience performatively to see the phenomenon ultimately at issue for themselves.[23] This is a large part of

---

[22] From a Heideggerian perspective, the last explanation is the most problematic; it not only illustrates another way in which aesthetics can come to serve "enframing" through neuroscience; it also shows how the enigma of art gets "explained" away in the process. (See Livingstone's own remarks to this effect at http://neuro.med.harvard.edu/faculty/livingstone.html [accessed 23 August 2010].)

[23] This chapter faces the same problem, in that it rather brazenly puts into words some of the insights Heidegger seems deliberately to have left unstated. I think such hermeneutic audacity justified by that fact that Heidegger's readers have not yet seen these important matters (and others surely remain unseen still). If Heidegger seems to overestimate readers' perspicacity, we should remember that his original audience (viz., "the Art-Historical Society of Freiburg") would have known that his understanding of art in "The Origin of the Work of Art" was paired with his complementary critique of aesthetics because, as Kelly points out, "the title of the colloquium at which Heidegger first presented an early version of the 'Origin' essay (and which he coorganized) was entitled 'The Overcoming of Aesthetics in the Question of Art.'" (See Kelly, *Iconoclasm in Aesthetics*, 35.)

what makes Heidegger's later works even more elusive and challenging for contemporary philosophical readers than *Being and Time*. By drawing on Heidegger's early as well as his later works, however, I think we can clearly understand the enduring philosophical challenges that his phenomenological approach to art seeks to surmount.

1.3. The Phenomenological Difficulty Heidegger
Introduces Van Gogh to Address

The basic problem, we have seen, is that the way artworks function in the background of our everyday experience cannot be adequately described in aesthetic terms (as a subject's experience of an art object) because: (1) aesthetics presupposes the subject/object dichotomy; (2) this subject/object dichotomy emerges only at a secondary level of experience, when our primary, integral engagement with the world of practical equipment breaks down; and (3) secondary structures of experience like the subject/object dichotomy cannot recapture the primordial level of our engagement with the world (the level from which they originally derive), because any such description of an external object "on hand" for a subject misses precisely *what it is like* to encounter "equipment" in a hands-on way. Objective descriptions of equipment bypass the very "equipmentality of equipment [*Zeughaften des Zeuges*]" (PLT 32/GA5 17) – as Heidegger phrases the point in "The Origin of the Work of Art" (still using the technical terminology of *Being and Time*) – because these descriptions of what is objectively "on hand" fail to notice, let alone capture, what it is like to be integrally involved with equipment in engaged, "hands-on" use. The fundamental problem, then, is: How can such engaged use ever be adequately described and communicated?

It is this difficult attempt to describe phenomenologically "what equipment in truth is" (PLT 32/GA5 17) – that is, to convey what it is like to encounter something when we are not aware of it as an object at all but, instead, are completely immersed in our practical engagement with it – that motivates Heidegger not just to mention but genuinely to introduce Van Gogh's painting, which he next presents simply "as an example of a common sort of equipment – a pair of farmer's shoes" (PLT 32/GA5 18). In Van Gogh's most famous painting of *A Pair of Shoes* (1886), Heidegger believes we can "discover what the equipmental being of equipment is in truth" (PLT 33/GA5 18). In other words, Heidegger thinks Van Gogh's painting reveals what it is like genuinely to encounter a shoe in its use as a shoe. As he puts it:

The farming woman wears her shoes in the field. Only here are they what they are. They are all the more genuinely so, the less the farming woman at work thinks about the shoes, or senses them at all, or is even aware of them. (PLT 33/GA5 18)

Heidegger thus introduces Van Gogh's painting of (what he takes to be) a farmer's shoes in order "to facilitate the visual realization" of "equipmentality," that primordial modality of existence in which we are integrally involved with our world and so encountering equipment in a nonthematic, hands-on way (a nonthematic encounter with what Heidegger dubs the "reliability" of the shoes, that is, their inconspicuous being as equipment in use).[24]

Yet, this is a deeply paradoxical move, as Heidegger himself realizes, because Van Gogh's painting does not picture shoes being used as equipment; it pictures shoes merely standing there like objects in a still-life painting! We will thus remain caught in an aesthetic experience, Heidegger acknowledges, "as long as we simply look at the empty, unused shoes as they stand there in the picture" (PLT 33/GA5 19). The deep puzzle here, then, is: How is Van Gogh's picture of "empty, unused shoes" standing there like objects supposed to help us uproot and transcend the subject/object dichotomy lying at the heart of modern aesthetics? To put the puzzle in Heidegger's terms: How is our experience of a painting of a pair of shoes standing there like objects supposed to lead us back to a preobjective encounter with "equipmentality"? How can a picture help us find a way out of the age of the world picture? How, in other words, can aesthetics transcend itself from within?

Here Heidegger has set up a genuine aporia – or better, an *Holzweg*, a "forest path" or, more colloquially, "a path to nowhere." It is not a coincidence that *Holzwege* is the title Heidegger gave to the book of essays that opens with "The Origin of the Work of Art." As Heidegger hints (in the otherwise empty page he had inserted into the book, before its first page), an *Holzweg* is a path through the woods made by foresters (and known to backwoods hikers as well as to the locals who follow these paths to gather their own firewood, as Heidegger himself did). Such a path eventually comes to an apparent dead-end, but this dead-end – seen differently – turns out to be a "clearing" (or *Lichtung*), that is, a place in the forest from which the trees have been removed. Such a clearing thus offers an unexpected vista, an epiphany that, although it results only from walking a particular path for oneself, can nevertheless seem to come from out of the middle of nowhere. As Heidegger suggests, an encounter with a forest "clearing" from which the trees have been removed – that is, an encounter with *nothing*, initially – makes it possible for us to notice the light through which we ordinarily see the forest. In his terms, a clearing redirects our attention from entities to being, that usually unnoticed ontological light through which things ordinarily appear. And if we can notice the light through which we see, then we can also notice that things show up differently in different lights,

---

[24] I take up the notorious *whose shoes* controversy in Section 3.

and so begin to realize that being exceeds any of its particular manifestations and, indeed, makes them all possible.[25] Seeing differently, we might
thus say, can turn an apparent dead-end into the occasion for an ontological epiphany.

2. SEEING DIFFERENTLY: FROM THE NOTH-ING
OF THE NOTHING TO THE ESSENTIAL STRIFE
OF EARTH AND WORLD

With this crucial idea of *seeing differently* in mind, let us notice a related aporia
that appears a bit earlier in Heidegger's text. While developing his phenomenological critique of the way the modern conception of what "things"
are implicitly structures and so distorts the aesthetic understanding of art,
Heidegger observes that when this "subject-object relation is coupled with
the conceptual pair form-matter," and this conceptual matrix is combined
with the "rational/irrational" and "logical/illogical" dichotomies,

> then representation has at its command a conceptual machinery which nothing
> can stand against [*eine Begriffsmechanik, der nichts widerstehen kann*]. (PLT 27/GA5 12)

Heidegger seems to mean us to take his words seriously: Aesthetic representation now possesses "a conceptual machinery which nothing can
stand against." Taken seriously, however, these words leave no room for
Heidegger's hope of transcending aesthetics. We reach a dead-end, that
is, until we hear these words differently, as instead suggesting that (the)
nothing can indeed stand against the otherwise irresistible conceptual
machinery of aesthetics.

That might sound bizarre at first, but remember that, for Heidegger,
the nothing is not nothing at all but, rather, does something; "the nothing itself noths or nihilates [*das Nichts selbst nichtet*]" [P 90/GA9 114], as
he notoriously put it in 1929.[26] This active "noth-ing" of the nothing was

---

[25] A similar phenomenon attracted numerous painters to New Mexico. For the famous Taos
School, beauty was not only about what one saw (the sweeping vista of mountain and val-
ley) but just as much about the light through which one saw it. In the quick and dramatic
shifts of light that characterize the high desert plateau (especially around sunset and
sunrise, or when the clouds suddenly roll in during monsoon season), the usually unnoticed light though which we see suddenly becomes radiantly self-evident. The experience
of coming to "see the light" through which one sees can be transformative for anyone,
but it has proven particularly attractive for painters, photographers, and, most recently,
cinematographers. (Tellingly, those who have lived there the longest, the natives of the
Taos Pueblo, have no word for "art" because they understand *everything* they do as art.
Heidegger's conviction that what one learns from a great work of art should come to shape
the way one sees everything else is not, I think, so different.)

[26] This famously chagrined Carnap, for whom such a seeming hypostatization of negation
was the very epitome of metaphysical nonsense. Friedman even suggests that this sentence effectively represents the moment that split the so-called analytic and continental

the first name Heidegger came up with to describe the phenomenological manifestation of that which both elicits and eludes complete conceptualization, an initially inchoate phenomenon we encounter when we go beyond our guiding conception of what-is. To experience this "noth-ing" is to become attuned to something that is not a thing (hence "nothing") but which conditions all our experiences of things, something that fundamentally informs our intelligible worlds but that we experience initially as what escapes and so defies our "subjectivistic" impulse to extend our conceptual mastery over everything. With the help of Heidegger's strange thought that only this "nothing" can stand against the conceptual machinery of aesthetics, we are now poised to understand his phenomenological interpretation of Van Gogh's painting.

To turn a dead-end into a clearing one has to see it differently. Notice how Heidegger looks at Van Gogh's still-life painting of a seemingly ordinary pair of well-worn shoes. The pivotal moment in Heidegger's meditation takes place when he attends to the fact that "[t]here is nothing surrounding this pair of farmer's shoes" (PLT 33/GA5 18–9).[27] Although the English translations obscure this (and no other interpreters seem to notice it), it is nevertheless clear that for Heidegger this nothing is not nothing at all. Heidegger literally says:

Surrounding this pair of farmer's shoes there is nothing, in which and to which they can belong ... [*Um dieses Paar Bauernschuhe herum ist nichts, wozu und wohin sie gehören könnten...*] (PLT 33/GA5 18–9)

Heidegger thrice introduces Van Gogh's *A Pair of Shoes* by employing the word "nothing" in precisely this ambiguous way; as we will see, this is how he begins every extended description of Van Gogh's painting. The crucial phenomenological question, then, is: What would it mean to really see this

---

traditions asunder. (See Michael Friedman, *A Parting of the Ways: Carnap, Cassirer, and Heidegger.*) Because "The Origin of the Work of Art" rethinks and develops this phenomenon of the "nothing" in terms of the "earth," the essay helps us better grasp what Heidegger was groping toward with that initially obscure formulation from 1929.

[27] "From Van Gogh's painting we cannot even determine where these shoes stand" (PLT 33/GA5 18) – or "to whom they belong" (GA5 18 note a), Heidegger adds in a note he made in the margins of his copy of the 1960 Reclam edition, clearly in response to Meyer Schapiro's criticism. On this basis, Schapiro concludes that (1) "Heidegger changed his interpretation of Van Gogh's painting" and (2) "ended up admitting that he was uncertain about whose shoes they were." Schapiro's second conclusion misses the point of Heidegger's note, which is that *no one* – neither he nor Schapiro – can be certain about who originally wore the shoes that Van Gogh painted in *A Pair of Shoes* (1886). Yet, this turns out to be largely irrelevant to Heidegger's view (as we will see in section 3). Meyer's first conclusion is thus mistaken as well; Heidegger retracts nothing essential from his phenomenological interpretation of Van Gogh (as we will also see). (See Meyer Schapiro, "The Still Life as a Personal Object – A Note on Heidegger and van Gogh (1968)," 142 note 9; and David Craven, "A Series of Interviews: Meyer Schapiro and Lillian Milgram Schapiro with David Craven," 161.)

FIGURE 2. Vincent van Gogh, *A Pair of Shoes*, 1886, Van Gogh Museum, Amsterdam, The Netherlands. Reproduced by permission from Art Resource, NY. Photo credit: Art Resource, NY.

"nothing," to encounter it not as nothing at all but, quite differently, as that "in which and to which" the shoes can indeed belong?[28] (See Figure 2.)

If, following Heidegger, one attends long enough to the "nothing surrounding this pair of farmer's shoes," meditating (with sufficient patience and care)[29] on "the undefined space" (PLT 33/GA5 19) in Van Gogh's

---

[28] Heidegger is not the only one who thinks that the key to the enduring appeal of Van Gogh's much beloved painting, *A Pair of Shoes* (1886), is to be found in the poignant way it depicts absence making itself present. Cliff Edwards, who spent "many hours in Amsterdam's Van Gogh Museum with this painting," suggests that "Vincent, in these empty shoes, painted absence," although, as we will see, Edwards means something different than Heidegger does by this. (See Edwards, *The Shoes of Van Gogh: A Spiritual and Artistic Journey to the Ordinary*, 52, 54.)

[29] As noted earlier, Klee became extremely important for the later Heidegger, who would spend many "hours [alone] with Klee's paintings." When Heidegger's art-historian friend Petzet helped make a television program about Klee, Heidegger watched it and vehemently objected to the way the "random movement of the camera forces the eye to take certain leaps that hinder an intensive, quiet viewing as well as a thoughtful staying-with (or a "lingering thinking-after," *verweilendes Nachdenken*), which each single work and the relations within it deserve." Petzet was so convinced by Heidegger's criticism that a

painting – the strange space that surrounds these shoes like an underlying and yet also enveloping atmosphere – one can notice that inchoate forms begin to emerge from the background but never quite take a
firm shape; in fact, these shapes tend to disappear when one tries to pin
them down. The background of the painting not only inconspicuously
supports the foreground image of the shoes but, when we turn our attention to this ordinarily inconspicuous background, we can see that it continues to offer up other inchoate shapes that resist being firmly gestalted
themselves. This intriguing phenomenon is more obvious in some of Van
Gogh's other paintings. (That Van Gogh seems to have embedded his own
hat-wearing visage into the sole light that illuminates his famous "Café
Terrace at Night" is perhaps easiest to see.)[30] Clearly, "Vincent recognized
that something important happened in the old shoes painting, for he
went on to experiment several times with the theme," and if one studies
another of Van Gogh's paintings titled *A Pair of Shoes* (this one from the
following year, 1887), it is hard to miss the faces half-emerging from the
background in the upper right corner of the painting, or the Christ-like
figure in the upper left.[31]

technologically mediated viewing necessarily "missed the tenderness and intimacy that
flourish between Klee's lines" that Petzet resolved never again to make a television program about art. (See H. Petzet, *Encounters and Dialogues with Martin Heidegger*, 146, 150.)
[30] See http://upload.wikimedia.org/wikipedia/commons/7/7e/Vincent_Willem_van_Gogh_
015.jpg (accessed 9 August 2010).
[31] (See http://www.vangoghgallery.com/catalog/Painting/379/Pair-of-Shoes,-A.html [acces-
sed 9 August 2010]; Edwards, *The Shoes of Van Gogh*, 51.) Some art historians are so
convinced that such subliminal figures were intentional on Van Gogh's part that their
presence has been used not only to interpret his mental health but even to try to authen-
ticate his disputed works. My own experience suggests that some people can see these
figures quite easily, while others apparently cannot. The scientific "skeptic," Michael
Shermer, plausibly suggests that apophenia, the tendency to make sense out of apparent
nonsense (or not-yet-sense), evolved in human beings because missing a real pattern has
potentially much higher evolutionary costs than noticing a false one; e.g., mistaking the
wind in the grass for a lion is much less dangerous than the reverse (see Michael Shermer,
"Patternicity: Finding Meaningful Patterns in Meaningless Noise"). Of course, making
sense of what initially seems senseless also surely has immense evolutionary benefits (giving rise to science itself (!), e.g.), and I agree with art historians that at least some of
the "patterns" in Van Gogh's backgrounds are not in fact meaningless data (upon which
one simply projects one's own subjective associations). Still, Shermer's hypothesis opens
the door to the phenomenologically problematic possibility that only those who have
inherited an evolutionarily nonuniversal tendency toward a kind of hyperactive pattern-
recognition might be able to appreciate Heidegger's point. If so, an interesting question
would then be whether such a trait is more prevalent in artists, poets, sculptors, and the
like? That might support Heidegger's understanding of the essence of artistic creation,
but it might also limit the force of his call for us to *learn* to practice "dwelling" – i.e., a
poetic sensitivity and openness to other possible meanings – if such an openness is largely
hard-wired. The crucial question, then, is whether such an openness can be learned, or at
least improved upon (in a way that does not involve seeking to impose a universal form on
the diversity of human cognition). Absent empirical study of the matter, it is not clear how

Heidegger would later describe this phenomenon as "the tension of emerging and not emerging," and it is central to his remarks on the painting of Paul Cézanne and Paul Klee.[32] As Young nicely shows, Heidegger especially admired Klee's later works such as *Saint from a Window* (1940, the year Klee died), in which the eponymous image in the painting's foreground barely manages to emerge from the muted cacophony of other images half-suggesting themselves from the background. Here the tension between emerging and withdrawing is almost as palpable as the central figure, which seems to be disappearing back into the subtly dynamic background from which other figures continue to suggest themselves. In a note Heidegger made beneath his sketch of Klee's *Saint from a Window*, Heidegger asks: "If one erases the 'image'-character [from a picture], what [is left] to 'see'?" He answers in another note by quoting Klee himself: "The inner structure organizing the picture itself thus begins to come to the fore – and come toward truth, *coûte que coûte* [whatever the cost]."[33]

optimistic one is entitled to be here. As Vincent wrote to his brother Theo on 26 August 1882: "They [our parents] will *never* be able to understand what painting is. They cannot understand that the figure of a laborer – some furrows in a ploughed field, a bit of sand, sea and sky – are serious subjects, so difficult, but at the same time so beautiful, that it is indeed worthwhile to devote one's life to expressing the poetry hidden in them." (See Van Gogh, *The Complete Letters of Vincent van Gogh*, letter #226, emphasis added.) I have taken Van Gogh's sad and wonderful sentiment as an epigraph for this chapter because it fits perfectly – *like an old pair of shoes*, I would suggest – with Heidegger's understanding of Van Gogh. This is not surprising; Heidegger read Van Gogh's famous correspondence with his brother with great enthusiasm, so much so that by 1919, Van Gogh and Martin Luther had become Heidegger's two main exemplars of authenticity. (I thank Charles Guignon for drawing my attention to this fact.)

[32] In a birthday note written to the poet René Char in 1971, Heidegger said of Cézanne that: "In the late work of the painter, the tension of emerging and not emerging has become onefold, transformed into a mysterious identity. Is there shown here a pathway that opens onto a belonging-together of poet and thinker?" (Heidegger's note is quoted by Petzet, *Encounters and Dialogues with Martin Heidegger*, 143–4. See also HR 310–11 and Young's insightful treatment of Heidegger's later work on art in *Heidegger's Philosophy of Art*.)

[33] (Heidegger's unpublished notes on Klee are partly reproduced by Günter Seubold in "Heideggers nachgelassene Klee-Notizen"; see 8, 11.) In his later works, Klee increasingly erased the lines that typically distinguish a painting's foreground image from its background, populating this background with numerous other figures that enter into a viewer's awareness to greater and lesser degrees. (A black and white reproduction of Klee's *Saint from a Window* can be found in Young's *Heidegger's Philosophy of Art*, 160.) Thus Klee's late works, Heidegger suggests, paint the inconspicuous tension of emerging and withdrawing, thereby foregrounding the usually unnoticed opposition of foreground and background that allows painting to work. The "cost" of what Young calls Klee's "semi-abstraction" (*Heidegger's Philosophy of Art*, 160) concerns the fact that Klee's paintings sacrifice the longstanding tradition of a clear and unambiguous central image. Of course, Klee is far from alone in bearing this cost, but his semi-abstraction did help open the door for the abstract and conceptual art movements that followed, the merits of which Heidegger remained more skeptical about, as his acquaintance with them was minimal (as Young shows). If, in the terms of the early Heidegger, Van Gogh helps lead us back from the presence of an on-hand object to the encounter with hands-on equipmentality,

For Heidegger, to put it simply, Klee's late paintings preserve the phenomenological struggle of emerging and withdrawing, and so bring the usually inconspicuous tension between foreground and background itself to the fore, thereby offering us a glimpse of the underlying structure hidden within all art. Yet, this phenomenological "tension of emerging and not emerging" that Heidegger finds in Klee and Cézanne, I want to suggest, he discovered first in Van Gogh's *A Pair of Shoes* (1886), specifically, in the way Van Gogh's painting manifests what "The Origin of the Work of Art" famously calls "the essential strife" between "earth and world" (PLT 49/GA5 35).

We can encounter this phenomenological "strife" for ourselves if we can recognize the way that what initially seems like "nothing" in the background of Van Gogh's painting continues to tantalizingly offer itself to our understanding while also receding from our attempts to order what it offers us into any firm, settled meaning. Thus, when Heidegger defines the phenomenon of "earth" as "the essentially self-secluding" (PLT 47/GA5 33), he quickly qualifies this definition by specifying that:

The self-seclusion of earth is not a uniform, inflexible staying under cover; rather, it unfolds itself in an inexhaustible abundance of simple modes and shapes [*eine unerschöpfliche Fülle einfacher Weisen und Gestalten*]. (PLT 47/GA5 34)

"Earth," in other words, is an inherently dynamic dimension of intelligibility that simultaneously offers itself to and resists being brought fully into the light of our "worlds" of meaning and permanently stabilized therein, despite our best efforts. These very efforts to bring the earth's "inexhaustible abundance of simple modes and shapes" completely into the light of our worlds generates what Heidegger calls the "essential strife" between "earth" and "world":

The world grounds itself on the earth and the earth juts through the world.... The world, in resting upon the earth, strives to raise the earth completely [into the

---

Klee seems to leave us half-submerged within such equipmentality. Or, to put this in a later Heideggerian light, one could say (with Young) that "whereas, like Cézanne, Klee thematizes the presencing of world, unlike Cézanne, the works [of Klee] explicitly present us with the presencing of other worlds as well." (Ibid., 162.) What Young says here of Cézanne can also be said of Van Gogh. Indeed, Van Gogh can be situated between Cézanne and Klee, in that Heidegger discovers at least one other world slumbering in *A Pair of Shoes*, viz., the world of a farmer (to which we return in section 3). Indeed, in the terms Heidegger still uses, he says that Klee depicts "no object" but, instead, "the nothing coming to presence [*Nichts Anwesendes*]" (Seubold, "Heideggers nachgelassene Klee-Notizen," 11), which is precisely the insight that Heidegger finds first in Van Gogh. For Heidegger, Van Gogh, Cézanne, and Klee also stand in close proximity to "East Asian 'Art'" – specifically, to "Zen" painting (e.g., the famous tradition of the "Enso" or circle painted in a single stroke, like the famous one by the Zen master Hakuin) – which, Heidegger similarly suggests, "is in itself not concerned with a 'representation' of what is, but rather with the approach of humanity to the enveloping nothingness" (ibid.).

light]. As self-opening, the world cannot endure anything closed. The earth, however, as sheltering and concealing, tends always to draw the world into itself and
keep it there. (PLT 49/GA5 35)

In Heidegger's view, for a great artwork to *work* – that is, for it to help
open and preserve a meaningful "world" for a community (whose members
come to embody that meaning in their lives) – this artwork must maintain
an essential tension between the *world* of meanings it pulls together and
the more mysterious phenomenon Heidegger calls "earth." *Earth,* in his
analysis, both informs and sustains this meaningful world and also resists
being interpretively exhausted by it. The earth provides that "combination
of recalcitrance and support" that allows a great artwork to quietly pulsate
with an "inexhaustible abundance" of possibilities while also maintaining
the sanctity of the uninterpretable within the very world of meanings it
conveys.[34]

Like the notorious "nothing" that (Heidegger wrote in 1929) "makes
possible the manifestation of entities as such for human existence [or
"being-here," *Dasein*]" (P 91/GA9 115), the "earth" is thus Heidegger's name
in 1935–36 for what he most frequently calls "being as such," a dynamic
phenomenological "presencing" (*Anwesen*) that gives rise to our worlds of
meaning without ever being exhausted by them, a dimension of intelligibility we experience *both* as it calls for and informs *and* as it overflows
and escapes our attempts to pin it down.[35] Heidegger will again evoke the
"nothing" to important effect in his later work (as we will see in Chapter 7).
In 1935, however, he seems to have grown dissatisfied with his broadly misunderstood "nothing noths" terminology, for he now seeks to redescribe
and more carefully elaborate the mysterious phenomenon he had initially
called the "noth-ing" in terms of the "essentially self-secluding earth," the
recalcitrant nature of which becomes palpable in its resistance to our best
efforts to bring the phenomenon fully into the light of our intelligible
worlds. In fact, we can observe this refining redescription taking place in
Heidegger's interpretation of Van Gogh, if we pay close attention.

2.1. From the Phenomenology of Van Gogh's Painting
to the Ontology of Art

Heidegger's most famous interpretation of Van Gogh's painting pivots
again on an ambiguous use of "nothing," to which Heidegger now adds an

---

[34] (See Carman, "Heidegger, Martin: Survey of Thought," p. 979.) This "earth," as we will
see, is also the phenomenon Heidegger has in mind when he refers to the "un-truth"
of truth" as "the originating region of the not-yet-disclosed, the un-unconcealed [*des
Noch-nicht (des Un-) Entborgenen*]" (PLT 60/GA5 48).

[35] Heidegger begins to anticipate his 1935 thinking of the essential conflict of earth and
world in 1929, when he adds: "The nothing does not merely serve as the counterpart of
beings; rather, it originally belongs to their essential unfolding [a later note specifies: "the
essential unfolding of being"] as such." (P 91/GA9 115)

elliptical, intimating locution ("And yet...") in order to encourage his audience to hear a subtle shift and so notice the meaning suggested by his otherwise superfluous addition, "and nothing more." Heidegger's use of this ambiguous locution ("and nothing more") had become a well-established rhetorical trope for him by 1935; it was his preferred method for introducing the idea of that "nothing" we encounter when we move beyond the totality of entities toward that which makes it possible to encounter entities the way we do. Heidegger established the pattern in 1929's "What Is Metaphysics?" by deliberately employing just such ambiguous locutions seven times in a row, referring to "entities themselves – and nothing besides [*und sonst nichts*]," "entities themselves – and nothing further [*und weiter nichts*]," "entities themselves – and beyond that, nothing," etc., then driving the point home with the rhetorical question: "Is this only a manner of speaking – and nothing besides?" (P 84/GA9 105)

Seen in this light, the fact that Heidegger repeats the same rhetorical strategy when he introduces Van Gogh's painting becomes unmistakable:

A pair of farmer's shoes and nothing more. And yet. [*Ein Paar Bauernschuhe und nichts weiter. Und dennoch.*]

From out of the dark opening of the worn insides of the shoes the toilsome tread of the worker stares forth.... The shoes vibrate with the silent call of the earth, its quiet gift of the ripening grain [i.e., "earth" makes "world" possible by inconspicuously *giving* itself to the world] and the earth's unexplained self-refusal in the fallow desolation of the wintry field [i.e., it is also constitutive of earth that it *resists* this world by receding back into itself]. (PLT 33–4/GA5 19)

As my editorial insertions seek to clarify, the point of Heidegger's phenomenological interpretation of Van Gogh's painting of the farmer's shoes is not to engage in an armchair anthropology of farming but, rather, to suggest that attending to the "nothing" in Van Gogh's painting reveals the deepest level of "truth" at work in art, namely, the essential tension in which the phenomenologically abundant "earth" both makes our intelligible worlds possible and also resists being finally mastered or fully expressed within any such "world."

If attending to the mysterious nothing allows us to recognize the dynamic tension between "earth" and "world" preserved in Van Gogh's painting, then we have thereby encountered what is for Heidegger the inner tension at the heart of art, a tension that not only drives art and keeps it alive but also allows humanity's understanding of being to unfold historically. "Art" in this essential sense – which Heidegger also calls "poetry" or *poiêsis*, that is, *bringing into being* – can be understood as an unending creative struggle to express that which conditions and informs our worlds of meaning and yet resists being exhaustively articulated in the terms of these worlds.[36] The

---

[36] Remember that for Heidegger, the particular worlds great artworks open have a finite lifespan, because they depend not only on the materiality of the work but also on those

conflict preserved in Van Gogh's painting – between emerging into the light and receding into the darkness, revealing and withdrawing, "emerging and not emerging" – is for Heidegger the basic structure of intelligibility as it takes place in time.

Indeed, Heidegger's description of this essential conflict between earth and world can be understood as his attempt to phenomenologically elaborate his distinctive understanding of truth as the inherently ago-nistic manifestation of *a-lêtheia*, that is, "truth" conceived ontologically as historically variable "un-concealment" or "dis-closure." It is, I would say, the *hyphen* in *a-lêtheia* – the joining together, literally "under one" (*hypo + hen*), of revealing and concealing – that Heidegger develops as the essential strife between world and earth. With world and earth, in other words, Heidegger seeks to name and so render visible the quietly conflic-tual structure at the heart of intelligibility, the unified opposition that allows "being" to be "dis-closed" in time. Since *Being and Time* at least, Heidegger had insisted on the "equiprimordiality" or "co-originality" (*Gleichursprünglichkeit*) of "truth" and "untruth" (BT 265/SZ 222), build-ing on Husserl's phenomenological axiom that the emergence of one thing or aspect of a thing into intelligibility requires the concealing of another. (Taken to its extreme, this axiom allows Heidegger to sug-gest that the totality of what-is stands in the place of and so conceals the "nothing" from which it emerges. The "earth" is his response to the problem that this seems to make all creation *ex nihilo*, as we will see.) For Heidegger, the fact that there can be no revealing without concealing (and vice versa) is a necessary feature not just of perception or cognition but of intelligibility in general.[37]

The truth disclosed by Van Gogh's particular ("ontic") work of art is thus *ontological*. That is, the tension between emerging and withdrawing that is visible in Van Gogh's painting implicitly conditions all artistic crea-tion, which (we have seen) means all bringing-into-being, hence all histor-ical intelligibility. Heidegger thus goes so far as to claim that:

"preservers" who struggle to keep that world open to the future. (For a remarkably clear, phenomenological interpretation of Heidegger's "earth" in terms of the those aspects of a tradition that can *never* be clarified, see Mark Wrathall, *How to Read Heidegger*, 71–87.)

[37] Perhaps this helps explain why Heidegger placed Klee "higher than Picasso" (see Seubold, "Heideggers nachgelassene Klee-Notizen," 6). While Klee's semiabstraction brings the tension between revealing and concealing itself to the fore (and so teaches us about the necessarily partial nature of perception and of our experience of intelligibility more gen-erally), Picasso's cubism seems to follow the modern, subjectivist impulse by seeking to represent all the aspects of a figure simultaneously. (The stupendous facility of Picasso's painting suppresses the tension inherent in this impossible ambition. Had Heidegger rec-ognized it, he might have been more sympathetic to Picasso's cubist works.) Thinking in these terms also helps us recognize a similar tension at work in Heidegger's own attempt to develop a philosophical version of the musical art of the fugue (as we will see at the beginning of Chapter 6).

The world is the self-disclosing openness of the broad paths of the simple and essential decisions in the destiny of an historical people. The earth is the spontaneous forthcoming of that which is continually self-secluding and to that extent sheltering and concealing. World and earth are essentially different from one another and yet are never separated.... The work-being of the work consists in the fighting of the battle [*der Bestreitung des Streites*] between world and earth. (PLT 49/GA5 35–6)[38]

As "earth," in other words, intelligibility tantalizingly offers previously unglimpsed aspects of itself to our understanding and yet also withdraws from our attempts to order those aspects into a single fixed meaning. As "world," we struggle nevertheless to force a stable ordering onto this inexhaustible phenomenological abundance, however temporarily. In this way, "earth" both supports and resists "world," tantalizingly eliciting, always informing, and yet also partly escaping all our attempts to permanently stabilize our intelligible worlds, to assign a firm shape to things once and for all.

The "essential strife" of this *a-lêtheiac* struggle between concealing and revealing, earth and world, is precisely what Heidegger thinks Van Gogh renders visible in *A Pair of Shoes* (1886).[39] What we can thus learn from a work of art like Van Gogh's painting – in which this usually inconspicuous tension is masterfully captured and conveyed – is that our intelligible worlds are shaped by what we take from and make of a dynamic phenomenological abundance that we can never fully grasp or finally master. By partly informing and yet always also partly eluding our attempts to order those elements the earth offers to our understanding into a single, final historical "world," the abundant earth preserves itself for future orderings, for worlds still yet to be disclosed.[40] For Heidegger, then, the essential tension

---

[38] Heidegger obviously tones down his rhetorical presentation of such "conflicts" in his post-War work, but this Heraclitean tension of unified oppositions remains even in his much less agonistic thinking of "the fourfold" in the 1950s. In this fourfold, such oppositions continue to join the (subtly reconceived) "earth" to "the heavens," and "mortals" to "the divinities," along two linked axes. (See, e.g., "The Thing" and "Building Dwelling Thinking" in PLT.) As this suggests, *the "earth" in Heidegger's later "fourfold" is subtly different from the "earth" in "The Origin of the Work of Art."* Put simply, the later earth loses much of its mystery (becoming a more literal stand-in for the earth on which we dwell), a mystery that Heidegger transfers over to the fourfold as a whole. (See Young, *Heidegger's Philosophy of Art*, 40–1.)

[39] As Heidegger puts it: "What happens here? What is at work in the work? Van Gogh's painting is the revelation [*Eröffnung*] of what equipment, the pair of farmer shoes, *is* in truth. This entity steps out here into the unconcealment of its being. This unconcealment is what the Greeks called *alêtheia*." (PLT 36/GA5 21) In the 1956 "Addendum" to "The Origin of the Work of Art," Heidegger refers to this dynamic union of "clearing *and* concealing" whereby being becomes intelligible in time as "the movement of the clearing of self-concealment as such" (PLT 84/GA5 71–2).

[40] This holds true, moreover, whether these worlds are more monolithic historical epochs implicitly held together by great works of art like the Greek temple, or initially much smaller and ultimately more pluralistic historical worlds like the one that could take

between "world" and "earth" – that dynamic back-and-forth whereby some things (or aspects of things) cannot emerge into the light of our intelligible worlds without others withdrawing into the background (which means that it is impossible for everything to take place in intelligibility all at once) – names the basic conflict in the structure of intelligibility, the conflict that is ultimately responsible for ontological historicity (the fact that the intelligibility of what-is must unfold historically, and thus changes with time).

2.2. Representing Nothing: Transcending Aesthetic Subjectivism from Within

Once we recognize the crucial role played by Heidegger's subtly ambiguous use of the nothing, we can see that Heidegger's only other major reference to Van Gogh's painting (in 1935's *The Introduction to Metaphysics*) again follows the same basic sequence of phenomenological steps. This important passage turns once more on the double meaning of (the) "nothing," which Heidegger again seeks to suggest with the subtly ambiguous locution, "nothing besides":

A painting by Van Gogh: a pair of tough farmer's shoes, nothing besides [*sonst nichts*]. The picture really represents nothing [*Das Bild stellt eigentlich nichts dar*]. Yet, what *is* there, with that you are immediately alone, as if on a late autumn evening, when the last potato fires have burned out, you yourself were heading wearily home from the field with your hoe. (IM 37–8/GA40 38)

Readers often take Heidegger's deliberately provocative claim that "[t]he picture really represents nothing" as a flat-footed assertion that Van Gogh's painting does not represent shoes.[41] But that obscures Heidegger's deeper point and, in fact, would make no more sense than if, beneath *La Trahison des Images* ("*The Treachery* [or *Treason*] *of Images*)" (1929) – René Magritte's realistic representation of a pipe against a blank background – Magritte had not painted the famous words, "This is not a pipe [*Ceci n'est pas*

---

shape around Van Gogh's painting and Heidegger's attempt to "preserve" its phenomenological truth (insofar as Heidegger's efforts sufficiently inspire his successors).

[41] This, however, *is* the point of Heidegger's understanding of the ancient Greek temple. Potentially confusing matters, Heidegger introduces the Greek temple and tragic drama similarly, by suggesting that: "A building, a Greek temple, displays nothing" (PLT 41/GA5 27); and: "In the tragedy nothing is staged or displayed theatrically" (PLT 43/GA5 29; but note the telling absence of the qualifier *eigentlich*, "really, genuinely, or authentically"). In these cases, Heidegger's point is the more straightforward one that the Greek temple and drama are literally not "re-presentations" of anything (because there was not some object standing before them that they sought to re-present). The temple is thus quite different from Van Gogh's painting of the shoes, which for Heidegger *really, genuinely, or authentically* represents (the) nothing. Indeed, Heidegger seems only to have noticed and developed his own ambiguous use of "nothing" in the final version of his essay, precisely where it fit with his phenomenological understanding of Van Gogh (cf. HR 140–1/UK1 14).

FIGURE 3. René Magritte, *La Trahison des Images*, 1929, Los Angeles County Museum of Art, Los Angeles, CA. © 2010 C. Herscovici. London/Artists Rights Society (ARS), NY. Reproduced by permission from Art Resource, NY, and ARS. Digital Image © 2009 Museum Associates/LACMA/Art Resource, NY.

une pipe]" but, instead, "This is not a *representation* of a pipe." For, Magritte's most obvious point is that a representation of a pipe (be it pictorial or linguistic) is not itself a pipe. The surreal effect of *The Treachery of Images* comes from the way it encourages us to confront the usually unnoticed distance between representations and the things they represent. "This is not a pipe" calls the very obviousness of representation into question, and so points toward the mysteries concealed beneath the system of representation we usually take for granted.[42] (See Figure 3.)

The effect of Heidegger's provocative claim about Van Gogh's *A Pair of Shoes* is similar. When Heidegger states that "[t]he picture really represents nothing," he is not advancing the bizarre claim that Van Gogh's painting of a pair of shoes does not represent shoes. The fact that Van Gogh's painting represents shoes is the first thing anyone notices about it and also

[42] Although Magritte's painting initially appears "as simple as a page borrowed from a botanical manual" (as Michel Foucault nicely describes it), the mysteries of the painting are quickly multiplied by the vague pronoun reference in "This is not a pipe": "This" could refer to the image of the pipe, the words beneath it, or the entire ensemble. (See Foucault, *This Is Not a Pipe*, 19.)

(as we have seen) the first thing Heidegger himself mentioned about it: Van Gogh's picture "represents [*darstellt*] a pair of farmer's shoes" (PLT 19/ GA5 3). Heidegger is not retracting that claim now but, instead, building upon it, suggesting that Van Gogh's painting does more than just represent a pair of shoes: Van Gogh's painting "really, properly, or authentically" (*eigentlich*) represents (the) nothing. Indeed, it represents (the) nothing in a way that ultimately allows us to transcend aesthetic representation from within – by getting us back in touch with the more basic level of human existence that the order of objective representations presupposes but cannot fully recapture.[43]

The suggestively ambiguous phrase, "nothing out of the ordinary," might make a good title for Heidegger's attempt to show how the mysterious "nothing" emerges from Van Gogh's painting of a seemingly ordinary pair of shoes. For Heidegger, it is not that the person who broke in these empty shoes, although absent from the painting, nevertheless remains present there in his or her very absence. It seems true, as Cliff Edwards suggests, that the almost palpable presence of that missing person whose feet shaped the shoes Van Gogh painted quite naturally leads those who study this painting carefully to wonder, *Whose shoes* were these originally? And that question, in turn, fuels the controversy still surrounding Heidegger's interpretation of the painting (as we will see in section 3). For Heidegger, however, the "nothing" that is visible in Van Gogh's painting is not the haunting presence of these shoes' absent owner but, instead, the equally paradoxical (and no less phenomenologically discernible) appearance of that which is neither an entity nor merely nothing at all and yet conditions our experience of all entities.[44]

---

[43] It is true that for Heidegger Van Gogh's painting is not wholly representational – and should not, in the end, be understood representationally – but this is because it really represents (the) nothing, and does so in a way that exceeds and so transcends aesthetic representation from within. "The picture which shows the farmer's shoes ... [does] not *only* make manifest what these isolated entities are as isolated entities.... [Rather, the picture allows] unconcealment as such to happen in relation to the totality of what is" (PLT 56, emphasis added/GA5 43). Heidegger's "if they manifest entities at all" has been deliberately excised from this quotation because the doubt it expresses derives from the fact that in this quotation he is also discussing Meyer's poem "Fountain" (the second elision) which, as we have seen, Heidegger does not interpret as re-presenting some actual fountain in the way Van Gogh's painting of *A Pair of Shoes* does obviously re-present an actual pair of shoes (among the other things that it does). Heidegger's doubt thus suggests that he thinks Meyer's poem is more like the completely nonrepresentational Greek temple than the initially representational painting.

[44] (See Edwards, *The Shoes of Van Gogh*, 54.) Heidegger even seems to be generalizing from his phenomenological description of Van Gogh's painting when he writes: "And yet – beyond what is, not apart from but, rather, before it, there is still something else that happens. In the midst of all that is an open place comes to presence. There is a clearing. Thought from the perspective of entities, this clearing has more being than entities do. This open center is therefore not surrounded by what is; rather, the clearing center itself encircles all that is, like the nothing which we scarcely know." (PLT 53/GA5 39–40)

What Heidegger really wants to suggest, I think, is not just that the nothing emerges from the ordinary – that the nothing makes itself visible in Van Gogh's painting of an ordinary pair of shoes – but also the reverse, that what we now think of as "ordinary" first originated out of the "nothing," through the essential struggle between earth and world. For, in Heidegger's view, initially extraordinary creations, once brought into being, eventually become stabilized in intelligibility and so perceived as merely "ordinary" (in much the same way that what begins as a revealing poetic insight eventually gets routinized into a worn-out cliché).[45] As he puts it:

> Does truth, then, originate out of nothing? In fact it does, if by "nothing" we mean no more than that which is not an entity, and if "an entity" represents that which is objectively on hand [*Vorhandene*] in the normal way – a [way of conceiving of] "what is," the merely putative truth of which comes to light and thereby becomes shattered by the standing-there of the work. (PLT 71/GA5 59)

In other words, the encounter with the nothing in the work of art "shatters" the taken-for-granted obviousness of the modern theoretical framework in which subjects seek to master external objects, a framework implicit in the basic aesthetic view according to which subjects undergo intensive experiences of art objects. For Heidegger, the phenomenological encounter with Van Gogh's painting undermines the obviousness of the modern worldview by returning us directly to the primordial level of engaged existence in which subject and object have not yet been differentiated. Indeed, Heidegger thinks that aesthetics transcends itself from within in the encounter with Van Gogh's painting because this encounter with the work of art brings us back to this engaged level of existence in a particularly lucid and revealing way. This lucid encounter, moreover, is supposed to help us transform our guiding sense of what beings are, leading us beyond both the modern and late-modern understandings of being as objects to be mastered and as resources to be optimized. But how exactly?

Heidegger thinks we can transcend modern aesthetics from within if, in what begins as an ordinary aesthetic experience of an object (Van Gogh's

---

45 Here we see the deeper point behind Heidegger's aforementioned phenomenological dictum: "What seems natural to us is presumably just the familiarity of a long-established custom which has forgotten the unfamiliarity from which it arose." (PLT 24/GA5 9) Richard Rorty repeatedly emphasizes this underlying affinity between Nietzsche and Heidegger in his *Essays on Heidegger and Others*, but the insight goes back beyond Nietzsche to Emerson and the Romantics. Indeed, Heidegger's view is close to Emerson's conviction that: "The poets made all the words, and each word was at first a stroke of genius.... Language is fossil poetry." The "genius" of such poetic "naming," moreover, is presented by Emerson as salvific receptivity to nature rather than as subjectivistic creation *ex nihilo*; "not art, but a second nature, grown out of the first [nature], as a leaf out of a tree." Because "genius realizes and adds," "[g]enius is the activity which repairs the decay of things." (See Emerson, "The Poet," *Essays and Lectures*, 451, 457.)

painting of a pair of shoes) that stands opposite us (as if external to our own subjectivity), we notice and carefully attend to the way these shoes take shape on and against an inconspicuously dynamic background (the "nothing developed as "earth"), a background that turns out not to be nothing at all but, rather, to both support and overflow the intelligible world that emerges from it.[46] Our experience of an aesthetic object transcends itself here because, in order to encounter Van Gogh's artwork in its full phenomenological richness (by recognizing the struggle between "earth and world" preserved in the painting), we can no longer approach the meaning of this work as if this meaning were contained within an external object standing apart from us or else projected by our subjectivity onto it. Our phenomenological encounter with Van Gogh's painting shows us that its meaning is neither located entirely in the object standing over against us nor simply projected by our subjectivity onto an inherently meaningless work; instead, the work's meaning must be inconspicuously accomplished in our own implicitly dynamic engagement with the work. Through our engagement with Van Gogh's painting, Heidegger thus suggests, we can lucidly encounter the very process by which we are always-already making sense of our worlds.

It is crucial for Heidegger that we not reinterpret this encounter as a subject's selective cognitive and perceptual uptake of an objective world. What we encounter in art is something more deeply rooted in existence that the modern subject/object dichotomy skates right over. Our encounter with the work teaches us that that meaning does not happen solely in the art object or the viewing subject but instead takes place, we could say, *between* us and the work. This, again, is an *ontological* truth; it holds true of (human) existence in general. To be *Dasein* is to be "the being of the '*between*'" (HCT 251/GA20 346–7), as Heidegger first put it in 1925 (cf. BT 170/SZ 132). This means that our encounter with Van Gogh's painting helps us to realize and so *become what we are*. For, what we lucidly encounter in art is our making-sense of the place in which we find ourselves, a fundamental "world-disclosing" that is always-already at work in human "existence," our standing-out into intelligibility. For Heidegger, our encounter with Van Gogh's painting discloses what we already are, most fundamentally, but without realizing it – namely, *Dasein*, "being-here,"

---

[46] Another way to experience this "essential strife" of earth and world in Van Gogh's painting is to attend to the way the painting's subtly rich and dynamic background not only supports but also envelops the foreground image of the shoes. The shoes belong so integrally to their background that they can even appear to recede back into it. Notice, for example, how both shoes (esp. the left one) seem almost to melt back into their own black shadows, and how the lightest colors "behind" the shoes bleed over the edges of these shoes thanks to Van Gogh's thick brushwork (especially between the two shoes and along the right edge of the right shoe). In such ways, as Heidegger suggests, "the earth ... tends to draw the world into itself and keep it there" (PLT 49/GA5 35).

the active making intelligible of the place in which we find ourselves. Art teaches us to become what we already are by allowing us lucidly to undergo the transition from understanding and experiencing ourselves as meaning-bestowing subjects standing over against an objective world to recognizing that, at a deeper level, we are always implicitly participating in the making-intelligible of our worlds.[47]

2.3. Heidegger's Postmodern Understanding of Art

This implicit struggle whereby being becomes intelligible in time, we have seen, is the very essence of art, the "poetic" heart of creation responsible for both providing and renewing our sense of what-is. As Heidegger puts it:

everything with which humanity is endowed must, in the [poetic] projection [that "brings-into-being" or makes things newly intelligible], be drawn up from out of the closed ground [i.e., from the "earth" understood as the untapped possibilities still concealed within the tradition] and set upon this ground. (PLT 75–6/GA5 63)

Humanity's ontological "endowment" (our sense of what entities are) ultimately springs from the phenomenon of earth through the poetic "naming-into-being" (or making intelligible) at the heart of art. Moreover, Heidegger adds (showing that he was indeed a "conservative revolutionary" in 1936 at least), Western humanity's sense of being can only be changed historically through the creative discovery of possibilities hidden within the tradition that has come down to us.[48] Only by disclosing the tradition's hidden heritage can we hope to reshape our communal sense of what is and what matters, thereby redrawing the basic contours of this tradition,

---

[47] In *Being and Time* (1927), the claim that existence always-already "stands-out" into temporally structured intelligibility is presented as a phenomenological description of how we ordinarily encounter ourselves when we are not paying attention to the encounter. In "The Origin of the Work of Art" (1935–6), however, such "existence" no longer just describes the way we always-already are; it now becomes an existential task to *become* Dasein by *realizing* what we already are. Heidegger will even go so far as to say that the goal of "The Origin of the Work of Art" – "the step toward which everything that has been said up to now leads" (PLT 66/GA5 54) – is to help us learn from art to *become what we are*. To "resolutely" own up to what human existence most truly is, Heidegger writes, means entering into the essential conflict of "earth and world" and thereby encountering the "self-transcendence" of existence in "the sober standing-within the extraordinary awesomeness of the truth that is happening in the work" (PLT 67–8/GA5 55). "The Origin of the Work of Art" thus suggests that art is a particularly direct and revealing actualization of the human essence. For, to be a human being, in Heidegger's terms, is to realize oneself as a world-discloser, struggling to world the earth in the right sort of way (as the next section explains). (On this important "perfectionist" question of how we become what we are, see chapter 4 of *Heidegger on Ontotheology*, and my "Heidegger's Perfectionist Philosophy of Education in *Being and Time*.")

[48] For an interpretation of Heidegger's views on this point that moves him closer to the liberal-democratic tradition, see Guignon's "Meaning in the Work of Art."

making it easier to see beyond the limits of our ontotheology and so create new possibilities for human understanding and action. In this way, art
remains capable of helping us redraw the lines that establish our basic
sense of what-is and what matters.

For art to accomplish this revolutionary task, however, the artist must be
able to see something beginning to take shape where others see nothing at
all. All true creators discern the inchoate contours of something previously
unseen and – as if playing midwife to being – help draw it into the light of
the world.

Because it is such a drawing, all creation is a drawing-up (like drawing water from
a well). Modern subjectivism, of course, misinterprets creation as the product of
the genius of the self-sovereign subject [and so imagines that the genius creates *ex
nihilo* by projecting his or her idiosyncratic subjectivity onto an otherwise meaningless world].... The poeticizing projection comes out of nothing in the sense
that it never derives its gift from what is familiar and already there. But in another
sense it does not come out of nothing; for what it projects is only the withheld
determination of historical existence [*Dasein*] itself. (PLT 76/GA5 63–4)

As this suggests, at the very core of Heidegger's understanding of art is
an encounter with a "nothing" that is not simply nothing at all but, rather,
designates possible meanings still concealed within the "tradition," which
preserves historical intelligibility as it has come down to us. The inchoate contours of that which is not yet a thing need to be drawn out in an
original way in order to release the possibilities inherent in this tradition
(including the roads not taken, forgotten, or bypassed), and so create or
renew humanity's ontological inheritance for the future. Put otherwise,
artistic creation requires the exercise of an active receptivity we might call
ontological "response-ability," that is, an ability to respond to the inchoate
ways in which being offers itself to intelligibility. For, in Heidegger's terms,
only such an ability will prove capable of bringing that which was hidden
in the "noth-ing" (or still slumbering in the "earth") into the light of our
historical worlds.

To participate in such creation, the artist needs to be receptive to what
"The Origin of the Work of Art" calls the "rift-design" or "fissure" (*Riß*) that
joins the world to the earth. By "creatively" and selectively responding to
the abundance of ways in which being genuinely offers itself to us, the artist establishes one of these possibilities, bringing it into the light of day for
the first time, just as Michelangelo legendarily spent weeks carefully studying the subtle network of veins and fissures running through that famous
piece of marble before he could set his "David" free from the stone. This is
not to say that David was the only possible form slumbering in that particular piece of marble; the grain and texture running through it might have
been taken up by the artist and creatively gestalted in other ways, thereby

giving birth to other, more or less different sculptures.[49] In any such case, however, "the establishing of truth in the work is the bringing forth of a being such as never was before and will never come to be again" (PLT 62/ GA5 50). In artistic creation, the artist responds to what offers itself, creatively discerning and helping to realize the outlines of a new world in the manifold possibilities offered up by the earth. As Heidegger puts it:

> There certainly lies hidden in nature a rift-design, a measure and border, and, tied to it, a capacity for bringing-forth – that is, art. But it is equally certain that this art hidden in nature becomes manifest only through the work, because it is lodged originarily in the work. (PLT 70/GA5 58)

In Heidegger's view, then, all great artists learn to recognize and respond to the complex texture of edges, lines, and breaks that together constitute an open-ended "basic design" or "outline sketch" (PLT 63/GA5 51), which the artist then creatively gestalts in order to bring at least one of those "inexhaustible" shapes still hidden in the earth into the light of the world.

To gestalt the hints nature offers us in one way is necessarily not to gestalt them in another, but Heidegger thinks that Van Gogh's *A Pair of Shoes* (1886) preserves the hints of other possible gestalts in its quietly dynamic tension between what takes shape in the foreground and what recedes into the background.[50] For, in Van Gogh's painting, what recedes into the phenomenological background does so in such a way that, rather than completely disappearing behind the foreground image, it continues to manifest a complex texture of rifts and fissures that suggest the

---

[49] Heidegger sometimes suggests, more problematically, that there are unique ways of gestalting the inchoate forms the earth offers us that *best* respect what was there. Although that is sometimes true, I think Heidegger should have been clearer that there are usually multiple ways of bringing things out in their ownmost. For, this fits better with his ontological pluralism and takes nothing crucial away from his view that in an ontologically disclosive truth "event" (as e.g. when Michelangelo gestalts David from that piece of marble) entities, human being, and the being of entities all come "into their own" simultaneously. (This is what Heidegger means by the "event" of *Ereignis*, as we have seen, hence the aptness of the initially strange-sounding translation of this term of art as "enowning" instead of "event of appropriation," which risks suggesting something more subjectivistic than Heidegger intends). Indeed, what is crucial in such an event of enowning is that not only are the entity and the human being (here the marble and Michelangelo himself) fully realized in this act of world-disclosure, but being's fullest (postmodern) way of manifesting itself in intelligibility is also realized here (since such events allow us to understand the being of entities neither in terms of modern objects to be controlled or late-modern resources to be optimized but, instead, as informing and yet also exceeding all our pre-existing designs), and this *requires* ontological pluralism.

[50] It is probably not a coincidence that Heidegger's thinking of the mysterious and yet familiar "rift structure" that joins earth and world should emerge from his phenomenological meditation on Van Gogh's painting of *A Pair of Shoes*. Shoes are, after all, precisely the place where the earth ordinarily makes contact with our worlds.

possibility of other gestalts, new ways of drawing out what simultaneously offers itself to and withdraws from our grasp, even ones that challenge the habitual ways in which we have come to see things (as an ordinary pair of shoes, for example). As Heidegger thus writes, a truly great artistic "beginning ... always contains the undisclosed abundance of the unfamiliar and extraordinary, which means that it also contains the strife with the familiar and the ordinary" (PLT 76/GA5 64).

Heidegger's view that the hints intelligibility offers us can be gestalted in more than one way makes him an *ontological pluralist* (or *plural realist*), but he does not believe that just anything goes. As his thoughts on the "rift-structure" permeating intelligibility suggest, Heidegger firmly believes that there is a coming into being in nature itself that the bringing into being through art should serve. This means that there must be limits on what the artist can creatively impose that arise from the things themselves. The "abundant" dimension of intelligibility Heidegger calls "earth" has to genuinely resist the artist's creative efforts to bring it into the light of the world at some point (or, more likely, points), or else art would just be a frictionless subjective projection or hallucination (or even a deeper ontological destructiveness masquerading as creativity), rather than an ontologically maieutic gestalting that finds a genuinely creative way to be grounded in and genuinely responsive to the ways things show themselves. The importance of acknowledging that there is always something in intelligibility that resists our merely subjective designs (rather than Carnap's famous critique) seems to be the main reason Heidegger stopped talking about the "nothing" and began referring to the "earth." The point is that all genuine creativity, all bringing-into-being, requires us to learn to recognize and respect (what we could think of as) the *texture* of the texts with which we work. This mean that all artists – indeed, all those who would bring-into-being in a meaningful way, whatever media we work with – must learn to draw creatively upon a phenomenological abundance that cannot be entirely appropriated, finally mastered, or definitively manipulated.[51]

Here, then, we can see the phenomenological intuition behind the contrast sketched in Chapter 1. For, it is this idea – that true art emerges from a creative response to the genuine possibilities of being – that allows Heidegger to contrast those drastically different ways of comporting ourselves toward that which shows itself to us: namely, the active receptivity of a postmodern responsiveness to the phenomenological "abundance" of being (at one end of the spectrum of ontological responsiveness) and (near

---

[51] With earth and world, then, Heidegger deconstructs and undercuts the form/matter dichotomy, seeking to teach us to recognize and respond to the inchoate forms that always-already inhere in the phenomenological matters themselves. Heidegger thus makes the case that creation should be grounded not in geographical but, instead, in ontological indigeny in his "Memorial Address" (in DT).

the opposite end of this spectrum) the endless domination of that modern subjectivism that treats everything as an object to be mastered or (at the extreme antipode) the obtuse reductiveness of that late-modern enframing that understands and so relates to everything as an intrinsically meaningless resource to be optimized. The simplest way to understand the stark difference between these poetic and technological modes of revealing Heidegger opposes, I have suggested, is to think in terms of the contrast between an ontological midwifery that respects the limits and creatively seeks to draw out the natural potentialities of the matters with which it works, as Michelangelo legendarily set his "David" free from the marble or, less hyperbolically put, as a skillful woodworker attends to the inherent qualities of particular pieces of wood (subtleties of shape and grain, shades of color, weight, and hardness), while deciding what (or even whether) to build from that wood. In precisely the same way, Heidegger contends, "[t] he authentic interpretation must show what does not stand there in the words and yet is said nevertheless" (IM 173/GA40 171). For Heidegger, in other words, an "authentic" hermeneutics must work creatively to bring forth the hidden riches of a text in the very same "poetic" way that a skilled woodworker learns to "answer and respond above all to the different kinds of wood and to the shapes slumbering within wood – to wood as it enters into human dwelling with all the hidden riches of its nature" (WCT 14/ GA8 17).

The distinctive character of this postmodern responsiveness to the abundance of being stands out most clearly when we contrast it with our defining late-modern tendency toward the kind of technological making that imposes form on matter without paying any heed to its intrinsic potentialities, in the way that, for example, an industrial factory indiscriminately grinds wood into woodchips in order to paste them back together into straight particle board that can then be used flexibly to efficiently construct a maximal variety of useful objects. Or, to take another example, think of the way our institutions of higher education increasingly seek to remake students into whatever society currently values, rather than helping students identify, cultivate, and develop their intrinsic skills and capacities and yoke these to serving their generation's emerging needs.[52] The fundamental difference between what we could simply call the *modern* and *postmodern* ways of comporting ourselves toward our worlds is thus fairly obvious (however tricky it might be to categorize difficult cases) insofar as we have not yet become happy "enframers," blithely content with the empty optimization imperative ("Get the most for the least!"), often incapable of believing in the intrinsic meanings that emerge between being and human being, and so relatively impervious to noticing them.

[52] For a development of Heidegger's arguments to this effect, see *Heidegger on Ontotheology*, ch. 4.

To emphasize the crucial difference at stake here, Heidegger pointedly asks: "But where in the manipulations of the industrial worker is there any relatedness to such things as the shapes slumbering within wood?" (WCT 23/GA8 26) If such a relatedness cannot be found, then something crucial has gone missing.[53] For, without such an ontological responsiveness capable of discerning and developing what is really there, human beings lose touch with what Heidegger understands as the source of genuine meaning. Although our late-modern metaphysics leads us to assume that all meaning ultimately comes from us, as the result of our subjective "value positings," Heidegger is committed to the less subjectivistic and more phenomenologically accurate view that, at least with respect to that which most matters to us (the paradigm case being love), what we care about most is not entirely up to us, not simply within our power to control, and this is a crucial part of what makes it so important. Here Kierkegaard seems to have taught Heidegger the fundamental problem with taking our modern idealization of autonomy to its limit; if something matters to us solely because we decide that it does, then we can also decide that it no longer matters.[54] By contrast, to learn from art how to understand the being of entities in a postmodern way means dedicating ourselves to cultivating and developing the ontological responsiveness that allows us to recognize and encounter entities as being richer in intrinsic meanings than we are capable of doing justice to conceptually, instead of thoughtlessly taking them as intrinsically meaningless resources awaiting optimization. In this way, we learn to approach the humble things, other animals, and human beings that constitute our worlds with care, humility, patience, thankfulness, and (as we will see in Chapter 5) even awe, reverence, and love.[55]

---

[53] Heidegger does not rule out a poetic receptiveness within technological settings. Instead, he suggests that such settings tend to undermine receptivity, and that we need to recognize how they do if we are to find meaning in them nonetheless. (On this use of technology against technologization, see *Heidegger on Ontotheology*, ch. 2. For a nice phenomenological exploration of this point, see Matthew B. Crawford, *Shop Class as Soulcraft: An Inquiry Into the Value of Work*.)

[54] If the modern enlightenment ideal could ever be fulfilled, Kierkegaard suggests, this perfectly autonomous individual would be like "a king without a kingdom," the absolute sovereign of a realm of consummate meaninglessness. Experiencing the ultimate arbitrariness of all freely chosen substantive values, such an "absolute ruler" finds that he "really rules over nothing" because he "remains subject to the dialectic that rebellion is legitimate at any moment." (See Kierkegaard, *The Sickness Unto Death*, 100.)

[55] Heidegger suggests in the later "Afterword" that the humble but difficult "task" (*Aufgabe*) of "The Origin of the Work of Art" is "to see the riddle [or mystery] ... that art itself is," not "to solve the riddle" (PLT 79/GA5 67). In his insightful book on art, Alexander Nehamas similarly observes not only that "we can be attracted to things of which we are not yet fully aware," but that in fact "everything we love is a step beyond our understanding." The main difference is that Nehamas describes in terms of "love" and "beauty" what Heidegger calls "being" and "earth." In both cases, however, the crucial phenomenon is of "something calling me without showing exactly what it is calling me to," as Nehamas nicely puts it. (See Nehamas, *Only a Promise of Happiness: The Place of Beauty in a World of Art*, 71, 76, 78.)

Such a subjectivism-humbling lesson in ontological responsiveness is precisely what Heidegger thinks great art like Van Gogh's *A Pair of Shoes* can help teach us. In "Hölderlin and the Essence of Poetry" (1936), Heidegger presents the German Romantic poet Friedrich Hölderlin as the "poet of poetry" because Hölderlin's poetry expresses poetically what poetry *is*; Hölderlin's poetry names-into-being the fact that poetry itself is essentially a naming-into-being.[56] In the same way, "The Origin of the Work of Art" presents Van Gogh as the painter of painting. For Heidegger, Van Gogh is the painter who paints what painting really *is*, because his painting of *A Pair of Shoes* (1886) captures and preserves that essential tension between revealing and concealing, "earth" and "world," which is at work in all *art*, indeed, in all creation, all bringing into and maintaining in intelligibility. By painting "the truth of painting" (to borrow Derrida's apt phrase), Van Gogh discloses the truth of art and so helps us learn to see what we could even call "the truth of truth." For, by preserving the dynamic struggle between earth and world, withdrawing and emerging, in all its "bound frenzy," Van Gogh allows us to encounter phenomenologically what Heidegger means when he describes ontological truth as *alêtheia*, namely, the essential tension between revealing and concealing that can be found at the heart of all intelligibility as it takes shape in time. This is why Heidegger's postmodern hope is that Van Gogh can help teach us to understand and encounter not only painting or art but even what it means to *be* in a *postmodern* way, one that no longer preconceives everything we encounter as inherently meaningless objects to be mastered or resources to be optimized, but instead helps us learn to discern and develop creatively the inherent meanings of things and others, to be open to the hints they offer and dedicate ourselves to *working* to bring forth such hints responsively, and responsibly, into the world.

What drew Heidegger to Van Gogh, then, was not just their mutual affinity for rural life, their shared awareness of the way its pastoral rhythms are rooted in nature's cycles and bespeak a fundamental faith that hard work can bring forth the earth's hidden bounty. Heidegger seems to have been deeply moved by the way half-formed figures seem to struggle to take shape in the background of Van Gogh's paintings, less in clear lines than in the thick texture of the paint, brush strokes, and deep fields of color. (Even the most accurate representations of Van Gogh's late paintings barely intimate their amazing use of paint, color, and brush-stroke, which helps explain why there is simply no substitute for encountering these paintings in person. In this too, Van Gogh's work subtly resists the combination of representation and efficient ordering on which our age of technological reproduction relies.) These two sources of attraction work together

---

[56] See EHP, 51–65; "The Origin of the Work of Art" builds on the very same romantic view: "Language, by naming entities for the first time, first brings entities to word and to appearance." (PLT 73/GA5 61)

for Heidegger. It is the mysterious bounty of the strife between world and earth that comes through in the subtle but dynamic tension between what shows itself and what recedes in Van Gogh's paintings. In Heidegger's interpretation, Van Gogh's *A Pair of Shoes* (1886) preserves the essential strife whereby the "nothing noths," both calling for and partly eluding conceptualization. His painting thereby allows us to encounter the way the earth both yields to and resists our worlds and so, out "of the calm of great riches, ripens and dispenses what is inexhaustible" (IM 164/GA40 118).

3. RESOLVING THE CONTROVERSY SURROUNDING HEIDEGGER'S INTERPRETATION OF VAN GOGH

Heidegger's artful and ambitious effort to show phenomenologically how aesthetics can transcend itself from within in an encounter with Van Gogh's painting has not been well understood, and Heidegger's attempt, as part of that effort, to link Van Gogh's painting with the deep spiritual wisdom of rural life proved highly controversial (to say the least). Unfortunately, this controversy has subsequently distracted readers from understanding what Heidegger was really trying to do in "The Origin of the Work of Art." By working through this controversy here, however, I think we can finally resolve it, learn its most important lessons, and so put it behind us.

As we have seen, Heidegger assumes that the shoes Van Gogh painted belong to a farming woman. The standard but unfortunate translation of *die Bäuerin* – literally "the female farmer" – as "the peasant woman" is not just classist but misleading. That the shoes disclose the world of a *farmer* is important for Heidegger precisely because the farmer's world is deeply attuned to the struggle with the earth; the farming woman works the earth daily, caring for, struggling with, and ultimately depending on the earth to nurture and bring forth her harvest.[57] Heidegger suggests that no one is

[57] Schapiro misses this point; his Marxian presuppositions lead him mistakenly to assume that "Heidegger's argument throughout refers to the shoes of a *class* of persons." Heidegger's guiding intuition is instead suggested by Yi-Fu Tuan's observation (in another context) that "the very existence of the farm and the hard work necessary to maintain it remind us that nature is not wholly accommodating," i.e., that the earth must inform but is never entirely within the farmer's control. As Heidegger himself later wrote: "The farmer's doing does not challenge the soil of the field; instead, it gives the seed over to the powers of growth; it shelters the seed in its thriving." (HR 270/GA79 27) For Heidegger, the traditional farmer is a paradigmatic figure, an exemplary embodiment of the *poietic* mode of disclosure that patiently struggles with the earth in order to creatively bring forth what is hidden there. This romantic figure contrasts most starkly with the technological mode of revealing that imposes predetermined ends on nature with minimal regard for any of its meaningful solicitations or inherent possibilities. The technologization of such farming in "mechanized agribusiness" is thus for Heidegger a sacrilegious profanation, and so a particularly ominous sign of our ongoing desecration of the source of genuine meaning, a technologization of the *poietic* itself, as it were. This helps explain, but does not at all excuse, Heidegger's scandalously insensitive (indeed, rather inhuman) comparison

more immediately attuned to the struggle between earth and world than the experienced farmer, long intimate with "the uncomplaining fear as to the certainty of bread" as well as "the wordless joy of having once more withstood want" (PLT 34/GA5 19). Of course, farmers forced to abandon their farms in the Dust Bowl might find Heidegger's vision of the earth as that which, from out "of the calm of great riches, ripens and dispenses what is inexhaustible" (IM 164/GA40 118) to be a romantic exaggeration.

Nevertheless, during the Great Depression era of the 1930s, "the earth" really was Heidegger's chosen name for that "inexhaustible" dimension of intelligibility experienced not only by farmers while farming but also by poets while poetizing, painters while painting, thinkers while thinking, and, indeed, by all those who create by patiently and carefully seeking to bring something long nurtured and concealed in a protective darkness into the light of day. That such metaphors also suggest pregnancy might help explain why Heidegger imagines the farmer as a woman, despite the fact that the shoes in Van Gogh's painting appear rather masculine to our contemporary aesthetic sensibilities. Or Heidegger might simply have assumed that the shoes belonged to a female farmer because the exhibition in which he originally saw Van Gogh's 1886 painting of *A Pair of Shoes* was probably populated with some of Van Gogh's many paintings from 1884–5 of women engaged in farm work (women digging in the fields, planting, harvesting and peeling potatoes, and so on) or simply sitting for him. (See Figure 4.)[58]

In fact, however, we have no way of knowing exactly which paintings Heidegger saw at the 1930 exhibit of Van Gogh's works in Amsterdam he later recalled having visited. The debate surrounding Heidegger's interpretation of Van Gogh's painting can be traced back to the fact that initially it is not even clear which painting Heidegger is referring to when "The Origin of the Work of Art" invokes an allegedly "well known painting by Van Gogh, who painted such shoes several times" (PLT 33/GA5 18). If Heidegger was aware that Van Gogh painted no fewer than five works

---

of this technologization of farming with the murder of millions of human beings in the Nazi death camps. His own sense of "shame" got in the way, but he should instead have recognized the death camps as by far the most sacrilegious and devastating form of technological desecration ever devised. (See Schapiro, "Further Notes on Heidegger and van Gogh," 150, my emphasis; Yi-Fu Tuan, "Time, Space, and Architecture: Some Philosophical Musings," 23; and also my *Heidegger on Ontotheology*, 82–4 and "Rethinking Levinas on Heidegger on Death," 68–73.)

[58] The Van Gogh Museum catalogues this painting as *Head of a Peasant Woman with Dark Cap*, 1885. (I have chosen to include this image because of its intriguing resemblance to the figure I shall call "the little old woman who lived in the shoe.") See also e.g. Van Gogh, *Farming Woman Digging* (1885) and *Farming Woman Digging up Potatoes* (1885), <http://www.vangoghgallery.com/catalog/Painting/406/Peasant-Woman-Digging.html> and <http://www.vangoghgallery.com/catalog/Painting/408/Peasant-Woman-Digging-Up-Potatoes.html> (accessed 9 August 2010).

FIGURE 4. Vincent van Gogh, *Head of a Dutch Peasant*, 1884, Musée d'Orsay, Paris, France. Reproduced by permission from Art Resource, NY. Photo Credit: Réunion des Musées Nationaux/Art Resource, NY.

titled *A Pair of Shoes* between 1886 and 1888 (plus several other pairs of wooden farmer's clogs, leather clogs, and paintings of more than one pair of shoes), then he does not seem to have thought this fact significant. The art historian who was closest to Heidegger, Heinrich Petzet, proposes that the "various versions [of Van Gogh's *A Pair of Shoes*] each show the same thing," and this might well be what Heidegger himself thought (if he ever even thought about it): Each of these paintings manifests the struggle between earth and world.[59] Perhaps that is true (although I think some do so much better than others), but there are lots of other differences between these paintings; anyone who studies them will soon see that they are not even all paintings of the same pair of shoes. Given the subsequent fame of Heidegger's essay, it is perfectly understandable that both art historians and phenomenologists would want to determine precisely which painting Heidegger was referring to in "The Origin of the Work of Art" so as to be able to evaluate his interpretation for ourselves.[60] When the eminent art historian Meyer Schapiro took up the task of identifying the painting in the 1960s, however, the mystery concerning which painting Heidegger was referring to ended – and a new controversy began.

Schapiro wrote to Heidegger to find out when and where he had actually seen Van Gogh's painting; Heidegger, then nearing eighty years of age, recalled having seen it at an exhibition in Amsterdam in 1930, so Schapiro cross-referenced all the works that could possibly have been exhibited there with Heidegger's own descriptions of the painting in his essay. In the end, Schapiro concluded not just that Heidegger had melded several paintings together in his memory but that, in so doing, Heidegger had mistaken as the shoes of a female farmer shoes that in fact belonged to Van Gogh himself. The significance of Schapiro's famous criticism has been hotly debated ever since. Art historians have typically taken Schapiro's claim that Heidegger mistakenly attributed Van Gogh's own shoes to a farming woman as a devastating objection that pulls the rug out from under Heidegger's entire interpretation of the painting, whereas philosophers sympathetic to Heidegger usually conclude that Schapiro's objection simply misses Heidegger's point.[61] (These philosophers thus treat Heidegger's apparent error of attribution as if it were of no more significance than the hauntingly similar fact that the work he attributed to Duns Scotus in his Habilitation thesis was shown subsequently to have been written instead by Thomas of Erfurt.)[62]

[59] See Schapiro, "A Note on Heidegger and van Gogh," 136; Petzet, *Encounters and Dialogues with Martin Heidegger*, 134.

[60] Unintentionally illustrating the danger here, Jameson confidently refers to "Van Gogh's well-known painting of the peasant shoes," then presents his readers with the wrong painting. (See his *Postmodernism*, 6, and the color plate immediately facing 10.)

[61] As Babette Babich reports, Schapiro's objection was widely understood by art historians as having "conclusively discredited Heidegger's essay ... by discounting its objective legitimacy or accuracy." (See Schapiro, "A Note on Heidegger and van Gogh," 136; Babich, "From Van Gogh's Museum to the Temple at Bassae: Heidegger's Truth of Art and Schapiro's Art History," 155.) The intriguing fact that philosophers and art historians typically reach such different judgments about the significance of Heidegger's alleged attribution error has itself become the impetus for an interesting philosophical reflection. (See Kelly, *Iconoclasm in Aesthetics*, 20–54.)

[62] The noteworthy exception here is Wayne Martin, who addresses this "fateful omen for Heideggerian historiography" in his *Theories of Judgment: Psychology, Logic, Phenomenology* (104).

To wit, Dreyfus simply dismisses the question of who the shoes originally belonged to as "irrelevant to how the picture works."[63] Although Dreyfus is ultimately right, his dismissal is much too quick to convince the many who disagree. For, Schapiro's criticism does indeed constitute a devastating objection to Heidegger's interpretation of Van Gogh, if that interpretation is understood in the standard way. According to what most readers take to be the sequence of phenomenological steps in Heidegger's interpretation of Van Gogh, Heidegger begins (1) with the assumption that the shoes belong to a farmer, an assumption that then allows him (2) to invoke that struggle with the earth with which the farmer's world is so closely attuned, so that he can finally (3) postulate this earth/world tension as the ontological truth of art. On this reconstruction of his argument, however, if Heidegger is wrong that the shoes were used by a farmer while farming (and he surely is wrong about this, as we will see), then the phenomenological bridge he is trying to build between a particular ("ontic") work of art and the ontological truth of art in general would collapse before it even gets off the ground, severed at its very first step.

Indeed, Heidegger's entire interpretation of Van Gogh as the painter of the ontological truth of painting implodes if its first step is merely an idiosyncratic and arbitrary projection on Heidegger's part – or something worse. And that is precisely what Schapiro alleges. Here is the verdict he delivers:

> Alas for him, the philosopher has deceived himself. He has retained from his encounter with Van Gogh's canvas a moving set of associations with peasants and the soil, which are not sustained by the picture itself. They are grounded rather in his own social outlook with its heavy pathos of the primordial and earthy. He has indeed "imagined everything and projected it into the painting."[64]

As this attempt to link Heidegger's thinking of earth with "the soil" and his "social outlook" suggests, Schapiro's famous criticism has an obvious political subtext. To put it bluntly, Schapiro is insinuating that Heidegger projected his own National Socialist-tainted associations onto Van Gogh's work, then mistook these "blood and soil" projections for the truth of the painting.[65] Even detached from the political subtext that motivates it, Schapiro's allegation – that Heidegger's interpretation of Van Gogh's painting is really nothing more than a projection of Heidegger's own subjective

---

[63] See Dreyfus, "Heidegger's Ontology of Art," 409.
[64] See Schapiro, "A Note on Heidegger and van Gogh," 140.
[65] Derrida recognizes this political subtext and suggests that Schapiro's reduction of earth to soil misses precisely what remained most unorthodox and challenging about Heidegger's Nazism, viz., his philosophical attempt to replace the Nazis' identity-defining philosopheme of the blood-drenched "soil" with his own conception of the nontotalizable yet existence-supporting "earth." (See Jacques Derrida, *The Truth in Painting*, 272–3; *Of Spirit*; and my discussion of this point in *Heidegger on Ontotheology*, 135 note 103.)

biases – constitutes a potentially formidable objection to Heidegger's attempt to move beyond the subject/object dichotomy at the heart of aesthetics. For, if Heidegger's interpretation really just covertly reinstalls his own subjective perspective, then his attempt to transcend aesthetic subjectivism from within looks dubious at best.

Heidegger's response to this particular objection (which he anticipates in "The Origin of the Work of Art") is simply to turn it around. Heidegger maintains, in effect, that any objection that he is merely projecting is merely a projection on the part of the objector. As he puts it (in the line Schapiro throws back at him in the quotation given earlier):

> It would be the worst self-deception to believe that our description had first pictured [or imagined, *ausgemalt*] everything thus as a subjective act and then projected it onto the painting. (PLT 35–6/GA5 21)

Here, however, we seem to reach a deadlock. To Schapiro, Heidegger's anticipatory denial of projection looks like an unconscious confession, what Freud called a *denegation*, that is, a disavowal that really confirms the truth of what it denies (the classic example of which is: "I have no idea what my dream meant, Dr. Freud, I only know it was *not* about my mother!").[66] To Heidegger, Schapiro would seem to have deceived himself in the "worst" way; by projecting projection onto Heidegger's essay, Schapiro's interpretation will have been led astray by its own maliciousness. Is there no way to avoid leaving the debate in such an unfriendly state, where the explicit avowal of "not A" is taken as an unconscious confession of "A," no one's motives remain above the hermeneutics of suspicion, and art interpretation threatens to collapse into the relativism of competing subjective projections?[67]

The way out of this unhappy impasse is to take Heidegger's phenomenology much more seriously, as we have done here. What we have seen is that, rather than just asserting his interpretation of Van Gogh, Heidegger

---

[66] One problem with such hermeneutic denegation detection is that it becomes very difficult to circumscribe its legitimate application. To someone like Derrida, every "clearly," "obviously," "of course," "to be sure," and so on, begins to look like an author's unconscious confession of a repressed uncertainty (except, apparently, when Derrida himself employs such emphatic expressions of certainty). The specific problem here, moreover, is that Schapiro overlooks the fact that philosophers like Heidegger are trained to anticipate and respond to likely objections. (Such training, which comes from studying the history of philosophy, gets reinforced if one's own work becomes famous and so subject of the criticisms of numerous others, as happened to Heidegger with the publication of *Being and Time* in 1927.) In the sentence in question, Heidegger shows that he recognizes that he is saying something that will sound idiosyncratic to readers – and how could he not recognize that? The sympathetic way to respond to his considered denial of projection, then, is to look for an alternative explanation for his description of the farming woman – a figure that, his next sentence goes on to say, he *literally* saw in his encounter with Van Gogh's painting.

[67] Schapiro's own Marxian-Freudian interpretation of Van Gogh's painting – which holds that for "an artist to isolate his worn shoes as the subject of a picture is for him to convey

provides a *phenomenological argument* for it, that is, a series of steps meant to take his audience from an experience of a particular "ontic" work of art to an encounter with the ontological truth of art in general. Insofar as we can personally experience the phenomenological sequence of steps to which Heidegger refers, we ourselves can attest to the truth of his interpretation (and if we cannot experience that sequence, or we experience something else instead, then we can seek to redescribe, refine, or contest his interpretation for ourselves). It is in this spirit, then, that I would like to suggest that we can finally resolve this longstanding controversy simply by summarizing and so clarifying what we have already implicitly seen to be the real sequence of steps in Heidegger's phenomenological interpretation of Van Gogh's painting.

When Heidegger discusses Van Gogh's *A Pair of Shoes* (1886), I have shown, his analysis takes us from: (1) experiencing Van Gogh's painting as an aesthetic object (a painting of a pair of shoes apparently on hand for our viewing); to (2) attending to the nothing (that is, the way the painting's background continues to suggest other possibilities that nevertheless resist being fully gestalted and so brought into the foreground); to thereby (3) encountering the essential tension between earth and world (the inconspicuous struggle between revealing and concealing implicit in "what *is* there"), and so finally (4) coming to see for oneself what it is like to walk in a farmer's shoes (by encountering for oneself, in the artwork, the same struggle to bring forth the bounty of the earth into the light of the world). We can see this quite clearly by looking at one of the crucial passages we examined earlier again, this time with the four steps in Heidegger's phenomenological transition explicitly labeled:

[1] A painting by Van Gogh: a pair of tough farmer's shoes, [2] nothing else. The picture really represents nothing. [3] Yet, what *is* there, with that you are immediately alone, [4] as if on a late autumn evening, when the last potato fires have burned out, you yourself were heading wearily home from the field with your hoe. (IM 37–8/GA40 38)

These four steps, taken together, form the phenomenological bridge that allows us to move from an interpretation of a particular work of art to the

a concern with the fatalities of his social being" – seems equally open to the charge of subjective projection. And Schapiro's way of developing this interpretation of Van Gogh's painting – which unblinkingly suggests that the shoes are "morbid," "deviant," deformed," "unsightly," "depressed and broken" – tends to reinforce rather than diminish such an impression. The same can also be said of Schapiro's incredible assertion that the late Van Gogh was "a man of the town and the city" rather than someone who identified with the rural countryside and the farmers' working "relation to nature." (See Schapiro, "A Note on Heidegger and van Gogh," 138, 140; and Schapiro, "Further Notes on Heidegger and van Gogh," 147. See also Derrida, *The Truth in Painting*, 367–8, where Derrida quotes from letters in which Van Gogh expresses his distaste for "city dwellers" and his sense of being "in his element" as a painter of farmers and their rural world.)

ontological truth inherent in all art (indeed, in all coming-into-being). In other words, these are the four steps in the phenomenological argument whereby Heidegger discovers what he calls the *a-lêtheiac* "essential strife" between "earth" and "world" – that is, the tension of emerging and withdrawing implicit in all intelligibility – in Van Gogh's *A Pair of Shoes* (1886).

We can unpack that third step – and better understand its connection to the fourth – by more closely examining Heidegger's curiously specific assertion:

> Yet, what *is* there, with that you are immediately alone, as if on a late autumn evening, when the last potato fires have burned out, you yourself were heading wearily home from the field with your hoe. (IM 37–8/GA40 38)

Initially this certainly sounds, as Schapiro alleges, like a highly idiosyncratic projection of Heidegger's own subjective prejudices onto Van Gogh's work. Of course, art historians like Schapiro commonly observe that in late works like *A Pair of Shoes* (1886), Van Gogh seems to devote as much care and attention to his use of color and brush strokes as he does to representing the fairly simple subject at the center of the painting.[68] What is so interesting about this for us, however, is that if one attends carefully to what emerges from "[o]ut of the dark opening of the well-worn insides of shoes" (PLT 33/GA5 19) – attending specifically to the lighter patches of color that emerge from the dark opening of the shoe on the right – one can indeed discern the head (hair bonnet and face in profile), torso, and arms of what could easily be a woman, carrying a hoe (a small shovel), with what could even be a yellow-orange "fire" smoldering behind her. I have tried to isolate this figure in the following detail (see Figure 5).

Insofar as we too can discern "the little old woman who lived in the shoe" (as I like to call this figure which I am convinced Heidegger himself saw), then I think we can be certain (*pace* Derrida) that Schapiro did in fact correctly identify the precise painting Heidegger was discussing: *A Pair of Shoes* (1886). But this also means that Heidegger is not using Van Gogh's painting as a jumping off point for his own free-associations (as Schapiro assumes). Instead, Heidegger is drawing directly on his own phenomenological encounter with the painting when he describes "what *is* there" (IM 37–8/GA40 38) in the work's inconspicuous earth/world struggle.[69] This,

---

68 Even Schapiro eventually found it important to draw our attention to "[t]he thickness and heaviness of the impasto pigment substance, the emergence of the dark shoes from the shadow into the light, the irregular, angular patterns and surprisingly loosened laces extended beyond the silhouettes of the shoes," apparently without ever realizing how close he was coming to Heidegger's phenomenological interpretation of Van Gogh's painting. (See Schapiro, "Further Notes on Heidegger and Van Gogh [1994]," 146.) As Heidegger wrote, "even the much-vaunted aesthetic experience cannot get around the thingliness of the artwork" (PLT 19/GA5 3–4).

69 Joseph Kockelmans makes the same mistake as Schapiro when he confidently asserts of Heidegger's description that "it is obvious that all of this cannot be *seen* in the picture"

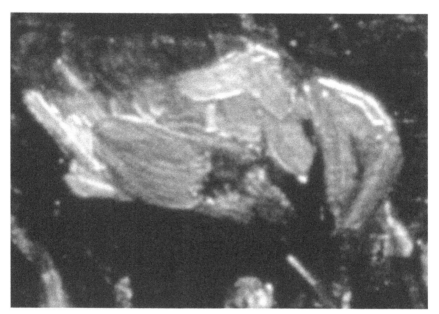

FIGURE 5. Detail of Vincent van Gogh, *A Pair of Shoes*, 1886, Van Gogh Museum, Amsterdam, The Netherlands. Reproduced by permission from Art Resource, NY. Photo credit: Art Resource, NY.

moreover, would also explain what Heidegger means when (immediately following the quotation Schapiro throws back at him) he writes:

If anything is questionable here, it is rather that we experienced too little in the vicinity of the work and that we expressed the experience too crudely and *too literally.* (PLT 36, emphasis added/GA5 21)

and so concludes that Heidegger is not "describing" Van Gogh's painting at all. (See *Heidegger on Art and Art Works*, 128.) As I shall now go on to show, Heidegger is indeed *describing* his experience of Van Gogh's painting (an experience grounded phenomenologically in his discernment of the figure I have isolated). I also do not think Heidegger is engaging here in the Husserlian practice of phenomenological "free-variation" in order to try to isolate the essence of shoes (as Crowell ingeniously suggests in "Phenomenology and Aesthetics"). By the time he has come into his own as a philosopher, Heidegger never engages in this Husserlian practice. In fact, at the very outset of "The Origin of the Work of Art," Heidegger explicitly rejects any attempt to understand the essence of art by "collecting ... characteristics from what exists" as "impossible [because question-begging; such a method must already know *what art is* in order to know what instance of art to focus on] ... and, where practiced, a self-delusion" (PLT 18/GA5 2–3). Instead, Heidegger develops his own (quite different) method of *phenomenological attestation*. This method describes everyday phenomena in terms of widely recognized formal features that (when properly understood) reveal the ontological structures conditioning that everyday phenomenon, and this interpretation is thereby presented for confirmation or disconfirmation by an interpretive community (as I explain in "Death and Demise in *Being and Time*" and "Rethinking Levinas on Heidegger on Death").

If Heidegger was *literally* describing the figure he saw emerging from "[o]ut of the dark opening of the well-worn insides of shoes" (PLT 33/ GA5 19) in Van Gogh's *A Pair of Shoes* (1886), as I think it now clear that he was, then what Heidegger offers us is not merely the projection of his own subjective associations onto a blank canvas but, instead, a meaningful gestalting of something from what is really there, something we too can phenomenologically confirm for ourselves.[70]

This is important, because to make something from what is really there – something that is neither obviously determined by what offers itself to us nor simply ignores what offers itself to us in order to impose its own subjective idea – this is what all true artistic creation does, according to Heidegger's view (as we saw in section 2.7).[71] Indeed, every "authentic" hermeneutics must do this; to genuinely interpret any great work of art, "you yourself" have to struggle to bring forth its hidden riches, just as the farmer must struggle with the earth to bring forth the bounty nurtured within it.

---

[70] Heidegger perhaps hints at this further in a rather mysterious 1944–5 Dialogue ("The Teacher Meets the Tower Warden" [or "Tower Keeper," *Türmer*, literally "Towerer," i.e., the one who lives in the tower – the translator seems to miss that this is an oblique reference to Hölderlin] at the Door to the Tower Stairway"). The entire dialogue (which I hear as a discussion between the philosopher and the poet *in Heidegger*) circles around an event (which precedes the dialogue) in which the philosophy "teacher" was profoundly unsettled by a "wondrous" painting, a "painting which for me is no longer an object ever since I encountered it in its wondrousness" (CCP 129/GA77 198). The painting is never described, but it is presented (by the poetic, Hölderlinian figure in the dialogue) as "a true find, … [which] is everything" (CCP 106/GA77 164). The dialogue distinguishes "a reconnoitering *of* the painting," i.e., an understanding of the work in worldly terms (which is quickly set aside as mere "connoisseurship"), from "a reconnoitering *through* the painting" (CCP 110/GA77 170), i.e., a coming to see the world through the work (instead of the reverse). It is the latter "reconnoitering" (*Kundschaft*), this seeing in terms opened up by the painting, that the Hölderlinian figure celebrates as bringing with it "the gift of a message [*Kunde*], if not an original testimony [*Ur-Kunde*]; I mean a message that comes to us inceptively [*anfänglich*, as a beginning]" (ibid.). We learn, moreover, that this inceptive message is still the (perfectionist and literally revolutionary) one that brings us full circle "back to that place where we truly [*eigentlich*] already are" (CCP 111/GA77172). This fascinating dialogue even opens with an oblique reference back to the "Afterword" to "The Origin of the Work of Art." Picking up where that famous essay had then ended (in the mid-1940s, Heidegger had yet to write its 1955 "Addendum"), the dialogue begins with the same call for us to learn simply to see, rather than to try "to solve," the wondrous riddle or enigma of great artwork.

[71] This is, e.g., what Heidegger seeks to do when he describes the farming woman Van Gogh painted. We can say that this figure is not obvious because no one has ever mentioned it before. Even if it seems obvious in retrospect (as masterful artistic gestalts often do), we can nevertheless imagine gestalting those bits of color and paint otherwise (at least around the edges). This, then, is quite different from a "hidden eye picture" or even the subliminal images Mark Tansey cleverly conceals in the background of his work, which can be hard to see but, once seen, cannot be seen in any other way. (See e.g. Tansey's *West Face*, 2004.) In effect, Heidegger is offering us his own creative gestalt – his own way of "worlding" this patch of earth – in order to exemplify the very view he is seeking to convey. I have tried to do the same, in turn, for the "nothing" in Heidegger's essay.

To engage in such phenomenological hermeneutics, we could thus say, is to encounter oneself as a *farmer of meaning*. For, such an encounter allows us to understand for ourselves what it is like when the earth comes to inform our worlds with a genuine, partly independent meaning, one that we ourselves, helped bring brought forth through a creative struggle and yet did not simply make up or project onto the work. When we catch ourselves in the act of making-sense of an artwork in this way, then we experience for ourselves that fundamental making-sense – whereby world discloses earth – from which, for Heidegger, all genuine meaning ultimately derives.

Here, then, we reach the important fourth and final step in Heidegger's phenomenological interpretation, which still needs to be unpacked and explained. As we saw in section 1.3, Heidegger claims that by experiencing the subtly dynamic tension between earth and world in Van Gogh's painting, we can thereby come to encounter the same primordial level of practical meaning that is unknowingly known by the farmer who uses her shoes "without noticing or reflecting" on them (PLT 34/GA5 19). From what has been said, we can now understand just how that is supposed to be possible. In our phenomenological encounter with Van Gogh's painting, we catch ourselves in the act of struggling to impose a stable world of meanings on an inherently dynamic intelligible domain that both informs and resists this world. To thus find ourselves "worlding the earth" in our encounter with art, we have just seen, is to experience for ourselves essentially the same struggle as the farmer who must patiently wrestle with the earth in order to bring forth the crops long cultivated and concealed in the earth's protective darkness into the light of her world. In our encounter with Van Gogh's painting, we thus learn for ourselves what it is like to walk in a farmer's shoes – the shoes where earth and world meet, both literally and figuratively – because we too have experienced the way the earth both informs and exceeds the world of meanings we take from it, enduring the same struggle to world the earth (albeit on a smaller scale) in our own hermeneutic and phenomenological engagement with Van Gogh's painting (and, indeed, with Heidegger's texts).[72]

The most important point to grasp here, then, is that Heidegger does not maintain (as it is easy but nonetheless mistaken to assume) that Van Gogh's painting allows us somehow first to directly intuit the world of a farmer as she nonthematically encounters it so that, by getting in touch with her farming world, we can thereby come to experience the "essential tension" between earth and world with which a farmer is intimately familiar. That cannot be right because it begs the question, assuming the

---

[72] As Heidegger laconically puts this rather complex point: "Truth happens in Van Gogh's painting. That does not mean that something on hand is correctly portrayed but, rather, that the totality of what-is, world and earth in their counter-play, attains unconcealment in the becoming manifest of the equipmental being of the shoe-equipment" (PLT 56/GA5 43).

aporetic step that Heidegger realizes needs to be explained (as we saw in 1.3) – namely, how can we move from an aesthetic experience of a painting on hand like an object to an encounter with the "equipmentality" of equipment? It is thus crucial to see that Heidegger does not first assume that the shoes in the painting belong to a farmer so that, by alluding to this farmer's lifeworld, he can subsequently introduce the essential struggle between earth and world as the truth of the painting. If that were the sequence of steps in Heidegger's argument, then not only would he be knowingly begging his own question but, worse, Schapiro's telling criticism that the shoes in Van Gogh's painting could not in fact have been used by a farmer to form would constitute a completely devastating objection to Heidegger's interpretation. For, *Schapiro is certainly right that the shoes in the painting could not have been used by a farmer while farming*, for the simple reason that the Dutch farmers Van Gogh painted wore wooden clogs in the damp potato fields, not leather shoes like those worn by the farmers Heidegger knew in Southern Germany, which would have quickly rotted from the damper soil of the Netherlands! So, if Heidegger had sought simply to move from what he assumed were a pair of *farmer's* shoes to an intimation of the earth/world struggle familiar to farmers, and then from there to the essence of art, Schapiro's objection would indeed dynamite the phenomenological bridge Heidegger builds from an ontic work of art to the ontological truth of art in general.[73]

[73] Derrida and Babich both seek to unsettle the controversy by, in effect, developing Heidegger's suggestion that we cannot tell with certainty "to whom [the shoes] belong" (OBT 14/GA5 18 note a) – a brief marginal comment Heidegger seems to have jotted down in response to Schapiro. Thus Derrida dedicates more than one hundred pages to multiplying a seemingly unending succession of skeptical questions meant to suggest that the identity of the shoes is radically undecideable, because we cannot be sure to which painting Heidegger referred, whether the shoes in question even form a pair, and so on. Babich argues that, even if we grant to Schapiro that Van Gogh owned the shoes in the painting, this does not mean they were Van Gogh's shoes in the decisive sense. On the basis of the same historiographical evidence Schapiro appeals to (Van Gogh's letter to his brother, Gauguin's account of Van Gogh's studio, etc.), Babich nicely shows that Van Gogh bought the pair of shoes in question not in order to wear them himself but rather, "like the rough beer steins Van Gogh also collected, … in order to paint them," thus leaving open the question of who originally broke them in. Yet, this line of reasoning remains open to the response that, as Kelly starkly puts it: "The Painting is van Gogh's, according to Schapiro, because [Van Gogh] invested himself in it, because his subjectivity is *embodied* (not merely *represented*) in it. This idea – that embodied subjectivity is constitutive of what modern art is – is what Schapiro affirms and Heidegger denies." Although Kelly effectively changes the terms of the debate here, he nicely brings us to the crux of the issue. For Schapiro (on Kelly's reconstruction), Van Gogh's very act of painting the shoes transforms them into an expression of his own subjectivity, whereas for Heidegger, Van Gogh's painting shows us a way beyond the subject/object metaphysics that Schapiro presupposes. In the end, though, the real problem for all those who would defend Heidegger by arguing that the shoes originally were used by a farmer is that this line of defense overlooks Schapiro's most telling objection. (This is understandable, because the objection does not come

What I want to suggest, however, is that this longstanding controversy can finally be resolved when we recognize that Heidegger's phenomeno- logical interpretation of Van Gogh's painting actually follows a different sequence of steps. As we have seen, Heidegger moves from: (1) experiencing an objective painting of unused shoes (in the standard aesthetic way); to (2) noticing and attending to the dynamic "nothing" in the background of the painting and thereby (3) encountering the earth/world struggle implicit in the work; to finally (4) intimating, from this earth/world struggle, what a farmer's inconspicuous use of shoes as equipment is like. The trick missed by Schapiro (along with virtually every other reader of Heidegger's famous essay) is that it is only attending to the "nothing" that makes itself visible in the background of Van Gogh's painting that first allows us to encounter the essential tension between world and earth for ourselves, and it is this encounter – with the tension between that which comes forth into the light ("world") and that which nurtures this coming forth and yet also shelters itself in the darkness ("earth") – that allows us to understand, as though from the inside, *what it is like* to walk in the shoes of a farmer.

Once we understand the real sequence of steps in Heidegger's phe- nomenological argument, moreover, we can see that the second part of Schapiro's objection (that the shoes did not belong to a farmer *but to Van Gogh himself*) would, even if correct (which remains controversial), only temporarily complicate the inference from step 3 to step 4 – that is, the

through clearly in Schapiro's work; I owe my understanding of it to conversations with the art historian David Craven, who interviewed Schapiro several times and discussed it with him.) Schapiro's seemingly incontrovertible objection is that the shoes Van Gogh painted could not have been used by a farmer while farming because the Dutch farmers Van Gogh painted wore wooden clogs in the field, not leather shoes, which would have rotted quickly from the damp conditions in the muddy potato fields (since this preceded the adoption of rubber soles). Kockelmans implicitly acknowledges the force of Schapiro's criticism by attempting to dodge it, claiming that Heidegger is not in fact describing Van Gogh's painting but only using it as a phenomenological jumping off point to evoke the different shoes of the farmers with which he was familiar. The fatal problem is that Kockelmans's way of reading Heidegger's crucial "and yet" as a transition away from Van Gogh's paint- ing and toward the farmers with whom Heidegger was familiar completely misses the real force of his deliberately ambiguous use of the "nothing," and so also misses the way Heidegger's phenomenological descriptions of the painting seek to build a direct bridge from the ontic painting to the ontological truth of art. Kockelmans seems to presuppose that the ontic and ontological are heterogeneous domains (again understandably, as this was a central tenet of the orthodox Heideggerian scholars of the last generation and continues to be proclaimed by influential critics such as Haberilias), but such a mistaken view would (as Heidegger's critics allege) place Heideggerian phenomenology outside the realm of meaningful communal adjudication. (See Jacques Derrida, *The Truth in Painting,* esp. 257–382; Babich, "From Van Gogh's Museum," 157–8; Kelly, *Iconoclasm in Aesthetics,* 51; and Kockelmans, *Heidegger on Art and Art Works,* 126–32. Harries repeats Kockelmans's mistake in his otherwise insightful monograph, *Art Matters: A Critical Commentary on Heidegger's "The Origin of the Work of Art."*)

move from encountering the conflict between earth and world to understanding what it is like to walk in a farmer's shoes. The complication is only temporary, because this is a move Heidegger could have made just as easily by discussing the world of Van Gogh himself (to whom Schapiro himself attributes the shoes in the painting). For, in Heidegger's interpretation of him, Van Gogh surely understood the earth/world struggle at least as lucidly as the farmers he painted. Thus, Heidegger could just as easily have moved from (1) discerning the nothing and thereby (2) encountering the earth/world struggle to (3) understanding this struggle as the ontological truth of art to finally (4) seeing what it is like to walk in the shoes of a painter like Van Gogh, who devoted his life as an artist "to expressing the poetry hidden in" the everyday world all around him (as Van Gogh himself writes in the eloquent and arresting passage I have chosen as an epigraph for this chapter).

Indeed, Heidegger's larger point (the point conveyed by his provocative references to "you" and "you yourself") is that Van Gogh and these farmers lived the same struggle in different ways, and so do all of us *meaning farmers*, that is, all of us who genuinely create by discerning inchoate contours and so struggling to help give birth to something that previously remained hidden in darkness. Art thus teaches us not to try to banish the darkness that surrounds the light of intelligibility, but to learn to see into that ubiquitous "noth-ing" so as to discern therein the enigmatic "earth" that nurtures all the genuine meanings that have yet to see the light of day. Insofar as we can learn from Van Gogh (or other similarly great artists) to see in this poetic way ourselves, Heidegger suggests, we will find ourselves dwelling in a postmodern world permeated by meaningful possibilities.

Of course, the meaning of "postmodernity" itself is currently rather heavily contested. The next two chapters will seek to sort through the main senses the "postmodern" has today and to demonstrate the continuing relevance of Heidegger's own postmodern approach, the resonant call for us to remain sensitive to the inexhaustibility of the meanings permeating our everyday "reality." By staying attuned to what we could thus call *polysemy*, we will test Heidegger's postmodern approach in close hermeneutic readings of two celebrated "postmodern" works: U2's hit song, "Even Better than the Real Thing," and Alan Moore and Dave Gibbons's much-lauded "postmodern masterpiece," the comic book mini-series, *Watchmen*. These chapters, as works of post-Heideggerian hermeneutics, will seek to bring out what is really there in these works of "postmodern" art without claiming to exhaust their meaning. These chapters thus struggle, in Heidegger's terms, to creatively gestalt the rift-structure these postmodern texts offer us in a way that respects their texture and yet, rather than simply standing awe-struck before them, discloses some of their previously hidden meanings. Heidegger suggests that if such interpretations are "authentic" and "original" – that is, grounded in genuine insights and capable of inspiring the interpretive efforts of others – then they will have emerged from a personal struggle with the texts they interpret, and that personal dimension will probably continue to be obvious in what follows.[74] Of course, such interpretations must also hold themselves open to the possibility of more or less radical redescriptions by others as well. For, that too is how the conversation continues sometimes (as we will see in Chapter 5). With such ideas in mind, then, let us turn to see how a sympathetic altercation (or *Auseinandersetzung*) with these popular postmodern works might aid the philosophical effort to take the temperature of our times.

---

[74] Ironically, my interpretations of Moore and Gibbons's *Watchmen* as "a deconstruction of the hero" and of Heidegger's *Contributions to Philosophy* as "a philosophical fugue" (the two oldest chapters here) – like my thesis that Heidegger's critique of technology can only be understood by way of his views on ontotheology – interpretations that were initially greeted as somewhat outlandish, now seem to have become influential enough that I am occasionally confronted with the response that these views are not so much oddly idiosyncratic as patently obvious. (This is an improvement over that unanswerable objection I heard earlier: "If you are right about that, then why hasn't anyone else seen it before?") Thus some of my views, at least, seem to have passed from the first to the second of William James's stages in the reception of an idea: "First, you know, a new theory is attacked as absurd; then it is admitted to be true, but obvious and insignificant; finally it is seen to be so important that its adversaries claim that they themselves discovered it." If I feel some trepidation about the arrival of that third stage, I remind myself that "originality" can only truly me au helping to give rise to insights in others. (Still, while plagiarism might be the sincerest form of flattery, it is also the least ethical response to that "anxiety of influence" Bloom recognized.) I can thus hope that my more recent and still strange views presented here – on the little old woman who lived in Van Gogh's shoe, e.g., and on the nothing in Heidegger's essay – may yet face a similar fate. (See James, *Pragmatism: A New Name for Some Old Ways of Thinking*, 87; and Bloom, *The Anxiety of Influence: A Theory of Poetry*.)

4

"Even Better than the Real Thing"?

Postmodernity, the Triumph of the Simulacra, and U2

> My head is somewhere in between...
> You're the real thing
> Even better than the real thing.
> > U2, "Even Better than
> > the Real Thing"

1. POSTMODERNITY: BEYOND THE BRUTAL SIMPLIFICATIONS OF MODERNITY

As fans of the rock band U2 will recognize, I take both my title and my epigraph from the second song on U2's 1991 album, *Achtung Baby*. U2's lead singer, Bono, famously declared that U2 entered its "postmodern" phase with *Achtung Baby*. *Achtung*, of course, standardly translates as a command for "Attention!" – but it also literally connotes "respect" or "care" (for that to which one should have been moved to "attend" in the first place) – and in what follows I shall suggest that attending to and thinking carefully about some of the philosophical ideas and themes underlying U2's work from their "postmodern" period that begins with *Achtung Baby* can cast a mutually illuminating light on both U2 and "postmodernity."[1] In the first

---

[1] U2's almost oxymoronic album title is drawn, in a typical instance of postmodern "sampling" (a practice that can be traced back as least as far as the French Situationists' influential use and defense of *détournement*; see Knabb's *Situationist International Anthology*), from Mel Brooks's film *The Producers* – where the humorous greeting "*Achtung*, baby!" is met by a Nazi with the scolding response, "The *Führer* would never say *baby*!" (See Bill Flanagan, *U2 at the End of the World*, 171). The title of U2's self-avowedly "postmodern" album thus suggests the power of responding to fascism with humor. *The Joke*, as Milan Kundera suggested (in his novel of the same title), is what dictatorial regimes cannot tolerate, because the joke calls into question the unwritten rules on which their repression depends. (This is a common refrain in Slavoj Žižek's work; e.g., in *The Sublime Object of Ideology* and *Did Somebody Say Totalitarianism? Five Interventions in the (Mis)use of a Notion*.) Nevertheless, I will suggest, U2 *also* means their album title to be taken unironically; put simply, U2 intends for the

two sections I think primarily from Heidegger's philosophy toward U2, but, reversing this direction in the final section, my chapter concludes with an extended analysis of "Even Better than the Real Thing," a song I take to be particularly suggestive for the post-Heideggerian attempt to think through U2, beyond the triumph of the simulacra, and toward a genuine postmodernity.

What, then, does it mean today to be "postmodern"? That is not intended to be a trick question, but it may sound like one (at least to those "already in the know"), because the very idea that we should be able to precisely specify the singular meaning of a philosophical concept is a characteristically modern assumption, that is, just the sort of assumption postmodernists seek to get beyond. Of course, the modern pursuit of unambiguous precision proved to be stunningly successful for the mathematical sciences, which developed and so reinforced modernity's defining project of gaining control over the objective world through our knowledge, thanks largely to the Copernican revolution in which, rather than observe the way nature behaves independently of us, we "strap nature to the rack" and force "her" to answer our questions.[2] This modern project of "Tryin' to throw your arms around the world" (as if "trying to throw his arms around a girl," a variation U2 employs in the ninth song on *Achtung Baby*) continues to generate undeniable technological and medical advances, along with equally undeniable and unwanted side-effects (including environmental devastation and the innumerable other inhumanities generated by our rapacious struggle to control and profit from this knowledge over nature) and real dangers (from that slow erosion of our sense of the meaningfulness of life that Heidegger analyses to more dramatic threats of looming global catastrophe, whether nuclear, environmental, economic, biogenetic, or even nanotechnological).

Indeed, our increasingly exact calculations allowed us to extend our technical mastery of the natural world so far that, to mention just two (not unrelated) examples, we have been able to construct buildings and planes that do not fall from the sky (without sufficient provocation) as well as an unmatched military-industrial arsenal capable of enforcing our tenuous geopolitical dominance (which, in turn, provides our newest enemies with that "sufficient provocation").[3] What such connections suggest is that

---

audience to become their "baby," a beloved being asked to attend to a deeper dimension of meaning. (On the direct connections between Situationism and art and popular music, see Greil Marcus, *Lipstick Traces: A Secret History of the Twentieth Century*, and Sadie Plant, *The Most Radical Gesture: The Situationist International in a Postmodern Age*.)

[2] Bacon's notoriously misogynistic formulations of the modern project now look, in retrospect, rather revealing. (See Francis Bacon, *The New Organon*.)

[3] The unhappy fact that this supposed geopolitical dominance did not actually protect our planes and buildings – or, more important, the people within them – raises the thorny issue of what, if anything, such dominance does protect, besides the most avaricious and destructive economic interests.

even the best efforts of our modern mathematical sciences have not been able to master the domains we apply them to without generating *rebound effects*, in which what we seek to master at least partly escapes and then returns with a vengeance. We see these rebound effects all around us, in our political headlines as well as in the mounting environment crisis still too often excluded from these same headlines. Seeking to draw our heads outside the lines that corral our thinking, postmodern theorists such as Baudrillard and Derrida sometimes describe these effects as *the revenge of the real*, a scenario in which (as with those symptoms Freud called *the return of the repressed*) we are revisited by destructive effects ultimately attributable to our very efforts to control, suppress, deny, or exclude that which cannot be assimilated efficiently to the existing order. In response, these postmodernists follow Heidegger in seeking to isolate and overturn those destructive but usually unnoticed modern assumptions that function both to devastate our world and to preemptively neutralize our critiques of this destruction (rendering these critiques as ineffectual as protestors confined to predesignated "protest sites").

Surprisingly, however, some avowedly "postmodern" scientists (of which there are more than a few) seem to believe that the best way to eliminate such devastating rebound effects is to master nature still more precisely, for example, by employing nonmonotonic logics that do not presume bivalence, using fractal models capable of predicting the behavior of extremely complex systems, and so on – in short, by giving us more precise mechanisms of control, more finely grained conceptual mappings of the real, better predictive hypotheses, calibrated with such complex precision that, finally, nothing will exceed our grasp, our "arms" (conceptual and military – in U2's fortuitous ambiguity) thrown entirely "around the world."[4] From a post-Heideggerian perspective, this sounds like a prescription for a more intense dosage of the very radiation that made us sick in the first place, but it is not immediately clear what other rational alternatives remain open to us, since our modern obsession with prediction and control seems to have painted us into a conceptual corner in which all the solutions we can think of that might help involve more prediction and control – as if we could get our addiction to control under control if we just had a bit more self-control.[5] The very persistence of such fantasies of control,

---

[4] See the litany of scientific figures Lyotard cites in *The Postmodern Condition: A Report on Knowledge*.

[5] And yet, is it so obvious that we cannot do so? What is meditation, for example, if not a proven path whereby one learns to control one's way beyond control? The paradox, put in Heideggerian terms, is that we must decide to learn *Gelassenheit*, the "releasement" or "letting be" that helps us transcend the "subjectivism" of modernity's subject-centered worldview and recognize that the great sophist Protagoras was wrong: Humanity is *not* the measure of all things. Such antianthropocentric insights help us experience our connection to a greater whole, a reality that transcends us and to which we belong, part to whole,

moreover, suggests that, however disastrous some of the consequences of modernity's "subjectivistic" drive toward total control are proving to be, the source of this drive is to be found in the intrinsically limited nature of our own cognitive capacities and our often laudable resistance to all such limits – a resistance sometimes called *freedom, progress,* or even *life,* forces no one wants to stand against, especially because the struggle whereby we finite beings seek to achieve the impossible continues to help generate our most cherished scientific, medical, and technological advances, many of which we surely do not want to forfeit. So, if modernity has painted us into this conceptual corner historically, how might we go about getting out of it? That is another way of asking the general question of *post*modernity.

In an insightful analysis of the terrorist attacks of September 11, Derrida describes the way "repression in both its psychoanalytic sense and in its political sense – whether it be through the police, the military, or the economy – ends up producing, reproducing, and regenerating the very thing it seeks to disarm." Does not U2, whose own work emerged internationally as a critique of the cycle of terrorist and counterterrorist violence (remember their powerful 1983 song, "Sunday Bloody Sunday"), frequently draw our attention to the same problem? In "Peace on Earth," for example, Bono warns: "Where I grew up there weren't many trees / Where there was we'd tear them down / And use them on our enemies / They say that what you mock / Will surely overtake you / And you become a monster / So the monster will not break you / And it's already gone too far." Theorizing such effects in terms of the logic of *autoimmunity,* in which the forces in us that seek to keep out "the other" grow so excessive that they begin to destroy the health of the system they are supposed to protect, Derrida calls for an "immuno-depressant" response by which we would seek to "limit the mechanisms of rejection and to facilitate toleration."[6] Derrida articulated an earlier version of this strategic response in terms of what he rather cleverly called "hauntology" (the logic of *being – haunted* by alterity), suggesting that we must accept the fact that every concept "is in advance contaminated, that is, pre-occupied, inhabited, haunted by its other," and so stop attempting the various exorcisms that inadvertently animate these specters and give them a stage on which to appear. Instead, Derrida liked to say, we should work to transform our *ghosts* into *guests* by offering our others our hospitality.[7] U2 evokes this rebound effect in a particularly haunting way in

like organisms in an holistically interconnected environment. Indeed, the *holy,* Heidegger suggests (and I shall develop this suggestion later), is what allows us each to experience such a connection to the whole, one that can help restore that sense of interconnectedness and belonging that we are no longer quite comfortable describing as our "spiritual" health (although "mental" health is too narrow a term).

[6] See Giovanna Borradori, ed., *Philosophy in a Time of Terror: Dialogues with Jürgen Habermas and Jacques Derrida,* 99, 188 note 7.

[7] Derrida thus articulates what is in effect an unreachable *regulative ideal,* although he resists that conclusion, insisting that, impossible or not, only the concrete realization

"Until the End of the World" when Bono sings: "In my dream I was drowning my sorrows / But my sorrows they learned to swim," and Bono even seems to recommend the same response as Derrida, describing the peacemaking gesture in which: "I reached out for the one I tried to destroy."[8]

Following Derrida (and so Heidegger, whom Derrida himself mostly follows), many postmodernists call for us to resist extending the demand for unambiguous precision typical of modern mathematical science into the domain of ordinary human life. The ironic lines of "Zooropa" similarly caution against our unthinking technological extension of modern fantasies of control: "Zooropa ... better by design / ... / Through appliance of science / We've got that ring of confidence," and in "Zoo Station" U2 advocates that we should instead be "Ready for the shuffle / Ready for the deal / Ready to let go of the steering wheel." Rather than embracing the modern drive toward complete control through the universal extension of unambiguous mathematical precision, these postmodernists echo the Heideggerian call for us to learn to develop what we could think of as a sensitivity to the unpredictable nature of poetic *polysemy*, that is, an attunement to the inexhaustibly *multiple meanings* known to all careful readers of poetry, and probably experienced by aficionados of all the other poetic arts, all the divine arts of "making" that (as we saw last chapter) bring new things into existence. Of course, if our modern bridges are going to stay up, a steel girder must *either* be capable of bearing certain weight and stress tolerances *or* not. For a poem to work, however, it need not mean *either* one thing *or* another – indeed, quite the opposite. I shall show in the conclusion that this is the case with U2's "Even Better than the Real Thing," but let us begin with an uncontroversial example of poetry.

Treat the following as a multiple-choice question, if you like. Consider e. e. cummings's densely suggestive line: "... if you are glad / whatever's living will yourself become." Is the real, true, or genuine meaning of this line that if we are "glad" (that is, happy, willing, bright, and cheerful), then: (A) we will find ourselves becoming one with the life all around us; or (B) we

---

of *unconditional* "hospitality" is genuinely deserving of the name. (See Jacques Derrida, *Specters of Marx: The State of the Debt, the Work of Mourning, and the New International*, 160.)

[8] Already in "Sunday Bloody Sunday" (1983), U2 issued an overtly Christian call for the forgiveness necessary to break the cycle of terrorist violence (invoking "The real battle yet begun / to claim the victory Jesus won"). Drawing on the work of René Girard, Charles Taylor develops a similar view of "a Christian counter-violence" that would avoid that scapegoating of enemies (which externalizes unacknowledged forces within us and demonizes them, rather than recognizing and seeking a transformative appropriation of those forces). For Taylor, however, the Gospel suggests that one should dedicate oneself to a peaceful "transformation which reaches to overcome the fear of violence not by becoming lord over it, by directing it as an annihilating force against evil, but which rather aims to overcome fear by offering oneself to it; responding with love and forgiveness, thereby tapping a source of goodness, and healing," which places Taylor closer to Tutu, Mandela, and Derrida than to Girard and the early Bono. (See Charles Taylor, *A Secular Age*, 708.)

should choose to identify our will with whatever is living; or (C) we become the "living will" of whatever we encounter (whether we choose to or not); *or* (D) we should will ourselves to become one with vital force possessed by all things, including ourselves (so as to actualize that life within us that allows us to grow along with all other living things)?[9] An attunement to poetic polysemy suggests that this question is badly posed as an "either/or." Where poetry and the subtle density of everyday life are concerned, the question, "What does it *really* mean?" cannot truly be answered with *either* A, B, C, *or* D, but only with E: *All of the above (and more).*

If this is true of a single line within a poem, how much more true will it be of that poem as a whole, let alone of the poet's entire oeuvre? (Or of the relation of that oeuvre to its world, and ours?) And if it is also true of my experience of a single leaf falling through the sunlit morning onto the path before me – or a remark you utter that changes me in some indefinable yet irrevocable way – or the look on the face of a stranger I have not quite forgotten, each of these experiences singular moments of a single day, then how much more true will it be of the life in which those moments resonate together? And of all the other lives that I might, in turn, somehow impact and subtly realign? This exuberant insight – that mere existence is unspeakably deep, that meaning is inexhaustible, that "every atom of gold [sunlight] is the chance of blossoming fruit" (as Baudelaire famously put it) – sometimes seems to me to be the postmodern insight *par excellence.* In it, we can recognize postmodernism's neoromantic refusal of the modern scientific rejection of romanticism, and so discern the premodern roots of postmodernism. The romantic exuberance that often accompanies this wonderful insight is perhaps also the source of the postmodern movement's visionary fervor and those occasional evangelical excesses that seem to have turned so many against it.

And yet, the minute we begin to imagine that we have placed our fingers on the living pulse of *the* postmodern, do we not risk betraying the polysemy of the very concept of "postmodernity," as if mistakenly believing that the postmodern impulse itself could be defined precisely and unambiguously along a single axis of meaning? Or, to make the same point in another way (and so note the first of several *paradoxes of reflexivity* haunting the postmodern project): If postmodernity should be defined by its call for a sensitivity to polysemy, then presumably we should also understand postmodernity itself polysemically, as possessing multiple meanings, which would mean that postmodernity should mean more than just the call for polysemy – and, in fact, it does. Ironically, the postmodern is even in danger of meaning too much. We now use the adjective "postmodern" to describe not just philosophical ideas but the vast array of cultural "texts" embodying these ideas, texts found all along that increasingly obsolete continuum

---

[9] See e. e. cummings, *Collected Poems*, "New Poems," #315.

spanning "high" and "low" art, a distinction the postmodern movement undermines by lavishing its theoretical attentions on objects that previous generations rarely stooped to examine. As a new generation of "highbrow lowbrows" mobilize postmodern insights and theories to analyze everything from television ("*Lost* is the postmodern *Gilligan's Island*"), to comic books ("Alan Moore's *Watchmen* is a masterpiece of postmodern literature"), to Hollywood movies ("Quentin Tarantino's combination of nonlinear narrative and pulp sensibility gives his films their postmodern texture"), to pop music ("U2 entered its postmodern phase with *Achtung Baby* and celebrated it with the *Zooropa* tour"), to architecture ("The rejection of the coldly-functional, geometric austerity of the modern Bauhaus movement helps explain postmodern architecture's resistance to any integral style and its promiscuous hospitality to competing and even contradictory stylistic elements"), to conceptual art ("There seems to be a mutual affinity between U2 and the postmodern artists Jeff Koons and Cindy Sherman"), to philosophy ("Baudrillard may be the greatest of the avowedly postmodern philosophers, but Lyotard is probably the most famous"), and even to religion ("Postmodern theologians heatedly debate whether God *is* humanity, nonappearance, or absence, but postmodern Christians should simply insist that *God is love*").

Thus, if one tries to infer the meaning of postmodernism by induction from the disparate uses of the term that one overhears (even in the circles of the learned), one may begin to suspect that the concept of the "postmodern" has become so saturated with different meanings that it risks collapsing under the weight of their competing pulls and so fracturing into a disordered multiplicity, the various facets of which only arbitrarily bear the same name. *Postmodern* begins to look like one of those words used so frequently, and in such a bewildering variety of ways, that it has lost all purchase and specificity. Overloaded with meanings, it loses all meaning; for, if everything is "postmodern," then postmodernity becomes meaningless. This is the reflexive paradox mentioned above: Approached in its own terms, postmodernity risks suffering a kind of *death by polysemy*, its meaning drawn and quartered, again and again, until nothing remains.

2. THREE MORE MEANINGS OF POSTMODERNITY

It seems to me, then, that in order to understand postmodernity, we need to navigate carefully between the twin excesses of *modern singularity* and *postmodern multiplicity*, the Scylla of the only One and the Charybdis of the infinitely Many. I shall thus risk a more schematic approach, setting out what, to my ear at least, seem to be three more ways in which it makes good sense to describe something as "postmodern." Of course, postmodern polysemy suggests that it is a bit arbitrary to discuss only three more senses of postmodernity: Why stop at three?

Here I take some solace from the idea that a great poem always means more than one thing and yet does not mean everything at once, for that latter would drown out all the poem's particular meanings in a dissonant cacophony or, perhaps, a mystical harmony or fusion (a point to which we will return in Chapter 6).[10] At the same time, however, a truly great poem always holds itself open to meaning more than I currently realize. (Thus, on explaining my sense of a poem as fully and carefully as I can, I will nevertheless be aware that I am far from exhausting its meaning; and hence someone else can say to me, "I think it means something else than what you've said, namely, the following...," and I will often be able to see just what she means.) According to this Heideggerian view, then, the postmodern call for us to attend to polysemy is best taken as a hopeful request for a poetic sensitivity to the inexhaustibility of meaning rather than an insistence on the static infinity of meaning, as an "always more" rather than an "everything at once." (In such a postmodern attunement, as Bono suggests in "Zooropa," "I don't know the limit / The limit of what we got.") This is to take postmodernity to be suggesting, in other words, that the future for which it calls is not here yet, or, better, that it arrives only in the moment of

---

[10] I should acknowledge that, at least in the form of *song*, we sometimes experience a poem that seems to mean *everything* (if only by presenting some aspect of experience so powerfully that we seem to sense everything else reflected in and so connected by it), an experience that transports us beyond the mundane realm of differentiated human meaning in an ecstatic feeling of transpersonal, mystical union with the All. As Schopenhauer – and, following him, the early Nietzsche – recognized, the medium of *music* more easily facilitates such a mystical experience than any of the other arts (as the full title of Nietzsche's great early work already suggests: *The Birth of Tragedy from the Spirit of Music*). Indeed, music may be more likely to facilitate such an experience of mystical union than any other ordinary experience, with the exception of sex itself, at least if it is understood in the transpersonal sense suggested by Plato's *Symposium*. (I shall return to this connection in the conclusion.) I have not tried to apply Heidegger's philosophy of art in any systematic way to the pre-existing aesthetic genres (for the reasons explained in the introduction), but the following questions remain pertinent here: How should we understand Heidegger's critique of aesthetic enframing in relation to music? More important, how might music embody and so help facilitate the spread of the kind of postmodern understanding of being for which Heidegger calls? My sense is that the music that best embodies the earth/world tension will not be as seamlessly polished as U2's music now is (like almost all popular music today). Indeed, insofar as U2's musical world preserves its relation to Heidegger's earth, it probably does so mainly in the passionately unsonorous timbre of Bono's vocals (unfortunately increasingly erased by studio overproduction), which nicely suggest the band's attempt to express a world of meanings that cannot be exhausted, as well as in some of the lyrics, on which I shall mostly focus here. (Thinking about this issue also suggests the deeper point behind Jay-Z's polemic against "Autotune," the widespread computer software most responsible for erasing the distinctive imperfections of human vocal timbre and so technologically homogenizing the sound of many of today's most popular vocalists, in genres ranging from Pop to Rap, a trend first catalyzed by Cher's 1998 hit song "Believe," with its suggestively titled, Autotuned chorus – an apparent paean to enframing: "Do you believe in life after love?")

moving (however incrementally) beyond the destructive aspects of modernity. This postmodern future is not simply implicit in the past (as some of Heidegger's own formulations, like "the beginning ... stands *before* us" [HR 111/GA16 110], risk suggesting), but instead requires the creative efforts of those who would yet "invent" it (that is, literally, enter into it) in order to remain genuinely "futural," that is, open or yet to come.[11] Without endless apology, then, here are the three other main senses of postmodernity we most often hear when we direct the postmodern sensitivity to polysemy back upon the concept of postmodernity itself.

First, to be *postmodern* means *to seek passage beyond modernity* (as we saw in detail last chapter). In other words, "postmodernity" does not name a new historical epoch that is already here, a new age that came after modernity, as one trend might follow another, but, rather, the ongoing endeavor to get free of those modern assumptions that have been most disastrous for our world and in the grip of which we remain so stubbornly caught. To be postmodern, then, is to be on the way or in transition toward another understanding and approach to being, one that not only (1) *transcends* (in the Hegelian sense of negating the negative while preserving the positive at a higher level, but without Hegel's modern assumption that this dialectical *Aufhebung* ultimately serves the teleological aim of generating an all-encompassing conceptual system) our continuing *modern* obsession with extending the human subject's dominance and control of an objective world, but that also (2) "twists free" (in a Heideggerian *Verwindung*) of our distinctive late-modern self-objectification, which increasingly reduces all entities, modernity's celebrated human subject now included, to the ontological status of an intrinsically meaningless "resource" (*Bestand*) standing by merely to be optimized and ordered for efficient and flexible use. This sense of postmodernity also harmonizes closely with the work of such post-Heideggerian thinkers as Levinas – who insists that "infinity" *is* only in the act of "infinition" (that is, the ethicopoetic act of bringing something new into this finite world), an act that must speak to the finite world in order to be understood and so cannot radically break with the past once and for all – and also, albeit in a more complicated way, with Lyotard's thinking of our "postmodern condition" (as we will see shortly).[12]

---

[11] Was not U2's attempt to remind us of this very "futurity" of the future one of the driving impulses of their avowedly postmodern "Zooropa" tour? Slogans like "It's your world, you can change it" flashed across the screens during performances, while songs like "Acrobat," "Zooropa," and "Always" exhorted the audience to "dream out loud." Perhaps this was even partly anticipated on *Rattle and Hum* (the album prior to *Achtung Baby*), where "Love Rescue Me" already celebrated that utopian, revolutionary moment when "I've conquered my past / The future is here at last / I stand at the entrance to a new world I can see. / The ruins to the right of me / Will soon have lost sight of me."

[12] See Emmanuel Levinas, *Totality and Infinity: An Essay on Exteriority*, and my "Rethinking Levinas on Heidegger on Death."

What is so misleading here, however, is that many self-described post-modernists do not use the term *postmodernity* simply as a handy label for the latest challenges to modern assumptions in their particular fields. Instead, apparently hypostatizing and generalizing these developments, they sometimes treat postmodernity to name the new age into which they seem to think they have already irreversibly entered, as if all that needs to happen now is for the rest of us to catch up to where they already are. Such extreme vanguardism, despite its occasional nuggets of truth (for who could deny the great poetic visionaries their defining experiences of a genuinely postmodern revelation?), nevertheless risks degenerating into a naive and dangerously Pollyannish optimism, one that blithely mistakes our late-modernity for a genuine postmodernity. Such rose-colored spec-tacles can blind us to the uncomfortable fact that the modern assumptions we need to twist free of remain deeply and pervasively entrenched in the fundamental but unnoticed ontotheological principles of vision and divi-sion by which we go about making sense of our worlds (as the two previous chapters have sought to show). None of us lives unaffected by the mod-ern subject/object divide or by the late-modern reduction of everything to intrinsically meaningless resources standing by for optimization. None of us are postmodern saints, in this modern world and yet not of it. Still, all of us remain capable of achieving temporary experiences in which the subject/object divide dissolves into a unified being-in-the-world (especially with the aid of art, music, meditation, sport, or religion), and many of us do at least occasionally have an experience of belonging to something that genuinely matters independently of our own goals and desires. (Whether we describe such experiences with names drawn from poetry or religion might be irrelevant, were it not for the way theologians have too often rein-terpreted such experiences so as to falsely suggest that they remain beyond the reach of us mere mortals – an important matter I shall return to in the conclusion.)

Otherwise put, none of us is a postmodern island, but we do have post-modern experiences, some subtle and some profound, which means that there exist, here and there, postmodern archipelagoes jutting out from our modern past into a territory that has yet to take the firm shape of a new land, a genuine "new age" or widespread and relatively coherent historical postmodernity of the kind Heidegger dedicated his thought to preparing – albeit in what he thought was likely to be the rather distant future. To many today, it is not even clear that such a promised land ever could rise from the various mists now darkening our future horizons. Those who doubt that any much new postmodern world is even in the offing find it most suggestive to emphasize the frequent identification of postmodernity with wander-ing and nomadism, with Deleuzean "deterritorialization" and the sojourn without hope of homecoming, with Moses and all those who can only point toward a utopia they know themselves unable to take up any final residence within. Others of us welcome such fellow-travelers but wonder if they will be able to keep their good cheer indefinitely while underway toward a goal they believe they can never reach.[13] We thus think it important, if only to keep hope alive long enough for it to become more than hope, not simply to elevate means above ends, not to permanentize a holding-pattern, not to substitute Nietzsche's "constant overcoming" for the possible arrival of Heidegger's "last God," this being one of the names Heidegger used (as we will see in Chapter 6) to try to help us envision our collective entrance into a genuine historical postmodernity, an historical age in which we, or more likely our descendents, have entirely transcended our late-modern reduction of reality to resource by (to take the most likely path, the one explored in Chapter 3) coming together to recognize and celebrate our belonging to the *earth*.[14]

Let us turn to the second sense. Postmodernism is usually taken to mean an "incredulity toward metanarratives," as Lyotard famously put it in *The Postmodern Condition*, the most influential book ever written about postmodernism.[15] If narratives are the stories we tell ourselves and each other in order to make sense of our lives (by discerning meaning in the historical trajectory of our existence), then a metanarrative would be a perspective from which we could adjudicate between the different and competing narratives currently struggling with one another (tacitly or actively) to tell us our story the most authoritatively. This, moreover, is why one so often hears that postmodernists are *relativists*. If we cannot believe in any standpoint from which we might reasonably adjudicate between competing interpretations of our historical situation, then we are indeed consigned to relativism (and its ethico-political bedfellows, cynicism and interest-driven *Realpolitik*). Fortunately, so the received view goes, "postmodernism" thus understood immediately undermines itself (in a second paradox of reflexivity). For, what is Lyotard's historical claim that we no longer believe in metanarratives but itself another metanarrative? If Lyotard offers us a metanarrative about the end of metanarratives, then he falls into the trap of a liar's paradox (the most straightforward example of which is "This sentence is false," a statement that, if true, must be false, but then, if false, must be true, and so on, in an endless circle or Möbius strip). Put simply, *if Lyotard were right, then we would not believe him*.[16] This is how

---

[13] If such worries get raised by the bleak portrait of "wandering" or "drifting" painted by U2's postmodern appropriation of Johnny Cash on *Zooropa*'s "The Wanderer," they may be partly assuaged by listening to "Kite" on *All That You Can't Leave Behind*.

[14] I develop these ideas further in Chapter 6 and in "Ontology and Ethics at the Intersection of Phenomenology and Environmental Philosophy."

[15] See Jean-François Lyotard, *The Postmodern Condition*, xxiv. Here Lyotard explicitly warns (although critics commonly overlook this), that with this definition he is "[s]implifying to the extreme."

[16] "The [Cretan] liar's paradox" takes its name from a legendary man from Crete who asserted that: "All Cretans are liars." U2 provided audiences with a provocative example

Lyotard is commonly understood, and so quickly dismissed. Yet, this dismissal of Lyotard as self-undermining is much too quick. Like many other dismissals of postmoderism, it commits what logicians call "the straw-man fallacy," rejecting a simplified caricature so as not to have to grapple with an idea in all its complexity and force. In fact, Lyotard's considered view is much more specific than his "extremely simplified" definition of our "postmodern condition," taken out of context and treated as a perfectly general thesis, leads hasty readers (or nonreaders) to conclude.[17]

As the subtitle of *The Postmodern Condition: A Report on Knowledge* suggests, Lyotard's focus is on *knowledge* as it is embodied and transmitted by contemporary institutions of higher education. The important question his famous book addresses is: *What justifies knowledge and the institutions responsible for embodying and transmitting it?* Lyotard argues that we can no longer answer this question the way the philosophical founders of the modern university did. On Lyotard's reading of the German idealists like Fichte, who (along with Schleiermacher and Humboldt) were largely responsible for founding the University of Berlin at the dawn of the 19th century, the point of the modern *University* was either (1) to *unify* the disparate domains of knowledge or (2) to progressively *emancipate* humanity. In the two intervening centuries, however, we have witnessed both (1) the increasing specialization and consequent fragmentation of the various fields of knowledge (undermining our modern faith that knowledge would eventually justify itself by giving rise to a unified understanding of all reality) as well as (2) the uncoupling of scientific progress from the advancement of human freedom (which has led us to grow skeptical about the modern enlightenment's optimistic belief that the growth of knowledge necessarily expands human freedom). Lyotard's famed thesis concerning our "incredulity toward metanarratives" is in fact limited to these two specific examples. His view is that we no longer believe in the metanarratives of *unity* and *emancipation* by which modern philosophers sought to justify knowledge and its institutions, and it is in precisely this sense that we are in a *postmodern* condition. There is thus nothing self-undermining about saying so, nor even in Lyotard's further argument that these two modern metanarratives have now been supplanted historically by the "postmodern" metanarrative of *optimization*, in which all "legitimation ... is based on its optimizing the system's performance" – although I do think it would have been much less confusing if Lyotard had instead referred to this more

of the liar's paradox on their *Zooropa* tour by flashing across giant video screens the message "Everything you know is wrong." For the claim that Lyotard's postmodern thesis is self-undermining (because, being a metanarrative itself, it is caught in a paradox of reflexivity), see, e.g., Reed Way Dasenbrock, "Slouching Toward Berlin: Life in a Postfascist Culture." As I shall now show, however, this widely influential reading is based on an illegitimate overgeneralization of Lyotard's actual view.

[17] See, e.g., Gianni Vattimo, *Nihilism and Emancipation: Ethics, Politics, and Law*, 5–6.

accurately as our "late-modern" condition. For, as we saw in Chapter 2, the progressive spread of the optimization imperative that Lyotard documents (following a Heidegger) emerged from the way we have turned the techniques and procedures devised for controlling an objective world back on the modern subject itself, leading to a late-modern dissolution of this modern subject and its historical self-understanding, without yet putting any more meaningful historical self-understanding in its place.[18] (Thus we find ourselves confronting that historical situation described by U2 in *Zooropa's* "Numb," in which "Too much is not enough.")

Nor does Lyotard cynically simply accept (what he calls) "the postmodern condition" (the condition we have more accurately called *late-modernity*), as critics often assume. Instead, he advocates a *Trojan horse strategy* according to which we should recognize – and provisionally appeal to – this dominant logic of optimization in order to transcend it from within.[19] Lyotard's crucial claims here are (1) that knowledge domains are finite and so eventually become exhausted unless we encourage "paralogy," that is, paradigm-altering transformations of the fundamental assumptions (or "metaprescriptives") underlying and guiding the various knowledge domains, and (2) that such transformations are the most likely source for the emergence of any new historical logic other than the empty optimization imperative. Lyotard argues that the hegemonic knowledge system will accept appeals to paralogy precisely because paralogy promises to *optimize* knowledge (by helping researchers transcend the finite resources of any fixed knowledge domain). Yet, Lyotard suggests, paralogy will also work from within the optimization economy to encourage a fundamental paradigm-shift, which he believes might yet emerge like some metastatic growth from a particularly fecund region of knowledge (ecology, let us hope, rather than cybernetics). In this way, Lyotard thinks we might successfully generate a new justification for knowledge in general (and for institutions responsible for embodying and transmitting such knowledge), a justification that would eventually supplant the empty optimization imperative of late modernity, which itself displaced the modern metanarratives of unity and emancipation (and only then, *pace* Lyotard, would we enter into a genuine *postmodernity*). Thus, although many details of Lyotard's analysis remain questionable (and certainly call for much further thought), he is basically offering a neo-Heideggerian vision for how we might actually go about transcending our current historical self-understanding, that nihilistic reduction of all knowledge and meaning to "optimal input/output matrices" that Lyotard misleadingly calls *The Postmodern Condition*. Lyotard

---

[18] See Lyotard, *The Postmodern Condition*, xxiv.

[19] This Trojan horse strategy also nicely characterizes the "postmodern" spirit of "Zooropa," in which U2 seeks to move us through the banality of corporate slogans into the "guiding light" of "uncertainty" in order to encourage us to "dream out loud" and so "dream up the world [we want] to live in."

is really better understood as a *strategic late-modernist*, then, one who (following Heidegger) suggests that we must face up to our increasingly nihilistic historical predicament clearly and even provisionally accept its terms if we are ever to discover a path leading through and beyond it.[20]

Third, and finally, postmodernism is often taken to connote *the fragmentation of the subject*. The "unholy trinity" of Marx, Nietzsche, and Freud developed their hermeneutics of suspicion to suggest, each in a different way, that the heroic modern conception of an autonomous subject firmly in control of an objective world was an illusion, a surface appearance or projected fantasy concealing the deeper truth that subjectivity is a battleground for forces of which we often remain unaware. These great critics of modern subjectivity focused on domains that philosophers often overlook (such as economics, biology, and mental illness) in order to argue that the subject is a product of more or less unconscious drives for *respect* (Marx, following Hegel), *power* (Nietzsche, generalizing Darwin), and *erotic fulfillment* (Freud, developing Plato).

Compared to these critical analyses, which broke down the modern subject into its component forces, the positive visions of Marx, Nietzsche, and Freud were notoriously underdeveloped, but each did at least try to imagine how a postmodern age might be built up from the fragments of modern subjectivity. Thus Marx envisioned a socialist utopia of mutual respect, in which advances in technology would eliminate the need for the alienating labor that estranges us from ourselves (and so prevents the formation of any satisfying self-understanding), thereby allowing each of us to cultivate (and be *recognized* by others for) his or her unique contributions. (Hence Marx's famous formula for socialism: "From each according to his ability, to each according to his need.") Nietzsche, playing his part in the postmodern drama, announced the death of the God who had guaranteed the privileged status of human subjectivity, predicting the emergence of a "higher type" of human being who would face up to the death of God, embrace the dangerous truth that life is will-to-power, and so set out to reshape human beings the way artists sculpt clay. (Hence *Thus Spoke Zarathustra*'s notorious doctrine of "the *superman*: Humanity is something that should be *superseded*.")[21] Finally, and with comparative modesty, Freud called for the achievement of a new and more austere autonomy, one in which the widespread practice of psychoanalysis would enable us to transmute our neurotic misery into ordinary unhappiness by helping us relinquish our unfulfillable (and paradigmatically modern) subject-centered fantasies, reconcile ourselves to the unquenchable desires that drive us (by acknowledging and then finding socially acceptable ways to sublimate

---

[20] See Lyotard, *The Postmodern Condition*, xxiv, 65. For an explanation and defense of Heidegger's remarkably similar views, see Chapters 3 and 4 of my *Heidegger on Ontotheology: Technology and the Politics of Education*.

[21] I develop these points in Chapter 5. See also Nietzsche, *Writings from the Late Notebooks*, 71.

and express these drives), and thereby reclaim and reintegrate the self. (Hence Freud's well-known psychoanalytic slogan: "Where *id* was, *ego* shall be.") One would need at least two axes to measure the impact of these "postmodern" visions, however, because the considerable influence each of these great iconoclasts exerted historically seems to have been met by an at least equal and opposite reaction (due in no small measure to the way the Nazi and Communist appropriations of Nietzsche and Marx distorted their teachings).

Even if the postmodern visions of Marx, Nietzsche, and Freud worked like powerful magnets, repelling as much as they attracted, the influence of their different ways of analyzing subjectivity into its component forces has been immense, leaving an indelible imprint on the self-understanding of our current historical epoch of late-madernity. For, what emerged historically from this three-fronted dissolution of modern subjectivity was the even broader fragmentation and fracturing of identity we now see expressed in the common claim that "postmodernity" (or what we would call late-modernity) is an age without an integral style, one that – lacking any robust sense of its own positive identity – borrows freely from all other styles in its "postmodern pastiche," famously employing such hospitable techniques as bricolage, *détournement*, and sampling.[22] Not surprisingly, the initial resistance to this fragmentation of the modern self was considerable. It is perhaps most prominently visible in the enduring influence of Kierkegaard's idea that "purity of heart is to will one thing" (hence Kierkegaard's own passionate belief that he could not be *both* a writer *and* a husband, and his famous call for the decisiveness of an *either/or*), a call Heidegger carries over in *Being and Time*'s secularized appeal for each of us to resolutely choose a defining life project (or "ultimate for the sake of which") that will allow us to integrate our various senses of self in the achievement of an *authentic* identity (a vision not so different from Freud's, as the existential psychoanalytic movement enthusiastically observed).[23]

Yet, many contemporary post-Heideggerian thinkers came of age in France during a time (1960–90) when the influence of Marx, Nietzsche, and Freud were powerfully reinforced by what Gary Gutting describes as "the structuralist decentering of the subject," that is, the ambitious development of Saussure's linguistic theory of signs into a general semiotics,

---

[22] It is only here, at this second degree of remove, that we encounter the kind of cultural "postmodernism" that Marxians like Jameson dismiss as a "superstructural expression" of underlying economic forces. (See Jameson, *Postmodernism, or, The Cultural Logic of Late Capitalism*, 5. See also Žižek's polemical and rather superficial critique of Gilles Deleuze's "postmodernism" as an extension of, rather than an escape from, the logic of late capitalism in *Organs without Bodies: On Deleuze and Consequences*.)

[23] On Heidegger's view of authenticity, see my "Heidegger's Perfectionist Philosophy of Education in *Being and Time*." On Heidegger's influence on existential psychoanalysis, see Guignon's "Authenticity, Moral Values, and Psychotherapy," and Keith Hoeller, ed., *Heidegger and Psychology*.

which sought to explain all phenomena by analyzing the structural inter-play of signs instead of the subjective intentions of human beings (hence Lévi-Strauss's antianthropological proclamation that "the ultimate goal of the human sciences ... [is] not to constitute but to dissolve man"). It is not surprising, then, that these more contemporary post-Heideggerians almost unanimously advise us to abandon the quest for a unified identity as, at best, an illusory nostalgia for something we never really possessed and, at worst, a neurotic reaction to the vertiginous anxiety of freedom that leads us (as some might suggest it led the early Heidegger himself) to rush into the arms of an awaiting authoritarian regime, each of which promises us the final reassurance of its one true answer.[24] These French neo-Heideggerians instead call for us to transcend modern subjectiv-ity (and even its echo in the early Heidegger's valorization of the robust, *authentic* self), as we can see, for example, in Foucault's famed prediction of the passing of the era of modern subjectivity ("the end of man"), Derrida's tireless deconstructions of the myths of complete "self-presence," Lacan's neo-Freudian analysis of subjectivity as an ultimately hollow construction, Deleuze and Guattari's "schizoanalysis" celebrating the divided self, and perhaps even in Baudrillard's post-Marxist diagnosis of our late capitalist "triumph of the simulacra," the victory of an age in which our growing pref-erence for artificiality comes to displace our desire for anything real.[25] This last phenomenon especially, I shall now suggest, brings us directly into the sphere of U2's own distinctive postmodern experiment, and so requires us to recognize and confront the real dangers of their postmodern ven-ture ("I'm ready," *Achtung Baby* begins by resolutely repeating). Let us thus examine the stakes of U2's postmodern experiment, asking whether U2 has shown its dangers to be worth risking – and if so, how?

3. U2 AND POSTMODERNITY: *ET TU, BONO?*

U2 has been blessed with a long and influential musical career, one that has passed through an interesting variety of stages and styles. My goal here is simply to facilitate further thinking about U2's famous experiment with postmodernity, the "postmodern phase" they self-consciously entered into with *Achtung Baby* and celebrated in the complex and almost overwhelming

[24] See Gary Gutting, *French Philosophy in the Twentieth Century*, 213–352 (quotations from 225 and 261); Lévi-Strauss, *The Savage Mind*, 13. On the latter critique, see Vattimo, *Nihilism and Emancipation*, 20. Bono too recognizes fascism as a reaction to the anxiety-provoking truth of uncertainty. As he said in an interview: "The fascists at least recognize the void, their pseudo-strong leadership a reaction to what feels like *no* leadership.... Fascism is about control. They know what we won't admit: that things are out of control." (See Flanagan, *U2 at the End of the World*, 172.)

[25] The canonical works here are Foucault, *The Order of Things*; Derrida, *Of Grammatology*; Deleuze and Guattari, *Anti-Oedipus*; Lacan, *Écrits*; and Baudrillard, *Simulacra and Simulation*.

pop-cultural pastiche of the *Zooropa* tour. The obvious question for us, then, is: Which of the four different senses of postmodernity we have explored best allows us to understand the meaning and significance of U2's own distinctive postmodernism? As you may not be surprised to hear, I think the answer is, *All of the above, and more.* In order to see why, let us address a fairly obvious criticism of U2's postmodern experiment.

It is very tempting to understand U2's paradigmatically postmodern song (on which we will now focus), "Even Better than the Real Thing," as a celebration of the allegedly "postmodern" condition Baudrillard characterizes as *the triumph of the simulacra.* How else are we to understand this song's oft-repeated, eponymous chorus ("Even better than the real thing") than as an embrace (whether ironic or not) of a world that is coming to prefer surfaces to depths, images to reality, sex to love, the fake to the genuine? Insofar as U2's famous song does seem to celebrate this "postmodern" triumph of the simulacra, then must we not suspect that its popularity worked to reify that triumph, thereby making U2 into agents, willing or (if the song is meant ironically and that is lost on most listeners) unwilling, of the most nihilistic aspects of such "postmodernity"? Whatever their intentions (and other good deeds), would we not then feel moved to castigate U2 for spreading this triumphant "postmodernity" around the world, like a virus embedded in a catchy hook?

There is no way around it: That is precisely the risk U2 took with "Even Better than the Real Thing," and some superficial listeners may indeed have taken the song in exactly this way and never gone any further, a fact U2 and their fans will have to come to terms with in order to take responsibility for this "postmodern" venture. At the same time, however, I think we can see that this gamble was not an unworthy one. For, if we think about what has been said thus far, we can begin to recognize that there is something else going on in "Even Better than the Real Thing" than a simple capitulation to superficiality and the allure of the artificial. In fact, I know of no sophisticated proponents of any such allegedly "postmodern" celebration of glittering surfaces over mute depths. Some postmodern thinkers, like Baudrillard and Derrida, follow Nietzsche and deny the very existence of any such depths, but in so doing they banish the contrast between surface and depth on which this distorted image of postmodernism depends. This rather common picture of "postmodernity" thus appears to be an unfortunate caricature advanced by superficial critics seeking to portray themselves, by contrast, as sober defenders of tradition and common sense. Such critics thereby fail to notice that the very "common sense" we inherit from the tradition is shaped by the prejudices of modernity, and so functions not only to advance our political and scientific ideals but also to reinforce our internalization of the nihilistic and destructive aspects of the modern worldview (as we saw in the first two chapters). The crucial question remains, then, how might we "twist free" of such a nihilistic, *late-modern* "triumph of the simulacra," thereby transcending it into a genuine *postmodernity*"? It is precisely here, I think, that U2 can help.

Let us remember where we began: The postmodern call for a sensitivity to polysemy suggests that, if U2's "Even Better than the Real Thing" is *genuinely postmodern*, then its meaning cannot be reduced to any straightforward embrace of a single axis of postmodernity, including those nihilistic, late-modern phenomena Baudrillard describes as "the triumph of the simulacra." If the rest of our analysis applies as well, then this song should also suggest an attempt to forge a path through and beyond the problematic aspects of our historical age by attuning us to a more genuinely meaningful experience, and to do so even while the song resists being reduced to any single meaning or simple self-identity. So, does it? I think so, but as they say: The Devil (or God) is in the details.

The lyrics of "Even Better than the Real Thing" are clearly written to a lover ("Give me one more chance, let me be your lover tonight"), perhaps originating as a poetic appeal to a specific lover for another chance (or two, suggesting a certain recidivist repetition of the pattern). If that was its inspiration, however, the song's meaning quickly changes. For, as a song, it is also addressed to a broader audience ("Give me one last chance, and I'm gonna make you sing"), and thus seems to transform this entire audience into the beloved. In so doing, however, it loses its force as an appeal to a particular lost love for a second (or third) chance and becomes an affirmation of the very powerful communal experience that, we can easily imagine, would repeatedly pull Bono and the other members of U2 away from the arms of any particular lover. ("You're the real thing / Even better than the real thing.") Of course, if one insists on hearing the song as addressed to a specific lover, then it seems to celebrate sex above love: With its singer promising an ecstatic but superficial experience ("Gonna blow right through ya like a breeze / ... we'll slide down the surface of things"), "Even better than the real thing" risks suggesting that sexual ecstasy is better than the experience of genuine love.

Notice, however, that if these same lyrics are heard differently – as addressed to an audience, especially a live audience – then, the meaning of these words is subtly but radically realigned. The implication becomes that U2's relation to its audience is "Even Better than the Real Thing," but no longer in the simulacra-triumphant sense that mainstream Western culture does increasingly celebrate sex rather than love. "Twisting-free" of that nihilistic, late-modern vision, the song instead comes to evoke and celebrate the experience of a profound feeling of communal love that transcends and is "even better" than erotic love, an experience in which we can all be taken "higher" and "higher" and "higher" (as the band sings) without ever reaching that fatal point (which the French call *la petite mort*, "the little death") where, like Icarus, our wings "melt" and we fall back down to earth. Heard in this communal register, the erotic meaning that "I'm gonna make you sing" has when addressed to a particular lover becomes transformed, ele-vated into a celebration of communal singing as an ecstatic experience that builds upon the feeling of self-transcendence that transpires in erotic love between two individuals. (This universalization of love – by which U2 seeks to transmute the entire audience into a beloved – works, as Plato observed in the *Symposium*, by generalizing from the particular; it is thus striking that in concert Bono sometimes performs the same gesture in reverse, bringing a particular audience member onto stage in order to sing to her personally, as a particularization of the general audience he seeks to reach through her.)

With the very idea of an ecstatic communal experience transcending erotic love, we begin to tread, I would suggest, into the territory Heidegger calls the *holy*, that which heals us by making us feel whole, raising us up by allowing us to feel ourselves a part of a greater whole to which we genuinely belong. "Even Better than the Real Thing," then, would indeed celebrate the real pleasures of erotic sexuality insofar as these transcend themselves into the communal experience of universal love. Such a love transcends the bounds even of the community in which it is experienced, and so works (erotically, ethically, spiritually, politically) to both reinforce and expand the bounds of those communal bonds by extending the feelings of unity, sympathy, and belonging beyond the contingent limits of a group – and toward that universe experienced in love that both inspires and beckons for such an unlimited embrace.[26] Does the embrace and demand (*Achtung, Baby!*) at the heart of that experience of universal love include and call on me as well? Yes, and *you, too*, if we hear even the band's name polysemically. That is perhaps the deepest message of the *postmodern* U2, which is, at the same time, the *Christ-ian* U2. And by "Christ-ian" I mean Christ-emulating rather than "Christian theology" following, in other words, striving to live (and live up to) Christ's own teachings of universal love (rather than the more narrowly circumscribed and exclusionary creedal statements of the particular churches).

I think Christianity itself was born out of such a fundamental attune-ment of universal love – born, that is, in Christ's own powerful experience of and subsequent call for us too to experience what it is like genuinely *to love everyone and everything*, without imposing borders or distinctions. (In this Christianity represents a significant ethical modification of Judaism, which

---

[26] Such a "promiscuous urge to love without boundary or measure" need not be "unlimited" to the point of meaninglessness, as Harry Frankfurt suggests in his provocative attempt at a *reductio* of the Christian celebration of "divine love" as "infinite and unconditional." As experienced by human beings, at least, such love need only repeatedly exceed and so expand the limits previously placed on *which* individuals and groups we will love. Such experiences feel real and inspiring, and so should not simply be dismissed as something "[f]inite creatures like ourselves ... cannot afford," however "unreasonable" they doubt-less remain. (See Frankfurt, *The Reasons of Love*, 63.)

seems to me to have emerged from an importantly different fundamental attunement, namely, that awesome experience of wonder before the mere fact that reality exists – that *there is something* rather than nothing at all – an experience Christ transforms simply by seeing this reality through the eyes of unlimited love.) If this is right, then understanding "Even better than the real thing" in these terms allows us to recognize U2's postmodern experiment as continuous with, and so not some bizarre deviation from, the artistic trajectory the band has followed all along. U2's postmodern swerve can thus be seen as another switchback on the mountainous path the band has followed as they continue seeking ways to express effectively (and so let be felt in our late-modern world) their enduring commitment to the immeasurable and uncontainable ethical, aesthetic, spiritual, and political implications of the genuinely polysemic experience that postmodernists and Christians (or at least Christ-ians) might yet agree to call *love, charity,* or *peace* (no single element of which can long exist without the others – the words and actions of many prominent, self-described "Christians" notwithstanding).

If I express a certain caution here when predicting that postmodernists and Christ-ians "*might* yet agree," even as Rorty, Vattimo, Caputo, and numerous others seem to be building just such an alliance between postmodernism and Christianity, this is not only because *postmodernity* (as a movement seeking *transition beyond*) reminds us not to foreclose the very "futurity" of the future (the ineliminable unpredictability in virtue of which the future remains yet to come) – a reminder nicely reinforced by U2's Christ-ian teaching (*apropos* of "love") that: "She moves in mysterious ways." My caution also stems from my enduring respect for another "postmodern" strand of anti-theological religious thinking, namely, that heritage running from Kierkegaard through Derrida (and beyond), which valorizes social alienation and the radical individuation it facilitates as an alternative and at least equally genuine and important dimension of religious experience.[27] It thus seems appropriate, by way of conclusion, to suggest that U2's own postmodern Christ-ianity might help inspire us to fruitfully combine postmodernity's competing spiritual pulls toward both the universal and the particular. In this spirit, I close this chapter with the inspired and, I hope, inspiring words from U2's "One": "One life / But we're not the same / We've got to carry each other / Carry each other..."

---

[27] Following in the footsteps of Kierkegaard and Nietzsche, Derrida resists any strong ideal of religious communitarianism in which the individual would feel "herded by a religious community." As he puts it, "I have never believed that it is possible to synthesize the existence of any individual, in any case not my own, and therefore I believe that dissociation is inescapable." (See Mustspha Chérif, *Islam and the West: A Conversation with Jacques Derrida*, 51, 66. See also the essays by Rorty and Vattimo in Mark Wrathall, ed., *Religion After Metaphysics*, and their subsequent interview in Santiago Zabala, ed., *The Future of Religion*. Here my own intuitions remain closer to Kierkegaard and Derrida than to Vattimo and Rorty.)

5

Deconstructing the Hero

The Postmodern Comic Book

> Obviously, if you're going to be doing something new, then to a degree you're destroying – [Laughs] – whatever preceded it.
>
> Alan Moore[1]

> But by my love and hope I beseech you: Do not throw away the hero in your soul! Hold holy your highest hope!
>
> Friedrich Nietzsche, *Thus Spoke Zarathustra*[2]

Our identities as individuals and as groups are shaped, in ways both subtle and profound, by our heroes. If our enemies (and the other "villains" in our psychic narratives) help give us a sense of who we are *not*, of what we stand *against*, then, conversely, our heroes help tell us who we *are*, what we stand *for*.[3] Indeed, as Heidegger recognized, the heroes we choose focus our sense of what is most important in life, shaping our feel for which battles we should fight as well as how we should go about fighting them. Thus, those who chose Martin Luther King Jr. as their hero, for example, pursued very different goals, and pursued them in a very different manner, than those who heroized Adolf Hitler.[4] Despite the obvious differences, however, in both cases the chosen hero functioned like a mirror, reflecting back to the group an idealized image of itself, an ideal concentrated and so given an almost superhuman form. What happens, then, when we

---

[1] A lot turns on how one interprets this laughter – e.g., as anxious, malicious, or *both*. I hear it as both, and hence as expressing the same ambivalence about heroes as *Watchmen* itself. (See Barry Kavanagh, "The Alan Moore Interview.")

[2] Nietzsche, *Thus Spoke Zarathustra*, 156.

[3] This functional definition of the hero suggests that one of the dangers of a group with enemies but not heroes – a group our society sometimes seems to be becoming – is that such a group will only define itself negatively, in terms of what it is *against*, and so become ever more empty, hostile, and closed-in on itself.

[4] Between 1933 and 1938, this latter group unfortunately included Heidegger himself. (On this issue, see later in this chapter and my *Heidegger on Ontotheology*, ch. 3.)

shatter these mirrors? What does it mean when we seek not just to destroy our heroes – to gleefully expose their feet of clay in order to reduce them to their human, all-too-human failings – but to deconstruct the very idea of the hero?[5] Does this deconstruction of the hero argue for – or against – the historical dispensability of the hero? Why do modern Enlightenment thinkers, existentialists, and postmodernists give such different answers to this question? What is at stake in their disagreement?

In pursuit of these questions, we will follow a perhaps surprising itinerary, one that leads back to the masterworks of the great existentialists by way of a postmodern comic book.[6] Written by Alan Moore and illustrated by Dave Gibbons, *Watchmen* is best known as the comic book with which comic books "grew up."[7] *Watchmen* helped accomplish this coming

---

[5] It is important to realize that "deconstruction" (*Destruktion, Abbau*) is not the same as "destruction" (*Zerstörung*). I shall discuss the particular deconstructive strategy employed by Moore later, but for a detailed philosophical discussion of "deconstruction," see *Heidegger on Ontotheology*, ch. 1.

[6] In referring to what may well be one of the great works of postmodern literature, I shall nevertheless avoid the embarrassed euphemism, "graphic novel"; Moore himself rejects this term as a ploy meant to help market comic books to adults. Still, it is difficult to ignore the embarrassment to which such marketing responds. (Michael Chabon, in what is basically a graphics-free "graphic novel" about superhero comics, *The Amazing Adventures of Kavalier & Clay*, recognizes "the opprobrium and sense of embarrassment that would forever … attach itself to the comic book" (75). But Chabon also describes the truly American art form of the comic book as "something that only the most purblind of societies would have denied the status art" (574–5). See also *Unbreakable*, in which Shyamalan makes his case for comics.) A few words about the philosophical study of comic books are thus in order here, as a maximally unapologetic apology for what follows. As the great sociologist Pierre Bourdieu observed, academics are traditionally the dominated members of the dominant class. Owing to this position in the field of cultural capital, we tend unconsciously to turn our backs on our humbler origins and become eager apologists for "high-brow" cultural commodities (opera, orchestra, foreign films, fine wine), while remaining blind to (if not deluded about) the fact that we thereby help legitimate the class divisions such rarefied cultural commodities serve. At the same time, we also tend to denigrate "low-brow" media such as rap music, Hollywood movies, television shows, or, heaven forefend, comic books. (See Bourdieu's *Distinction: A Social Critique of the Judgment of Taste*.) Such unreflexive prejudices may be common, but they are unworthy of a philosopher, who should indeed know (themselves) better. As something of a "high-brow low-brow," a philosopher (or "lover of wisdom") who has long felt love for and drawn wisdom from Hollywood, rap, and – longest of all – comic books (from which I first learned to read), I could hardly refuse when Jeff McLaughlin kindly asked me to contribute a chapter for his book, *Comics as Philosophy* (the origin of this current chapter). For, *Comics as Philosophy* nicely implies that we should treat comics *as philosophy*, clarifying and discussing the ideas these comics contain, instead of just using comics to illustrate pre-existing philosophical theories. Demonstrating the inherent philosophical content of a comic is a more fitting way to give comics their intellectual due than simply showing that they make for good philosophical examples, which (as in the case of Hollywood films, for which comics increasingly serve as the templates) far fewer would deny.

[7] When discussing the maturation of mainstream comic books, Moore is always quick to share the credit (and blame) with Frank Miller. One thinks immediately of *Watchmen* and

of age not by celebrating the *development* of its heroes (as in the romantic *Bildungsroman* tradition stretching back to Homer's *Odyssey*) but, rather, by developing its heroes precisely in order to deconstruct the very idea of the hero, overloading and thereby shattering this idealized reflection of humanity and so encouraging us to reflect upon its significance from the many different angles of the shards left lying on the ground.[8]

1. SHATTERING: FRAGMENT OF A *BILDUNGSROMAN*

With *Watchmen*, comic books came of age, and, in a sense (a coincidence that is not merely coincidental), we grew up together. During 1986–1987, while *Watchmen* was being published, I was an eighteen-year-old freshman at UC Berkeley, living in overcrowded dorms and working part-time at "The Best of Two Worlds," a once great but now defunct comic book store on Telegraph Avenue, right around the corner from the legendary "People's Park." Although I tried to play it cool, this was a dream job for me, as some of my most memorable childhood pilgrimages had been to this very store. To get there, my younger brother and I had to convince one of our parents to drive us (sometimes with a lucky friend or two) from Davis (ninety long minutes away) to Berkeley, where, after being dropped off (always for too brief a time), we hurried past pan-handlers, drug-pushers, mentally ill homeless (quite obviously off their medications), street artisans and performers, plus a wide assortment of colorful locals (I later learned some of their names – the Bubble Lady, Polka-Dot Man, Hate-Man – they sounded like tragically fallen heroes and were embraced by the countercultural Berkeley community as antiheroes), all of whom seemed completely unlike anyone we had ever seen before. As a result, "The Best of Two Worlds" felt like it was located in the eye of a slightly threatening and deeply intriguing storm called "Berkeley."[9]

The owner of "The Best of Two Worlds" – despite being, as comic collectors might say, "a few issues short of a complete run" – knew exactly what he was doing when he hired me. Like most of the core staff I took much of my salary in comics, which meant (because of the difference between

The Dark Knight Returns, but those seminal comics, which forever changed the comics genre, were made possible by earlier work, including Miller's darker reinvention of *Daredevil* and Moore's romantic transformation of *The Swamp Thing*. (For abundant testimony to Moore's worldwide influence, see Millidge, ed., *Alan Moore: Portrait of an Extraordinary Gentleman*.)

[8] One can most easily recognize Homer's *Odyssey* as an early *Bildungsroman* by focusing on the coming of age story of Telemachus embedded within it. *Beowulf* belongs in this genre as well.

[9] This perhaps helps explain why I would choose to go to Berkeley rather than to the more overtly heroic Air Force Academy (one of my own early versions of what Sartre called a "radical choice," a significant parting of the ways on the path of life), and why *Watchmen* would so fascinate me. Clearly (in retrospect), I was already in the grip of an ambivalence concerning the hero that *Watchmen* intensified.

wholesale prices and employee discounts) that we were actually paid very little, and the store benefited from the combined expertise of a group of hardcore comic book fans. Growing up, I was the kid who the owners of the local comic book shop called when they were unable to answer some customer's question; now I was surrounded by comic experts who knew at least as much esoteric minutiae as I did.[10] We employees each had our areas of particular expertise; as befitted a small-town boy, mine was superhero comics. One of the older employees – a diffident artist who exuded that air of bitter superiority any fan of "The Simpsons" would recognize from Matt Groening's grotesque but knowing caricature ("Worst. Episode. Ever.") – took a perverse pleasure in turning me on to *Watchmen*, which was then coming out each month.

To begin to imagine the impact of *Watchmen* on die-hard superhero comics fans like me, visualize a train wreck taking place in twelve monthly installments. I may not yet have recognized *Watchmen* as a deconstruction of the hero, but certainly I realized (with that combination of horror and fascination known to rubberneckers everywhere) that here my precious heroes were being *shattered* before my very eyes, taken apart from the inside out, in the pages of the medium that had always loved and cared for them, and in a style that demonstrated an obvious mastery of this medium that it now set out to implode. As I sift once again through the rubble, it is, moreover, clear to me – for to reread *Watchmen* is to be stunned once again by the brutal clarity of this masterful deconstruction of the hero – that Moore and Gibbons knew exactly what they were doing.

2. REREADING, RETROACTIVE DEFAMILIARIZATION, AND THE UNCANNY

Perhaps the first thing one realizes upon rereading *Watchmen* is that it *requires* rereading. *Watchmen* was written to be reread; indeed, it can only be read by being reread.[11] That may sound paradoxical, but upon rereading

---

[10] I could easily have told you all the first appearances and crossovers of the major and minor heroes, plus every issue ever drawn by the leading artists of the day (Miller, Byrne, and Sienkiewicz loomed largest for me then), but some of my coworkers knew every obscure British fanzine that had ever published a story written by Moore, for example, or exactly what was happening in the then burgeoning world of "underground comics" (for which several of them were busy writing and drawing), or which comics were likely to make the best financial investment (one of my coworkers presciently bought a near mint copy of *Superman* #1 for $10,000; it would probably sell now for more than half a million dollars). It was here that I first found the kind of concentration of creative intellectual talent that I had expected from UC Berkeley itself, but did not encounter there until I started taking advanced philosophy and political theory courses.

[11] *Watchmen*'s first and last images are essentially the same, a device that (as with the first and last paragraphs of Nietzsche's *Zarathustra*) conveys the circularity of the text and so signals the necessity of rereading it. See Alan Moore and Dave Gibbons (with colorist

Watchmen it becomes painfully obvious that the meanings of almost every word, image, panel, and page are multiple – *obviously* multiple.[12] In *Watchmen*, the meanings are primarily multiplied by the fact – and this is painfully obvious when one finishes the series and then rereads it – that, from the first panel (a blood-stained smiley-face, looking like a clock counting-down to midnight, floating in a gutter of blood), the parts all fit into a whole one grasps only in the end (although in retrospect the hints are everywhere).[13] Because that end is so unsuspected and surprising (I shall reluctantly spoil it in the next section), the parts are given a new and different meaning by their place in it. This new meaning, moreover, immediately strikes home as the true meaning of the work, thereby subverting and displacing the first reading.

Rereading *Watchmen*, we thus undergo the same kind of *retroactive defamiliarization* we experience when, rereading Aeschylus's *Oresteia*, we blushingly

John Higgins), *Watchmen*, I.1.i and XII.32.vii. (I refer to *Watchmen* throughout by listing, respectively, the issue, page, and [where relevant] panel number to which I am referring.) See also *Watchmen* XI.23.iii, where the young man who is continually reading the comic (within the comic) hints: "I gotta read 'em over."

[12] As *Watchmen* XI.1.iv–v nicely suggests: "this jigsaw-fragment model … aligns itself piece by piece…. These reference points established, an emergent worldview becomes gradually discernible." Moore explains (in Kavanagh's "The Alan Moore Interview") that "with Watchmen, what we tried to do was give it a … kind of crystalline structure, where it's like this kind of jewel with hundreds and hundreds of facets and almost each of the facets is commenting on all of the other facets and you can kind of look at the jewel through any of the facets and still get a coherent reading." This multidimensional polysemy leads Moore to add (echoing remarks Nietzsche made more sardonically about *Zarathustra*) that *Watchmen* is "tailor-made for a university class, because there are so many levels and little background details and clever little connections and references in it that it's one that academics can pick over for years." That is true, but for the most part I leave the monumental task of cataloguing all of the interconnections to others (several Web sites undertake this daunting task). I might warn them, however, that if they can exhaustively explain the meaning of an artwork, eliminating the earth/world tension by completely "worlding" the earth, then they have thereby undermined its claim to being a true artwork. (I explain this paradox in Chapter 3 and in "The Silence of the Limbs: Critiquing Culture from a Heideggerian Understanding of the Work of Art.")

[13] *Watchmen* uses several other devices to multiply meanings, including, most notably, the story within a story (the books, article, journal, magazine, and comic book within the comic book), which then become multiple allegorical frameworks for interpreting the story in which they are placed. Each issue also employs a different recurrent theme and symbol (named in the issue's title and revealed in a quotation given fully, and revealingly, only on that issue's last page). My favorite example of this device can be found in issue five, "Fearful Symmetry," in which the entire issue is amazingly symmetrical in its panels, colors, figures, and so on. (To see this, compare the first and last pages, then work inward to the amazing centerpiece on 14–15, in which the two pages are a "fearfully symmetrical" reflection of one another.) The point is not only subtly to display a formal mastery of the medium, but also to suggest the necessarily isomorphic and symmetrical relation of life to death – an important and recurring theme throughout the book (cf. V.15.i with V.12.xiii).

realize that on our first reading we had been taken in, along with King Agamemnon himself, by the beautiful duplicity of Queen Clytemnestra's early speeches, for now we recognize that her artful words, seductive on a first reading, drip with venom on a second. Or, to use a more recent example, we experience the same kind of retroactive defamiliarization when, viewing M. Night Shyamalan's *The Sixth Sense*, we share the protagonist's stunning realization that he himself is a ghost, a realization which displaces and reorients our entire sense of the film. (Of course, one does not need actually to re-view *The Sixth Sense* – to view it twice – because Shyamalan, apparently not trusting his audience, embeds a reviewing within it, in the form of a series of flashbacks. Thanks to this rather heavy-handed move – which, to be fair, only Aeschylus never condescends to make – to view *The Sixth Sense* is already to re-view it. This retroactive defamiliarization is precisely what the film version of the *Watchmen* was unable to capture, despite Zack Snyder's almost obsessive faithfulness to the original, and why the film thus flattened out the comic's essential ambiguity and so fell relatively flat in turn.)[14] In Moore and Gibbons's *Watchmen*, Aeschylus's *Oresteia*, and Shyamalan's *The Sixth Sense*, rereading effects this retroactive defamiliarization by undermining and displacing the familiar sense that emerged from and guided the first "reading," changing our minds about what we thought we understood by leading us to recognize that in fact we had not understood what we thought we understood.

With such retroactive defamiliarization, we experience what Heidegger called the "uncanny" (*unheimlich*, literally, "unhomelike"). Although this is rarely thematized, we can only experience this uncanniness (this *Unheimlichkeit* or sense of "not-being-at-home") somewhere that we have first been at home. One's *first* reading of a new text, like one's first visit to a new city or one's first encounter with a new person, might be strange, different, disorienting, even anxiety-provoking, but it cannot be *uncanny*.[15] The experience of the uncanny emerges only with "rereading," when what

[14] The theatrical version of the film eliminated the pirate comic within the comic (although this has been restored in the "Director's cut" version). Because the pirate comic made the most obvious case that the resolute pursuit of heroics can turn you into a villain (showing that the road to hell is paved with heroic intentions), cutting this darkly allegorical tale from the film softened the negativity of the comic's ending and so undermined its profound ambivalence about the future of heroes.

[15] For Heidegger, we constantly experience *Angst* (even our moments of profound joy remain "anxious") because our existential condition itself is ultimately "uncanny" (*unheimlich*). We are never fully at home in the world, Heidegger suggests, because there is nothing about the structure of the self that can ever definitively tell us what to do with our lives. (On this point, see my "Heidegger's Perfectionist Philosophy of Education in *Being and Time*.") Nonetheless, we do not *experience* the uncanny on our first time through something, because the uncanny only becomes tangible to us against the contrast-class of feeling ourselves to be already at home in something. (This, at any rate, is the view that emerges from reading Heidegger's and Freud's insights into uncanniness side by side. See Freud, "The 'Uncanny,'" in *Collected Papers*, vol. 4, esp. 394–9.)

seemed familiar suddenly becomes strange – and *estranging*; it is as if we are gripped by that upon which we have lost our grip. (Here I am using "reading" in the broad postmodern sense, which applies to the lives we lead as well as the texts we more literally "read," since, as Derrida provocatively put it, "There is nothing outside the text" – which does not mean that there is no reality outside books but, instead, that what we like to call "reality" is itself composed of texts that require reading and interpretation, whether or not we notice such everyday hermeneutics.)[16] When rereading uncanny works, we find ourselves no longer at home in our first reading; we realize that the first reading was not a "reading" properly so-called, since (we now realize) we had not yet understood the text on that first reading, although we assumed, of course, that we did understand it, and so we learn (or at least are encouraged to learn) to become more reflective about the course that we have been following with unreflective self-assurance. Shattering this self-assurance – with the realization that we were ignorant of our own ignorance – has been, since Socrates at least, one of the first pedagogical steps (and stumbling blocks) of the philosophical education.

Uncanny works, moreover, in that they must be reread in order to be *read*, teach us something fundamental about reading itself, namely, that at least some of the great works survive and perpetuate themselves not by statically maintaining eternal truths, or even simply by offering successive generations the same experience again and again, but rather by being deep enough – that is, resonant enough, *meaningful* enough – to continue to generate new readings, even those revolutionary rereadings that radically reorient our original sense of the work. It was by helping to effect just such a revolutionary reorientation of the entire genre of superhero comics that *Watchmen* established itself as a great work, an enduring example of postmodern deconstruction. This means that *Watchmen* is not only a work of rereading, a work that we have to reread simply in order to read, but that *Watchmen* itself has to be understood as a rereading of the history of comic books. *Watchmen* gives us a revisionary history that asks (as one astute observer put it), "What would have happened to us if costumed heroes had appeared in reality around the same time they appeared in the American pop consciousness?"[17]

3. DECONSTRUCTION, THE UNHAPPY REALIZATION OF FANTASY, AND NIHILISM

The animating idea in the background of *Watchmen* is as simple as it is compelling: What if superheroes were real? What would it *really* be like if

---

[16] See Derrida, *Of Grammatology*, 158.
[17] On this revisionary history of comics, see esp. *Watchmen* V.29–32 and Sridhar Pappu, "We Need Another Hero."

comic book heroes walked among us? By taking this question with deadly seriousness, *Watchmen* shows that previous comics in fact failed to do so. Yes, Peter Parker had his share of personal problems, but he (let alone his impact on his world) only seems real until one reads *Watchmen*. If, moreover, the *Spiderman* movies did a surprisingly good job of seeming real (and so helping to suspend the disbelief of mass audiences), this was thanks not only to the inspired casting of the main character (Tobey Maguire had already established a Peter Parker–like screen persona in *The Ice Storm* and *Wonder Boys*); it was also because the movies were influenced by a recent retelling of *Spiderman*, which is itself part of a series of deliberately more adult and realist reprisals (namely, Marvel's "Ultimate" versions of its most famous comics), a series inspired in large part by the dark realism of *Watchmen*. (Thus, however ungenerous the sentiment, Moore is not entirely wrong when he denigrates such work as *Watchmen*'s "deformed bastard grandchildren.")[18]

In effect, *Watchmen* makes the case that if our superhero fantasies were realized, our world would be radically altered, and not for the better. In this way it asks us, "Which world would you rather live in?"[19] In the alternative reality that forms the backdrop for *Watchmen*, America won the Vietnam war (with the help of the earth's only super-powered hero, "Dr. Manhattan"). Nixon was never impeached, since an especially right-wing hero ("The Comedian") killed Woodward and Bernstein before they could break the Watergate scandal. There are no longer any superhero comics (apparently no one wants to read about them in a world with actual superheroes; in fact, many ordinary people hate these heroes, who they perceive, correctly in most cases, as right-wing pawns of a repressive government). Instead, very dark Pirate comics now dominate the market (in this reality, unlike our own, no censoring "comics code" was ever imposed because the government protected the genre that inspired the heroes on whom it became politically dependent). The cold war is being won by America, thanks to our having enlisted Dr. Manhattan. Unfortunately, this American "superman" (or "God") has Russia terrified about its chances of

[18] Moore now bemoans this aspect of *Watchmen*'s influence, saying: "When I did *Watchmen*, I thought, great, people are going to feel compelled to look at the clever storytelling involved and they'll feel compelled to match me or better me in coming up with ways for telling stories. But instead, it seems what most people saw was the violence, the grimness, the layer of atheist pessimistic politics that was glossed over it. That's what got regurgitated and recycled" (Moore, "Interview with Jonathan Ross") Neil Gaiman's epic *Sandman* saga might be the only mainstream comic that succeeded in meeting *Watchmen*'s challenge (of course, one needs to read the entire *Sandman* series to appreciate this). Indeed, Gaiman's *Sandman* would be my nominee for the title of greatest comic book ever written.

[19] See *Watchmen* I.31 ("Under the Hood," 5). It is not uncommon for the fantasy genre to contain a critique of fantasy (as, e.g., Anne Rice's vampire novels seek to convince us that we would not really enjoy being immortal), and one can always suspect that such a move is motivated more by "sour grapes" than by an embrace of the human condition as such.

survival, so when Dr. Manhattan decides to leave the earth (humanity having become no more interesting to him than ants are to us), an atomic world war (and planet-destroying nuclear holocaust) seems imminent.[20] It is a bleak vision, to be sure, but one made entirely compelling by the unprecedented wealth of background detail Moore and Gibbons weave deftly into the story.

Moore did not need Jean Baudrillard (perhaps the greatest of the post-modern philosophers) to tell him that "the idea is destroyed by its own real-ization," that the "extreme" development of an idea (which takes that idea beyond its own limits, end, or terminus, into "a state of ex-termination") can thereby destroy it – as, for example, sex is destroyed by "porn," which is "more sexual than sex"; the body by "obesity," which is "fatter than fat"; violence by "terror," which is "more violent than violence"; informa-tion by "simulation," which is "truer than true"; time by "instantaneity," which is "more present than the present"; and as, in *Watchmen*, the hero is destroyed by the superhero, who is more heroic than any hero, but whose extreme "heroics" are no longer recognizable *as heroics*.[21] Moore seems to know instinctively (or else he has, like *Watchmen*'s Ozymandias, stud-ied "a hundred different philosophies") that one of the most powerful deconstructive strategies involves provisionally accepting an idea, thesis, position, or worldview, then working from inside it to extend it beyond its limits until it is eventually made to collapse under its own weight, like a plant forced to bear fruit too heavy for its own branches.[22] I would call this strategy *hypertrophic deconstruction* (after Nietzsche, who recognized that "a hypertrophic virtue ... may bring about the decay of a people as much as a hypertrophic vice").[23] *Watchmen* deconstructs the hero by developing its heroes – extending traditional hero fantasies beyond their limits – to the point where the reader comes to understand that these fantasies, realized, become nightmares.

Watchmen begins, tellingly, with the hero "Rorschach," a hypertrophic development of the Batman archetype. Batman himself, of course, was already a later version of *The Shadow*, a character himself drawn from the

---

[20] Moore lampoons the reactionary, right-wing nature of the superhero, e.g., when he shows the heroes meeting during the Nixon years in order to discuss forming a new team to fight the evils of "promiscuity," "anti-war demonstrations," "campus subversion," "drugs," and "black unrest" (see *Watchmen* II.10.ii, II.11.iv, and VIII.29–31).

[21] See Jean Baudrillard, *The Vital Illusion*, 46–9: "Everywhere we see a paradoxical logic: the idea is destroyed by its own realization, by its own excess. And in this way history itself comes to an end ... [subsequent] history presents itself as if it were advancing and contin-uing, when it is actually collapsing."

[22] See *Watchmen* XI.31 (9 of "Nova Express"). Thus Moore describes *Watchmen* (in "The Alan Moore Interview") as "taking these ordinary characters and just taking them a step to the left or right, just twisting them a little bit.... *Watchmen* was at the time about as far as I could imagine taking the mainstream superhero comic. It seemed to take it to some place that was so completely off the map."

[23] See Nietzsche, *On the Advantage and Disadvantage of History for Life*, 8.

notoriously gritty "detective" genre of pulp fiction.[24] With Rorschach, however, Moore gives us such an extreme version of the archetypal "hard-nosed detective" character that not only Bogart but the entire *film noir* genre (even such ultraviolent films as John Woo's *The Killer*) looks squeaky clean by comparison. *Watchmen*'s intentionally shocking first words (coldly staccato and already slightly disjointed) establish its dark and violent mood: "Rorschach's Journal. October 12th, 1985: Dog Carcass in alley this morning, tire tread on burst stomach. This city is afraid of me. I have seen its true face."[25] As this notion of "seeing" the "true face" already hints, Rorschach takes his name (and his mask, which he views as his own true "face") from the famous "ink-blot test" in which a psychiatrist asks an analysand to interpret an image that has no fixed meaning of its own in order thereby to gain access to the analysand's unconscious as it is revealed in the meanings the analysand *projects* onto the image.[26] By opening (and "closing") the comic with Rorschach, Moore implies that comic book heroes are projections of the fantasies of their readers – as well as of their authors.[27] *Watchmen*'s

---

[24] (As Mungo Thomson reminds me, it was this pulp aspect of Batman that Frank Miller so influentially revived in *The Dark Knight Returns*, revitalizing *Batman* by reconnecting the comic to its pulp origins.) If one views comics from a sufficient distance, one finds oneself confronting the phenomenon that Joseph Campbell – the great Jungian analyst (whose interpretations of myth revealingly applied Jung's concept of the "archetype" to the idea of the hero) – provocatively titled *The Hero with a Thousand Faces*.

[25] (See *Watchmen* I.1.i; on this "true face," cf. VI.17.iv–vi, VI.21.ix, and VI.26.iv.) Rorschach's journal also replicates the detective's "voiceover" in classic *film noir*. In Greek drama, the mask amplifies the voice and so focuses and expresses, rather than hides, the person within (a point nicely suggested by Jim Carrey's character in the movie, *The Mask*). Rorschach takes this so far that he disappears into his mask. Night Owl (his former partner) represents a more skeptical ambivalence toward the adoption of the mask of the hero, which (Moore implies) is a kind of "Jesus costume" through which the hero seeks to provide a kind of secular salvation (cf. VII.8.vi–vii, VII.24/vii, and VII.9.viii).

[26] See *Watchmen* V.18.vi–vii.

[27] (For the connection between Rorschach and the comic within the comic, see V.22.vi–vii, which employs the near homophone, "Raw Shark.") In part to head off the facile response that the idea of comics as projection is merely a projection of Moore himself, the plot of *Watchmen* VI is framed by an ingenious recurring device in which Rorschach himself is subjected to a Rorschach test, a test that he tellingly reverses so that it reveals the unconscious projections of the psychiatrist seeking to administer the test. As a result, the psychiatrist comes to understand his own careerist ambitions as social ideals the internalization of which has alienated him from what he truly cares about, namely, helping people (see *Watchmen* XI.20.vii). Deconstructing these projections puts them out of play, and so confirms the motto from Nietzsche that bookends the issue: "If you gaze [for long] into the abyss, the abyss gazes also into you," (See *Watchmen* VI.28.iv–ix.) In the end, the psychiatrist recovers his humanistic ideals, but then dies – in a noble but futile act of ordinary heroism – because of them. The ending of this subplot is thus more ambivalent about the hero than the conclusion of the comic within the comic itself, which straightforwardly suggests that the attempt to be a hero turns one into a monster. This very contrast represents an ambivalence about the future of the hero, the question *Watchmen* itself concludes by posing (as we will see).

development of Rorschach as a character makes clear Moore's contention that these wishful superheroic fantasies of power stem not just from a deep fear that we are powerless to live up to our own ideals, but also from an even deeper fear that these ideals themselves are mere projections with which we cover over and so conceal from ourselves "the real horror" that "in the end" reality "is simply an empty meaningless blackness."[28] Thus we learn, for example, that Rorschach was driven to become a "masked hero" by the neglect, abuse, and abandonment he suffered as a foster child, that his right-wing ideology is itself a construction with which he tries in vain to please a father he never knew, and that the truly horrific evil he encountered soon after putting on his mask led him to reject his humanity in favor of this mask and so become empty, a blank onto which others project their own fears – becoming, in philosophical terms, a *nihilist*. (As Rorschach puts it: "Existence is random, [it] has no pattern save what we imagine after staring at it for too long. No meaning save what we choose to impose.") Although Moore presents us here with one of *Watchmen*'s brilliantly twisted versions of the "secret origins" device common to all superhero comics, Rorschach's *nihilism* – his defining conviction that reality is ultimately meaningless – cannot simply be dismissed as a symptom of the personal psychological traumas that led him to become a "hero."

Instead, Moore presents nihilism as a psychological state shared by almost all the heroes in *Watchmen*. Initially Moore suggests that, given the black-and-white, all-or-nothing mentality of the kind of person who would become a hero (a person who wants to believe in "absolute values" but encounters only "darkness and ambiguity" in the world), nihilism is a natural fall-back position.[29] It is as if, rebounding from an inevitable collision with moral ambiguity, such a hero precipitously concludes that, since our values are not absolute, they must be relative – their absolutism having led them falsely to assume these alternatives to be exhaustive.[30] Later, however,

[28] See *Watchmen* VI.28.vii–ix. It is consistent that Rorschach, a character whose very name is synonymous with "projection," should project his understanding of all meaning as projection onto the world.

[29] At least for those who do not simply delude themselves. See *Watchmen* I.5 ("Under the Hood," 5) and compare *Watchmen* VIII.27–28 (in which the old, naively optimistic – indeed, delusional – hero is, in effect, slain by the public). See also VI.10.iii, in which Rorschach describes his mask (made from the fabric of a space-age dress ordered by Kitty Genovese – one of *Watchmen*'s innumerable, brilliant little details) in symbolically *absolutist* terms: "Black and white. Moving. Changing shape … but not mixing. No grey. Very, very beautiful."

[30] Following Nietzsche, Heidegger rejects the superficiality of the *either* absolute *or* else relative dichotomy: "We have disavowed an absolute truth. That does not mean, however, that we advocate the thesis of an only relative truth; relativity is merely arbitrariness. The rejection of the standpoint of the absolute truth means, at the same time, the rejection of all relations between absolute and relative. If one cannot speak in this sense of an absolute truth, neither can one speak of relative truth" (LQ 74/GA38 88). For Heidegger (here in 1934 at least), the dimension of truth to which human beings do have access (which

Moore deepens this explanation by suggesting that such nihilism is the natural complement of a thoroughly scientific worldview. As I mentioned earlier, "Dr. Manhattan" is *Watchmen*'s only truly superpowered being; he is a hero of the "Superman" archetype, but his seemingly omnipotent power over matter comes from his own advanced scientific understanding of, and consequent control over, the physical world at the subatomic level. In Dr. Manhattan, Moore embodies our near-deification of science – and its dangers. (With Dr. Manhattan, Moore presents us with a concentrated embodiment of that historical current Heidegger calls "subjectivism.") *Watchmen* tells us not only that Dr. Manhattan "symbolized mankind's problems," but that his name was itself chosen for its "ominous associations," namely, the government-controlled scientific project that produced the first atomic bomb, and so, more broadly, science's godlike power to control nature and its perilous consequences.[31] *Watchmen* thus says that: "We are all of us living in the shadow of Dr. Manhattan"; this "shadow" is the dark side of science – the nihilism of a thoroughly objectified and thereby dis-enchanted world, a world science takes to be intrinsically value-free, and so ultimately meaningless (a meaninglessness which nuclear annihilation threatens to realize).[32] Hence, when told about the murder of another hero, Dr. Manhattan's revealing reply is: "A live body and a dead body contain the same number of particles. Structurally, there is no discernible difference. Life and death are unquantifiable abstracts. Why should I be concerned?"[33]

In the end, *Watchmen* not only deconstructs the motivations of its individual heroes (who become heroes to please their mothers, because

he conceives in phenomenological terms as "the manifestness of entities which joins and binds us to the being of entities") "is quite enough for a human life" (LQ 68/GA38 79).

[31] *Watchmen* XI.22.ii and IV.12.viii.

[32] *Watchmen* IV.32 ("Dr. Manhattan: Super-Powers and the Super Powers," III). The first image after that sentence is a barely disguised "Jolly Roger" (see V.1.i), a skull and cross-bones that, here, symbolizes Rorschach and the projection of meaning onto an empty world. The implication – that Rorschach's nihilism is itself a clear-eyed view of the world science reveals – is reinforced at VIII.18.ix.

[33] *Watchmen* I.21.iii; see also the main debate in IX (through which Moore implies that poetry, not science, will save us). As Night Owl explains (in another of Moore's ironically self-referential passages), "in approaching our subject with the sensibilities of statisticians and dissectionists, we distance ourselves increasingly from the marvelous and spell-binding planet of imagination whose gravity drew us to our studies in the first place." At the same time, however, Night Owl also contends that: "A scientific understanding ... does not impede a poetic appreciation of the same phenomenon. Rather, the two enhance each other"; thus Night Owl expresses the hopeful side of Moore's deep ambivalence toward comics (see *Watchmen* VII.30–1) an optimism that is reinforced by the facts (1) that Night Owl comes out of retirement at the end of *Watchmen* and (2) that *Watchmen*'s signature smiley-face is restored by the recognition that science covers-over the miraculous nature of the everyday (see esp. IX.27.i–iii). Indeed, even Dr. Manhattan has a decisive experi-ence in which the statistical improbability of each individual human life strikes him as a kind of scientific "miracle" (X.27.i), yet his own response will be to leave this "compli-cated" earth in order to create life for himself (XII.27.iii–iv).

of traumatic childhoods, repressed homoerotic urges, naively absolutist worldviews, sadistic desires to inflict violence on others, fetishes for costumes, equipment, night patrols, and so on). By presenting nihilism as the simple, unvarnished truth about life in a godless universe, Moore seeks to deconstruct the would-be hero's ultimate motivation – namely, to provide some kind of secular salvation and so attain a mortal form of immortality.[34] If there is no God, who will save us? This is the basic question to which *Watchmen*'s heroes seek to respond. (Thus the old hero implores the young, would-be heroes who had briefly gathered before him, even as they walk away: "Somebody has to do it, don't you see. Somebody has to save the world.")[35] The hero rises above normal human beings by *saving* them, and, through this secular salvation, he or she lives on in their memory. Ozymandias, the hero who most lucidly realizes all this, unapologetically seeks to put himself in the place previously thought to be occupied by God.[36] His ability to shoulder this superhuman responsibility – by choosing to sacrifice millions of innocent lives in a bid to save the world from nuclear annihilation – not only makes him a hero with which most of us cannot identify, it also puts him above, and so alienates him from, humanity in general.[37]

Although *Watchmen*'s heroes all subscribe to the nihilistic belief that reality is ultimately meaningless, they are *heroes* precisely in so far as they embrace this nihilistic belief and nevertheless seek a path leading beyond it, something the tragic hero has done since the time of Homer by pursuing the mortal "immortality" of *glory* (think especially of Achilles and Sarpêdon in *The Iliad*).[38] By suggesting that all such paths out of nihilism

---

34 When Dr. Manhattan departs for Mars, the juxtaposed text wonders about "the cold distant God" in whose hands fate rested: "Was He really there? Had he been there once, but now departed?" Rorschach describes his own defining epiphany in similar terms: "Looked at sky through smoke heavy with human fat and God was not there. The cold, suffocating dark goes on forever and we are alone." See *Watchmen* III.21.vii and VI.26.ii. (Oblique references to the Holocaust abound in *Watchmen*; see e.g. II.30 ["Under the Hood," 8] and the many appearances of "Krystalnacht.")

35 *Watchmen* II.11.vii.

36 See *Watchmen* II.9.ii–iii; XII.27.ii.

37 In another baldly self-referential moment, Moore (under the pretext of analyzing the pirate comic contained in *Watchmen*) writes: "In the final scenes, thanks to the skillful interplay of text and pictures, we see that the mariner," i.e., Ozymandias, "is in the end marooned from the rest of humanity in a much more terrible fashion." (See *Watchmen* V.31: "Treasure Island Treasury of Comics," 61.)

38 Recall the famous speech of Sarpêdon (a mortal son of Zeus seeking the mortal "immortality" of *glory*): "Ah, cousin, could we but survive this war / to live forever deathless, without age, / I would not ever go again to battle, / not would I send you there for honor's sake! / But now a thousand shapes of death surround us, / and no man can escape them, or be safe. / Let us attack – whether to give some fellow / glory or to win it from him." (Homer, *The Iliad*, 291.) Of course, Homer challenges this view in *The Odyssey* (in Book 12), when the shade of Achilles suggests that he actually made the wrong

may be either hopeless or horrific, and that the heroes' motives for seeking them are either dangerous or else unworthy of our admiration, *Watchmen* develops its heroes precisely in order to ask us if we would not in fact be better off without heroes. In order to suggest a response, let us examine the perhaps surprising conceptual roots of *Watchmen*'s "postmodern" cynicism in the modern Enlightenment, and then show that the existentialists too deconstructed the hero, but that their deconstructions suggest very different conclusions.

4. FRAMING THE FRAME: SHOULD HISTORY DISPENSE WITH THE HERO?[39]

Does the apparent paucity of real heroes in our culture suggest that we are living in a post-heroic age? If not, should we seek to dispense with heroes? Isaiah Berlin famously maintains that Romanticism's tendency toward hero-worship helped spark the flames of fascism, and so he suggests that, after the terrible conflagration of the Holocaust, for one human being to hero-ize another is a dangerously childish refusal of "Enlightenment," and thus

decision when he chose a heroic death that ensured him glory instead of a long but humble life. We could thus say that Moore pursues a deconstruction of the hero already begun by Homer himself. If the hero embraces the tragic *in order to find some path beyond it*, moreover, then this helps explain why "The Comedian" does not really seem to be a hero; he embraces the nihilism of the world only for the licentious freedom it permits him (as if following the maxim derived from Dostoyevsky's *The Brothers Karamazov*: "If God is dead, then everything is permitted"). (See *Watchmen* IV.19.vi.)

[39] Why approach *Watchmen* from this angle? The very title, *Watchmen*, as a reference to Juvenal's "*Quis custodiet ipsos custodes*" ("Who watches the watchmen?" or, as we might now say, who polices the police?), is intended primarily as a political question (see *Watchmen* XI.18.ix, which quotes from the conclusion of the speech that J.F.K. was supposed to read the day he was assassinated: "We in this country, in this generation, are by destiny, rather than choice, the watchmen on the walls of world freedom"). But this reference also implicitly raises the postmodern question of the interpretive frame (a problematic question because it seems to generate an infinite regress): From what perspective can one justify one's own hermeneutic perspective? (On this issue, see Jacques Derrida, *The Truth in Painting*, 37–82.) One of the most influential views of postmodernism equates it (misleadingly, as we saw last chapter) with the claim that there can be no privileged interpretive "metanarrative" (whether Marxist, Freudian, or even existential) from which to adjudicate between competing interpretive perspectives. I think the more defensible view to rely on here is Heidegger's own postmodern idea that no one interpretive frame can *exhaust* the meaning of a true work of art (an idea that in the present context can be combined with Heidegger's warning that the task of seeking to situate one's own perspective is endless, since one can never "get back behind one's thrownness," two points I explain in "The Silence of the Lambs"). Here it is also relevant to recall that in comics, the action always happens outside or between the frames, which are themselves frozen, and that this is esp. true of *Watchmen*, which refuses to employ force lines, blurred backgrounds, and any of the other visual shorthand comics use to convey a sense of motion *within* a single, framed panel. (I owe the latter point to Mungo Thomson, the former to Scott McCloud's *Understanding Comics: The Invisible Art*.)

an historically retrogressive resistance to what was for Kant the "essential destiny" of "human nature": We human beings must grow up, emerge from our "self-imposed immaturity," and have the "courage" to think for ourselves.[40] Have we indeed reached the point in history when, in pursuit of autonomy, we need to put away such childish things – as heroes? Or is the intense cynicism of the times perhaps merely a burnt shell that hides (and thereby also shelters and protects) an inextinguishable human need for something better: Hope, ideals, a future worth pursuing, and heroes to help lead us there? If one takes the history of the West and subtracts all the stories of its heroes, what remains? Can there even be a *meaningful* history – a history worth living – without heroes?

These are fateful questions, for history concerns the future at least as much as the past. We "exist" (from the Latin, *ek-sistere*, to "stand out") historically. As Heidegger saw, we enact the life-projects that render us intelligible – to ourselves and to others – only by projecting the past into the future and so constituting the intelligibility of the present. History is a congealing of this basic temporality; it is time made thick. Indeed, without the historical dimension of intelligibility, our existence would be desiccated, massively impoverished; the temporal frame through which we live would be too transient to sustain the thick worlds of meaning that make us who we are. We cannot meaningfully be without history; so, can history be meaningful without its hero stories?[41] If the West began to confront such

---

[40] See Isaiah Berlin, *Three Critics of the Enlightenment: Vico, Hamann, Herder*. See also Habermas's virulent, neo-enlightenment suspicion of heroes: "It seems to me that whenever 'heroes' are honored, the question arises as to who needs them and why.... [O]ne can understand Bertolt Brecht's warning: 'Pity the land that needs heroes'" (in Borradori, ed., *Philosophy in a Time of Terror*, 43). Cf. Levinas's depiction of Romanticism's "heroic conception of human destiny," in which "the individual is called upon to loosen the grasp of the foreign reality that chokes it," in *On Escape* (1935), 49–55; and Immanuel Kant, "An Answer to the Question: What Is Enlightenment?" in *Perpetual Peace and Other Essays*, 41, 44. Ironically, in order to advocate the sober self-guidance that is supposed to lead us beyond such heroizations, Kant employs an unmistakably *heroic* rhetoric, proclaiming that "the motto of Enlightenment" is "*Sapere Aude!*" ("Dare to Know!"), and pitting Enlightenment "resolve and courage" against the "laziness and cowardice" of "lifelong immaturity" (41). This is not merely a rhetorical inconsistency, but helps us see that Kant advances his critique of *other*-heroization (a form of heteronomy) from the perspective of a particular kind of *self*-heroization (autonomy). In other words, rather than a critique of heroization in general, Kant pits one kind of hero (the self) against another (the other than oneself).

[41] Heidegger's technical answer to this question in *Being and Time* is: No; our temporality is fundamentally an attuned disposedness that projects into the future only by implicitly taking over roles (teacher, husband, parent, etc.). We cannot help but take over "the repeatable possibilities of existence" (BT 443/SZ 391), in other words, and so we can at best do so reflexively, by recognizing the implicit role played by role-models, exemplars, or "heroes" in always-already disposing us toward the particular roles through which we come to understand ourselves. The unthinking appropriation of existential roles in inauthentic heroization thus becomes explicit (or at least lucid) in authentic heroization.

fateful questions as the last millennium drew to a close, this was due not only to the eschatological despair that drives millennialism and thereby betrays our (more or less conscious) belief that *history is over* – a thanatological belief that in fact has been haunting the cultural unconscious of the West for almost two thousand years but which, as our technology becomes ever more destructive, is in increasing danger of being self-fulfilling.[42] This fateful questioning of the hero also emerges even more directly in those philosophical countermovements to millennial despair (postmodernism, postcolonialism, postimperialism, and the like), which often seek to get us beyond our destructive desires to get beyond (our limits, borders, finitude, and so on).

In *Watchmen* (a work that, as mentioned earlier, is now widely regarded as a masterpiece of "postmodern literature"), the imminence of just such a self-fulfilling apocalypse is one of the major points of departure for the plot. Recall that *Watchmen*'s signature image (which appears on *Watchmen*'s first cover as well as its first and last panels) depicts a blood-stained happy-face, the blood transforming the smiley into a millennium-clock twelve minutes (that is, twelve issues) away from midnight.[43] Ozymandias – the heroic "world's smartest man," who uses his intelligence to avert nuclear holocaust in the shocking culmination of the story – tells an interviewer earlier that: "I believe there are some people who really do want, if only subconsciously [*sic*.], an end to the world.... I see the twentieth century as a race between enlightenment and extinction."[44] If Ozymandias sounds like Isaiah Berlin here, however, we need to recall that Ozymandias intentionally kills millions of innocent people ("half of New York") in a successful bid to convince cold-warring nations on the brink of a nuclear war that they are being attacked by an alien species and so must put aside their differences and band together in order to survive.[45] This is no mere

[42] Our unconscious solution to the long-anticipated arrival of the millennium was ingenious and revealing; we simply transformed our millennial despair into a technical problem (the quickly forgotten "Y2K Bug"), and then channeled our fears into practical attempts to solve this "glitch in the programming." This explains why the dangers of the "Y2K Bug" were so incredibly exaggerated (viz., because it served as a stand-in for our deeper fear of the end of time or apocalypse), and so also revealed our (pre-9/11) optimism that we could "de-bug" death from the human genetic "program" (perhaps the ultimate goal of science). (On Heidegger's own understanding of the danger of this self-fulfilling prophecy, see Chapter 7.)

[43] See *Watchmen* I.1.i and XII.32.vii.

[44] See *Watchmen* XI.32 (10 of "Nova Express"); ironically, here "the world's smartest man" confuses the subconscious with the unconscious. Showing himself to be an extreme disciple of Enlightenment, Ozymandias will later speak of ushering "in an age of illumination so dazzling that humanity will reject the darkness in its heart" – and, as he says this, he finds himself confronting a "disappointed" god-figure. (See *Watchmen* XII.17.ii–v.)

[45] Mungo Thomson informs me that this plot device comes from a 1950s' episode of *The Outer Limits* called "The Architects of Fear" (starring Robert Culp, who later figured prominently in the 1980s' TV show "The Greatest American Hero," in which the action,

triumph of consequentialist reasoning over the deontological ethics of the Enlightenment. Read carefully (which, I have argued, is the only way it can be *read*), *Watchmen* clearly calls Ozymandias's "less obvious heroism" into question along with the more traditional "schoolboy heroics" of the other heroes, who proved incapable of resolving a world crisis of such magnitude.[46] Thus, in all the ways we have seen (and more), *Watchmen*'s deconstruction of the hero suggests that perhaps the time for heroes has passed, and this, as we will see next, distinguishes this postmodern work from those deconstructions of the hero in the existential tradition that preceded and helped generate the postmodern movement.[47]

5. EXISTENTIAL DECONSTRUCTIONS OF THE HERO

Existentialism, that philosophical tradition previously best known for radical questioning (the tradition that, with Heidegger, gave us the very

drama, and comedy revolve around the Moore-like question, "What happens when you give a 'normal,' gainfully-employed, family-man superpowers?"), and he points out that Moore cites "The Architects of Fear" at the end of *Watchmen* (it is playing on a TV in the background in XII.28ii–iii). Moore's plot device also borrows freely from H. P. Lovecraft's "The Call of Cthulhu" (1928) (although this aspect of the comic was also cut from the film). When asked, "Who'd believe an alien invasion?", Ozymandias responds by quoting the principle that guided the Nazis' anti-Semitic propaganda: "People swallow lies easily, provided they're big enough" (*Watchmen* XI.36.iii). *Watchmen*'s climax thus complicates Žižek's hypothesis that: "Disaster films might be the only optimistic social genre that remains today, and that's a sad reflection of our desperate state. The only way to imagine a Utopia of social cooperation is to conjure a situation of absolute catastrophe." (See Žižek, "Disaster Movies as the Last Remnants of Utopia.")

[46] Cf. *Watchmen* XII.27.i with XI.13.vi and XI.23.i: The obvious parallels between Ozymandias and the would-be savior of his hometown in the pirate comic suggest that Ozymandias's "innocent intent" to save the world has destroyed him, undermining not only the "schoolboy heroics" of the traditional superhero but also his own darker and "less obvious heroism" (XII.17.i). The very name *Ozymandias*, moreover, implicitly connotes the futility of all dreams of empire. (In *Watchmen*, Ozymandias personifies that empire of capitalist imperialism, which wears a liberal-democratic mask, now often referred to cynically as "neo-liberalism"; Moore was responding to Thatcher's neo-Reaganite policies.) As Moore obviously knows (but does not say in *Watchmen*), the arrogant lines quoted from Shelley (on XI.28: "My name is Ozymandias, king of kings:/Look on my works, ye mighty, and despair!") are, in Shelley's poem, found engraved on the base of an ancient monument that now lies shattered and half-buried in the sand. (This context helps one understand Dr. Manhattan's final answer to Ozymandias: "Nothing ever ends"; see XII.27.v. Cf. the epigraphy of my *Heidegger on Ontotheology*.)

[47] By the end of *Watchmen*, Ozymandias changes the fragrance line he sells from "Nostalgia" to "Millennium" (see XII.31.iv) because he has helped shift the cultural mood from a retrospective pessimism to a forward-looking optimism. Yet, "Millennium," a word with thanatological undertones, is an odd name for a product meant to embody the victory of "Enlightenment" over "extinction," and so helps (along with the neo-Nazi aesthetics of the advertising campaign for "Millennium," one of many ways in which Moore associates Ozymandias with Nazism) to signal the darker undercurrents of *Watchmen*'s conclusion.

concept of *deconstruction*), questioned, but did not overturn, the great importance Western history has always accorded to the hero. ("Always," here that means – since we are talking about Western history – beginning with our own beginning: Our founding myths are mostly hero stories and, as Xenophanes and Plato already complained long ago, these are far from being morally unambiguous tales.) In fact, of the three greatest existential philosophers, Nietzsche and Heidegger both found it easier to give up their own devout Christianity than to stop believing in heroes.[48] The third, Kierkegaard, transformed Christian faith itself into an heroic act, heroizing faith in provocatively contemporary terms: Kierkegaard's "knight of faith" is essentially a secret identity, an identity "the public" can never see. Wrapping this existential riddle inside the enigma of his own authorship, Kierkegaard permitted himself to describe his hero (which is also an obvious attempt at self-heroization) only while masking his own authorial identity with various pseudonyms.[49] This doubly secretive strategy for self-heroization is repeated by Rorschach – the hero and antihero (really, he is both) who initially occupies the shifting center of *Watchmen* – when he chronicles, and so seeks to justify, his own would-be heroics in "Rorschach's Journal," a literary device that serves both as an homage (ironic or not) to the tradition of the detective's voiceover in *film noir* and, more importantly, as a symbolic stand-in for the projected fantasies of the comic book as such. It is thus telling that *Watchmen* not only opens with this "Journal" but closes

[48] Heidegger explicitly rejected the label "existentialist" in The Letter 'On Humanism,'" but that was really because *he did not want to belong to any club that would have Sartre for a member* (or, more precisely, that would allow Sartre, rather than Heidegger himself, to write the "existentialism" club charter, which Heidegger in fact rewrites in his own image in "The Letter"). I hope that my employment of heroic terms ("the three greatest") in a context concerned with questioning such terms will not be seen as begging the question with which we began. I do recognize that it tips my hand a bit, or rather that it would, if my epigraph from Nietzsche had not done so at the outset by indicating one of the philosophical intuitions guiding me here, *viz.*, that, however problematic, heroes are indispensable for history-making (which, in turn, is needed to transcend the nihilism of the age). I should perhaps also respond to the criticism that I myself am guilty of heroizing Nietzsche, Heidegger, and Moore. On Nietzsche and Heidegger's closely related definitions of the hero (see below), this is true: I not only admire aspects of their thought, but have made those aspects part of my own philosophical identity through a series of creative interpretive appropriations (or hermeneutic *introjections*). There are, of course, many senses in which I do not want to be anything like them (!) – were that not the case, then my self-constituting interpretations of their work would not need to be particularly creative. If, as I maintain in my opening paragraph, a hero functions as an individual or community's idealized self-projection, a projection that helps focus their guiding sense of self, then certainly these thinkers (among others) play that role for me. This entire chapter, moreover, in that it argues for the indispensability of heroes, can be understood as a response to the charge that such heroization constitutes a telling criticism.

[49] Although both Kierkegaard and Rorschach keep their identities secret, their masks confer rather than disguise their "true" identities, amplifying and focusing the self, character, or "personality" speaking through the mask.

with it as well (and "closes" precisely by leaving *open* – however seemingly pessimistic its suggestions on this score – the question of whether or not comic books have any future).[50]

Why, then, do the three greatest existentialists vehemently resist the Enlightenment suggestion that the time for heroes is past? It is important to understand that these existentialists inherited two great but conflicting traditions: On the one hand, the modern Enlightenment revolution (which celebrated Reason *über alles* and so stripped the holy halos from the heads of earlier saints and saviors, leaving only a "de-auratized," halo-free world), and, on the other hand, the Romantic counterrevolution (which sought to resacralize the world by recognizing that the sources of meaning always exceed the current forms of human understanding).[51] Kierkegaard, Nietzsche, and Heidegger recognized that the Enlightenment yielded powerful and important insights into the "transcendental" structures that make existence as we know it possible, but they also believed that the possible *should* always "transcend" existence as we know it, and so they held that human beings, in order to lead lives worth living, need to celebrate the romantic *imagination* that creates the possible as well as the enlightened *reason* that discovers the actual.[52] It is, however, precisely this Romantic current in the existentialists' work (succinctly expressed by Nietzsche's anti-Enlightenment quip: "Not only light but also darkness is required for life by all organisms") that renders existentialism vulnerable to criticism from those neo-Enlightenment movements that seek to move us historically beyond our need for heroes.[53]

---

[50] See *Watchmen* I.1.i; XII.32.vii; and cf. V.12.vi; *Watchmen* is "closed" only in the sense that a line is closed when it is made into a circle. On the question of the dispensability of the hero, Moore himself now seems deeply ambivalent. In Kavanagh's "The Alan Moore Interview," Moore says: "at the time I think I had vain thoughts, thinking 'Oh well, no one's going to be able to follow this, they'll all just have to stop producing superhero comics and do something more rewarding with their lives.'" Yet, the penultimate scene of *Watchmen* is of two aging heroes preparing to return to their "adventuring" (see XII.30.ii).

[51] See Max Horkheimer and Theodor Adorno, *Dialectic of Enlightenment: Philosophical Fragments*.

[52] It is perhaps not too great an oversimplification to point out that a significant strain of the intellectual (or "spiritual," *geistlich*) history of the last few centuries can be sketched as a series of skirmishes in the ongoing conflict between Enlightenment and Romanticism: The Enlightenment throws off the "dogmatism" of a religious worldview; Romanticism rejects the triumph of Enlightenment rationality as sober but unsatisfying; the existentialists seek to rehabilitate Romanticism's call for meaning within a broadly Enlightenment framework; Berlin and other liberals reject this Romantic counterrevolution as politically disastrous and call for a return to the Enlightenment; postmodernists rebel against this return to the privileged metanarrative of Reason while nevertheless reviving its suspicion of heroes, master-concepts, and so on.

[53] See Nietzsche, *On the Advantage and Disadvantage of History for Life*, 10. These "neo-Enlightenment" views can, but need not, share the Enlightenment belief that reason is *sufficient* for happiness (the view Nietzsche denigrates as "Socratic optimism" in *The Birth of Tragedy*).

This vulnerability can be seen most clearly in the fact that Kierkegaard's *heroization* of faith stands or falls along with the fate of the hero in general. For, put simply, if there can be no *heroes*, then there can be no *heroizations*.[54] This same vulnerability holds, albeit in a more complex way, for Nietzsche's own heroic struggle against historical nihilism, the existential mission that animates Nietzsche's work as a whole and that is at the heart of his self-proclaimed magnum opus, *Thus Spoke Zarathustra*. *Zarathustra*, of course, is the text that gave us the very idea of the "superman" (*Übermensch*), Nietzsche's personification of the neo-Darwinian idea that *history is not over*, since humanity too "is something that shall be superseded."[55] Indeed, Nietzsche equates belief in the hero with hope for the future (as the epigraph over this chapter indicates: "But by my love and hope I beseech you: Do not throw away the hero in your soul! Hold holy your highest hope!"). Those individuals who would participate in the creation of a

---

[54] If nothing can be an X, then nothing can be made into an X. No liquid, no liquefaction, no heroes, no heroization, and so on. (Someone might object, e.g., that while there are no demons, there are certainly *demonizations*. But a person "demonized" is transformed rhetorically into something that does not actually exist, which helps explain why such rhetorical moves are so objectionable. As I noted earlier, however, even Kant himself proved incapable of abiding – in his *rhetoric* – by this strict logic of Enlightenment.) A would-be "enlightened Kierkegaardian" might try to avoid this problem by insisting that, since Kierkegaard distinguishes the "knight of faith" from the "tragic hero" in *Fear and Trembling*, he does not in fact "heroize" faith. Yet, not only is Kierkegaard's distinction quite idiosyncratic (since a knight is the very paradigm of the medieval hero), the distinction also turns on Kierkegaard's questionable claim that we can understand the tragic hero, but not the knight of faith. (Can one really "understand" Hector or Achilles, let alone Oedipus or Antigone? Not, I would argue, without becoming sufficiently like them.) As Andrew Cross shows, moreover, Kierkegaard's knight and hero stand in a relation of isomorphic interdependence, each completing the other (each is the other's "better nature"; see Cross, "Faith and the Ethical in *Fear and Trembling*"). If Cross is right, then even within Kierkegaard's idiosyncratic conceptual vocabulary, one can say that Kierkegaard gives us a "poetic heroization" (or "heroic poeticization") of faith. (The concepts of the hero I have analyzed in this chapter, however, remain significantly broader than Kierkegaard's own.) Alternatively, a postmodern Kierkegaardian might try to argue that we cannot say that the Knight of Faith is a heroization of Kierkegaard himself, since Kierkegaard entirely disappears behind (or into) his pseudonymous masks, such that even his signed works and journals are (allegedly) just further masks. That response, however, only extends the parallel with Rorschach (who also disappears into his mask), while missing the general point that there is almost never a superhero without an unknown "secret identity" (seeming exceptions, like Wolverine, fit the pattern on closer examination). Not only is this secret identity unknown to the heroes' admirers, but their public character is usually perceived to be the very opposite of their heroic self (think, e.g., of the "nerdy" Peter Parker and Clark Kent, who look cowardly because they are always "running off when trouble starts," and also of Kierkegaard's vicious caricature in *The Corsair*). This opposition, we can imagine, continues to motivate their compensatory heroics (potentially into the kind of vicious shame/exhibition cycle Moore analyzes in works such as *Miracleman*).

[55] See Nietzsche, *Thus Spoke Zarathustra*, 124: "*I teach you the superman*. Humanity is something that shall be superseded."

more meaningful future need to be inspired by the great heroes of the past, Nietzsche thought, ultimately so as to overcome these heroes and thereby become "overheroes" – or, better, "superheroes" – that is, even greater heroes for the future. The "superhero" (another Nietzschean conception) is someone who becomes a hero by superseding the hero who inspired him or her. (As *Zarathustra* says: "For this is the soul's secret: Only when the hero has abandoned her, is she approached in a dream by the superhero [*Über-Held*]."))[56]

Under the influence of the comics Nietzsche unintentionally helped inspire, we tend to think of *Superman* as a type of superhero, but on Nietzsche's view, it would be more accurate to say that all superheroes are variations of the "superman" archetype. (Applied to the history of comic books, this overly reductive view can be surprisingly revealing.)[57] The "superman" personifies Nietzsche's idea that the creation of a future worth living in requires the continual supercession of the past, while his "superhero" symbolizes his component claim that in order to help create that future, we must supersede even the *heroes* of the past. (Thus, in the fourth and final book of *Zarathustra*, Zarathustra himself finally becomes the superman only by superseding the greatest heroes of the past, "the higher men," each of whom represents a different peak of past human achievement.) One of the lessons Nietzsche drew from his (mis)reading of Darwin was that to survive in a competitive environment organisms cannot remain static but must continue to grow and develop over the generations. By helping us supersede even our greatest past achievements, the Nietzschean superhero serves the "constant overcoming" – or "will to power" – whereby "life" keeps itself alive.[58]

---

[56] See Nietzsche, *Thus Spoke Zarathustra*, 231.

[57] *Watchmen* clearly recognizes that "superheroes" need not literally have "super powers." (On this point, to which I return later, see also Moore's *Supreme* comics and Chabon's *The Amazing Adventures of Kavalier & Clay*, 74–77 and *passim*.) The creation of America's famous "Superman" in 1938 was in part an ideologically motivated response to the Nazis' glorification of the Aryan superman (an idea that, in so far as the Nazis conflated it with an equally superficial appropriation of Nietzsche's "blond beast," they almost completely misunderstood). Chabon's retelling nicely replaces Superman with own Houdini-esque hero, "The Escapist," in order to transform the common anticomics charge of *escapism* into a celebration of comics' "noble" and "necessary" ability to liberate the imagination and so help us escape oppressive regimes and realities (see 575–6, 582, 620). It would thus be illuminating to read Chabon's heroization of escape – as resistance to tyrannical "senses of reality" (to borrow Berlin's language) – in terms of Levinas's idea that "escaping is the quest for the marvelous," the "need to get out of oneself, that is, *to break that most radical and unalterably binding of chains, the fact that the I is oneself*" (*On Escape* [1935], 53, 55).

[58] Here Nietzsche thought he was criticizing Darwin when he was really making almost the same point. (See *Thus Spoke Zarathustra*'s section "On Self-Overcoming," 225–8, and John Richardson, *Nietzsche's New Darwinism*.) Max Scheler appropriates this Nietzschean idea when he characterizes "the hero" as the exemplary embodiment of "life values." (See Manfred Frings, *The Mind of Max Scheler*.)

Nietzsche thus believed that without the continued emergence of new heroes, "superheroes," we will have no future – whether this absence of a future means the literal annihilation of human civilization (as in *Watchmen*), or the endless repetition of an old value system that becomes increasingly worn-out and meaningless to us (as in *Zarathustra*). Since, for Nietzsche, only a superhero should dare to undertake the dangerous venture of questioning the heroes of the past, this means that *past heroics may be questioned only for the sake of future heroics*; we should overcome our heroes only to become heroes ourselves. Thus, Nietzsche's deconstruction of the hero never calls into question the idea of the hero as such. It is Moore who uses *Watchmen*'s two main "superhero" candidates – Ozymandias and Dr. Manhattan – to demonstrate the dangers of this Nietzschean ideal. As we have seen, Ozymandias succeeds, where even his hero Alexander the Great did not, in unifying the world, but at the cost of alienating himself from humanity by rising so far above them. Thanks to a more extreme version of this alienating transcendence, the superficially more Superman-like "Dr. Manhattan" becomes a "God" rather than a human being (as *Watchmen* makes clear), eventually abandoning our world to go create one of his own.[59] Nevertheless, Nietzsche maintains, however dangerous the idea of the superhero remains, we cannot give it up without risking the future itself.[60]

Heidegger, the last and most complex of the three great existentialists, explicitly chooses Nietzsche as his own philosophical "hero" and so, as a faithful Nietzschean, seeks to overcome Nietzsche – with all the paradox (and hermeneutic violence) that notoriously involves.[61] In other words, Heidegger's attempt to supersede his hero Nietzsche follows from an acceptance (and critical appropriation), not a rejection, of Nietzsche's own conception of the hero. In fact, with *Being and Time*'s notion of "authentic historicality" (BT 429–439/SZ 376–77), Heidegger explicitly formalizes an idea he learned from his appropriation of Nietzsche, namely, that the true heritage of an otherwise stultifying tradition is best kept alive via "reciprocative rejoinders," sympathetic but critical appropriations of the

[59] See *Watchmen* XI.14.vii. Ozymandias describes his own transformation into a "super-human" (*Watchmen* X.32), but Moore makes clear that the catchphrase announcing Dr. Manhattan, "The superman exists, and he's American," was actually a corruption of "*God* exists and he's American" (cf. IV.13.i and IV.31). Moreover, Dr. Manhattan's human name, Osterman, connotes Easter (*Oster*), and thus divine rebirth, a connotation rein-forced by the Christ-like pose in which he is first reborn (see IV.10.iv), and by the end of *Watchmen* he is no longer a human being at all (see XII.18.ii).

[60] For a critique of Nietzsche's dangerous conception of the hero, see Alexander Nehamas, "Nietzsche and 'Hitler.'" Interestingly, Moore's Ozymandias calls into question Nehamas's rejection of Nietzsche's "evil hero" by providing precisely the kind of example Nehamas himself finds "difficult to imagine" (101).

[61] For a sympathetic reconstruction of Heidegger's controversial critique of Nietzsche, see Chapter 1.

"heroes" of the past by which we develop and update our chosen hero's mission or example so that it will be capable of meeting the changed demands of our contemporary world.[62] Not surprisingly, then, Heidegger supersedes Nietzsche and Kierkegaard (even as he critically appropriates their views) when, in 1927's *Being and Time*, he deconstructs the hero, seeking to describe the structural features of the process whereby individuals and social groups constitute fundamental aspects of their own identities by "choosing their heroes."

In Heidegger's view, although the heroes we choose fundamentally shape our sense of self, initially we choose our heroes without even being aware that we are choosing them, and, moreover, we tend to choose from the same predetermined array of stock heroes as everyone else. By simply taking over a hero society has prepackaged for us, we are doing what Heidegger calls choosing "the anonymous anyone" for a hero (BT 422/SZ 371). Whether the hero unreflexively embraced is Michael Jordan, Albert Einstein, or Marilyn Manson, such conformist (or "inauthentic") heroization helps perpetuate the status-quo sense of what matters in life, be it athletic excellence, scientific genius, or a route to rebellion already mapped out by the status quo – and so a rebellion that (like the aforementioned political protest that accepts its confinement to a "pre-determined protest area") tends unintentionally to reinforce the very order it rebels against.[63] Nor am I necessarily any closer to owning my own identity simply in virtue of having chosen a more marginal figure – such as John Muir, Ansel Adams, or Julia "Butterfly" Hill – as the hero who inspires my defining existential projects (here, say, "deep-ecological" environmentalism) and so my sense of self. In terms of *authenticity* (*Eigentlichkeit*, more literally "ownedness"), what matters is not the type of hero chosen so much as the way that hero is chosen and made my own.

For, Heidegger believed it possible, in a "moment of vision," to step back from the heroes we have "always-already" chosen, adopt a second-order perspective on those choices, and choose again, in full awareness that we are choosing a hero, and that doing so lucidly can help us own our own

---

[62] Habermas revealingly (if, as usual, reductively) traces back to Kierkegaard Heidegger's understanding of historicality (often misleadingly translated as "historicity"); see Habermas, *The Future of Human Nature*, 5–11.

[63] This is not to denigrate Marilyn Manson (or Einstein, or Michael Jordan); what really matters, for Heidegger, is that such a "hero" be chosen *authentically* by a particular individual as his or her hero, with all that entails (see later). The same could obviously be said of the many different comic book heroes, which function similarly. (Hence, those who know comic books can often get a quick sense of what matters to one another just by finding out which comic book heroes were favorites: Wolverine? Fierce rebellion coupled with integrity and loyalty to friends. X-Men in general? A hope that the exceptional "gifts" for which one is ostracized will also allow one to contribute to the struggle for good. Superman? Hope that American ideals will win out in the end. Spiderman? Intelligence and the wisecracking courage to stand up to the world's bullies. And so on.)

lives in a way that will restore our sense of the meaning, weight, and integrity of our actions.[64] With such "authentic" heroization, what is crucial is the "reciprocative rejoinder" mentioned earlier, whereby we critically appropriate our heroes by interpreting and updating their "mission" so that it speaks to the changed demands of our own world. In this way, we keep alive what our hero stood for in our own lives, rather than simply admiring our hero from afar, worshiping them from a safe distance. When we choose our heroes inauthentically, we do not really have to do much (to "Be like Mike," apparently I simply need to drink Gatorade), and, moreover, our society will subtly reassure us that we have made the right choice (since, sticking with this example, our society continually reinforces its bread-and-circuses celebration of professional athletics).[65] When we choose our heroes authentically, however, we take more upon ourselves (here, I would actually dedicate myself to becoming like my hero Mike, and I would also have to take responsibility for my interpretation of what that demands), and the result is much riskier (for I actually need to try, and thus am quite likely to fail, to become like Mike in some exemplary respect).[66]

Authentic heroization thus requires us to chart a difficult middle course between the Scylla of deifying or idolizing our heroes, placing them so far above ourselves that we do not even try to follow in their footsteps, and the Charybdis of simply reducing them to their human, all-too-human failings in such a way that they fail to inspire us to try for ourselves something we would not otherwise dare.[67] If we choose our heroes authentically,

---

[64] In Heidegger's words: "The authentic repetition of a possibility of existence that has been – the possibility that Dasein may choose its hero – is grounded existentially in anticipatory resoluteness; for it is in resoluteness that one first chooses the choice of that which first makes one free for the struggle of loyally following in the footsteps of that which can be repeated." (BT 437/SZ 385) See also Charles B. Guignon, "Authenticity, Moral Values, and Psychotherapy," and my "Heidegger's Perfectionist Philosophy of Education in *Being and Time*."

[65] None of us are immune from such influences, of course. A few years ago I attended a meeting of the North American Nietzsche Society in which Nietzsche scholars read papers on the subject of "Nietzsche and Sport"; one after another, they each maintained that Nietzsche would have loved the same culturally banalizing professional sporting events they themselves seemed to worship – from afar.

[66] In *Watchmen*, too, the "public" – nicely embodied in the shifting scene surrounding the appropriately Kierkegaardian figure of the newspaper vendor – is distinguished by the refusal of its members to take responsibility for their decisions.

[67] Remember that the superhero need not have superpowers (only one does in *Watchmen*); they need only be truly exceptional, i.e., to have elevated themselves above the ordinary run of humanity, usually through the dedicated cultivation and development of their natural gifts. This might also help explain why the classic heroes of the Greeks (Perseus, Hercules, Orpheus, Sarpêdon, etc.) were imagined as demigods, situated halfway between other mortal human beings and the Gods, but with no hope of ever entering the pantheon of Gods (as Aeneas does in later Roman myth), and so striving instead for the mortal immortality of glory. Is believing in heroes thus necessarily elitist? Probably. (In later works like *Miracleman* and *Top Ten*, Moore imagines worlds where everyone has

moreover, then we, like Ozymandias at the end of *Watchmen*, will not be able to find any reassurance outside ourselves that we have made "the right choice," and like Heidegger himself (when he chose to believe in the initial promise of Hitler's "revolution"), it will always be possible that we are making a horrible mistake.[68] Authentic heroics require learning to live with this uncertainty. Following in the footsteps of our heroes thus encourages us to follow Nietzsche's exhortation to "live dangerously," to risk an absolute commitment (a commitment in which our very identity is at stake), since only such a risk, Kierkegaard and Heidegger suggest, can give existential weight and meaning to our lives.[69]

6. SPARKS IN THE DARKNESS

If we look for people who made no mistakes, who were always on the right side, who never apologized for tyrants or unjust wars, we shall have very few heroes and heroines.
   Richard Rorty, *Achieving our Country*[70]

In the end, *Watchmen*'s postmodern ambivalence concerning the hero places it somewhere between the Enlightenment rejection of, and the existentialist commitment to, the idea of the hero. In this, *Watchmen* reflects a tension underlying our own age, in which we late-moderns rather obsessively return to confront the relation between our past and its different possible futures – as though seeking with increasing desperation to control

superpowers, but these abilities are always differentially distributed, just as abilities are in our world.) But elitism as such is not objectionable so long as the elite is in no way a fixed group, predetermined by tradition or heredity. (The latter explains why *Star Wars* went so terribly wrong when the later prequels naturalized the force: Lucas's misguided introduction of the "midichlorian count" transformed the Jedis into a group whose membership gets determined by genetics rather than the cultivation of skills through dedication, practice, courage, self-control, etc.) So long as we do not know where heroes will emerge from ahead of time (and we do not), then there is nothing too objectionable about recognizing that, as a matter of fact, not everyone can become a hero. Not everyone can, but anyone might, so every person deserves the opportunities to cultivate and develop his or her own gifts. (Here I follow Cavell's response to Rawls's charge that perfectionism is elitist; see "Heidegger's Perfectionist Philosophy of Education in *Being and Time*," 460–1, note 9.)

[68] See Hubert L. Dreyfus, "Mixing Interpretation, Religion, and Politics: Heidegger's High-Risk Thinking." In the final pages of *Watchmen* (XII.27.iv–vii), Ozymandias seeks reassurance from Dr. Manhattan (who has become nearly omniscient), asking him, "I did the right thing, didn't I? It all worked out in the end." Dr. Manhattan answers simply: "Nothing ever ends." Ozymandias's confidence is clearly shaken, and the final image of him (looking away from his own shadow, which is now larger than he is) leaves open the question of whether "the world's smartest man" will be able to live with his uncertainty concerning his own heroics.

[69] See Hubert L. Dreyfus, *On the Internet*, esp. 73–107. See also Žižek's critical appropriation of Dreyfus's Kierkegaardian critique in "Rhetorics of Power," *Diacritics* 31:1 (2001), 98–103.

[70] Richard Rorty, *Achieving our Country: Leftist Thought in Twentieth-Century America*, 45.

the direction of history (which slips free nonetheless, like a bar of wet soap, from the tightening grasp of this subjectivistic impulse).

Even if one believes that there is something admirable in the desire to live without heroes, the problem remains that we have not woken up and walked with our eyes wide open into the clear light of a postheroic tomorrow. Instead, we as a culture have simply discovered the decadent pleasure of destroying the heroes we create. Indeed, building up sham heroes only to destroy them the next week or month – once the fare only of the tabloids – seems to have become our most popular national pastime. The obsessive delight the public takes in tormenting the very athletes and entertainers they formerly idolized (Britney Spears, Lindsay Lohan, Tiger Woods, and on and on) seems like an unhappy stalemate, our culture's way of oscillating endlessly between the Romantic celebration and the Enlightenment rejection of the hero.[71] Concealed, however, behind this spectacle of a "star-studded" popular culture saturated with "malicious delight" (*Schadenfreude*, a German word for an increasingly American disposition) is the fact that we not only degrade our sham heroes (in whose company I would include not only the aptly named *American Idol* and its ilk but almost all our culture's precious "stars"), we also ignore or quickly forget the real heroes who emerge despite it all (Julia Hill, Rachel Corrie, Mark Bingham, Wesley Autrey, to name but a few), heroes with the capacity to disrupt our cynical complacency, realign our felt-understanding of what matters, and so give focus to our guiding sense of self. When greatness as such is suspect, and quickly subjected to vicious persecution, in the end we are left with only conformity, cultural banalization, and the triumph, by default, of sad mediocrity. Although I look forward to a dawn beyond our own twilight of the idols, our dusk of "stars" made mostly of paper-thin tinsel (easily torn and foresworn), I do not believe we are entering into – or should seek to enter – a time without heroes, a postheroic age.

I would suggest instead that when a genre seems to commit suicide – as philosophy did with Kant, Heidegger, and Wittgenstein, and as the superhero comic did with *Watchmen* – this apparent suicide is usually better understood as an attempted martyrdom, that is, a sacrifice with a redemptive intent, a striving for rebirth, even if in a different form. When the greatest representatives of a genre seek to end it, perhaps this is because they sense (on some level) that no field can long survive without being periodically revitalized by such sacrifice and rebirth. Certainly it is no coincidence that many of the comics that followed *Watchmen* sought to respond to its challenging deconstruction of the hero, and that the result greatly enriched the comics medium as a whole. Twenty-five years later, mainstream comics continue to occupy a post-*Watchmen* landscape, one in which *Watchmen*'s

[71] Thanks to Steve Crowell for suggesting this last point.

ambivalence about the hero has become nearly ubiquitous.[72] Even in the darkest of contemporary comics, however, a careful reader can still recognize the sparks from that ongoing struggle to imagine and create the kinds of heroes who will prove themselves capable of inspiring the denizens of this complex and morally ambiguous world, a struggle that seeks to keep alive (as the dream of the hero, with all its risks, has always done) our hope for a better future.[73] This hope (which, really, is hope itself) we can deconstruct but never destroy.

If this is right, then perhaps the aforementioned imperative to "grow up" is itself founded on a faulty understanding of maturity – indeed, on a *child's* understanding of maturity, one that presupposes a world divided into two discrete groups, the children and the grown-ups. By the time we have become what children call "grown-ups" ourselves, however, we come to understand (at least if we are honest) that maturation is not an achievement that can be accomplished once and for all but is, rather, an ongoing process in which we must continue to confront and find our way through the challenges that face – and in many cases follow from – our current self-understanding. This ongoing maturation process (more Eriksonian than Hegelian) requires us periodically to exchange one mask for another ("mask" is the synecdoche *Watchmen* consistently uses for "hero"); yet, is anyone ever really maskless? Heidegger reminds us that: "*Persona* means the actor's mask, through which the sound of his saying resounds." (WCT 62/GA8 65) (It is from the Latin *persona*, "mask," that we get the word "personality.") We all "prepare a face to meet the faces that we meet" (as T. S. Eliot wrote).[74] Since we thus give voice to being, Heidegger suggests that "we can think of human beings as the *persona*, the mask of being" (WCT 62/GA865). Perhaps the question then becomes: Why do we put on

---

[72] This work includes Frank Miller's revival of Batman, *The Dark Knight Returns* (which, like so much of Miller's work, embraces the very hero Moore's deconstruction showed to be so problematic, while developing Moore's ideas of superman as a dupe of the government and, later, as a kind of god), Neil Gaiman's *Sandman* (a brilliant *Bildungsroman* of the fantasy genre that masterfully reconstructs the hero *Watchmen* deconstructed), Moore's own later work (such as *Miracleman* – an insightful, neo-Nietzschean fable – *Supreme*, *Top Ten*, *Tom Strong*, and *The League of Extraordinary Gentlemen*), as well as – at the very heart of the mainstream – the death and multiple rebirths of *Superman* himself and the very popular *Ultimate* work by Brian Michael Bendis, Mark Millar, and many others. As these works increasingly come to influence even more popular genres such as film and television, the tensions they embody become ever more central to our cultural self-understanding, as Heidegger's vision of the work of art suggests. Nonetheless, comparing *Watchmen* to a more recent work like *Kick-Ass* (which was already being made into a film before Millar even finished writing the comic), puts one in mind of Marx's famous quip that history repeats itself, but "the first time as tragedy, the second as farce."

[73] For a discussion of three such attempts (comics in which "The Thing" is Jewish, "Rawhide Kid" is gay, and "Captain America" is Black), see Alan Jenkins, "Minority Report," 36–38.

[74] See Erik Erikson, *The Life Cycle Completed*; T. S. Eliot, "The Love Song of J. Alfred Prufrock," *The Wasteland and Other Poems*, 4.

the masks we do, the ones we grow so accustomed to that they come to feel like our own faces? What does it mean to "take responsibility for your own face" (something Sartre suggests every adult must do)? If we cannot simply take off our masks once and for all, then how do we exchange one mask for another, for one less confining, one that better amplifies our voice and so allows us to us speak out more clearly, more resoundingly and with greater nuance, one in which we can more fully recognize ourselves? In the spirit of these lingering questions (but without claiming finally to resolve them), let us return to Heidegger's work, examining his thinking about how issues of sound and voice might actually help us make the transition to another understanding of being.

6

The Philosophical Fugue

Understanding the Structure and Goal of Heidegger's Contributions to Philosophy (From Enowning)

> All essential thinking calls for its thoughts and sentences to be mined, like ore, every time anew.
>
> Heidegger (CP 15/GA65 21)

After Chapter 3 explained Heidegger's postmodern view of ontological meaning as inexhaustibly plural or polysemic, Chapters 4 and 5 took this view as their philosophical point of departure for exploring two popular works of "postmodern" art. We will now return to the question of the nature and implications of Heidegger's own postmodernism by examining what is probably his most difficult and least well understood work, the much vaunted and vilified *Contributions to Philosophy (From Enowning)*.

My thesis is that this notoriously difficult text is best understood as an innovative philosophical application of the musical art of the fugue.[1] Recognizing Heidegger's *Contributions* as a fugal composition allows us to understand this esoteric text's basic structure and goal, and so to avoid several influential misreadings of the work, which allege that *Contributions* is Heidegger's second *magnum opus*, that it is Heidegger's attempt to write aphoristically (à la Nietzsche), or that it or that it has no structure and so is nothing but a failed "heap." Undermining those misreadings, I shall instead suggest that in the *Contributions* Heidegger is "fuguing," exploring his underlying subject – *Ereignis* or "enowning" – through a series of linked meditations whereby he seeks to elaborate and develop the inner philosophical possibilities and implications of this polysemic term of art that is so important to his later work.

The musical model of the fugue is well chosen for such a task, because it allows Heidegger to explore the fullest possible resonances of the polyphonic phenomenon of enowning, and to do so in a way that serves the

---

[1] I first developed this thesis in the 1990s (as I explain in my acknowledgments; see also Ch. 3, note 74).

later Heidegger's overarching goal of helping us think our way through the historical transition from modernity to postmodernity. The musical genre of the fugue is nicely ambiguous in precisely this respect, in fact, because fuguing is an artistic practice with an essential tension at its core (the kind of productive conflict Heidegger thinks we will find at the heart of all true art, as we saw in Chapter 3): The art of the fugue is torn between the paradigmatically modern desire for the exhaustive elaboration of a theme and a postmodern recognition of the impossibility of ever completely satisfying that desire. The greatest practitioners of the fugue (most notably J. S. Bach) show that fuguing is driven by the relentless modern impulse to completely explore the possibilities of a theme, by manically (if not maniacally) multiplying variations on this basic theme and introducing them into what thereby becomes an increasingly dense texture of musical notes.[2] At the same time, however, that impulse toward completion must find a way of coming to terms with the impossibility of its satisfaction, because at a certain point (and part of the art of the fugue is to see – or hear – just how far this point can be pushed), when too many overlapping variations have been generated, the entire effort begins to collapse into an indiscernible wall of noise. (We could thus say that, in Heidegger's terms, Bach – like Van Gogh, Hölderlin, and Michelangelo – was an artistic postmodernist *avant la lettre*.)

Given Heidegger's conviction that the only way to reach a genuine postmodernity is by transcending modernity from within (as we saw in the first three chapters), his innovative philosophical experiment with the musical model of the fugue remain a deeply intriguing effort, even if it too risks its own collapse into meaningless noise.[3] For Heidegger this risk is worthwhile, because the goal of his painstaking elaboration of the possibilities of "enowning" is nothing less than "the essential transition into the still possible transformation of Western history" (CP 57/GA65 82). The *Contributions'* fugal structure serves its extremely ambitious goal, I shall suggest, because the text is ultimately an attempt to re-attune humanity, that is, to foster a new, more thankful "fundamental attunement" (*Grundstimmung*) to the source of historical intelligibility, a comportmental attunement through

---

[2] This growing density cannot only be heard but seen as well, e.g., if one examines the increasingly crowded musical score for Bach's six-part fugue, "The Musical Offering." See <http://upload.wikimedia.org/wikipedia/commons/2/25/Kdf2.jpg> (accessed 14 August 2010).

[3] Heidegger's experimental use of language in the *Contributions* takes its own version of the fugal collapse into noise, as Polt nicely attests when he observes that: "The language is hypnotically repetitive and dense, consisting of formula after formula in which Heidegger tries to say everything unsayable all at once." (See Polt, *The Emergency of Being*, 2.) Indeed, the only impression many mainstream philosophers seem to have of this text is that it represents a complete collapse into Heideggerese "gibberish." Thus, in his mocking review of its English translation, Simon Blackburn suggests that Heidegger's "orchestra is only tuning up." (See Blackburn, "Enquivering," 45.)

which Heidegger thinks we can come to understand being in a postmodern way and so help inaugurate another historical age (thereby participating in a new Renaissance or "rebirth" of history). Although Heidegger chose not to publish the rather mixed results of his fugal experiment during his own lifetime, he nevertheless cherished the work for helping him develop the perspective of his later thought, and he firmly believed that future thinkers ("those to-come," *die Zu-künftigen*) would be able to appreciate and carry further his efforts to help us think our way into a postmodern age. Let us thus see if we can help vindicate his optimism.

1. INTRODUCTION TO HEIDEGGER'S *CONTRIBUTIONS TO PHILOSOPHY (FROM ENOWNING)*

Heidegger's *Contributions to Philosophy: From Enowning* (or *"Contributions," Beiträge*, as the work is popularly known) is a dense, strange, difficult, and – *pace* Otto Pöggeler and Friedrich-Wilhelm von Herrmann – also a deeply problematic text.[4] As Pöggeler's well-known remark that "a wind from Sils-Maria has blown through . . . the *Beiträge*" suggests, the *Contributions* is a text in which Heidegger is at his most Nietzschean (that is, hyperbolic, elliptical, allusive, fragmentary), even as he tries to get back behind Nietzsche, to Nietzsche's Hölderlinian sources, in order to accomplish what (looking back in 1951) Heidegger would characterize as the "most difficult task" of having had to extricate himself from Nietzsche's "ruinous" influence.[5] The

---

[4] Heidegger grouped his *Contributions* together with several roughly contemporaneous texts that he thought would help readers understand it (in his "Collected Works, Division III: Unpublished Treatises"), including *Mindfulness/GA66* (1938–9); GA67 (the first part of which is from 1938–9); GA69 (1938–40); and Heidegger's contemporaneous work on Hölderlin in GA75 (on which cf. Pöggeler, *Heidegger's Path of Thinking*, 178). These works help fill-in the background already provided by such important works as "The Origin of the Work of Art" (1935–6); Heidegger's lectures on Nietzsche stretching from 1936 to 1946; 1936–7's BQP/GA45; and 1941's BC/GA51. Heidegger claims at one point, dubiously, that his Nietzsche lectures "remain only foreground" for the *Contributions*, and that these other works all develop perspectives first opened up in the *Contributions'* third fugal part, *das Zuspiel* (see below and M 372/GA66 421). While the texts needed to fully understand and evaluate the *Contributions* are still being published, any attempt to render a final judgment on this work remains premature. For the most ambitious explication and critique of the work to date, see Richard Polt's impressively clear but interpretively contentious monograph, *The Emergency of Being: On Heidegger's* Contributions to Philosophy.

[5] On Heidegger's critique of "Nietzsche" as a synonym for our late-modern, technological epoch, a reading of Nietzsche that suggests that: "People have no idea how difficult it is truly to lose that thought again" (WCT 56/GA8 60), see Chapter 1. Pöggeler reports Heidegger's frequent lament that "Nietzsche ruined me [*Nietzsche hat mich kaputt gemacht*]" (in his "Besinnung oder Ausflucht? Heideggers ursprüngliche Denkens," 240–1; cf. Wolin, *The Politics of Being*, 198 note 25). See Pöggeler's *Martin Heidegger's Path of Thinking*, 281, for the famous remark that a philosophical sirocco from the birthplace of Nietzsche's own most "elevated" (or "theological," Heidegger would say) thought of eternal recurrence left its mark on the *Contributions*. This Nietzschean influence helps explain what Guignon

text's complicated pedigree helps explain why Reiner Schürmann, surely one of his generation's most perceptive readers of the later Heidegger, would complain of the *Contributions* that "at times one may think one is reading a piece of Heideggerian plagiarism, so encumbered is it with ellipses and assertoric monoliths."[6] In order to help us navigate a safe approach toward that elliptical and "monolithic assertion" that is most important for anyone seeking to understand Heidegger's postmodern hopes – namely, Heidegger's unexpected invocation of "The Last or Ultimate [*Letzte*] God" at the very climax of the *Contributions* – it helps first to know a bit about the *Contributions* remarkable history, which Schürmann refers to a bit elliptically himself as the text's "overdetermined legacy."

Von Herrmann was the editor of Heidegger's *Collected Works* (*Gesamtausgabe*) when the already famous *Beiträge zur Philosophie (Vom Ereignis)* was finally published in 1989 (as volume 65 of the *Collected Works*). In this capacity, von Herrmann tells us that the *Contributions'* publication was sped-up ahead of schedule in order to coincide with and so commemorate the centennial of Heidegger's birth. Still, more than fifty years elapsed between the writing of these "contributions" in 1936–8 and their publication in 1989.[7] These circumstances might not be remarkable, however, were it not for the fact that the *Contributions* had already become famous long before its 1989 publication, when it was greeted quickly – indeed, precipitously – by more than a few enthusiastic Heideggerians as "Heidegger's second *magnum opus*."[8] The enthusiasm distorting this judgment can be explained by the text's remarkable pre-publication fame, which can itself be traced back to the fact that Pöggeler had read the unpublished manuscript in the early 1960s. Then, in his influential 1963 study, *Martin Heidegger's Path of Thinking*, Pöggeler acted as an effective philosophical "PR man" for the

rightly characterizes as "the soteriological and apocalyptic 'meta-narrative'" underlying Heidegger's history of Being. (See Guignon's "Introduction" to *The Cambridge Companion to Heidegger*, 24.)

[6] Schürmann, "Riveted to a Monstrous Site: On Heidegger's *Beiträge zur Philosophie*," 313. (Schürmann's footnotes make clear his polemical implication that Derrida is the "Heideggerian plagiarist" he has in mind.)

[7] The publication of GA65 was sped up to be in time for the centennial of Heidegger's birth, against the letter if not the spirit of Heidegger's last *Gesamtausgabe* directives that (von Herrmann informs us) specified that the *Contributions* should not be published until after all the Marburg and Freiburg lectures; see his "Editor's Afterword" (CP 363/GA65 511). See also Alexander Schwan, "Heidegger's *Beiträge zur Philosophie* and Politics," 71.

[8] (See e.g. von Herrmann, "Way and Method in Philosophy: Hermeneutic Phenomenology in Thinking the History of Being," 185. The claim was also prominently echoed on the back cover of the first edition of *The Cambridge Companion to Heidegger*.) Pöggeler had long called the *Contributions* the sole major work of the later Heidegger (see e.g. "Heideggers Politische Selbstverständnis"). And von Herrmann continues to insist that: "As Otto Pöggeler has rightly and repeatedly pointed out, the *Beiträge zur Philosophie* are the major work of Heidegger's thinking of the history of Being" ("Way and Method," 56). I try to show here that this is all rather misleading.

Contributions, granting the text the status of an open secret by frequently quoting tantalizing snippets from it, dropping intriguing hints and promissory notes, and issuing incredible claims about the work's unparalleled importance for any philosophical understanding of Heidegger's "thought-path as a whole."

Some of the more extraordinary of these claims were subsequently widely disseminated and, ironically, have now ossified into a scholarly dogma that threatens to obstruct our access to a text that has finally become available first hand. To wit, Pöggeler went so far as to call the *Contributions* Heidegger's sole "major work proper [*das eigentliche Hauptwerk*]," a characterization he based on the claim that in the *Contributions* Heidegger outlined the complete "system" of thought that he spent the rest of his life developing in a piecemeal fashion.[9] It is incredible that this fantasy of having had exclusive access to the Heideggerian Rosetta stone (a hermeneutic fantasy of the first order, to be sure) has been so widely adopted.[10] For, with the actual publication of the *Contributions*, it has become clear that Pöggeler seriously mischaracterized the *Contributions*' organizational structure, which Heidegger explicitly (if rather mysteriously) tells us "is essentially other than a 'system'" (CP 56/GA65 81). It is thus not surprising that significantly varying judgments have begun to emerge concerning both the text's merits and its status within Heidegger's increasingly immense *oeuvre*. (His *Collected Works* are now scheduled to include more than one hundred volumes, and while three quarters of these have been published, an indeterminate number of other works continue to languish in the

---

9 See Pöggeler, "Heidegger und der hermeneutische Theologie," 481; referenced by Schürmann in "A Brutal Awakening to The Tragic Condition of Being: On Heidegger's *Beiträge zur Philosophie*," 104, note 2. As Schürmann notes, "Pöggeler ... kept his readers in suspense for a quarter of a century; as Heidegger's one major work, the *Beiträge* alone, he claimed, contain Heidegger's genuine thinking which the public lectures and courses were merely to make accessible to a more general audience" (ibid., punctuation corrected; cf. Pöggeler, *Martin Heidegger's Path of Thinking*, 116).

10 Of course, Heidegger does say things that encourage such a fanciful view (e.g., the previously noted passage at M 372/GA66 421). This helps explain why thinkers like Schwan – who envisions the *Contributions* as "a complete blueprint" developed in only "a truncated form" in the later philosophy (see his "Heidegger's *Beiträge zur Philosophie* and Politics," 72) – and von Herrmann adopt Pöggeler's dubious view so uncritically. Even Polt, a much more critical reader of the text, continues to disseminate the view that Heidegger's *Contributions* "sets the stage for all his late thought" (*The Emergency of Being*, 1). One can all too easily understand why a scholar like Pöggeler with sole access to a text might make such claims, but they are not born out by Heidegger's complicated body of work, which contains numerous *earlier* developments of the views elaborated in *Contributions* (as Chapters 2 and 3 showed in detail), as well as later revisions of some of its central claims (as I showed in *Heidegger on Ontotheology*). As I shall try to suggest in this chapter, however, one need not claim that the work says (or even anticipates) everything in Heidegger's later work in order to conclude that it does advance some extremely important ideas, especially concerning Heidegger's philosophical faith in the possibility of a genuine postmodernity, and that it does so in a suggestively postmodern way.

archives.)[11] For instance, the *Contributions* has been described by Rüdiger Safranski (much more modestly, but with a certain psychological perceptiveness) as a kind of "philosophical diary," while Schürmann himself characterized this "disconcerting document" as "a monstrous site." Schürmann implies that this dramatic appellation is not meant to connote "terrifying" (*ungeheuer*) so much as *demonstrative*, but – if Schürmann's own series of dense but provocative analyses of the *Contributions* are any indication – just *what* this text demonstrates will surely be a matter of contention for a long time to come.[12]

2. THE FUGUE: UNDERSTANDING THE STRUCTURE OF HEIDEGGER'S *CONTRIBUTIONS*

The *Contributions* as a whole is organized into seven "divisions." Yet, as Heidegger explains in the first of these seven sections (the "Preview" or "Glance Ahead," *Vorblick*), merely to call the major organizational units of the *Contributions* "divisions" is already to imply the very opposite of what Heidegger intends when he names them "*Fügungen*," a word that means "unifications" rather than "divisions" and, carrying multiple resonances, also connotes the working of fate in our existence. Through these polysemic *Fügungen*, in other words, Heidegger means to designate the way in which certain decisive events (the ordinary German meaning of *Ereignis*) not only come together to give shape to our lives but also, if properly understood, can even lead us to transform human history itself (by working to transform our underlying understanding of being – as we have seen).[13]

These, moreover, are not the only meanings of *Fügungen*. Crucial to understanding the text, I submit, is Heidegger's subtle suggestion that

---

[11] See Julian Young, *Heidegger, Philosophy, Nazism*, 40; and Elizabeth Livingston, "The Last Hand: Restrictions on Martin Heidegger's Papers in the Deutsches Literaturarchiv Marbach."

[12] (See Safranski, *Heidegger: Between Good and Evil*, 307; cf. M 382–3/GA66 433.) Schürmann's description – especially if placed alongside his observation that "these *Contributions* date from the years when Heidegger was painfully working through what he would later call his greatest blunder" and Boss's report that Heidegger's "own proper and fundamental self-realization was evidently reached with his waking discernment of that state of affairs that revealed itself to him as '*das Ereignis*'" – encourages us to recognize the *Contributions* as the central text for any psychologically informed reading of Heidegger's "turn." (See Schürmann, "Riveted to a Monstrous Site," 313; Boss, "Martin Heidegger's Zollikon Seminars" 13, 20. For Schürmann's other attempts to come to terms with Heidegger's *Contributions*, see "Ultimate Double Binds" and "Technicity, Topology, Tragedy: Heidegger on 'That Which Saves' in the Global Reich.") Polt concludes his detailed study of Heidegger's *Contributions* with the judgment that this "is a book saturated with emergency, drunk on apocalypse" (*The Emergency of Being*, 254), and so calls for a more calm and sober appropriation of its philosophical insights. That is what we too are attempting to do here.

[13] See CP 57/GA65 81–2 and later in this chapter.

the *Contributions'* complex organizational structure (which, recall, is "essentially other than a 'system'") can best be understood according to the musical model of the "fugue" (*Fuge*), standardly defined as a "polyphonic composition constructed on one or more short subjects or themes, which are harmonized according to the laws of counterpoint, and introduced from time to time with various contrapuntal devices."[14] In another context, Philippe Lacoue-Labarthe suggestively examines what I take to be the most important of these "laws of counterpoint" or "contrapuntal devices" at work in Heidegger's *Contributions*, namely, the phenomenon of the "*caesura*," which Hölderlin influentially theorized as "the pure word, the counter-rhythmic interruption." In ancient Greek drama, the *caesura* is the moment of the "*kata-strophê*," that is, literally, the introduction of a second voice that turns against a first voice and so divides the chorus, thereby transforming a monologue into a dialogue or multivoiced discussion.[15] If the Hölderlinian *caesura* is the "pure word" that interrupts and pluralizes the monologue that precedes it, then for Heidegger this word is clearly his avowedly "untranslatable" *Ereignis* – typically rendered into English as "enowning," "the event of appropriation," or even the "event" of ontological truth. *Ereignis* is a word that, implicitly folded in on itself ("en-owning" or *Er-eignis*), helps draw our attention to word formation itself, that is, to the world-disclosing action that (as we saw in Chapter 3) Heidegger takes to be the "poetic" (or *poietic*) essence of language, the source of language's ontologically regenerative capacity for "bringing into

---

[14] See CP 56–7/GA65 81 for Heidegger's defense of the "rigor," "unity," and "clarity" of this fugal construction. E.g., Heidegger justifies "*the rigor of the fugal-articulation* of this construction [der Strenge des Gefüges *im Aufbau*]" as an attempt to envision an alternative way of accomplishing what has always been for philosophy "the impossible," namely, "to grasp the truth of being as such in the fully unfolded richness of its grounded essence [*die Wahrheit des Seyns in der voll entfalteten Fülle seines begründeten Wesens begriefen*]." Pöggeler thus suggests the gentle criticism that: "Only slowly did Heidegger's thinking relinquish its wanting to ground" (*Martin Heidegger's Path of Thinking*, 130). But in fact, the postmodern pluralism that Heidegger proposes as the ontological "ground" of all future world-disclosing is not foundational in the ontotheological sense Heidegger criticizes, as we saw in Chapter 1. (On the definition of "fugue," see James Murray, et al., eds., *The Compact Oxford English Dictionary*, henceforth "OED," 642.)

[15] (See Lacoue-Labarthe, *Heidegger, Art, and Politics: The Fiction of the Political*, 45–6; and Hölderlin, *Essays and Letters on Theory*, 102.) Nietzsche's *The Birth of Tragedy from the Spirit of Music* suggests that this internal division of the chorus (which the caesura effects) reintroduces the tragic principle of individuation into what had originally been an ecstatic communal fusion known to the ancient mystery religions. Without recognizing the *Contributions'* fugal structure, Schürmann nevertheless suggests that as such a *caesura*, *Ereignis* is meant as Heidegger's own answer to what he (like Hölderlin and Nietzsche) takes to be a historical call for "decision," and thus the enactment of the latest in the series of "epochal breaks 'severing' (*caedere*) eras of truth" (Schürmann, "Riveted to a Monstrous Site," 316). As I have suggested, however, for Heidegger the postmodern understanding of being will not be epochal, because it will not "hold back" being as such.

being." That "enowning" is the *caesura* for Heidegger suggests, moreover, that Heidegger thinks this word helps disclose those decisive moments in which our Nietzschean late-modernity intersects with the "arrival of the future of Western thinking," thereby making possible the "transition [*Übergang*] to the other beginning" (CP 124/GA65 176).[16]

Heidegger is notoriously not shy about asserting such bold, almost incredibly ambitious claims in *Contributions to Philosophy (From Enowning)*. But how exactly is thinking through "enowning" supposed to help us to make a transition from modernity to postmodernity? What I shall try to show here is that Heidegger's answer to this question is embedded in the fugal "composition" of *Contributions*. This is not only because the work's fugal structure is what allows Heidegger to "polyphonically" elaborate the implications of "enowning" (*Ereignis*), the underlying theme of the work, but also because the contrapuntal development of this theme is what harmonizes *Contributions* as a whole and explains its overall movement, that is, the particular way in which it builds toward (what Heidegger originally intended to be) its symphonic climax. Recognizing the *Contributions* as an experiment in fugal composition will thus allow us understand how exactly Heidegger hopes to accomplish the work's postmodern goal, its attempt "to prepare for the transition" to "the other beginning" (CP 5/GA65 6). In order to train our ears to hear this overarching movement, however, we need first to develop a feel for the basic structure of the work, circumventing several influential misreadings of it along the way.

After the anticipatory "Preview," Heidegger gives the *Contributions'* second through seventh "fuguings" (*Fügungen*) deliberately polysemic titles: "The Echo of Reminiscence [*Der Anklang*]," "The Interplay or Playing Forth [*Das Zuspiel*]," "The Leap or Spring [*Der Sprung*]," "The Grounding or Founding [*Die Gründung*]," "The Ones To-Come or The Futural Ones [*Die Zu-Künftigen*]," and "The Last or Ultimate God [*Der Letzte Gott*]."[17]

---

[16] "The Transition to the Other Beginning" begins: "To grasp Nietzsche as the end of Western metaphysics is not [to make] an historical determination about what lies behind us but, rather, [it is to enter into] the arriving *historicity* of the future of Western thinking" (CP 124/GA65 176).

[17] One of the most interesting of these is *der Anklang*, by which Heidegger means a kind of *echo of reminiscence*. Among *Anklang*'s multiple connotations is the first glimpse of twilight, a glimpse that has a trace of dawn in it (as in "I hear 'traces' of Bach in that"). Heidegger's *Anklang* thus comes rather close to Benjamin's theory of "reminiscences" (based on his analysis of Proust's remembrances – the famous Madeleine – as well as Baudelaire's analogous understanding of the relation between current spleen and original Ideal). This "ringing echo" is literally a "reminiscence" triggered by a sound received through the ear, so we should recall that as the son of a Catholic Sexton, childhood memories involving the ringing of Church bells remained close to Heidegger's heart (see "The Secret of the Bell Tower," GA13 113–16). In IM, moreover, Heidegger describes the "call" in terms reminiscent of that "ringing of silence" in which Yahweh is said to have spoken to Abraham. *Das Zuspiel* is also interestingly polysemic: "Playing Forth, Interplay, or Pass"; it connotes the playing forth of certain themes from the "first beginning" within the

According to von Herrmann's influential interpretation, the *Contributions'* *Fügungen* illuminate different but interconnected "essential aspects of *Ereignis.*"[18] Unfortunately, this rather vague interpretation (and the editorial redaction of the text that it underwrites) risks concealing the fugal structure unifying the *Contributions*. For, in fact, only the second through seventh of the *Contributions' Fügungen* were written in 1936–7 and originally intended by Heidegger to be part of his philosophical fugue. By appending a final "division" on "being as such [*Das Seyn*]" to the *Contributions* as if it were the work's conclusion (when it is really a summarizing restatement of the text's major themes that Heidegger penned the following year, in 1938), von Herrmann's editorial redaction obscures the fugal structure of Heidegger's original text. Once we realize this, and so distinguish that later summarizing section from the original body of the work (recognizing that Heidegger's original text really ends with §256, not §281, nearly one hundred pages later), its organizing structure becomes much more readily discernible: *Contributions* is not composed of eight divisions but, instead, of seven thematic "fuguings" in which Heidegger contrapuntally explores and so develops (with steadily building urgency and brevity) the underlying theme of the work, namely, "the essential happening of being itself [*die Wesung des Seyns selbst*], which we name *enowning*" (CP 6/GA65 7).

As this suggests (and we have seen in earlier chapters), "enowning" (*Ereignis*) is Heidegger's name for the way in which "being as such" takes place historically when it is hermeneutically appropriated (or "enowned") by human beings in a distinctive way. More precisely, "enowning" describes the way "being as such" or "be-ing" (*Seyn*, the deliberately archaic name Heidegger uses in *Contributions* for the inexhaustible source of historical intelligibility) gets brought into our "being-here" (or *Dasein*) and made intelligible in a way that brings entities, our own being-here, and being itself into their own simultaneously. As we saw in Chapter 3, for example,

"other beginning (and thus the "interplay" of these two beginnings), as well as the play of space-time (i.e., "be-ing") in its approach to Dasein. Interestingly, Heidegger seems to have drawn the metaphor from soccer, where "the pass" is the *release* that makes playing together possible. (Heidegger himself played wing, the position for which passing – both giving and receiving – is the most important.) This "Playing Forth" also comes to suggest the giving of a gift in which the recipient does not know who gave it, although for Heidegger this unrecognized giver is being as such. (In his treatment of the theme of the gift, Derrida develops this idea by arguing that only an unconditional gift, a gift that would be neither given nor received as a gift, "the gift that is not present," would be a "gift" worthy of the name; see Jacques Derrida, *The Gift of Death*, 29.) *Der Sprung* ("The Leap") and *die Gründung* ("The Grounding") are directly related; the latter is "The Landing" from the neo-Kierkegaardian leap, an arrival at the site for building a new dwelling for historical humanity (hence Heidegger's claim that this "ground" is something we move toward rather than something from which we depart). I shall return to these interconnected fuguings, as well as to *die Zu-künftigen* ("The Futural Ones/Those To-Come") and *der Letzte Gott* ("the Ultimate God").

[18] See von Herrmann, "Technology, Politics, Art," 59.

when Van Gogh brings *A Pair of Shoes* (1886) into its own as a painting, he thereby also comes into his own as a world-disclosing artist, indeed, as an artist who discloses what art itself is (namely, the essential struggle between the phenomenological abundance of "earth" and the tacit coherence of "world"), and he thus allows being to show itself (in its ownmost, *postmodern* meaningfulness) as an historically inexhaustible tension of emergence and withdrawal.[19]

What, we might thus ask, does *Contributions*' 1936–7 meditation on "enowning" add to Heidegger's analysis of the poetic naming-into-being that he described as the very essence of art and the origin of historical intelligibility just a year or two earlier, in 1935–6's "The Origin of the Work of Art"? What "enowning" *emphasizes* (I would say) is Heidegger's conviction that these ontologically generative interpretive appropriations not only bring the being of entities and of human being-here into their own, but that they do so in ways that allow us to understand the being of entities in terms of being as such (to use Heidegger's terms), that is, as both informing and exceeding our ability to render entities intelligible in conceptual terms.[20] In other words, such an ontological truth event exemplifies the *postmodern* way in which being can take place for us. For, in such events we no longer implicitly understand and approach entities either as objects to be controlled by subjects (as in the modern understanding of being), or as inherently meaningless resources standing by to be optimized and ordered efficiently (as in the late-modern understanding of being). Heidegger believes that such ontological truth events can help move us into the postmodern understanding of being they exemplify. That is why

---

[19] This helps us understand Heidegger's view about the irreversibility of artistic creation (his claim, discussed in Chapter 3, that genuine artworks generate something that has never been before and will never be again). The definitive inexhaustibility of the "earth" dictates that intelligibility will never be permanently fixed, once and for all. It will always remain possible even for an irreversible work created through an appropriate gestalting of what the earth offers to become, in turn, the subject of another such artistic event in the future. This means that (although it is difficult to imagine) Michelangelo's David *could* be taken as the "earthly" basis of another creative act, as Rauschenberg's rightly famous work of "conceptual art," *Erased de Kooning* (1953), so powerfully suggests. In Heidegger's terms, the rift-structure permeating intelligibility is not fixed for all time, but is layered and changes in all sorts of complicated ways. For, when the earth is gestalted into a world it withdraws into itself again, and can thus become the subject for further gestalts in the future. While such creative acts remain irreversible when viewed retrospectively (because works of art join the artist and the work in a transformative event that changes them both), prospectively they nevertheless retain an ineliminable element of contingency, in that they "can never be verified or derived from what went before" (PLT 75/GA5 63). (I owe the former point, and its literal complications, to a helpful discussion with Mark Wrathall.)

[20] As Heidegger puts this crucial point here – in the esoteric language typical of the *Contributions*: "The *call* [that joins being and Dasein] is arrival and remaining-away in the mystery of enowning" (CP 287/GA65 408).

he writes (in the penultimate section of *Contributions*, §255, "The Turn in Enowning"): "Enowning has its innermost happening and broadest reach in the turn" (CP 286/GA65 407). For Heidegger, "the turn" (*die Kehre*) names the beginning of a new ontohistorical age, not simply the transformation between his early and later work – although (*pace* the current misunderstanding) the two *are* related.[21] The former is the "concealed ground" of the latter (as Heidegger suggests in the very next sentence). That is, Heidegger believed that the philosophical and stylistic transformation between his "early" and "later" work (a transformation he was engulfed in while writing *Contributions*) followed from his attempt to help inaugurate an ontohistorical transition beyond the modern understanding of being.

In light of these larger points, the distinctive hermeneutic question facing readers of Heidegger's *Contributions* might be posed as follows. If the underlying theme of *Contributions* is "enowning" (that is, the way both entities and human beings come into their own by disclosing "being as such" in its partly but never-completely fathomable phenomenological fullness), then how is this theme developed by the text's six "fuguings" (*Fügungen*) so as to provide this composition with its overarching movement and goal? Heidegger is clear that *Contributions* does possess such an overarching unity. As he puts it: "Each of the six fuguings of the fugue stands for itself, but only in order to make the essential onefold more pressing" (CP 57/ GA65 81). Indeed, in what at first glance looks like a wild run-on sentence, Heidegger presents the entire "essential onefold" that his six fuguings are meant collectively to convey:

[T]he "Interplay" between the first and the other beginning [–] out of be-ing's "Echo" in the distress of being's abandonment [–] for the "Leap" into be-ing [–] for "Grounding" its truth [–] as preparation for "The Ones to Come" [–] of "The Ultimate God." (CP 6/GA65 7)

As my dashes mean to suggest, the complete fugue that runs through and unifies Heidegger's text is developed through the contrapuntal juxtaposition of the *Contributions'* six consecutive fugal sections, or what Heidegger calls their "hidden inter-resonating" (CP 57/GA65 81). The six fugal sections that compose the *Contributions* are thus meant to work together so as to develop a complex but unified philosophical vision – a complicated movement we will seek to elucidate when we turn to the "goal" of the *Contributions* in the next section.

Already, however, just by recognizing the fugal composition of the *Contributions*, we can avoid Pöggeler's influential misconstrual of

---

[21] The misunderstanding currently in vogue – according to which Heidegger's famous "turn" has *nothing to do with* the transformation between his early and later views – is itself merely an over-corrective to the old misunderstanding, which reduced the "turn" to that personal level. (I discuss this matter at length in "The End of Ontotheology: Understanding Heidegger's Turn, Method, and Politics," 11–129.)

Heidegger's project as a self-defeatingly systematic break with the urge to philosophical system building, and thus as at best an ironic or parodic gesture. Such interpretations, which in the abstract might seem to fit the Nietzschean aspects of the style of the text, nevertheless seriously mischaracterize its tone, which is not only almost humorless (with the exception of some bitter sarcasm and the usual punning) but also – in the somber yet hopeful pitch of an elegy – even reverential.[22] The *Contributions'* elegiac tone is that of a *mournful celebration*, a paradoxical, Hölderlinian-Nietzschean ambivalence borne witness to in Heidegger's striking claim that: "The most terrible jubilation must be the dying of a god" (CP 163/GA65 230).[23] Despite this dramatic tension between Heidegger's Nietzschean obsession with the death of God and his secularized, Hölderlinian faith in the possibility of "His" return, the structure organizing the *Contributions* is more Bachian than Bacchanalian. Instead of mistaking the *Contributions* for a series of Nietzschean aphorisms, then, let us take seriously Heidegger's implication that his text is joined together according to the musical model of the fugue. Ringing the church bells was a formative childhood experience for Heidegger, and he often reaches first for auditory metaphors when he wants to convey something of that mutual interdependency of being and human being that the word *Ereignis* seeks to name and so disclose.[24] (Thus he writes, for example, that being "needs us and our essence just as the

[22] ("Nietzschean," at least according to a "modernist" interpretation of Nietzsche's style. For an insightful elaboration of the differences between the "traditional, modern, and postmodern" interpretations of Nietzsche's style, see Žižek, *The Ticklish Subject: The Absent Centre of Political Ontology*, 171.) Related considerations inform my decision to refer to this text by its now standard title, the *Contributions* or "*Beiträge*," which Pöggeler, following Heidegger himself, disparagingly calls its "*public*" title," as opposed to its "essential heading," its parenthetical subtitle "*(Vom Ereignis)*" (CP 3/GA65 3), as well as my adoption of Emad and Maly's rendering of Heidegger's "essential subtitle" as "*(From Enowning)*." "From" is an apt translation of Heidegger's *Vom* because it assumes that Heidegger's *Contributions* did in fact seek to make contributions to philosophy, contributions that come *from* his insights into enowning. For, Heidegger had not yet given up on all "philosophy" as "metaphysics" in the *Contributions* but, rather, is still seeking to rehabilitate "philosophy," at least "whatever in the future and in truth dares to be called philosophy" (CP 15/GA65 20). Thus, while readers such as Kisiel rightly detect irony in Heidegger's characterization of the title as "public" and the subtitle as "essential," this irony is not (*pace* Kisiel) directed at the very idea of making "contributions to philosophy." Instead, this irony conveys Heidegger's recognition that he is appropriating a once common but then already slightly dated German tradition of titling one's text *Beiträge zur Philosophie*. Since Heidegger intentionally gives his text this slightly stilted "public" title, the subtitle could also be rendered as *Of Enowning*, following the example of Derrida's *Of Spirit* (a title that is even more deliberately anachronous, and thus seems more parodic than ironic).

[23] For a revealing treatment of Heidegger's pervasive use of religious metaphor in the *Contributions*, see Schwan, "Heidegger's *Beiträge zur Philosophie* and Politics," 71–88.

[24] I again refer to Heidegger's little autobiographical essay from 1954, "*Vom Geheimnis des Glockenturms* [On the Mystery of the Bell-Tower]," GA13 113–16.

sound, even if it fades away unheard, needs the instrument from which it resounds" [CCP 155/GA77 237].) Joan Stambaugh's nice recognition of the *Contributions'* "preference for terms taken from the realm of sound" is best understood not as a self-conscious refusal of "ocularcentric" metaphors (as Stambaugh rather anachronistically suggests) but, rather, as evidence for the fact that in the *Contributions* Heidegger adopts the fugal form from music, thereby bringing the style of his writing into an intriguing and politically charged proximity to Paul Celan's fugal poetry.[25] As Celan's translator Michael Hamburger points out, a "fugal composition with words" is literally "an impossibility, of course, because words cannot be counterpointed if they are to remain intelligible."[26] Lines written atop one another like the successive contrapuntal themes of a fugue will quickly obliterate themselves, leaving only an indecipherable palimpsest. Fugal writing thus tends to experiment with the limits of legibility, as Heidegger's *Contributions* itself attests. In so far as it remains legible, however, sustained fugal writing will need to adopt the form of the fugue conceptually rather than literally. Ironically, this makes it difficult to recognize any experiment in fugal writing that does not simply fail by obliterating itself, drowning in the successive layers of meaning it unfolds.

It remains strange, nonetheless, that commentators should ever mistake the *Contributions* for a series of aphorisms. Aphorisms, in the very economy of their expression, quietly point back to the presence of the author who thought, penned, and polished them. The *Contributions'* fragments lack the wit and polish of aphorisms (reading instead more like a philosophical

---

[25] That this proximity to Celan remains politically charged is rightly suggested by the original title of Safranski's biography of Heidegger (*Ein Meister aus Deutschland*), which links Heidegger to the German "death" of the concentration camps that Celan evokes with a "terrible beauty" in his famous poem, "Death Fugue." There remains much to be said about Celan's relation with Heidegger. In the end, Heidegger reached the sad conclusion that "Celan is sick – hopelessly." Yet, the "sickness" afflicting Celan was "the survivor's wound" (as Hamburger says); his parents were both murdered in the death camps. In this connection, Blanchot seems, if not to blame Heidegger for the Shoah, then to accuse him of a profound complicity with it through his "silence" (which Blanchot calls "a wounding of thinking"). In Blanchot's letter in the January 22–28, 1988 *Le Nouvel Observateur,* he writes: "Heidegger's irreparable fault lies in his silence concerning the Final Solution. The silence, or his refusal, when confronted by Paul Celan, to ask forgiveness for the unforgivable, was a denial that plunged Celan into despair and made him ill, for Celan knew that the Shoah was the revelation of the essence of the West." Wolin too implies that Heidegger was at least partially responsible for Celan's suicide, but Lyons shows in meticulous detail that the facts are much more complicated than Blanchot and Wolin assume. (See Stambaugh, *The Finitude of Being,* 112–13; Celan, *Poems of Paul Celan,* 30–3; Safranski, *Martin Heidegger,* 421–5; and the much more detailed and significant treatment in James Lyon, *Paul Celan & Martin Heidegger: An Unresolved Conversation, 1951–1970*; Blanchot, *"Penser l'apocalypse"*; quoted in Ungar, *Scandal and Aftereffect: Blanchot and France since 1930,* 63; and Wolin, "Review of *Martin Heidegger: Between Good and Evil,* by Rüdiger Safranski," 6.)

[26] See Michael Hamburger, "Introduction," in Celan, *Poems of Paul Celan,* xxv.

shorthand, a series of fragmentary ideas poured onto the page and still waiting to be edited and elaborated).[27] In fact, Heidegger clearly goes to great lengths to erase his own authorial presence from the text – if only to try to augment the forcefulness of the philosophical perspective he advocates by effacing its individual origins and thus rendering its broader adoption less dependent on the idiosyncratic circumstances of a personal life-trajectory that nevertheless remains unmistakably Heidegger's own. (When Heidegger goes so far as to put "'I'" in scare-quotes when writing in the first person, moreover, one cannot help recalling that "fugue" also has a revealing psychological connotation: A "fugue state" designates "a flight from one's own identity, often involving travel to some unconsciously desired locality.")[28] We might thus say that, if Hegel in the *Phenomenology* plays the role of a phenomenological tour-guide, a guide whose presence becomes invisible precisely in so far as he disappears into his own tour, then Heidegger too disappears into the *Contributions*, much as a composer disappears into his own composition.[29] As an authorial composer absorbed into the fugue that he himself directs, Heidegger polyphonically elaborates a single theme through a series of successive, overlapping treatments,

---

[27] Jeff Malpas is more perceptive when he describes the *Contributions* as "a sort of 'source-book' for Heidegger's later thinking ... rather than its definitive expression." (Malpas, *Heidegger's Topology*, 214.)

[28] Such a fugue state "is a dissociative reaction to shock or emotional stress on the part of a neurotic, during which all awareness of personal identity is lost though the person's outward behavior may appear rational" (OED, 642). Taken together, these musical and psychological senses of "fugue" (which both derive from the Latin *fuga*, "*to flee*") would provide a provocative dual avenue of approach to the *Contributions*, in terms of its organization and something of its psychological motivations (suggesting another set of reasons for writing this strange and ambitious text). In this latter regard, recall Heidegger's report that he had to give himself over entirely to "thinking [*das Denken*]" daily at the same time in order to avoid doing himself psychological harm, and of his psychologist's claim that the epiphany of the event of enowning (*Ereignis*) hit Heidegger with the force of a psychoanalytic "cure." (See Boss, "Martin Heidegger's Zollikon Seminars,"8, 20.)

[29] Such authorial self-effacement is never perfectly complete. In *Subjects of Desire: Hegelian Reflections in Twentieth-Century France*, Judith Butler shows that no author can entirely efface those marks in their discourse that testify to the process whereby they enacted their own self-disappearance through writing. (On the signs or symptoms of this authorial self-erasure in the *Contributions*, see Schürmann, "Riveted to a Monstrous Site," 315–6.) The irony here is that Heidegger's effacement of his own authorial presence implicitly reinforces another impression suggested by calling these *Fügungen*; viz., that Heidegger sometimes seems to be writing here as a perfectly receptive vehicle of providence, as if indulging in the daydream of purely passive agency. It is not far from here to the ontotheological fantasy of being a self-grounding authority, an absolute sovereign whose words derive their unquestionable normative legitimacy from a source beyond communal adjudication (that this impression does not reflect the truth about Heidegger's *phenomenological* method is something I seek to show here and in Chapter 3.)

the cumulative effect of which is to try to help him – and *only secondarily us* – come to a fuller appreciation of the implications of the phenomenon of enowning.

A philosophical application of the art of fugue affords Heidegger an innovative means to meditate on, explore, and develop the riches of its subject, "enowning." For, by allowing the *Contributions* to remain structurally organized even as it breaks with the hierarchical demands of systematicity, the alternative model of "fuguing" provides Heidegger with a form that nicely accommodate the multiple, overlapping explorations thot allow him to develop his philosophically rich and suggestive underlying theme. Nonetheless, otherwise insightful scholars fail to recognize that the *Contributions* is composed according to the musical model of the fugue (an easy mistake to make if, under the influence of Pöggeler's reading, one too quickly "explains" the strangeness of Heidegger's text by reference to its "Nietzscheanism"), even as they inadvertently document its fugue-like structure. For example, Schwan writes:

> The outward construction of the work leads to many, often formulaic repetitions, producing a line of thought that does not really go anywhere.... The more pages Heidegger heaps up, the more the voluminous text becomes the document of an inner, albeit magnificent, yet nonetheless manifest foundering on the possibility of "making requisitely clear" the *Ereignis* or "event" of the truth of "Being." ... In the final analysis, the *Beiträge* are unable to offer that minutely worked out, structured philosophy of Being that Heidegger intended.[30]

Had Schwan recognized such "formulaic repetitions" as Heidegger's polysemic "fuguing" on the theme of enowning, he might have been able to see the big picture otherwise than as a failed structure, a heap. Schwan's is precisely the kind of impression one will have if one misses the text's fugal structure and – misled by the Pöggelerian dogma of "Heidegger's second *magnum opus*" – one reads the *Contributions* expecting the systematic organization familiar from his great early work, *Being and Time*, an organizational structure that it was never Heidegger's intention to provide in the *Contributions*.

3. HOW THE FUGAL STRUCTURE OF THE *CONTRIBUTIONS* SERVES ITS GOAL: POSTMODERNITY

So, if the *Contributions'* structure is fugal, then what goal does it seek to move us toward? And how does its fugal structure serve this goal?

---

[30] Thus I cannot agree with Schwan's judgment that the *Contributions* "fails to match even remotely the density of thought, content, and structure evidenced in" *Being and Time* (ibid.); put simply, Schwan is misled here by the radical stylistic differences between these texts. (See Schwan, *"Beiträge zur Philosophie* and Politics," 72.)

Heidegger's self-effacing style works to conceal this, but in the *Contributions'* six "fuguings" (*Fügungen*), he retraces the successive stages whereby he initially recognized the integrally related phenomena of "enowning" and "being as such" (the two central insights of his later thought), then he lays out the subsequent steps through which, by thinking these two phenomena in concert (as what he calls "the enowning of being as such"), he believes we can make the transition to an "other beginning" to Western history.[31] The *Contributions'* organizing *Fügungen* do not simply present "essential aspects" of *Ereignis* (as von Herrmann suggests); they articulate a linked series of successive steps meant to take us from first recognizing to fully understanding the significance of Heidegger's insights into the interconnected phenomena of enowning and being as such.

The *Contributions'* fugal composition thus works to develop a complex but unified set of consecutive claims, an overarching movement I suggest we can think of as a *fugal argument*. This overarching movement is what Heidegger calls the "essential onefold" of the *Contributions'* six fugal subjects, which (let us recall) he expresses as follows:

[T]he "Interplay" between the first and the other beginning out of be-ing's "Echo" in the distress of being's abandonment [*in der Not der Seinsverlassenheit*] for the "Leap" into be-ing for "Grounding" its truth as preparation for "The Ones to Come" of "The Ultimate God." (CP 6/GA65 7)

Heidegger's highly compressed statement of the *Contributions* fugal argument can be expanded as follows. We can recognize "being's abandonment" by experiencing the "distress" or "need" (*Not*) that follows from the fact that our current understanding of what entities are dissolves these entities into *nothing* but pure becoming (owing to the Nietzschean metaphysics underlying our atomic age). For, what appears to us (from within the fundamental conceptual parameters set by Nietzsche's ontotheology) as "nothing" should really be understood as the veiled appearance of "being as such" (CP 188/GA65 266), an "inexhaustible" phenomenological "fullness" (CP 266/GA65 382) that "beckons for" (CP 260/GA65 372) and yet also "overflows" (CP 176/GA65 249) all of our conceptualizations. (We will explore Heidegger's strange but crucial claim that the "nothing" should be understand as the veiled appearance of "being as such" in detail next chapter, but we should already have some sense for

---

[31] I take it that this is what Olafson is getting at when he remarks insightfully (if perhaps according to an overly Hegelian script) that the *Contributions'* "*pensées*" trace the "stages ... in the progress of a form of thought that undertakes to move toward a 'new beginning'" (see Olafson, *Heidegger and the Ground of Ethics: A Study of Mitsein*, 103 note 5), and perhaps what von Herrmann means when he says that "[t]he six divisions must thus be enacted in thought" ("Technology, Politics, and Art," 59).

what he is getting at from the explication, in Chapter 3, of Heidegger's phenomenological demonstration of the way the "noth-ing" makes itself felt in Van Gogh's painting.)[32]

In *Contributions*, Heidegger suggests that to see this "nothing" as the veiled appearance of being as such is to glimpse, in this seeming "nothing," an "echo" of the "first beginning" of Western philosophy. For, in that first beginning, "being as such" – that dynamic phenomenological "presencing" (*Anwesen*) that both elicits and exceeds definitive conceptual circumscription – was "inceptively" enowned for the West, interpretively appropriated and so rendered intelligible by "metaphysics" (as we saw in Chapter 1). If we can now recognize "being as such" as the inexhaustible phenomenological reservoir that made it possible for the "the history of metaphysics" to develop as a series of *different*, epoch-grounding understandings of the being of entities, then it finally becomes possible for us to experience the being of entities in a nonmetaphysical way. In Heidegger's terms, that means understanding "the being of entities" in terms of "being as such"; in other words, it means encountering entities as being richer in meaning than we are capable of doing complete justice to conceptually (the very *postmodern* view Heidegger sought to elaborate two years earlier in "The Origin of the Work of Art"). So, Heidegger's fugal argument concludes, to understand and experience intelligibility as "the enowning of being as such" is to "leap" into and thereby "ground" the "truth" (that is, the historical disclosure) of this other, postmodern understanding of being. Heidegger describes those who are capable of making this leap as a future-directed human community (a group he names "the futural ones") whose members, sharing this nonmetaphysical understanding of being, begin to disseminate a new historical sense of what matters, a postmodern understanding of being that Heidegger here calls "the last or ultimate God."

It is thus in the *Contributions* that Heidegger first explicitly elaborates what will henceforth become the two central phenomenological insights of his later work (enowning and being as such), and where he first attempts to spell out what he takes to be their momentous implications. Although these implications remain especially sketchy and elliptical in *Contributions*, it is nevertheless clear that for Heidegger their potential significance is not just narrowly "philosophical." Instead, the consequences of understanding "the enowning of being as such" include nothing short of "the still possible transformation of Western history [*die noch mögliche Wandlung der abendländischen Geschichte*]" (CP 57/GA65 82).[33] With his philosophical characterizations of the meaning and possibility of "other beginning" for Western

---

[32] See Heidegger's "From the First to the Other Beginning: Negation" (CP 125/GA65 178–9).

[33] Derrida thus describes Heidegger's project not as "ontohistorical" (Heidegger's term for it) but as "ontopolitological." (See Derrida, "Philopolemology: Heidegger's Ear

history, Heidegger seems to transgress into the domain of religion (if not theology); for, he goes so far as to equate this other beginning with the return of a "God." As he writes in the *Contributions*: "The ultimate God is not the end, but rather the other beginning in the immeasurable possibility of its history" (CP 289/GA65 412).

Indeed, in what was originally the climactic *Fügung* of the *Contributions* – the abrupt, culminating fugal section of the text that Heidegger calls "The Ultimate God [*Der Letzte Gott*]" – Heidegger first and perhaps most fully articulates and defends philosophically the historical possibility of what may initially be described as a secularized conception of historical "salvation."[34] Thanks to this section on "The Ultimate God," we are now in a much better position to understand Heidegger's famous and controversial pronouncement that: "Only another God can save us [*Nur noch ein Gott kann uns retten*]" (Q&A 57/GA16 671).[35] For with the publication of the *Contributions*, we can now recognize that Heidegger's haunting, posthumous pronouncement to the news magazine *Der Spiegel* (literally haunting, because deliberately posthumous) was not a spontaneous parapraxis

(*Geschlecht* IV).") "Ontopolitological" is Derrida's term for the way in which the understanding of being in the background of our social practices filters our decisions so that metaphysics comes to shape the very intelligibility of (what during the thirties Heidegger refers to as) the "domain of space-time" (*Zeit-spiel-raum*). Heidegger's idea that metaphysics, by ontotheologically "grounding" intelligibility, shapes the very being of *the political* has been highly influential in recent political theory. (This emphasis on the ontology of the political underwrites Ernesto Laclau and Chantal Mouffe's seminal *Hegemony and Socialist Strategy: Towards A Radical Democratic Politics*, and makes itself felt in the work of Badiou, Bourdieu, Connolly, Dallmayr, Rancière, Wolin, Žižek, and many others.)

[34] Von Herrmann's editorial placement of "*Die Kehre im Ereignis*" as the third of four sections in the seventh of eight "divisions" is appropriate in one sense (despite being part of the problematic editorial redaction which obscures the fugal structure of the core of the text), for it marks with a strange penultimacy a section that reflects the thinker's struggle with the ultimate metaphysical urge, the desire to speak one's *final* words (the "secret" words kept closest to one's heart and home but that, Nietzsche thought, precisely in their very "idiosyncratic individuality" may yet allow the individual to speak for humanity), to, as *Zarathustra* says, "speak your word and break!" (Nietzsche's idea that what is most distinctive to the great individuals best represents humanity as a whole is also presaged in Hölderlin's *Empedocles*, a work that strongly influenced *Zarathustra*.) Clearly, *Contributions* is a text deeply marked by Heidegger's tormented Hölderlinian-Nietzschean dream of a political realization of his own dearest philosophical ambitions. (See Nietzsche, *Thus Spoke Zarathustra*, 258. On the "universality" of the "distinctive," see Nietzsche's *Philosophy in the Tragic Age of the Greeks*, 23–4; Hölderlin, *The 'Ground' for Empedocles*" in *Essays and Letters on Theory*, 36, and Hölderlin's "Bread and Wine," in which Hölderlin writes of the suffering that precedes "naming that which is dearest [*nennt er sein Liebstes*]"; see *Hyperion and Selected Poems*, 182–3, translation modified.)

[35] Dreyfus proposes this "equally possible translation" in "Heidegger on Gaining a Free Relation to Technology," 105, 107 note 34. Cf.: "Only a God can save us" (the original English translation by Alter and Caputo) and "Only a God can still save us" (L. Harries' translation, see Q&A 57).

by which Heidegger unconsciously betrayed his Christian despair, and thus a "sad profession of impotence" (as Wolin influentially reads it). It was, instead, a deliberate allusion to "the wholly other" (*der ganz Andere*) "ultimate God" (CP 283/GA65 403), the figure with which Heidegger knew himself to have privately concluded his *Contributions*, and thus a reference Heidegger also had to have known would only make sense after the *Contributions'* publication – that is, as it turned out, more than three decades after the *Der Spiegel* interview.[36] If this is right, then to begin to unravel these long-standing mysteries of Heideggerian thought and scholarship (a task we will pursue further in the final chapter), we need to understand the philosophical work Heidegger is trying to do in "the ultimate God," an especially esoteric *Fügung* that, prior to von Herrmann's editorial redactions, had in fact been the final and climactic crescendo of the *Contributions*.

When we examine the fascinating combination of Hölderlinian, Nietzschean, and other influences that come together in Heidegger's mysterious call for "the ultimate God," we can see that the vision of philosophical salvation Heidegger famously invokes in the 1966 *Der Spiegel* interview is in fact the same positive philosophical project he had been elaborating since 1936–8, when (as we will see next chapter) he broke philosophically with the National Socialist pseudo-revolution as the most extreme symptom of the totalizing metaphysics of "enframing" (*Gestell*), the nihilistic worldview that (as we saw in Chapter 1) Heidegger traces back to the technocratic Nietzschean ontotheology of eternally recurring will-to-power.[37] This Nietzschean mode of revealing "preconceives" all entities as mere *Bestand*, forces endlessly coming together and breaking apart with no purpose other than their own unlimited, self-aggrandizing increase, and thereby "extends itself to a presumed 'eternity' that is no eternity but only the endless etcetera of what is most desolately transitory" (CP 287/GA65 409).

If Nietzsche's metaphysics threatens to empty history of its meaning (in the "eternal return" of technological homogenization and its underlying ontotheology), Heidegger's "other beginning" seeks to refill this emptiness through a postmodern understanding of being that leaves metaphysics – that is, *ontotheology* – behind. To fully understand how Heidegger conceives of this postmodern project in the *Contributions*, we would need to make sense of all the complex and sometimes competing influences that come

---

36 (See Wolin, *The Politics of Being*, 13.) Heidegger's interview with *Der Spiegel* was given Sept. 23, 1966, and published May 31st, 1976 (5 days after his death). The *Contributions* was written between 1936 and 1938 (its fugal core composed between 1936 and 1937), but not published until 1989.

37 For a careful analysis of Heidegger's views that nicely emphasizes Bultmann's influence, see Joachim L. Oberst, *Heidegger on Language and Death: The Intrinsic Connection in Human Existence*.

to a head in his philosophical soteriology of "the ultimate God." That is too huge a project to undertake here, but we can at least single out what is surely the most important of these influences, namely, that provided by Hölderlin's poetic vision of "the future," *das Zu-künft*, which literally connotes "the to-come."[38] Playing on this connotation with the utmost seriousness, Heidegger writes:

> Of those-to-come, Hölderlin came the farthest, and is therefore the most futural poet [*zukünftigste Dichter*, the "poet most to-come"]. Hölderlin is the most futural [*der Zukünftigste*, that is, the one most to-come], because he comes the farthest, and in *traversing* this distance he transforms what is greatest. (CP 281/GA65 401)

For Heidegger, in other words, Hölderlin was "the one who *poeticized the furthest ahead*" into the future (CP 143/GA65 204), and Hölderlin's vision was of a future "turning," or, in Heidegger's words, an "other beginning" for Western history.

Beginning in the student years he spent with Hegel and Schelling at the Lutheran Theological Seminary in Tübingen (in 1788–90, when the recent eruption of the French Revolution made the group's shared faith in a possible "spiritual" revolution in Germany seem much less utopian, if no less *dangerous*, than it does now), Hölderlin dedicated himself through his poetry to a "vernal renewal" of the German nation, "these people whom God has forsaken" (as he put it in *Hyperion*), a people who "live in the world like strangers in their own house."[39] Hölderlin's moving lamentations exercised a profound and important influence on the ambitions Heidegger harbored concerning the leading role that a poetically attuned philosophy could play in helping "*Germania*" discover and appropriate its own

---

[38] Heidegger makes this etymological connotation explicit when he hyphenates "*Zu-künft*" and "*zu-kommt*" (see *e.g.* GA65 401).

[39] (See Derrida, *Of Spirit: Heidegger and the Question*; Hölderlin, *Hyperion and Selected Poems*, 130.) As Benn says of Hölderlin's *Empedocles*, "the conception of salvation involved here is very different from the orthodox Christian conception" (see Benn's "Introduction" to Hölderlin's *Der Tod des Empedokles*, 27, 34). See also Heidegger's similarly fragmentary text, "Zu Hölderlins Empedokles-Bruchstücken" (1944), in GA75 331–9. In these fragments on fragments, Heidegger emphasizes the "*nonobjective nature*" (Ungegenständliche) of the Hölderlinian God, who does not stand over against us like an object but, instead, "comes near or far in an undecideable movement and thereby first comes to word" (GA75 332). The naming of this approaching "God" (for whose approach Heidegger still uses the language of the "rift" (*Riß*) from "The Origin of the Work of Art") is for Heidegger the first essential step of the "other beginning [*anderen Anfang*]" (GA75 335–6), i.e., the reintroduction of being as such into history, eclipsed and forgotten since its metaphysical reduction to the being of entities in the "first beginning" of the West. This fits my contention that for Heidegger this "God" is, in the end, another way of evoking the postmodern understanding of the being of entities in terms of being as such – that is (as we have seen), as genuinely meaningful, inexhaustibly polysemic, informing yet exceeding our conceptions, and so on.

national "identity."[40] For his part, Hölderlin suggested that the spiritual and political homelessness of the "God-forsaken" German people will only be ended when a new historical *"Göttertag"* is inaugurated and the "flight of the Gods" thereby reversed. This "reversal" is the Hölderlinian *Kehre*, and the eschatological vision underwriting it is the most important of the major influences that come together in Heidegger's momentous invocation of "the ultimate God" at the climax of the *Contributions*.

In his 1936–37 *Contributions*, his 1937–8 lecture course on the *Basic Questions of Philosophy*, and even his 1943 lecture on *Hölderlin's Hymn "The Ister,"* Heidegger philosophically appropriates and consistently characterizes the "turning" or "reversal" for which he calls in Hölderlinian terms, for example, as "a decision over the final flight or new advent of the gods." For Heidegger too, "the future of humanity will decide itself … in this turning" (CP 287/GA65 408).[41] But Heidegger rejects the German Idealist metaphysics implicit in Hölderlin's salvific vision, appropriating it instead in terms of his own secularized philosophical understanding of Western humanity's ontohistorical situation. Heidegger thus employs Hölderlin's language in order to help motivate his own deepest conviction that the current historical "night" of cybernetic technology can actually help awaken a phenomenological sensitivity to the inchoate possiblities inherent in things (as we saw in Chapter 3), a receptive comportmental attunement that remains capable of facilitating a history "healing" return of "the holy" (as he puts it in 1935), a spiritual "turn-toward-home" (*Heimkehr*, as he puts it in 1943, evoking Odysseus) that will help us effect a "homecoming through alterity" (a "becoming at home" by *passing through* our "not being at home" in the technological understanding of being). I shall try to explain what these crucial ideas mean as precisely as possible in the final chapter.

Let me just conclude by suggesting that the *Contributions'* musical model serves Heidegger's ambitious goal because music is one of the best ways to realign mood, and the *Contributions* is at bottom an attempt to re-attune humanity comportmentally by fostering a new, more thankful "fundamental attunement" (*Grundstimmung*). Of course, Heidegger's own "music" is linguistic and philosophical; *Contributions* seeks to use the written music of thoughtful words to help realign our sense of our ongoing human odyssey, bringing our existential *Aufenthalte* back home to the polysemy

---

[40] As Ananda Spike-Turner pointed out to me, Nietzsche's *Thus Spoke Zarathustra* begins with Nietzsche symbolically overcoming the event named in the title of Hölderlin's *The Death of Empedocles*: Empedocles throws himself into the volcano; Zarathustra carries his own ashes to the mountain to be reborn. Indeed, Hölderlin's *Empedocles* and Nietzsche's *Zarathustra* come together in a way that likely helped encourage Heidegger to revive the dangerous Platonic dream of the philosopher statesman, as noted earlier. (See also Véronique M. Fóti, "Johann Christian Friedrich Hölderlin," 29–30; and Mark Ralkowski, *Heidegger's Platonism*.)

[41] See also BQP 110/GA45 127.

of being and thus into a true postmodernity.[42] Heidegger's most famous names for this comportmental attunement will be "dwelling" (*wohnen*) and "releasement to things" (*Gelassenheit zu den Dingen*). What such dwelling should be phenomenologically attuned to – or dwell within – is that *Sache selbst* the *Contributions* calls "being as such," because (as we saw in Chapter 3) it is only by being open to that which is not yet here (the still inchoate noth-ing) that we can help bring it into being (thereby "enowning" being, entities, and ourselves in the same creative disclosure).

Of course, however philosophically appropriated, Heidegger's vision of a "turning" of the wheel of history remains, in a word, the dream of *revolution* (as we saw in Chapter 2).[43] Understanding the fugal structure of the *Contributions* helps us recognize that the ultimate goal of this text is to foment philosophically just such a revolution is our ways of understanding ourselves and the meaning and intelligibility of our worlds, and so to make a "transition" (*Übergang*, Nietzsche's word for a tragic undergoing that allows us to overcome something; Heidegger will later speak instead of *Verwindung*, "twisting-free") (CP 57/GA65 82) that leads us beyond our late-modern, "technological" eternal return of the same, "the endless etcetera of what is most desolately transitory."[44] I would add, finally, that despite the undeniable radicalism of this project – and the strikingly novel language Heidegger uses to describe and motivate this postmodern revolution in his *Contributions* – this is nevertheless the same revolution for which he already laid the philosophical groundwork in *Being and Time* by reconceptualizing the self as *Dasein*, being-here, that is, as a temporally structured

---

[42] For more on this revolutionary return home to ourselves, see Julian Young, *Heidegger's Later Philosophy*; as well as my *Heidegger on Ontotheology* (ch. 4) and "Heidegger's Perfectionist Philosophy of Education in *Being and Time*."

[43] After enthusiastically appropriating the language of "revolution" during the war (see e.g. N1 20, 203/NI 28, 234–5, discussed in my *Heidegger on Ontotheology*, 65 note 37), Heidegger renounces the label "revolutionary" in 1944–5, alleging that: "Everything revolutionary remains caught up in opposition. Opposition, however, is servitude." (CPC 33/GA77 51) This rather reactionary rejection of the revolutionary follows from Heidegger's disgust with the National Socialist (CPC 133/GA77 206) and Communist visions of "revolution," which he denigrates (superficially) as *merely* oppositional. As he writes: "I don't want to go forth 'against' anything at all. Whoever engages in opposition loses what is essential, regardless of whether he is victorious or defeated." (CPC 33/GA77 51) Nonetheless, the postmodern project to which Heidegger dedicates his later thought remains undeniably "revolutionary" in the literal sense of seeking to *turn* the wheel of history.

[44] In a text written shortly after *Contributions*, Heidegger makes this point explicitly by quoting Hölderlin's saying that: "For the most part poets spring up at the beginning and at the end of a world-epoch." Heidegger reinterprets Hölderlin's idea as follows: "Not only is the rise of history poetic [or *poietic*, i.e., a bringing-into-being], but above all the transition of one world epoch of history into the coming one is poetic. For such a transition takes place only as a going-under. ... The going-under is the rising dawn of the beginning." (See Heidegger's fragmentary text, "Own to Philosophy [*Das Wesen der Philosophie*]," translated by K. Maly in his *Heidegger's Possibility*, 152.)

making-intelligible of the place in which we happen to find ourselves. By developing his fuguing on the theme of "enowning" or *Ereignis, Contributions* seeks to help us recognize just how rich, meaningful – indeed, how philosophically *revolutionary* – the full implications of this seemingly simple world-disclosure might yet turn out to be.

7

The Danger and the Promise of Heidegger, an American Perspective

Enframing is, as it were, the photographic negative of enowning.

Heidegger (FS 60/GA15 366)

1. INTRODUCTION: THE DANGER AND THE PROMISE OF HEIDEGGER

Thanks to Heidegger, we have learned to hear the ambiguity of subjective and objective genitives in phrases with the form, "The X of Y." We needed to be taught to hear this ambiguity because it is concealed by the impossible simultaneity of its dual meanings. *Critique of Pure Reason*, for example, signifies both criticism *directed at* pure reason and criticism *belonging to* pure reason. Ordinarily, however, we hear the title of Kant's great work only as an objective genitive, as a critique directed at the earlier pretensions of pure reason (which, with Anselm and Descartes, went so far as to try to prove God's existence solely by analyzing the concept "God," as we saw in Chapter 1), and so not also as a subjective genitive, as a critique used by pure reason in order to circumscribe and secure its own legitimate domain. What is more, even after we learn to recognize that *Critique of Pure Reason* also means the critique that *belongs* to pure reason, we still cannot hear both meanings at the same time. This is because we hear one meaning instead of the other; what we hear occupies the place of what we do not. This point is nicely illustrated by the gestalt figure Wittgenstein made famous. (See Figure 6.)

Unless this figure has already been introduced as a "duck rabbit," we do not ordinarily notice that it has another aspect (that it can be seen as a rabbit), because the aspect we do see (the duck) stands in the place of the aspect we do not see (the rabbit), and we cannot see both the duck and the rabbit at once.[1] After we have recognized that the figure can be seen as

---

[1] See Wittgenstein, *Philosophical Investigations*, 194. Whether a naive viewer sees Wittgenstein's figure as a duck or as a rabbit seems to depend on the angle at which it is placed. As the

FIGURE 6. Wittgenstein's version of Jastrow's gestalt figure, redrawn by Mungo Thomson, 2010 (commissioned). Reproduced by permission from the artist.

either a duck or a rabbit, most of us can freely gestalt-switch back-and-forth between them. Yet, untutored viewers of gestalt figures such as Jastrow's duck-rabbit, a Necker cube, or a Janus vase do not initially see that there is anything they do not see, because what they do see stands in the place of what they do not see. The crucial point, for our purposes, is that we see what we see *instead* of what we do not.

I begin by rehearsing such seemingly obvious and rudimentary phenomenological lessons because I want to suggest that Heidegger, in a strictly analogous way, teaches us to see "the danger" of late-modern technologization as standing in the place of "the promise" of postmodernity. Heidegger's hope for the future, I shall show, turns crucially on helping us learn to make a gestalt switch whereby we come to see the promise *instead* of the danger – there, in the same place. When we examine the precise meaning Heidegger gives these philosophical terms of art, it will become clear that seeing the promise instead of the danger does not mean adopting some Pollyannaish optimism.[2] Rather, learning to see the promise instead of the

picture is rotated so that the "duck's beak" points north, this "beak" becomes increasingly likely to appear as the "ears" of the rabbit. As this suggests, neither the gestalt figures nor the subjective-objective genitives have an intrinsically dominant aspect (although in each precise case there is a dominant aspect which we tend to see instead of the other), and this constitutes a noteworthy difference from the danger-promise ambiguity, in which the danger more insistently eclipses the promise.

[2] "The greater danger consists in optimism, which recognizes only pessimism as its opponent" (N4 247/NII 393). I would suggest, nonetheless, that the old cliché of "seeing the glass as half full rather than half empty" turns out to be a rather appropriate image for the kind of gestalt switch Heidegger has in mind – if we add that the Heideggerian trick is to see the glass as *half-full of emptiness*.

danger means developing a phenomenological comportment attuned to what we can anticipate but never expect, that is, in a word, the future (and perhaps even, as Heidegger would say, the very *futurity* of the future – that which continues *to come* toward us phenomenologically from out of the horizon we call the "future" – a sense expressed by the German *Zukunft*, the French *avenir*, and the Latin *futūrus*: "to come," "to arrive or happen," "to come to be").[3]

For the same reasons, the title of this section and this chapter (a title I take from the European Parliament of Philosophers' international colloquium on "Heidegger: The Danger and the Promise") can also be heard in at least two different senses. First, "The Danger and the Promise of Heidegger" signifies what remains dangerous and promising *about* Heidegger. We tend to hear the title in this sense first, I think, despite the fact that what remains dangerous and promising about Heidegger's thinking cannot easily be reduced to a single "danger" or "promise." Heidegger's *dangerousness* may be most obvious in his unapologetic attempt to think "the inner truth and greatness" of National Socialism, but it is also clearly visible in his claim to have "dissolved the idea of 'logic' in the turbulence of a more originary questioning," in his reading of the entire history of Western metaphysics as increasingly "nihilistic," and in his never-relinquished endeavor to restore to thinking "a proper though limited leadership in the whole of human existence" (IM 213/GA40 208; P 92; 83/GA9 107, 105). Rather than multiplying examples of the dangers attendant upon Heidegger's thinking, or exploring their important interconnections (as I have done in *Heidegger on Ontotheology*), I shall risk a hypothesis that does not presume to stand entirely outside these dangers, as though diagnosing them from a safe distance. For, in my view, these dangers, undeniable though they are, cannot be entirely disassociated from "the promise of Heidegger," that is, from what remains promising about Heidegger's thinking – including, perhaps most importantly, the promise of postmodernity that his thought helps open up for us.

[3] This chapter started out as a paper I was invited to present to the European Parliament of Philosophers' international colloquium on "Heidegger: The Danger and the Promise" at the University of Strasbourg, France, in 2004. The announcement for this colloquium began: "To situate this project under the title 'Heidegger – the danger and the promise' [*sous le titre 'Heidegger – le danger et la promesse'*] is not only to engage reflection on the thinking of one of the most important philosophers of the 20th century, but it is also to propose an encounter with our historical destiny and its future. And, to speak more precisely about this question: Would not the future be a thing of the past?" The answer I shall suggest here is: Only if the thinking of a genuine postmodernity opened by Heidegger is a thing of the past. In my view, however, there is a future (indeed, more than one) disclosed by this thinking about how to transcend the ontotheological roots of global technologization. (Intriguingly, none of the other presenters at the Parliament of Philosophers recognized at the time that Heidegger himself had thought "the danger" and "the promise" in the intimate juxtaposition explored in this chapter, making the title of the Parliament's colloquium a fortuitous coincidence.)

Admittedly, it sounds provocative to maintain that what is promising about Heidegger remains linked to what is most dangerous in his thinking. It is, however, precisely this difficult and troubling juxtaposition of danger *and* promise that my title gathers together in order to think through.

This, then, is how I intend the "and" in this title: Heidegger's thinking remains dangerous *and* promising, in one and the same place. Of course, the "and" of this title can be understood differently. "The Danger and the Promise of Heidegger" could easily be taken as entitling one to specify the dangers of Heidegger's thinking, on the one hand, and then, on the other hand, to comment upon what remains promising about his work. This, however, presumes that we can take the measure of Heidegger's thinking by weighing its "pros and cons" in separate scales, which is not entirely true. If I think it more fitting to ask about what remains both dangerous and promising in Heidegger's thinking, this is not only because such a task accords nicely with Heidegger's cherished Hölderlinian maxim (from the late hymn, *Patmos*): "Yet, where the danger is, the saving power also grows." It is also because I believe – and sought to show in *Heidegger on Ontotheology* – that we can come to understand what remains most promising in Heidegger's thinking only by exploring what is most dangerous in his work.[4]

In that earlier book I showed, to sketch only the most striking example, how Heidegger's philosophical view of the relation between philosophy and the other sciences motivated his political attempt to transform the German university in 1933–4. This means that the direct connection between Heidegger's philosophy and his opprobrious commitment to National Socialism cannot be understood apart from his radical philosophical efforts to rethink and reform higher education, ultimately by uncovering and contesting the ontotheological roots of global technologization. Instead of using this dangerous connection as an excuse to dismiss Heidegger's promising views on education, however, I sought to show that his prescient critique of the university has only become more relevant since he elaborated it, and that, with the important philosophical corrections suggested for this philosophical research program by his so-called turn, the later Heidegger's mature vision for a re-ontologization of education merits the careful attention of all those of us who, like Lyotard (as we saw in Chapter 4), seek to understand the ontological roots and important implications of our own growing crisis in higher education. This is to suggest, in other words, that we cannot critically reconstruct and develop Heidegger's views on the future of education – one of the most promising

---

[4] Agamben points out that Heidegger himself did not consistently live up to his own thinking of the way the greatest danger opens onto the promise. Agamben appeals to "Hölderlin's principle" to suggest convincingly, *pace* Heidegger, that "precisely in the extreme situation of the camp appropriation and freedom ought to be possible." (See Giorgio Agamben, *Remnants of Auschwitz: The Witness and the Archive*, 75.)

dimensions of his thinking – without first understanding the philosophical depths of his commitment to Nazism, however dangerous those waters remain. While my first book is anything but an apology for Heidegger's disastrous Nazism, then, it does suggest that we recognize what remains most promising in his thinking only by coming to terms with what remains most dangerous about it. I have sought to show in the present work, moreover, that this intimate connection between danger and promise holds not only for Heidegger's long-developed vision for higher education and his resulting commitment to Nazism, but also for his controversial critique of our current "technological" ontotheology and his complementary vision of an "other beginning" for Western history, a postmodern beginning by which Heidegger suggests we can best regain a more meaningful future. It is this connection between the danger and the promise of Heidegger that I shall seek to elucidate further in this final chapter.

As I began by suggesting, moreover, we can also understand this title in a second sense, seemingly quite different from the way we have been reading it. "The Danger and the Promise of Heidegger" can be heard not as entitling an examination of what remains dangerous and promising *about* Heidegger's thinking but, instead, as calling for an elucidation of Heidegger's *own* understanding of "the danger" and "the promise." Indeed, we begin to appreciate the semantic riches concealed by the very economy of this title when we realize that Heidegger not only explicitly uses the concepts of "the danger" and "the promise" himself, but that the precise meanings he gives to these two concepts link them inextricably together. What is so suggestive, in other words, is that Heidegger does not just think "the danger" as well as "the promise"; he thinks "the danger *and* the promise" – and, moreover, he thinks the connection between the danger *and* the promise specifically in order to address the question of a future understanding of being. For Heidegger, the possibility of a meaningful postmodernity turns, as we have seen, on our discerning and transcending the ontotheological foundations of our late-modern, technological understanding of being. I shall thus focus in what follows on Heidegger's reasons for thinking these matters together, examining, in particular, the way they intersect with and give rise to Heidegger's provocative critique of "America." Doing so will not only help us elucidate one of the most mysterious claims at the heart of Heidegger's later thinking; it will also enable us to recapitulate, from another perspective, some of the central ideas we have explored in this book and further clarify some of their most suggestive philosophical implications.

2. HEIDEGGER ON THE GREATEST DANGER

Heidegger's conception of "the danger" can only be fully understood against the background of his famous critique of "enframing" (*Gestell*), our "technological" understanding of the being of entities. As we saw in

Chapter 1, Heidegger's critique of "enframing" *follows from*, and so can only really be understood in terms of, the understanding of metaphysics as "ontotheology" central to his later thought. Our endeavor to fathom Heidegger's own sense of "the danger" of technology must thus begin with a quick recapitulation of his profound but idiosyncratic conception of metaphysics as *ontotheology*.

Heidegger, as I understand him, is a great critical heir of the German Idealist tradition.[5] He builds upon the Kantian idea that we implicitly participate in the making-intelligible of our worlds, but maintains that our sense of reality is mediated by lenses we inherit from metaphysics. In effect, Heidegger historicizes Kant's "discursivity thesis," which holds that intelligibility is the product of a subconscious process by which we "spontaneously" organize and so filter a sensibly overwhelming world to which we are fundamentally "receptive."[6] For Heidegger, this implicit organization is accomplished not by historically fixed cognitive "categories" but, rather, by the succession of changing historical ontotheologies that make up the "core" of the metaphysical tradition. These ontotheologies establish "the truth concerning entities as such and as a whole"; in other words, they tell us both what and how entities *are* – establishing both their essence and their existence, to take only the most famous example. When metaphysics succeeds at this ontotheological task, it temporarily secures the intelligible order by grasping it both "ontologically," from the inside-out, and "theologically," from the outside-in. These ontotheologies come to provide the dual anchors that suspend humanity's changing sense of "reality," holding back the floodwaters of historicity long enough to allow the formation of an "epoch," an historical constellation of intelligibility, which is unified around its ontotheological understanding of the being of entities.

I have thus interpreted Heidegger's understanding of the ontotheological structure of Western metaphysics ("the history that we *are*") as advancing a doctrine of *ontological holism*. By giving shape to our historical understanding of "what *is*," metaphysics determines the most basic presuppositions of what *anything* is, ourselves included. This is why Heidegger writes that: "Western humanity, in all its comportment toward entities, and even

---

[5] Of course, for Heidegger "critical heir" is a pleonasm, since the calcified tradition can only be turned into a living heritage through those critical "reciprocative rejoinders" that update and alter the tradition so it can speak to the changed needs of the contemporary world. (For an insightful exploration of Heidegger's broader view, see Stephen Mulhall, *Inheritance and Originality: Wittgenstein, Heidegger, Kierkegaard*.)

[6] See my "Phenomenology and Technology," 195–201. On Kant's "discursivity thesis," see Henry Allison, *Kant's Transcendental Idealism: An Interpretation and Defense*, 65–8. For Heidegger, the "discursivity" (*Diskursivität*) "which belongs to the essence of understanding is the sharpest index of its finitude" (KPM 21/GA3 29–30), and "the understanding of being which thoroughly dominates human existence ... manifests itself as the innermost ground of human finitude" (KPM 160/GA3 228). (For more on this point, see my *Heidegger on Ontotheology*, 54 note 15.)

toward itself, is in every respect sustained and guided by metaphysics" (N4 205/NII 343). Ontological holism explains how the successful ontotheologies can function historically like self-fulfilling prophecies, pervasively reshaping intelligibility. Put simply, since all entities *are*, when a new ontotheological understanding of what and how entities *are* takes hold and spreads, it progressively transforms our basic understanding of *all* entities. By explicitly focusing and disseminating an ontotheological understanding of the being of entities, our great metaphysicians help establish the fundamental conceptual parameters and ultimate standards of legitimacy for each of our successive historical "epochs."

Nietzsche, we have seen, is the pivotal figure in Heidegger's critique of our technological epoch of enframing because, according to Heidegger's reductive yet revealing reading, Nietzsche's "unthought" metaphysics provides the ontotheological lenses that implicitly structure our current sense of reality. Nietzsche criticized what he (mistakenly) took to be Darwin's doctrine of "the survival of the fittest" by pointing out that life forms cannot survive by aiming at mere survival.[7] In a changing environment characterized by material scarcity and hence competition, life can survive only by continually overcoming itself, surpassing whatever stage it has previously reached. From the perspective of this inner "will" of life (what Nietzsche calls "will-to-power"), any state of being previously attained serves merely as a rung on the endless ladder of "sovereign becoming." Indeed, in Heidegger's view, Nietzsche understood "the totality of entities as such" *ontotheologically* as "eternally recurring will-to-power," that is, as an unending disaggregation and reaggregation of forces with no purpose or goal beyond the self-perpetuating augmentation of these forces through their continual self-overcoming. (In this, I suggested, Nietzsche effectively ontologized and so universalized insights that Darwin had already postulated in biology and Adam Smith in the economic domain.) Now, our Western culture's unthinking reliance on this implicitly Nietzschean ontotheology is leading us to transform all entities into *Bestand*, mere "resources" standing by to be optimized, ordered, and enhanced with maximal efficiency. As this historical transformation of beings into intrinsically meaningless resources becomes more pervasive, it increasingly eludes our critical gaze. Indeed, we late-modern Nietzscheans come to treat even ourselves in the nihilistic terms that underlie our technological refashioning of the world: No longer sovereign modern subjects seeking to master and control an objective world, human beings are becoming merely one more intrinsically meaningless resource to be optimized, ordered, and enhanced with maximal efficiency, whether capitalistically, psychopharmacologically, genetically, or even (as we have seen here) aesthetically.[8]

---

[7] See John Richardson, *Nietzsche's New Darwinism*.

[8] Heidegger is deeply worried that within our current technological constellation of intelligibility, the post-Nietzschean epoch of enframing, it is increasingly becoming the case

As this "technological" understanding of being takes hold and spreads, it dramatically transforms our relations to ourselves and our worlds. Yet, we tend not to notice these transformations because their very pervasiveness helps render them invisible, a seemingly paradoxical fact Heidegger explains by appeal to the "first law of phenomenology."[9] This "law of proximity" (or "distance of the near") states that the closer we are to something, the harder it is to bring it clearly into view (the lenses on our glasses, for example, or Poe's eponymous purloined letter), and thus that the more decisively a matter shapes us, the more difficult it is for us to understand it explicitly. Eventually, however, Heidegger thinks that either new ways of understanding the being of entities will emerge and take hold (most likely, as Kuhn suggests, out of the investigation of anomalous entities, like true artworks and humble things, which resist being reduced to the terms of the dominant ontotheology), or else our conception of *all* entities will be brought permanently into line with our spreading Nietzschean ontotheology. The latter alternative has never yet occurred historically (because no previous ontotheology succeeded in permanently entrenching itself), but the possibility that it could happen now is precisely what Heidegger calls "the danger" (*die Gefahr*), in the singular. It is this singular danger of a completely "technologically homogenized world-civilization" (GA13 243) that Heidegger often designates using such superlatives as "the greatest danger" and "the most extreme danger." The danger, in other words, is that our Nietzschean ontotheology could become permanently *totalizing*, "driving out every other possibility of revealing" (QCT 27/GA7 28) by enabling us to overwrite and so effectively obscure Dasein's "special nature," our defining capacity for creative world-disclosure, replacing it with the "total thoughtlessness" of lives lived entirely in the grip of the Nietzschean conception of all entities, ourselves included, as intrinsically meaningless resources on standby to be optimized for maximally flexible use (DT 56/G 25). For Heidegger, then, the danger has two isomorphic aspects: "Humanity is threatened with the annihilation of its essence, and being itself is endangered in its usage of its abode" (N4 245/NII 391).

It is, in fact, not so difficult to imagine that, in our endless quest for technological self-optimization, we might go so far as to unintentionally

---

that: "Only what is calculable in advance counts as being" (TTL 136/USTS 17). For, our technological understanding of being produces a "calculative thinking" (DT 46/G 13) that quantifies all qualitative relations, reducing entities to bivalent, programmable "information" (TTL 139/USTS 22), digitized data ready to enter into what Jean Baudrillard aptly describes as "a state of pure circulation" on the Internet. (See Baudrillard's *The Transparency of Evil: Essays on Extreme Phenomena*, 4; and Dreyfus's insightful monograph, *On the Internet*.)

9 For a detailed explanation and defense of Heidegger's use of the adjective "technological" to characterize our current mode of revealing, see *Heidegger on Ontotheology*, ch. 2, esp. 45 note 1 and 75 note 60.

reengineer our meaning-bestowing capacity for creative world-disclosure right out of our genetic makeup, thereby eliminating the very source of any meaningful future. Even short of such catastrophic scenarios, Heidegger suggests that if late modernity's technological "enframing" manages to secure its monopoly on the real, preemptively delegitimating all alternative understandings of being (by deriding them as "non-naturalistic," for example, and thus as irrelevant, ridiculous, nonserious, mystical, irrational, and so on), this enframing could effect and enforce a *double forgetting* in which we human beings lose sight of our distinctive capacity for world-disclosure *and* forget that anything has thus been forgotten. The greatest danger, put simply, is that we could become so satiated by the endless possibilities for flexible self-optimization opened up by treating our worlds and ourselves as resources to be optimized that we lose the very sense that anything is lost with such a self-understanding. (This is what Baudrillard calls "the triumph of the simulacra," and in Heidegger's terms it – along with the metanarrative of paralogism Lyotard describes – should really be characterized as *late-modern* rather than *postmodern* phenomena.) The possibility of such a double-forgetting explains the later Heidegger's strange, controversial, and seemingly paradoxical claim that the "greatest danger" is expressed in the "authentic need" of "needlessness" (GA79 56), his idea that we live in the age of greatest need precisely insofar as we experience ourselves as not needing anything at all.[10] It is, moreover, this concealed manifestation of the greatest danger – in which dystopia masquerades as utopia – that the later Heidegger comes to associate with "America."

3. AMERICA AND THE DANGER

When Heidegger first develops his conception of the danger in the late 1930s, he associates it primarily with the "total mobilization" of the Nazi war machine, which was then expanding to an unprecedented scale the metaphysical logic of "technicity" (*Technik*) or "machination"

---

[10] Thus we get Heidegger's provocative evocation of the great danger that I call (with a nod to Marx) *the problem of the happy enframer*: "What has long since been threatening man with death, and indeed the death of his own nature, is the unconditional character of mere willing in the sense of purposeful self-assertion in everything [i.e., "will-to-will," Heidegger's shorthand for the ontotheological unity of will-to-power and eternal recurrence]. What threatens man in his very nature is the willed view that man, by the peaceful release, transformation, storage, and channeling of the energies of physical nature could render the human condition, man's being, tolerable for everybody and happy in all respects" (PLT 116/GA5 294). Heidegger's postulation of a great "need of needlessness" initially sounds bizarre (he was writing at a time when nuclear energy promised to conquer material scarcity), but he develops here a line of thought long familiar to German philosophy (and not only critical theory), going all the way back to the Hippocratic tradition of diagnosing diseases of which the patient remains blissfully unaware. (See Raymond Geuss, *The Idea of a Critical Theory: Habermas and the Frankfurt School*.)

(*Machenschaft*) – Heidegger's first names for the historical mode of revealing he later calls enframing. In "The Turning in Enowning," the penultimate section of "The Ultimate God," the climactic "fugue" of *Contributions to Philosophy: From Enowning* (a section written between 1936 and 1937), Heidegger envisions this metaphysical logic reaching its conclusion in the dead-end of an historical age unable to recognize that it has rationally managed and controlled its own "future" right out of existence. In the ominous scenario he foresees:

> Humanity with its machinations might for centuries yet pillage and lay waste to the planet. This enormous hustle and bustle might "develop" into something unimaginable and take the seemingly rigorous form of the massive regulating of the desolate as such, while the greatness of be-ing remains closed-off because decisions are no longer undertaken about truth and untruth and their [*alêtheiac*] essence. The only thing that will still count [in this age of technological metaphysics] is reckoning the successes and failures of machinations. This reckoning stretches itself out into a presumed "eternity," which is no eternity but, instead, only the endless etcetera of what is most desolately transitory. (CP 287/GA65 408–9)[11]

Recognizing that this "desolate" mode of technological revealing is rooted in Nietzsche's metaphysics of "constant overcoming" (through which "the wasteland grows" [WCT 29/GA8 31]), Heidegger maintains that "[t]he bewitchment by technicity and its *constantly self-surpassing progress* is only *one* sign of this enchantment, by which everything presses forth into calculation, usage, breeding, manageability, and regulation" (CP 87/GA65 124, first emphasis mine).[12] In this total technological mobilization, the efficient "reckoning" that optimizes current actualities threatens to supplant the thoughtful discernment of inchoate possibilities.

Heidegger originally associates this danger with National Socialism, as his critical references to "breeding" in 1936–7 suggest. By 1940, however, when America directly enters the Second World War in response to the bombing of Pearl Harbor, Heidegger is no longer sure that Germany will win the massive arms race for global control that he thinks all nations are being driven into by the technological ontotheology underlying the age. Heidegger thus concludes his 1940 Nietzsche lectures dramatically, interpreting (for those students who have not already gone off to war) Nietzsche's notorious prophecy that: "The time is coming when the struggle for dominion over the earth will be carried on ... in the name of *fundamental philosophical doctrines*." According to the reading Heidegger will never

---

[11] It is worth noticing that what Heidegger will call the "promise" is already present (in its very absence) here in Heidegger's first description of the danger: "the greatness of be-ing *remains closed-off* because decisions are no longer undertaken about truth and untruth and their essence" (my emphasis).

[12] This is what Heidegger means when he writes: "Machination itself ... is the essencing of being as such [*die Wesung des Seyns*]" (CP 89/GA65 128).

subsequently relinquish, Nietzsche's ontotheological understanding of the being of entities invisibly shapes the historical unfolding of our contemporary world. For as we have seen, Nietzsche's ontotheological understanding of "the totality of entities as such" as "eternally recurring will-to-power" not only intensifies "the struggle for the unrestrained exploitation of the earth as a source of raw materials" (a struggle already implicit in the modern subject/object divide), it also generates our distinctively late-modern, reflexive application of that limitless objectification back upon the subject itself. This objectification of the subject works to dissolve the very subject/object distinction and so lays the ground for what Heidegger already recognizes in 1940 as "the cynical exploitation of 'human resources' in the service of the absolute empowering of will to power" (N3 250/NII 333).[13]

Heidegger thinks that the way Nietzsche's ontotheology reduces the subject to just another resource to be optimized renders it inevitable in the short-term that "humanity ... be forged and bred into a type, a type that possesses the essential aptitude for establishing absolute dominion over the earth" (N3 245/NII 327), but he is no longer sure that Germany is the nation that will prove itself equal to the metaphysical essence of the age and so inherit the destiny of global domination. Indeed, he expresses such dangerously "unpatriotic" doubts (for "all those who had ears to hear") in the final hour of this 1940 lecture:

> The question remains as to which peoples and what kinds of humanity ultimately ... will rally to the law of this fundamental trait and thus pertain to the early history of dominion over the earth. (N3 250/NII 332–3)

By 1969, however, at the height of the Vietnam war, there no longer seems to be any question in Heidegger's mind: "America" has become virtually synonymous with "the danger."

"As for America," Heidegger says during his 1969 seminar in France (not hesitating to pronounce his views on a land he would never deign to

---

[13] The fuller context runs: "Nietzsche's metaphysics, that is to say, the truth of the totality of entities as such ... is the fundamental trait of the history of our age, which is inaugurating itself only now in its incipient consummation as the contemporary age.... That is not to say, however, that the struggle for the unrestrained exploitation of the earth as a source of raw materials or the cynical exploitation of 'human resources' in the service of the absolute empowering of will to power will explicitly appeal to philosophy for help in grounding its essence, or even will adopt philosophy as its façade. On the contrary, we must assume that philosophy will disappear as a doctrine and a construct of culture, and that it can disappear only because as long as it was genuine it identified the reality of the real, that is, being, on the basis of which every individual entity is designated to be what it is and how it is.... *'Fundamental metaphysical doctrines' means the essence of self-consummating metaphysics, which in its fundamental traits sustains Western history, shapes it in its modern European form, and destines it for 'world domination.'* ... Nietzsche's metaphysics is at its core never a specifically German philosophy. It is European, global." In the *Gesamtausgabe* edition of this text, Heidegger explicitly identifies this global phase of fulfilled metaphysics with "the English empire" (GA50 82).

visit, despite numerous invitations from Americans deeply interested in his thought), "the reality of that country is veiled from the view of those [Americans who are] interested" in the question of being. The "reality" of "America," Heidegger proclaims, must be understood as "the collusion between industry and the military," that is, in terms of "economic development and the armament that it requires" (FS 56/GA15 359). To see that Heidegger is not only advancing another critique of America's notorious "military-industrial complex," we need to understand the context in which he introduces these remarks.

Discussing "the end of physics" with Jean Beufret and others, Heidegger recapitulates his argument from *Being and Time* that the positive sciences are each guided by an ontological preunderstanding of the ontic domains they study. For example, historians must presuppose an ontological understanding of what history *is*, biologists what life *is*, psychologists what consciousness *is*, and so on, simply to be able to pick out the appropriate objects to study. The "positive sciences" do not normally make the "ontological posits" guiding their empirical research explicit but instead take them over implicitly from the ontotheology underlying the age. When, usually in response to a scientific crisis, scientists come to focus explicitly on the ontological presuppositions guiding their "normal science," then in Heidegger's terms they are doing philosophy rather than science.[14] Here in 1969 Heidegger will thus suggest that physicists, as physicists, cannot question the *being* of physical entities, but instead tend unknowingly to take over – from the current ontotheological understanding of being – their preconception of the "physicality" of physical entities, which implicitly guides their scientific endeavors. When Heidegger asserts that "technology is not grounded in physics, but rather the reverse; physics is grounded upon the essence of technology" (FS 54/GA15 355), his point is thus that physics' guiding understanding of the being of physical entities is taken over from Nietzsche's "technological" ontotheology, which has already preunderstood the being of all entities as intrinsically meaningless forces serving only their own self-perpetuating increase.

Heidegger acknowledges that "nothing is more natural than to ask whether science will be able to stop in time" to avert the danger, but he maintains that: "Such a stop is nevertheless fundamentally impossible" (FS 55/GA15 358). Long before the explosive developments we have witnessed in biotechnology, the human genome project, stem-cell research, cloning, genetic engineering, gene splicing, and the like, Heidegger recognized that we would not be able to control the scientific objectification by which we seek to extend control over even our own human being. As Dreyfus succinctly explains, "the drive to control everything is precisely what we

---

[14] I explain and defend the logic of this view in *Heidegger on Ontotheology*, ch. 3.

do not control," because this drive toward increasing control over the human being follows from the deepest metaphysical presuppositions of the age.[15] As we saw in Chapter 2, modern *subjectivism*, the subject's relentless drive to master and control the objective world, redoubles itself in late-modern *enframing*, as the subject turns the techniques developed for controlling an external domain of intrinsically meaningless objects back upon itself. For Heidegger, then, the distinctive dictum of enframing is expressed in our growing conviction that: "The human can be produced according to a definite plan just like any other technological object" (FS 55/GA15 358).

What *distinguishes* our late-modern, technological enframing of all entities as resources to be optimized from the modern subject's total control and domination of the objective world, we have seen, is the reflexive application of this objectification back upon the subject itself. That which makes such late-modern enframing unique, however, is also precisely what makes possible the emergence of an historically unprecedented technological *danger*. For, it is this self-objectification of the subject that "dissolves" both self and world into the late-modern pool of intrinsically meaningless resources standing by for endless optimization. As Heidegger puts it here in 1969:

The most extreme danger [*die äußerste Gefahr*] is that man, insofar as he produces [*herstellt*] himself, no longer feels any other necessities than the demands of his self-production.... What is uncanny, however, is not so much that everything will be extinguished [*ausgelöscht*], but instead that this [extinction of the essence of human being, language, and tradition] does not actually come to light. The surge of information veils the disappearance of what has been, and prospective planning is just another name for the obstruction of the future. (FS 56/GA15 359)

It is no coincidence that Heidegger explicitly mentions "America" in the sentence that immediately follows this description of a dystopia blithely mistaking itself for utopia. Clearly, "America" is the name on the tip of Heidegger's tongue for a life lived in the eternal sunshine of the permanent present, for a humanity alienated from its own alienation, blind to the fact that the relation to the past preserved in language is being buried beneath an unprecedented "surge of information," and unaware that our prodigious capacity for generating far-reaching plans for the control of every foreseeable eventuality is in danger of blocking our path to the *future* – that is, the "opening" of a genuinely postmodern understanding of human beings and "an entirely new relation to nature" as overflowing with inchoate, meaningful possibilities (FS 55/GA15 358). In sum, then, when Heidegger names "America" as his sole example for "the emergence of a new form of nationalism ... grounded upon technological power" (ibid.),

---

[15] See Dreyfus, "Heidegger on the Connection Between Nihilism, Art, Technology, and Politics," 307–10.

his point is not simply that America has become the world's most advanced military-industrial complex but, rather, that we have become this by succeeding where the Nazis failed, by making ourselves into the most extreme expression of the technological ontotheology of the age. For Heidegger, America is the avant-garde of the greatest danger of ontohistorical technologization, the country working hardest to obscure the "most important ... insight that man is not an entity who makes himself" (FS 56/GA15 359).

Although it will be obvious to anyone who knows more about "America" than what they read in the newspapers that Heidegger's critique is terribly one-sided, he does diagnose this one terrible side with an unequalled depth of insight and prescience. Indeed, it is hard to deny that Heidegger was right to see "America" as blazing the trail toward the greatest danger of technology, since, guided by enframing's endless optimization imperative, we continue to develop a broad spectrum of cosmetic psychopharmacologies – from Prozac to Viagra – with which to eradicate whatever existential anxieties we cannot escape by throwing ourselves into an accelerating work world or distract ourselves from by means of our burgeoning entertainment technologies and other aesthetic diversions. So, is our self-proclaimed "superpower" really working out the will of the will-to-power and thereby increasing the danger that any other future becomes merely "a thing of the past"?[16] To open the discussion of this important question (which is all I hope to do here), allow me just one telling anecdote. In an article on the increasingly prominent role religious convictions have come to play in American politics (both abroad and at home), Ron Suskind, the former senior national affairs reporter for *The Wall Street Journal* (the unofficial newspaper of the American ruling class), reports on a conversation he had in 2002 with a "senior advisor to [then President George W.] Bush." This senior advisor, who was unhappy with a magazine article Suskind had written, said:

> that guys like [Suskind] were in "what we call the reality-based community," which he defined as people who "believe that solutions emerge from your judicious study of discernible reality." [Suskind] nodded and murmured something about enlightenment principles and empiricism. He cut [Suskind] off. "That's not the way the world really works anymore," he continued. "We're an empire now, and when we act, we create our own reality. And while you're studying that reality – judiciously, as you will – we'll act again, creating other new realities, which you can study too, and that's how things will sort out. We're history's actors ... and you, all of you, will be left to just study what we do."[17]

It was both alarming and revealing to hear such imperialistic hubris expressed so openly by one of President Bush's senior advisors. One thing it

---

[16] This is a quotation from the previously noted announcement of the French Parliament of Philosophers' international colloquium on "Heidegger: The Danger and the Promise."

[17] Ron Suskind, "Without a Doubt" (ellipses in original).

shows, from a post-Heideggerian perspective, is that recognizing historicity is not sufficient for actually transforming history. For, from this important insight that humanity's basic sense of reality changes with time, it does not follow that the American administration ever recognized the nature of our current historical reality, let alone that they succeeded in changing it. On the contrary, the Bush administration's delusions of "empire" seem only to have reified and reinforced the same ontotheologically grounded historical self-understanding that Heidegger already recognized in America in 1969, and before that, in Nazi Germany in 1940.

Of course, there is always something grotesque and misleading about such comparisons, by which we ignore hugely important differences in order to emphasize a deeper continuity that usually passes unnoticed. Granted, happily. A more interesting objection to what I have just said, however, would be the suggestion that the Bush administration, under the influence of religious fundamentalists like President Bush himself, did its best to reverse the technological control of human beings, as can be seen in from the way it outlawed the use of federal funds for new genetic lines for stem cell research, increased restrictions on abortion, reproductive freedom, cloning, and so on. To this my response would be as follows. First, that these changes were ontohistorically superficial and so relatively ineffectual, but if America ever truly abdicates its leading global role in the technological transformation of human beings into resources, other countries – as well as extra- and intranational entities (multinational biotech corporations and my home state of California, for example) – have already shown themselves more than eager to compete to assume that role themselves. Thus, even if America ever truly turned against more than a tiny spectrum of the technological enframing of humanity, this underlying enframing itself is not likely to stop anytime soon.

In fact, it will never stop, and this is the second point, without a prior diagnosis that recognizes and addresses the ontotheological roots of the problem, rather than simply seeking to ameliorate a few of its most obvious symptoms. For, such an effort, insofar as it succeeds, simply gives us a *symptom-free disease* – and what is that but another way of describing Heidegger's greatest danger? Third, and most important, what this objection misses is that transcending technological enframing does not require us to abandon biogenetic research and cloning, let alone reproductive freedom. Instead, Heidegger insisted, a true recovery demands not that we abandon our technological manipulation and control of human beings (which he recognized will not happen any time in the foreseeable future) but, rather, that we find ways to integrate these technological projects for increasing self-optimization into our basic sense of reality without allowing this sense of reality to be completely dominated by enframing's empty optimization imperative. Attaining such a "free" relation to technology, in other words, does not require us to avoid technologies (which would be a doomed strategy, giving technology's ceaseless spread); on the contrary, it demands of us that we learn to use particular technologies in ways that help us transcend technologization (WCT 23–5/GA8 26–8). Here the crucial goal is to *push through* the "greatest danger" of technologization by transcending our technological understanding of being – and this, in turn, requires an insight Heidegger first sought to communicate under the heading of *the promise*. I shall thus say a few words about what Heidegger means by "the promise," showing how the intimate connection between this promise and the danger of late-modern technologization expresses Heidegger's deepest insight concerning how the nihilism of late-modern enframing leads beyond itself, opening up a genuinely meaningful postmodern future.

4. FROM THE DANGER TO THE PROMISE

In "Nihilism as Determined by the History of Being" (1944–6), the important but difficult essay that forms the capstone of his voluminous *Nietzsche* work, Heidegger addresses the relationship between technology's greatest danger and "the promise" (*das Versprechen*). We have seen that the danger is Heidegger's dystopian scenario for the end of history, his depiction of what could happen if our late-modern understanding of entities as intrinsically meaningless resources on stand-by for optimization becomes permanently totalizing by driving out, co-opting, or preventing the formation of any postmodern ways of understanding ourselves and our place in the world. "*Yet, where the danger is, the saving power also grows.*" The point of Hölderlin's salvific insight, as Heidegger understands it, is not that it is always darkest before the dawn, but instead that the new day is discovered in another way of experiencing the greatest darkness. Midnight, seen otherwise, *is* dawn. That sounds paradoxical, but Heidegger believes that we discover what saves us precisely by deeply experiencing what most endangers us, and he first tries publicly to communicate his way of making sense of this idea in terms of "the promise."[18]

Heidegger's basic insight here is the secularized theological idea that being has *promised* itself to us, and that this "promise" cannot be broken even if we forget about it. Put in phenomenological terms, Dasein – our "being-here" – *is* the place where being takes place and becomes intelligible to itself, and we remain the place where being takes place, even if the way being takes place for us is by *not* taking place, or by becoming unintelligible to us. The "promise" is thus Heidegger's name for the insight that, although being shows up for us as nothing, this "noth-ing" (or "nihilating")

---

[18] Heidegger began to develop this same line of thought in a fictional dialogue written the previous year (in 1945), but his remarks on this crucial score were highly elliptical, and this part of his dialogue (or, more precisely, trialogue) was not published until 1995 (see CPC 11–3, 57, 103/GA77 17–21, 89–90, 157).

safeguards the future possibilities of being (as we saw in Chapter 3). Heidegger expresses this difficult idea as follows:

[I]nsofar as being is the unconcealment of entities as such, being has ... already addressed itself to [*zugesprochen*] the essence of humanity. Being has already spoken out for and insinuated itself in the essence of humanity insofar as it has withheld and saved itself in the unconcealment of its essence. Addressing [us] in this way, while withholding itself in staying-away, being is the promise of itself [*Sein ist das Versprechen seiner selbst*]. To think to encounter being itself in its staying-away means to become aware of the promise, the promise in terms of which being itself "is." (N4 226/NII 368–9)

In other words, being discloses itself in our way of understanding the being of entities. But our current, "technological" understanding of the being of entities – as eternally recurring will-to-power – reduces being itself to nothing, dissolves it into "sovereign becoming." Viewed from within enframing, then, being shows up as nothing; it "comes across" as "staying away," as Heidegger paradoxically expresses the point here.

Nevertheless, our technological understanding of being, which reduces being to nothing, is still an understanding of being. Recognizing our ineliminable ontological receptivity, Heidegger thinks, makes possible this crucial insight: *Rather than experience being as nothing, we can instead experience this noth-ing as the way being shows itself to us.* To experience being as nothing is to reach the fulfilled peak of Western nihilism. Yet, precisely this same experience – the most extreme point of technology's greatest danger – can be experienced differently: We "become aware of the promise" when, instead of experiencing being as nothing, we experience the "noth-ing" as being. In this simple gestalt switch, in which we pass from experiencing being as nothing to experiencing the "noth-ing" as the way being happens for us, we have passed, by simply turning in place, from the most extreme point of the greatest danger to the promise. With this gestalt switch from danger to promise we have taken both "the step back" beyond metaphysics and, at the same time, the first step into the postmodern future Heidegger calls "the other beginning."[19]

The relation of the danger to the promise of technology is thus very much like the relation of the duck to the rabbit in the figure of the duck-rabbit with which we began. Both can be gestalted otherwise; for, each has a second, nonsimultaneous aspect, which we can learn to see in the place of the first, as replacing it, standing in its stead. The difference is that, because the danger is a totalizing understanding, which tends nihilistically to make everything show up as an intrinsically meaningless resource, the danger is *replaced* by seeing the promise, that is, by experiencing the

---

[19] These two steps, taken together, bring us full circle back to ourselves, helping us to accomplish what *Heidegger on Ontotheology* calls that "revolutionary return to ourselves" central to Heidegger's educational thinking.

"nothing" of being as concealing and thereby preserving other ways of understanding ourselves and the meaning of our worlds. (An even better analogy for seeing the promise would thus be the phenomenological fact that, once we have seen the second aspect of the duck-rabbit figure, we can no longer go back to our initial understanding of the figure in terms of only one of its aspects.) We see the promise instead of the danger when, rather than see being as nothing, we learn to recognize this nothing as the "noth-ing or nihilating" of being (or as the "presencing" of being as such, which makes itself felt in its *difference from* enframing), for example, by learning to discern the way inchoate possibilities suggest themselves to us, allowing us to see something taking shape where initially we saw nothing at all. In such encounters (or *events*), entities show up not as intrinsically meaningless resources, but otherwise, namely, as being richer in meaning than we are capable of doing justice to conceptually, and thus as already exceeding, in the direction of postmodernity, the ontologically reductive confines of our late-modern epoch of enframing.

Here, then, we approach the same phenomenological matter explored in Chapter 3 from a slightly different angle. For, as we saw there, this "noth-ing" or verbal "nihilating" was Heidegger's first name, in 1929, for the phenomenological presencing that exceeds the ontological difference, the very same matter that his phenomenological ontology of art develops in terms of the essential conflict between earth and world in 1935–6. I would thus go so far as to suggest that Heidegger's recognition of the "nihilating" of the nothing as the action of being as such, an activity that exceeds and so cannot be explained in terms of the ontological difference between being and entities, is the defining experience at the heart of his so-called turn and the *sine qua non* of his "later" thought. It is therefore not surprising that, despite withering attacks from Rudolf Carnap and others, Heidegger never gave up this difficult notion. Instead, he struggled his whole life to develop this phenomenological insight more clearly, continually seeking new names with which to evoke the "be-ing" which gives itself to intelligibility ("earth," "being as such," written under a "cross-wise striking-through," the "it" of the "it gives/there is" [*es gibt*]) – as well as the *way* "it" gives itself ("the noth-ing," "the rift-structure," "the fourfold," "the difference," "the event of enowning") – which would not separate or hypostatize this be-ing or this giving (by treating intelligibility as the deliberate gift of a given entity, such as an ontotheological creator God).

We can see further evidence of this if we notice that, immediately following the discussion of America as the greatest danger we just examined, Heidegger tries to help his students think "the identity of being and nothing ... in departure from the ontological difference" (FS 56/GA15 361), that is, beyond our reigning, technological understanding of the being of entities. That segue will look like a bizarre nonsequitur, an abrupt change of topics, to anyone who does not see that, in 1969, Heidegger is still trying to help his students learn to make that same gestalt switch from danger to promise, which turns on recognizing that (as he succinctly states it here): "The nihilation of the nothing 'is' being" (FS 57/GA15 361). The passage from danger to promise from 1946 is thus only one of Heidegger's first attempts to communicate his central later notion of a "freeing" gestalt switch, a "lightning flash" in which we catch sight of an active phenomenological "presencing" that our technological ontotheology denies yet presupposes, coming thereby to exceed our late-modern understanding of being from within. In this gestalt switch we come to recognize that, as Heidegger nicely puts it (on what I cannot help but note was September 11, 1969): "Enframing is, as it were, the photographic negative of enowning" (FS 60/GA15 366). Despite Heidegger's many different attempts to communicate this crucial idea, Vattimo recounts that Heidegger remained deeply distressed by his sense that he had failed to develop this crucial phenomenological gestalt switch with the requisite clarity. Tellingly, Heidegger believed that his "insufficient elaboration of this intuited relation" between the danger and the promise remained a "failure of his thought" greater even than "the wretched business of his involvement with (alas!) Nazism."[20]

Of course, understanding such difficult matters has a temporality of its own, and cannot be forced. If I find it nicely ironic and perfectly fitting to think that a clarification of Heidegger's crucial insight into the relation between danger and promise should take place in America (since "Where the danger is, the saving power also grows"), I must nevertheless acknowledge that the seed for the way I have tried here to develop the connection between the danger and the promise – as dual and dueling aspects of the same underlying figure – was planted years ago, by one of Derrida's observations which has long haunted me. Only after reaching what I take to be the same point myself, do I now understand that Derrida already recognized, in 1981, Heidegger's crucial insight that the highest point of fulfilled nihilism belongs to two different planes – joining, in a single point, the danger of metaphysics and the promise of what exceeds it. Indeed, this is the *crucial point*, so to speak, of Derrida's lucid but unexplained observation that Heidegger's *Nietzsche* lectures are:

directed at gathering together the unity and the uniqueness of Nietzsche's thinking, which, as a fulfilled unity, is itself in a fair way toward being the culmination of occidental metaphysics. Nietzsche would be precisely at the crest, or ridge, atop the peak of this fulfillment. And thus, he would be looking at both sides, down both slopes.[21]

[20] Vattimo credits Hans-Georg Gadamer as the source of this telling remark. (See Vattimo, *Nihilism and Emancipation: Ethics, Politics, and Law*, 14.)

[21] See Derrida, "Interpreting Signatures (Nietzsche/Heidegger): Two Questions," 58. Before his untimely death, Derrida had agreed to participate in the meeting of the international Parliament of Philosophers (which he helped found), and his absence was thus quite palpably present at the meeting.

If this is right, then the connection between danger and promise I have developed here can, I hope, be understood as a belated homage to Derrida and a further clarification of his insight (and so also another reminder of how deeply ambiguous Heidegger's reading of Nietzsche turns out to be): Heidegger's Nietzsche is the pivotal thinker who both fulfills late-modern metaphysics and, in so doing, first opens the passage toward postmodernity. By reducing being to nothing, Heidegger's Nietzsche is the philosopher of the culminating end of the "forgetting of being" in the ontotheological tradition that began with Plato. Yet, because this late-modern end of ontotheology makes it possible for us to recognize this "noth-ing" not as nothing at all but, instead, as the subtle way being continues to make itself felt even in our technological age, Heidegger's Nietzsche is also the first philosopher of the other, postmodern beginning.

5. BEYOND ONTOTHEOLOGY: HOPE FOR THE FUTURE

As we have seen throughout this book, *ontotheology* is the dual attempt to conceptually grasp all of reality from both the inside-out (ontologically) and the outside-in (theologically) at the same time. The problem with ontotheology is not that it is impossible but, on the contrary, that the way our successive historical ontotheologies do in fact function to structure our historical sense of reality has increasingly come to undermine the meaningfulness of our very sense of reality. Many of the deepest problems haunting our age of enframing follow from the particular Nietzschean ontotheology in which our technological enframing is "doubly grounded." For, this Nietzschean ontotheology pre-understands the being of entities as nothing but eternally recurring will to power, that is, as mere forces coming together and breaking apart with no end beyond their self-perpetuating augmentation. As our sense of reality is shaped by this "technological" understanding of the being of entities, we increasingly come to treat all entities, including ourselves, as intrinsically meaningless resources, *Bestand* on standby merely to be optimized, enhanced, and ordered for maximally flexible use. Environmental devastation, our growing obsession with biogenetic optimization, the hijacking of higher education by empty optimization imperatives, the reduction of art to aesthetic experience, and the nihilistic erosion of all intrinsic meaning need to be recognized as symptoms of the underlying technological ontotheology that is "enframing" our sense of reality.

We have seen that these problems are as serious as they are deeply entrenched in the metaphysical presuppositions of modernity. Fortunately, Heidegger's work also helps suggest a treatment, and so a future for thinking. If we can learn to practice that phenomenological comportment he calls "dwelling," then we can become attuned to the phenomenological "presencing" (*Anwesen*) whereby "being as such" manifests itself. When this happens, we come to understand and experience entities as being richer in meaning than we are capable of ever fully doing justice to conceptually, rather than taking them as intrinsically meaningless resources awaiting optimization. In this way, we can learn to approach all things with care, humility, patience, gratitude, and perhaps, I have suggested, even awe, reverence, and love. Such postmodern experiences can become microcosms of, as well as inspiration for, the revolution beyond our underlying ontotheology that Heidegger teaches us we need in order to transcend our technological enframing and so set out to set our world aright. The task for a genuinely postmodern thinking is thus to help us discern and transcend our ontotheology and its devastating nihilistic effects, in our lives, our academic institutions, and our world at large.

What I have tried to show in this chapter is that Heidegger, in keeping with his most cherished Hölderlinian maxim, understands "the greatest danger" and "the promise" at the core of our technological age as two different ways of encountering precisely the same phenomenon, namely, *being* showing itself to us as *nothing*. In the danger, we see being as nothing; but when we see the nothing as the way being happens for us (as the "noth-ing" or "nihilating" of being), then we have entered into and so understood the promise that otherwise remains concealed within technologization. On an analogy with the gestalt figure of the "duck-rabbit," I have suggested that the danger and the promise can be recognized as the two competing aspects of the same figure, aspects that work to conceal one another by standing in the same place. Learning to see and experience the promise *instead* of the danger is thus literally *crucial* for Heidegger: The danger is the peak of historical nihilism, the very "fulfillment" of Western metaphysics (in which being becomes nothing); yet, seeing the promise, the obverse of the same phenomenon (recognizing this "noth-ing" *as* being), constitutes the initial "crossing" or transition into what he calls "the other beginning" of history, the first step, that is, into a *postmodern* age.

By examining the overlapping development of these esoteric but crucial views in Heidegger's thought (for example, in Heidegger's views on art and in his *Contributions*), I have sought to restore some of their phenomenological concreteness and historical particularity. Despite the vexing origins of these views, we have seen, Heidegger's insightful perspective on the increasingly global phenomenon of technological enframing helps us achieve a better grasp of the contemporary historical situation. Indeed, as I have tried to show throughout this book, a post-Heideggerian understanding of the dangers of late-modernity and the promise of a genuine postmodernity offers us neither blind optimism nor fatalistic despair but, instead, real hope for the future.

8

Against Conclusions

> Nothing ever ends.
>
> > Dr. Manhattan, in Moore and Gibbons's *Watchmen*

> Curiosity and idle chatter, in their ambiguity [that is, in the way they uproot concepts from the phenomena that give them their true meaning], ensure that what is genuinely and newly created is outdated as soon as it emerges before the public. It can first become free in its positive possibilities only when the idle chatter covering it over has become ineffectual and the "common" interest has died away.
>
> > Heidegger (BT 218/SZ 174)

As a vague but trendy ideological buzzword, "postmodernism" had its heyday in the 1970s, 80s, and 90s, running its course through humanities departments like the proverbial bull through the china shop, shattering established literary traditions (much as *Watchmen* deconstructed the hero) until finally even postmodernism's most enthusiastic early proponents began to turn against it, loudly proclaiming the "end of theory" and calling for a return to the simple reading of literature (as if there had ever been any such "simple reading" in literature departments, and "literature" and "theory" had not always walked down the halls of the academy with their hands entwined).[1] Today many mainstream philosophers seem relieved to have weathered the postmodern storm more or less unscathed. Some even evince an unmistakable air of superiority for not having allowed themselves to get caught up in the culture wars (as if defending a tradition against various "postmodern" critiques, usually by trying to ignore them, was not itself to take a side). These philosophers tend to use the word "postmodern" disparagingly (if at all), usually as a shorthand for "that-trendy-nonsense-they-read-in-the-other-Humanities-departments-instead-of-studying-

---

[1] Cf., e.g., Terry Eagleton's *Literary Theory: An Introduction* with his *The End of Theory*.

real-philosophy," or as a quick way to dismiss what they assume to be rather juvenile forms of cultural relativism.[2]

Indeed, in their least generous moods, many philosophers simply equate postmodernism with *bullshit*. As a technical term (for which we can thank Harry Frankfurt), "to bullshit" means *to care more about being interesting than about being correct*.[3] Now, we are all familiar with some of these sophomoric "bullshitters" and we can legitimately debate the use of the term in particular cases. But the indiscriminate application of Frankfurt's definition to post-Heideggerian thinking in general not only serves an obvious ideological function (as Žižek himself responds to the accusation), it also conceals the fact that the converse of "bullshit" is a real danger as well.[4] *To care more about being correct than about analyzing anything interesting* leads to the problem of excessive technicality (that is, to introduce another technical term, to *the boring*) and, worse, to a kind of "normal scientific" routinization of philosophical practice, one that tends to incorporate and build on the very presuppositions of modern and late-modern philosophy that Heidegger holds responsible for some of the deepest problems of the age, as we have seen here.[5]

The dismissive equation of postmodernism with relativism (an equation usually based on an acquaintance not with the philosophers discussed in this book but only with some of their most exuberant acolytes) is a bit more understandable. For, "relativism" is indeed a more succinct way of restating the most widespread definition of our "postmodern condition," namely, the thesis (based, we have seen, on a misleading simplification of Lyotard's view) that all metanarratives have become incredible, that is, that we can no longer believe in any overarching perspective that would allow us to adjudicate between competing interpretations of myriad historical phenomena. It certainly seems as if we will find ourselves consigned to relativism if there

---

[2] The unabashed ultracrepidarianism evident in most mainstream philosophers' use and abuse of "postmodernism" is itself provocative. It seems to suggest either an alarming like-mindedness, in which one is unlikely ever to be confronted with one's own ignorance (and so never corrected), or else, perhaps, a shared presumption that there can be no philosophical experts on postmodernism for one to consult (because the "postmodern" straw-men are assumed to subscribe to the self-undermining claim that "there is no truth").

[3] See Harry Frankfurt's famous essay "On Bullshit" in his *The Importance of What We Care About*.

[4] Žižek clearly realizes that he is often nominated for this insulting title. (See his analysis of the ideological function of the charge at the beginning of *In Defense of Lost Causes*, 1–2. That Žižek reiterates the same point at the beginning of *Living in the End Times*, 3 note 1, suggests that he continues to be confronted with the charge.) For a reconstruction and defense of the philosophical foundations of Žižek's work, see Adrian Johnston, *Žižek's Ontology: A Transcendental Materialist Theory of Subjectivity*.

[5] One of the most convincing critiques of such excessive technicality can be found in the title essay of Bernard Williams' *Philosophy as a Humanistic Discipline*, which contains Williams's final reflections on the future of philosophy.

is no rational way to decide between Marxian and Heideggerian readings of Melville's *Moby-Dick*, for example, let alone between liberal-progressive and neoconservative interpretations of America's legitimate role in foreign affairs. Of course, postmodernism understood in that superficial sense is easily dismissed as self-refuting (as we saw in Chapter 4): What is the thesis that all metanarratives have become incredible but another metanarrative, and thus an incredible one?[6] Although that dismissal is itself rather superficial, we need not enter into a detailed discussion of the various rejoinders more sophisticated defenders of relativistic views could deploy here, for the simple reason that *Heidegger himself is not a postmodernist in this widespread sense.*[7]

On the contrary, Heidegger clearly has a metanarrative of his own. As I have shown, the overarching account he provides of the "history of being" supplies his philosophical critique of the modern and late-modern understandings of being with a great deal of their normative force, thereby helping to contextualize and reinforce his critical phenomenological descriptions. The metanarrative Heidegger draws from the history of philosophy tells the story of the end of metaphysics as ontotheology. He would thus refer not to the end of metanarratives but, instead, to the end of the theological, that is, to the absence of any God's-eye view we could take on all that is so as finally to condemn or redeem it. As we saw in Chapter 1, however, this end of the theological is not the same thing as the death

---

[6] Similarly, we might ask: What is the trendy, allegedly "postmodern" claim that all philosophical and political views are ideological if not another ideology? And if it is an ideology, then whose interests does it serve? The answer seems to be: Those radical Nietzscheans who believe only in the empowerment of power, a field of struggles without appeal to any extra-ideological reality (those who say, e.g., "No position is ultimately any more legitimate than any other, so I shall commit myself to struggling for the empowerment of those similarly situated in the field of power). It should be clear that Heidegger is not a "postmodernist" in this increasingly widespread sense, either. For, he believes that human beings encounter what makes our lives matter only when we recognize the resistance of an extra-ideological dimension of intelligibility and then "world" this "earth" through creative disclosure. As we have seen, there usually will not be only one right way to follow the bent of that "earth" we encounter beyond our words and worlds (which means there is no room for the righteousness of those who believe they have a monopoly on the truth), but there will be self-contradictory ways of construing the encounter (which are thus self-undermining). Foremost among these will be understandings that undermine their own condition of possibility by denying that there is any "being" beyond our different understandings of being, as the Nietzschean strategy above tends to do (just like the "happy enframers" mentioned earlier). Such Nietzschean multiculturalism should thus be distinguished from a radical communitarianism in which communities are charged with preserving and developing the distinctive ontological insights that gave rise to their traditions, a more philosophically defensible species of postmodern multiculturalism to which Heidegger's own thinking of the postmodern lends itself.

[7] For a treatment that begins to do justice to the complexity of the philosophical problems surrounding relativism, see the essays collected in Michael Krausz, ed., *Relativism: Interpretation and Confrontation*.

of the divine. Under the influence of his creative interpretations of the great Romantic poet Hölderlin, Heidegger would in the end speak less of *the death of God* and more, perhaps, of an historical vacation of the divine. For, as *vacation* polysemically suggests, a return of the divine remains possible for Heidegger, but not as some resurrection of the ontotheological creator God. Instead, Heidegger suggests, we need to learn to embrace the absence of the divine in the right way. For, when we do, we can come to think of "gods" in a radically post-Christian sense, as historically transformative truth events that we encounter when we learn to discern the outlines of something where others have seen nothing, so as to creatively disclose new worlds of meaning.

Such ontological epiphanies not only inspire all enduringly meaningful creations (that is, all those works that disclose meanings at least partly independent of our pre-existing plans and designs); they also remain capable of transforming our fundamental sense of what it means for something to *be*, and so can in this Heideggerian sense be called *gods*. An event of ontological disclosure rises to the level of a god when this event brings the entity disclosed, the world-disclosing human being, and the disclosure of being itself *into their own* simultaneously (as we have seen). Such events are thus *postmodern gods*, because through them we no longer understand being in terms either of modern objects to be controlled or late-modern resources to be optimized but, instead, as something that both informs and exceeds – calls for and resists, elicits and overflows – all those efforts by which we disclose our historical worlds.[8] It is this exuberant insight, and so not some relativistic thesis about metanarratives, that forms the heart of Heidegger's distinctive postmodernism.

As this suggests, Van Gogh's *A Pair of Shoes* (1886) was just such a postmodern god *for Heidegger*. It will only become one for our age, however, if enough of us can encounter this work, or others that work just like it, and carry the "postmodern" insights such works disclose with us into our lives in ways that help catalyze a fundamental philosophical shift in our age's basic understanding of being, thereby setting-off a subtle but profound shift in our way of relating to all that is. That, I have suggested, is what Heidegger meant when he uttered those frequently quoted words: "Only

---

[8] Pointing out that such enduringly meaningful "events" of ontological disclosure can be found at the very heart of Heidegger's later thinking should, I think, make it obvious that Alain Badiou has been profoundly influenced by Heidegger, a fact obliquely attested to by the distorted, "anxiety of influence" criticisms Badiou frequently levels at Heidegger, most prominently in his *Manifesto for Philosophy* and *Being and Event*. (For more on Heidegger's relation to the divine, see e.g. Mark Wrathall's provocative essay on Heidegger's fourfold, "Between the Earth and the Sky: Heidegger on Life After the Death of God"; Julian Young's thoughtful book, *The Death of God and the Meaning of Life*; Ben Crowe's clear and careful study of *Heidegger's Phenomenology of Religion: Realism and Cultural Criticism*; and Ben Vedder's interesting work, *Heidegger's Philosophy of Religion: From God to the Gods*.)

another god can save us." That famous line was not the sad confession of despair Heidegger's critics take it to be but, instead, a dramatic restatement of his long-standing philosophical belief that only a radical shift in our fundamental understanding of being could succeed in moving our world out of the nihilistic ontotheological undercurrents that increasingly reduce everything we experience to *nothing* but intrinsically meaningless resources awaiting optimization. As that famous interview also makes abundantly clear, Heidegger did not believe this transformation could take place without a great deal of philosophical preparation. This book has thus sought to show – in several different but, I hope, mutually illuminating ways – why and how Heidegger thought learning to encounter that "noth-ing" differently could help us turn the wheel of history away from that nihilistic late-modern understanding of being and into a genuinely meaningful postmodernity.

To succeed in such an ambitious endeavor we need not, I think, fly our cultural and political elite to Amsterdam for a guided viewing of Van Gogh's *A Pair of Shoes* (however worthwhile such a project might well be). For, other works that work just like Van Gogh's hallowed painting of *A Pair of Shoes* (1886) remain much more plentiful than Heidegger himself seems to have imagined. I have tried to suggest that Heidegger's own writings, for example, can work for us in much the same way that Van Gogh's painting worked for him. Recognizing "the nothing" in "The Origin of the Work of Art" can transform our understanding of Heidegger's text just as his understanding of Van Gogh's painting was transformed when he first discerned the figure I have called "the old woman who lived in the shoe." Heidegger's very experience of painting – indeed, of art itself – was regestalted when he recognized the phenomenological emergence of that woman in Van Gogh's painting. Indeed, it was regestalted in such a way that Heidegger's understanding of the poetic world disclosure that essentially joins human being with being itself underwent the lucid transformation that his essay and subsequent works seek to evoke in readers, hoping to help lead us to the same insight for ourselves. There is reason to believe, then, that we can experience the same kind of transformative insight into the essence of creative world-disclosure any time we similarly discern something no one has caught sight of before and help it emerge into visibility (along with that disclosure itself), whether what we catch sight of in its emergence is the old woman in Van Gogh's shoe, the nothing in Heidegger's essay, or, perhaps, the *Contributions'* fugal structure, *Watchmen's* deconstruction of the hero, or even the central role played by ontotheology in the background of Heidegger's later thought as a whole (to mention just the main examples I have tried to illustrate in this book). Those and an indefinitely large number of other similar hermeneutic insights remain capable of regestalting our sense of the texts through which we understand ourselves and our worlds, and in so doing, they can help us better realize that to be a human being means, at bottom, to bring genuine meaning into the world (by disclosing the earth). If we can thereby come to understand the being of what is as intrinsically meaningful – and so learn to experience reality as always offering us true hints, suggestive outlines for us to receptively discern, creatively develop, and thereby help fulfill or realize – then we have already begun to move beyond the nihilism or meaninglessness of our current late-modern understanding of entities as intrinsically meaningless resources merely standing by for optimization.

That may sound simple, but I hope it does not sound too hubristic. For, without such experiences of our own, we are not actually engaging in the same kind of hermeneutic phenomenology Heidegger himself practiced and sought to inspire in others, and we will not be able to either confirm or contest his more general claims about historical world-disclosure for ourselves. In fact, for Heidegger it is a universal phenomenological principle that if we do not experience the phenomenon at issue for ourselves, then we cannot approach *any* interpretation of it from within the only domain in which the legitimacy of that interpretation is capable of being decided.[9] When we do experience the kind of hermeneutic epiphanies Heidegger evokes in "The Origin of the Work of Art" for ourselves, I have tried to show, these experiences teach us that the genuine meaning such epiphanies disclose is not entirely up to us, although of course it could not happen without our creative efforts. Over time, with enough such experiences, we can also come to learn that what we discern in such moments of epiphany (and then find ourselves creatively struggling to bring into the world), while really there, is not *all* that is there.[10] There will always be something more there, another insight yet to be found (and thus another future for the work), if the work truly is a great work of art in Heidegger's sense. For, as I suggested in Chapter 5, such great works remain deep enough – in other words, resonant enough, *meaningful* (that is, meaning-full) enough – to continue to generate new readings, even revolutionary rereadings that radically reorient the sense of the work that previously guided us. (Thus, for example, I can no longer see Van Gogh's painting without also seeing the figure of "the little old woman who lived in the shoe" emerging from

---

[9]   (I develop the case for this view in "Death and Demise in *Being and Time*.") This is by no means to argue against the importance of historically contextualizing great philosophical works, but only to suggest that such contextualizing should inform, but can never replace, an immanent reading of the *philosophical* meaning of those great texts (for the simple reason that context influences but never determines that meaning).

[10]   We are justified in initially presuming that what we see in such moments is really there, but we have phenomenological confirmation of that fact only insofar as others can also see it and so enter into a communal discussion concerning its meaning. If no one else can even begin to see what we see, then we have to face the hard fact that, as Heidegger says, a work without an audience to preserve its meaning does no work, however meaningful it might seem to be to its creator (or even to its would-be first preserver). Of course, great works often take many years to find an audience, so there is always hope.

the dark opening of the shoe on the right. This means, however, that I no longer see only that simple pair of shoes that I saw when I first looked at this painting. Now I see *both* the shoes *and* the woman, and, moreover, I see the painting as harboring numerous other possibilities as well.)[11]

In my own view, then, the works through which we are capable of learning to understand ourselves and our worlds in a postmodern light – as ontologically pluralistic or multiply meaningful – must surely be innumerable. Heidegger's own later work on the "thing" suggests that if we can learn to adopt an appropriately open and responsive phenomenological approach to things, then the works that remain capable of helping us come to understand being in a postmodern way can be found all around us – yes, even in popular songs and comic books. In my most optimistic moments, I sometimes think there is reason to believe that the postmodern lessons humble things and great artworks can teach us about meaning are already beginning to coalesce into another way of understanding what it means to be, one in which we no longer reduce everything we encounter, including ourselves, to either objects to be controlled or resources to be optimized. In such moments, I think I can see sparks in the darkness, hints large and small (from the growing deep-ecological movement to the fact that the OED just added the word "locavore" to its official lexicon – a Heideggerian word if ever there was one), which give me reason to believe that the postmodernity Heidegger dedicated his thinking to preparing is in fact already struggling to arrive.

This struggle will not be confined solely to books, obviously, but it will nevertheless remain a hermeneutic struggle over the meaning of all those "texts" (in the broadest, "postmodern" sense of the word) that constitute our worlds. And if *read* rhymes with *dead*, then *need* rhymes with *read*; that is, if a text can ever be finally read (if its meaning can be exhaustively enumerated in a series of propositions, for example), then no one need ever read that text again (since it will then be just as effective and more efficient to study that more economical enumeration). This means that those "texts"

---

[11] The same holds true of *Watchmen* (as I showed in Chapter 5): The second reading displaces the first, naïve reading. Because the first reading was blind to the deeper meaning that the second reading revealed, it cannot survive that second reading unchanged. That second reading thus shows the text to be multiply meaningful, and so to require this self-displacing, double reading in order to be understood. In so far as we explicitly refuse to reinstitute the naïve hermeneutic closure implicit in that first reading, moreover, that second reading remains open to future readings that will unfold new layers of the text – and, in so doing, perhaps even displace that second reading in turn, thereby becoming the basis of new readings (and so on, indefinitely). Yet, the comportment that remains resolutely open to such a recognition is not relativistic about its own understanding of the text, but instead "sticks to it without getting stuck with it," should that understanding get displaced or otherwise superseded in turn. (Here I am borrowing Haugeland's famous formulation of one of important lessons already found in Heidegger's existential analysis of death. For more on this point, see my "Death and Demise in *Being and Time*.")

that are amenable to final and definitive analysis are not great works. That should not be too surprising; not all works are great, obviously, and many seem to be exhausted rather quickly. Still, great works remain, as does our need to continue to read them, a deep need as world-disclosing beings to learn to discover meaning in the *texts* all around us. Insofar as these "texts" too are great works, then, in Heidegger's terms, they will continue to offer us meaningful worlds while still preserving the earth, thereby sheltering the possibilities of worlds yet to be born. For this same reason, however, such great works cannot be hopelessly vague, empty, or incomprehensible. They must be capable of meaning something definitive to us and yet be such that we never quite reach the bottom of them – even if we only truly learn that lesson when we, or someone else, finds a compelling way to turn another page.

References

Aeschylus, *The Oresteia*. D. Grene and W. D. O'Flaherty, trans. Chicago: University of Chicago Press, 1989.

Agamben, Giorgio, *Remnants of Auschwitz: The Witness and the Archive*. D. Heller-Roazen, trans. New York: Zone Books, 1999.

Allison, Henry, *Kant's Transcendental Idealism: An Interpretation and Defense*. New Haven: Yale University Press, 1983.

Babich, Babette. E., "From Van Gogh's Museum to the Temple at Bassae: Heidegger's Truth of Art and Schapiro's Art History." *Culture, Theory & Critique* 44:2 (2003), 151–69.

Bacon, Francis, *The New Organon*. L. Jardine and M. Silverthorne, eds. Cambridge: Cambridge University Press, 2000.

Badiou, Alain, *Being and Event*. O. Feltham, trans. London: Continuum, 2007.

Ethics: An Essay on the Understanding of Evil. P. Hallward, trans. London: Verso, 2001.

Manifesto for Philosophy. N. Madarasz, ed. and trans. Albany: SUNY Press, 1992.

Bartky, Sandra, "Heidegger's Philosophy of Art," in T. Sheehan, ed., *Heidegger: The Man and the Thinker*. Chicago: Precedent Publishing, 1981.

Baudelaire, Charles, *The Flowers of Evil and Paris Spleen*. W. H. Crosby, trans. Rochester, NY: BOA Editions, 1991.

Baudrillard, Jean, *Simulation and Simulacra*. F. S. Glaser, trans. Ann Arbor: University of Michigan Press, 1995.

The Transparency of Evil: Essays on Extreme Phenomena. J. Benedict, trans. London: Verso, 1993.

The Vital Illusion. J. Witwer, trans. New York: Columbia University Press, 2000.

Berlin, Isaiah, *Three Critics of the Enlightenment: Vico, Hamann, Herder*. Princeton: Princeton University Press, 2000.

Bernasconi, Robert, "Heidegger's Displacement of the Concept of Art." In M. Kelly, ed., *Encyclopedia of Aesthetics*, vol. 2. Oxford: Oxford University Press, 1998.

"The Greatness of the Work of Art." In J. Risser, ed., *Heidegger Toward the Turn: Essays on the Work of the 1930s*. Albany: SUNY Press, 1999.

Blackburn, Simon, "Enquivering." *The New Republic* (30 October 2000), 43–8.

Blanchot, Maurice, *"Penser l'apocalypse."* Le Nouvel Observateur (22–28 January 1988).

Blattner, William, *Heidegger's Being and Time: A Reader's Guide.* New York: Continuum, 2006.

Bloom, Allan, *The Closing of the American Mind.* New York: Simon and Schuster, 1987.

Bloom, Harold, *The Anxiety of Influence: A Theory of Poetry.* Oxford: Oxford University Press, 1997.

Borradori, Giovanna, ed., *Philosophy in a Time of Terror: Dialogues with Jürgen Habermas and Jacques Derrida.* Chicago: University of Chicago Press, 2003.

Boss, Medard, "Martin Heidegger's Zollikon Seminars." In K. Holler, ed., *Heidegger and Psychology.* Special issue of *Review of Existential Psychology and Psychiatry*, 1988.

Bourdieu, Pierre, *Distinction: A Social Critique of the Judgment of Taste.* R. Nice, trans. Cambridge, MA: Harvard University Press, 1984.

Braver, Lee, *A Thing of This World: A History of Continental Anti-Realism.* Evanston, IL; Northwestern University Press, 2007.

Brodsley, David, *L.A. Freeway: An Appreciative Essay.* Berkeley: University of California Press, 1981.

Butler, Judith, *Subjects of Desire: Hegelian Reflections in Twentieth-Century France.* New York: Columbia University Press, 1987.

Campbell, Joseph, *The Hero with a Thousand Faces.* Princeton: Princeton University Press, 1949.

Carman, Taylor, "Heidegger, Martin: Survey of Thought." In M. Kelly, ed., *Encyclopedia of Aesthetics*, vol. 2. Oxford: Oxford University Press, 1998.

Celan, Paul, *Poems of Paul Celan.* M. Hamburger, trans. New York: Persea Book, 2002.

Chabon, Michael, *The Amazing Adventures of Kavalier & Clay.* New York: Picador, 2000.

Chérif, Mustspha, *Islam and the West: A Conversation with Jacques Derrida.* T. L. Fagan, trans. Chicago: University of Chicago Press, 2008.

Connolly, William E., *The Ethos of Pluralization.* Minneapolis: University of Minnesota Press, 1995.

Craven, David, "A Series of Interviews: Meyer Schapiro and Lillian Milgram Schapiro with David Craven." *Res* 31 (1997), 151–68.

"Meyer Schapiro, Karl Korsch, and the Emergence of Critical Theory." *The Oxford Art Journal* 17:1 (1994), 42–54.

Crawford, Matthew. B., *Shop Class as Soulcraft: An Inquiry Into the Value of Work.* New York: Penguin, 2009.

Cross, Andrew, "Faith and the Ethical in *Fear and Trembling*." *Inquiry* 46:1 (2003).

Crowe, Benjamin D., *Heidegger's Phenomenology of Religion: Realism and Cultural Criticism.* Bloomington; Indiana University Press, 2008.

Crowell, Steven, *Husserl, Heidegger, and the Space of Meaning: Paths toward Transcendental Phenomenology.* Evanston, IL: Northwestern University Press, 2001.

"Phenomenology and Aesthetics; or, Why Art Matters." In J. Parry, ed., *Art and Phenomenology.* New York: Routledge, 2011.

Cummings, E. E., *Collected Poems.* New York: Harcourt, Brace and Co., 1923.

Dahlstrom, Daniel O., *Heidegger's Concept of Truth*. Cambridge: Cambridge University Press, 2001.

ed., *Interpreting Heidegger: New Essays*. Cambridge: Cambridge University Press, 2011.

Dallmayr, Fred, "Democracy and Postmodernism." *Human Studies* 10(1), 1986, 143–70.

The Other Heidegger. Ithaca and London: Cornell University Press, 1993.

Dasenbrock, Reed Way, "Slouching Toward Berlin: Life is a Postfascist Culture." In R. J. Golsan, ed., *Fascism's Return*. Lincoln: University of Nebraska Press, 1998.

Dawkins, Richard, "The Final Scientific Enlightenment." In J. Brockman, ed., *What Are You Optimistic About?* New York: Harper Perennial, 2007.

The God Delusion. Boston: Houghton Mifflin, 2006.

Denker, Alfred, Hans-Helmuth Gander, and Holger Zaborowski, eds., *Heidegger – Jahrbuch 1: Heidegger und die Anfänge seines Denkens*. Freiburg: Karl Alber, 2004.

Derrida, Jacques, *Copy, Archive, Signature: A Conversation on Photography*. G. Richter, ed. J. Fort, trans. Stanford: Stanford University Press, 2010.

The Gift of Death. D. Wills, trans. Chicago: The University of Chicago Press, 1995.

"Interpreting Signatures (Nietzsche/Heidegger): Two Questions." In D. P. Michelfelder and R. E. Palmer, eds. and trans., *Dialogue and Deconstruction: The Gadamer-Derrida Encounter*. Albany: SUNY Press, 1989.

Of Grammatology. G. Spivak, trans. Baltimore: The Johns Hopkins University Press, 1974.

Of Spirit: Heidegger and the Question. G. Bennington and R. Bowlby, trans. Chicago: University of Chicago Press, 1989.

On the Name. T. Dutoit, ed. D. Wood, J. P. Leavey, and I. McLeod, trans. Stanford: Stanford University Press, 1995.

"Philopolemology: Heidegger's Ear (*Geschlecht* IV)." J. P. Leavey, trans. In J. Sallis, ed., *Reading Heidegger: Commemorations*. Bloomington: Indiana University Press, 1993.

Psyche: Inventions of the Other, Vol. 2. P. Kamuf, ed. E. Rottenberg, trans. Stanford: Stanford University Press, 2008.

Specters of Marx: The State of the Debt, the Work of Mourning, and the New International. P. Kamuf, trans. New York: Routledge, 1994.

Spurs: Nietzsche's Styles. B. Harlow, trans. Chicago: University of Chicago Press, 1979.

The Ear of the Other: Otobiography, Transference, Translation. C. V. MacDonald, ed., P. Kamuf and A. Ronell, trans. New York: Schocken Books, 1985.

The Truth in Painting. G. Bennington and I. McLeod, trans. Chicago: University of Chicago Press, 1987.

Descartes, René, *Meditations on First Philosophy, with Selections from the Objections and Replies*. J. Cottingham, ed. and trans. Cambridge: Cambridge University Press, 1996.

Dreyfus, Hubert L., *Being-in-the-World: A Commentary on Heidegger's Being and Time, Division I*. Cambridge, MA: MIT Press, 1991.

"Heidegger on the Connection Between Nihilism, Art, Technology, and Politics." In C. B. Guignon, ed., *The Cambridge Companion to Heidegger*, 2nd ed. Cambridge: Cambridge University Press, 2006.

"Heidegger on Gaining a Free Relation to Technology." In Andrew Feenberg and Alastair Hannay, eds., *Technology and the Politics of Knowledge*. Bloomington: Indiana University Press, 1995.

"Heidegger's Ontology of Art," in H. L. Dreyfus and M. A. Wrathall, eds., *A Companion to Heidegger*. Oxford: Blackwell, 2005.

"Mixing Interpretation, Religion, and Politics: Heidegger's High-Risk Thinking." In Christopher Ocker, ed., *Protocol of the Sixty-first Colloquy of the Center for Hermeneutical Studies*. San Anselmo, CA: Center for Hermeneutical Studies, 1992.

On the Internet, 2nd ed., London: Routledge, 2009.

Dreyfus, Hubert L., and Sean Kelly, *All Things Shining: Reading the Western Classics to Find Meaning in a Secular Age*. New York: Free Press, 2011.

Eagleton, Terry, *Literary Theory: An Introduction*. Minneapolis: University of Minnesota Press, 1984.

The End of Theory. New York: Basic Books, 2004.

Edwards, Cliff, *The Shoes of Van Gogh: A Spiritual and Artistic Journey to the Ordinary*. New York: The Crossroad Publishing Company, 2004.

Eliot, T. S., *The Wasteland and Other Poems*. San Diego: Harcourt Brace Jovanovich, 1962.

Emerson, Ralph Waldo, *Essays and Lectures*. New York: Library of America, 1983.

Erikson, Erik H., *The Life Cycle Completed: A Review*. New York: Norton, 1982.

Feenberg, Andrew, *Critical Theory of Technology*. New York and Oxford: Oxford University Press, 1991.

Flanagan, Bill, *U2 at the End of the World*. New York: Delacorte Press, 1995.

Fóti, Véronique M., "Johann Christian Friedrich Hölderlin." In J. Wolfreys, ed., *The Continuum Encyclopedia of Modern Criticism and Theory*. New York: Continuum, 2002.

Foucault, Michel, *The Order of Things: An Archeology of the Human Sciences*. A. Sheridan, trans. New York: Vintage Books, 1970.

This Is Not a Pipe, J. Harkness, ed. and trans. Berkeley: University of California Press, 1983.

Frankfurt, Harry G., *The Importance of What We Care About*. Cambridge: Cambridge University Press, 1988.

The Reasons of Love. Princeton: Princeton University Press, 2004.

Freud, Sigmund, *Collected Papers*. 5 vols. New York: Basic Books, 1959.

Friedman, Michael, *A Parting of the Ways: Carnap, Cassirer, and Heidegger*. Chicago: Open Court, 2000.

Frings, Manfred, *The Mind of Max Scheler*. Milwaukee: Duquesne University Press, 1997.

Furtak, Rick Anthony, *Wisdom in Love: Kierkegaard and the Ancient Quest for Emotional Integrity*. Notre Dame IN: University of Notre Dame Press, 2005.

Gadamer, Hans-Georg, *Truth and Method*. R. Heinemann and B. Krajewski, eds. and trans. London: Continuum, 2004.

Geulen, Eva, *The End of Art: Readings in a Rumor after Hegel*. J. McFarland, trans. Stanford: Stanford University Press, 2006.

Geuss, Raymond, *The Idea of a Critical Theory: Habermas and the Frankfurt School.* Cambridge: Cambridge University Press, 1981.

Gover, Karen, "The Overlooked Work of Art in 'The Origin of the Work of Art.'" *International Philosophical Quarterly* 48:2 (2008), 143–54.

Gray, J. Glenn, *The Promise of Wisdom: An Introduction to Philosophy of Education.* New York: Lippincott, 1968.

Guignon, Charles, "Authenticity, Moral Values, and Psychotherapy." In C. Guignon, ed., *The Cambridge Companion to Heidegger,* 2nd ed. Cambridge: Cambridge University Press, 2006.

Heidegger and the Problem of Knowledge. Indianapolis: Hackett, 1983.

"Introduction." In C. Guignon, ed., *The Cambridge Companion to Heidegger,* 2nd ed. Cambridge: Cambridge University Press, 2006.

Heidegger and the Problem of Knowledge. Indianapolis: Hackett, 1983.

"Meaning in the Work of Art: A Hermeneutic Perspective." *Midwest Studies in Philosophy* 27:1 (2003), 25–44.

Gutting, Gary, *French Philosophy in the Twentieth Century.* Cambridge: Cambridge University Press, 2001.

Habermas, Jürgen, *The Future of Human Nature.* Cambridge: Polity, 2003.

Hammermeister, Kai, *The German Aesthetic Tradition.* Cambridge: Cambridge University Press, 2002.

Harries, Karsten, *Art Matters: A Critical Commentary on Heidegger's "The Origin of the Work of Art."* Dordrecht: Springer, 2009.

"Heidegger's Confrontation with Aesthetics." In M. Kelly, ed., *Encyclopedia of Aesthetics,* vol. 2. Oxford: Oxford University Press, 1998.

Hill, R. Kevin, *Nietzsche's Critiques: The Kantian Foundations of His Thought.* Oxford: Oxford University Press, 2003.

Hoeller, Keith, ed., Heidegger and Psychology. Special issue of *Review of Existential Psychology and Psychiatry,* 1988.

Hölderlin, Friedrich, *Der Tod des Empedokles.* E. M. Benn, ed. London: Oxford University Press, 1968.

Essays and Letters on Theory. T. Pfau, ed. and trans. New York: State University of New York Press, 1988.

Hyperion and Selected Poems. E. L. Santner, ed. and trans. New York: Continuum, 1994.

Homer, *The Iliad.* R. Fitzgerald, trans. New York: Doubleday, 1974.

The Odyssey. R. Fitzgerald, trans. New York: Vintage, 1990.

Horkheimer, Max, and Theodor W. Adorno, *Dialectic of Enlightenment: Philosophical Fragments.* G. S. Noerr, ed. E. Jephcott, trans. Stanford: Stanford University Press, 2002.

James, William, *Pragmatism: A New Name for Some Old Ways of Thinking.* New York: Cosimo, 2008.

Jameson, Frederick, *Postmodernism, or, the Cultural Logic of Late Capitalism.* Durham, NC: Duke University Press, 1991.

Jenkins, Alan, "Minority Report." *The Nation* (12 May 2003), 36–8.

Johnston, Adrian, *Badiou, Žižek, and Political Transformations: The Cadence of Change.* Evanston, IL: Northwestern University Press, 2009.

Žižek's Ontology: A Transcendental Materialist Theory of Subjectivity. Evanston, IL: Northwestern University Press, 2008.

Kant, Immanuel, *Critique of Pure Reason*. N. K. Smith, trans. New York: St. Martin's Press, 1965.

Perpetual Peace and Other Essays. T. Humphries, trans. Indianapolis: Hackett, 1983.

Kavanagh, Barry, "The Alan Moore Interview." In *Blather* (17 October 2000). http://www.blather.net/articles/amoore/alanmoore.txt (accessed 15 March 2003).

Kelly, Michael, *Iconoclasm in Aesthetics*. Cambridge: Cambridge University Press, 2003.

Kierkegaard, Søren, *The Sickness Unto Death*. A. Hannay, trans. New York: Penguin, 2004.

Klossowski, Pierre, "Nietzsche's Experience of the Eternal Return." In D. B. Allison, ed., *The New Nietzsche*. Cambridge, MA: MIT Press, 1973.

Knabb, Ken, ed., *Situationist International Anthology*. K. Knabb, trans. The Bureau of Public Secrets: Berkeley, 1981.

Kockelmans, Joseph J., *Heidegger on Art and Art Works*. Dordrecht: Nijhoff, 1985.

Krausz, Michael, ed., *Relativism: Interpretation and Confrontation*. Notre Dame, IN: University of Notre Dame Press, 1989.

Kripke, Saul A., *Naming and Necessity*. Cambridge, MA: Harvard University Press, 1980.

Kuhn, Thomas, *The Structure of Scientific Revolutions*. 2nd ed. Chicago: University of Chicago Press, 1970.

Kundera, Milan, *The Joke*. New York: Harper, 1993.

Lacan, Jacques, *Écrits*. B. Fink, trans. New York: Norton, 2006.

Laclau, Ernesto, and Chantal Mouffe, *Hegemony and Socialist Strategy: Towards a Radical Democratic Politics*. W. Moore and P. Cammack, trans. London: Verso, 1985.

Lacoue-Labarthe, Philippe, *Heidegger, Art, and Politics: The Fiction of the Political*. C. Turner, trans. Oxford: Basil Blackwell, 1990.

Lampert, Laurence, *Nietzsche's Teaching: An Interpretation of Thus Spoke Zarathustra*. New Haven: Yale University Press, 1986.

Lévi-Strauss, Claude, *The Savage Mind*. J. Weightman and D. Weightman, trans. Chicago: University of Chicago Press, 1968.

Levinas, Emmanuel, *Humanism of the Other*. N. Poller, trans. Urbana and Chicago: University of Illinois Press, 2003.

On Escape. B. Bergo, trans. Stanford: Stanford University Press, 2003.

Totality and Infinity: An Essay on Exteriority. A. Lingis, trans. Pittsburgh: Duquesne University Press, 1969.

Livingston, Elizabeth Amberg, "The Last Hand: Restrictions on Martin Heidegger's Papers in the Deutsches Literaturarchiv Marbach." *Journal of Information Ethics* 19:1 (2010): 110–25.

Lyon, James K., *Paul Celan and Martin Heidegger: An Unresolved Conversation 1951–1970*. Baltimore, MD: The Johns Hopkins University Press, 2006.

Lyotard, Jean-François, *The Postmodern Condition: A Report on Knowledge*. G. Bennington and B. Massumi, trans. Minneapolis: University of Minnesota Press, 1984.

Malpas, Jeff, *Heidegger's Topology: Being, Place, World*. Cambridge, MA: MIT Press, 2006.

Maly, Kenneth, *Heidegger's Possibility: Language, Emergence – Saying Be-ing.* Toronto: University of Toronto Press, 2008.

Marcus, Greil, *Lipstick Traces: A Secret History of the Twentieth Century.* Cambridge, MA: Harvard University Press, 1990.

Martin, Wayne, *Theories of Judgment: Psychology, Logic Phenomenology.* Cambridge: Cambridge University Press, 2006.

McCloud, Scott, *Understanding Comics: The Invisible Art.* New York: HarperCollins, 1993.

McLaughlin, Jeff, ed., *Comics as Philosophy.* Jackson: University Press of Mississippi, 2005.

Melville, Herman, *Moby Dick; or, The Whale.* Norwalk, CT: The Easton Press, 1977.

Millidge, Gary Spencer, ed., *Alan Moore: Portrait of an Extraordinary Gentleman.* Leigh-on-Sea, UK: Abiogenesis Press, 2003.

Moore, Alan, "Interview with Jonathan Ross." In *The Idler* (2003).

Moore, Alan, and Dave Gibbons, *Watchmen.* New York: DC Comics, 1986–7.

Mulhall, Stephen, *Inheritance and Originality: Wittgenstein, Heidegger, Kierkegaard.* Oxford: Clarendon Press, 2001.

Murray, James, et al., eds., *The Compact Oxford English Dictionary,* 2nd ed. Oxford: Clarendon Press, 1991.

Nehamas, Alexander, "Nietzsche and 'Hitler.'" In J. Golomb and R. S. Wistrich, eds., *Nietzsche, Godfather of Fascism?* Princeton: Princeton University Press, 2002.

Only a Promise of Happiness: The Place of Beauty in a World of Art. Princeton: Princeton University Press, 2007.

Neill, Alex, and Aaron Ridley, eds., *Arguing About Art: Contemporary Philosophical Debates.* London: Routledge, 2008.

Nietzsche, Friedrich, *Kritische Gesamtausgabe.* Giorgio Colli, Mazzino Montinari, et al., eds. Berlin: Walter de Gruyter, 1967–.

"On the Advantage and Disadvantage of History for Life." P. Preuss, trans. Indianapolis: Hackett, 1980.

Philosophy in the Tragic Age of the Greeks. M. Cowan, trans. Washington, DC: Regnery Gateway, 1962.

The Anti-Christ, Ecce Homo, Twilight of the Idols, and Other Writings. A. Ridley and J. Norman, eds. Cambridge: Cambridge University Press, 2005.

The Birth of Tragedy and Other Writings. R. Geuss and R. Speirs, eds., R. Speirs, trans. Cambridge: Cambridge University Press, 1999.

The Pre-Platonic Philosophers. G. Whitlock, ed. and trans. Urbana and Chicago: University of Illinois Press, 2001.

The Will to Power. W. Kaufmann, ed. W. Kaufmann and R. J. Hollingdale, trans. New York: Random House, 1967.

Thus Spoke Zarathustra. In W. Kaufmann, ed. and trans., *The Portable Nietzsche.* New York: Viking, 1982.

Writings from the Late Notebooks. Rüdiger Bittner, ed., K. Sturge, trans. Cambridge: Cambridge University Press, 2003.

Oberst, Joachim L., *Heidegger on Language and Death: The Intrinsic Connection in Human Existence.* London: Continuum, 2009.

Olafson, Frederick A., *Heidegger and the Ground of Ethics: A Study of Mitsein.* Cambridge: Cambridge University Press, 1998.

Heidegger and the Philosophy of Mind. New Haven: Yale University Press, 1987.

Pappu, Sridhar, "We Need Another Hero." *Salon* (18 October 2000). See: http://dir.salon.com/people/feature/2000/10/18/moore/index.html?pn=2.

Petzet, Heinrich Wiegand, *Encounters and Dialogues with Martin Heidegger, 1929–1976*. P. Emad and K. Maly, trans. Chicago: The University of Chicago Press, 1993.

Plant, Sadie, *The Most Radical Gesture: The Situationist International in a Postmodern Age*. London: Routledge, 1992.

Plato, *Symposium*. P. Woodruff and A. Nehamas, trans. Indianapolis: Hackett, 1989.

Cratylus, Parmenides, Greater Hippias, Lesser Hippias. H. N. Fowler, trans. Cambridge, MA: Harvard University Press, 1926.

Pöggeler, Otto, "Besinnung oder Ausflucht? Heideggers ursprüngliche Denkens." In Forum für Philosophie Bad Homburg, *Zerstörung des moralischen Selbstbewusstsein: Chance oder Gefährdung*. Frankfurt: Suhrkamp, 1988.

"Heidegger und die hermeneutische Theologie." In E Jüngel, ed., *Verifikationen: Festschrift für Gerhard Eberling*. Tübingen: Mohr Siebeck, 1982.

"Heideggers Politische Selbstverständnis." In A. Gethmann-Siefert and O. Pöggeler, eds., *Heidegger und die praktische Philosophie*. Frankfurt: Suhrkamp, 1988.

Martin Heidegger's Path of Thinking. D. Magurshak and S. Barber, trans. Atlantic Highlands, NJ: Humanities Press International, 1989.

Philosophie und Politik bei Heidegger. Freiburg: Alber, 1972.

Polt, Richard, *The Emergency of Being: On Heidegger's Contributions to Philosophy*. Ithaca: Cornell University Press, 2006.

Ralkowski, Mark A., *Heidegger's Platonism*. London: Continuum, 2009.

Reginster, Bernard, *The Affirmation of Life: Nietzsche on Overcoming Nihilism*. Cambridge, MA: Harvard University Press, 2006.

Richardson, John, *Existential Epistemology: A Heideggerian Critique of the Cartesian Project*. Oxford: Clarendon, 1986.

"Nietzsche Contra Darwin." *Philosophy and Phenomenological Research* 65:3 (2002), 537–75.

Nietzsche's New Darwinism. Oxford: Oxford University Press, 2004.

Nietzsche's System. Oxford: Oxford University Press, 1996.

Rorty, Richard, *Achieving our Country: Leftist Thought in Twentieth-Century America*. Cambridge, MA: Harvard University Press, 1998.

Essays on Heidegger and Others: Philosophical Papers Volume 2. Cambridge: Cambridge University Press, 1991.

Russell, Bertrand, *The Autobiography of Bertrand Russell*. London: Routledge, 2000.

Safranski, Rüdiger, *Heidegger: Between Good and Evil*. E. Oslers, trans. Cambridge: Harvard University Press, 1998.

Sallis, John, *Transfigurements: On the True Sense of Art*. Chicago: University of Chicago Press, 2008.

Sandel, Michael J., *The Case Against Perfection: Ethics in the Age of Genetic Engineering*. Cambridge, MA: Belknap, 2007.

Schapiro, Meyer, "Further Notes on Heidegger and van Gogh (1994)." In Meyer Schapiro, *Theory and Philosophy of Art: Style, Artist, and Society*. New York: George Braziller, 1994.

"The Still Life as a Personal Object – A Note on Heidegger and van Gogh (1968)." In Meyer Schapiro, *Theory and Philosophy of Art: Style, Artist, and Society.* New York: George Braziller, 1994.

Schmidt, Dennis J., *On Germans and Other Greeks.* Bloomington: Indiana University Press, 2001.

Schürmann, Reiner, "A Brutal Awakening to The Tragic Condition of Being: On Heidegger's *Beiträge zur Philosophie.*" In K. Harries and C. Jamme, eds., *Martin Heidegger: Politics, Art, and Technology.* New York: Holmes and Meier Publishers, 1994.

"Riveted to a Monstrous Site: On Heidegger's *Beiträge zur Philosophie.*" In T. Rockmore and J. Margolis, eds., *The Heidegger Case: On Philosophy and Politics.* Philadelphia: Temple University Press, 1992.

"Technicity, Topology, Tragedy: Heidegger on 'That Which Saves' in the Global Reich." In A. M. Meltzer, J. Weinberger, and M. R. Zinman, eds., *Technology in the Western Political Tradition.* Ithaca, NY: Cornell University Press. 1993.

"Ultimate Double Binds." *Graduate Philosophy Faculty Journal* 14:2–15:1 (1991): 213–36.

Wandering Joy: Meister Eckhart's Mystical Philosophy. R. Schürmann, trans. Great Barrington, MA: Lindisfarne Books, 2001.

Schwan, Alexander, "Heidegger's *Beiträge zur Philosophie* and Politics." E. Brient, trans. In K. Harries and C. Jamme, eds., *Martin Heidegger: Politics, Art, and Technology.* New York: Holmes and Meier Publishers, 1994.

Seubold, Günter, "Heideggers nachgelassene Klee-Notizen." *Heidegger Studies* 9 (1993): 5–12.

Kunst als Ereignis: Heideggers Weg zu einer nicht mehr metaphysischen Kunst. Bonn: Bouvier Verlag, 1996.

Shermer, Michael, "Patternicity: Finding Meaningful Patterns in Meaningless Noise." *Scientific American Magazine* (December 2008).

Sluga, Hans, "Heidegger's Nietzsche." In H. L. Dreyfus and M. A. Wrathall, eds, *A Companion to Heidegger.* Oxford: Blackwell Publishing, 2005.

Smith, Gregory Bruce, *Nietzsche, Heidegger, and the Transition to Postmodernity.* Chicago: University of Chicago Press, 1996.

Stambaugh, Joan, *The Finitude of Being.* New York: The State University of New York Press, 1992.

Suskind, Ron, "Without a Doubt." *New York Times Magazine* (October 17, 2004).

Swift, Jonathan, *Gulliver's Travels.* New York: Barnes & Noble Classics, 2003.

Taminiaux, Jacques, "The Origin of 'The Origin of the Work of Art.'" In J. Sallis, ed., *Reading Heidegger: Commemorations.* Bloomington: Indiana University Press, 1993.

Taylor, Charles, *The Secular Age.* Cambridge, MA: Harvard University Press, 2007.

Tefler, Elizabeth, "Food as Art." In Alex Neill and Aaron Ridley, eds., *Arguing About Art: Contemporary Philosophical Debates.* London: Routledge, 2008.

Thiele, Leslie Paul, *Timely Meditations: Martin Heidegger and Postmodern Politics.* Princeton: Princeton University Press, 1995.

Thomson, Iain, "Death and Demise in *Being and Time.*" In Mark A. Wrathall, ed., *The Cambridge Companion to Being and Time.* New York: Cambridge University Press, forthcoming 2011.

"Deconstructing the Hero." In Jeff McLaughlin, ed., *Comics as Philosophy*. Jackson: University Press of Mississippi, 2005.

"'Even Better than the Real Thing'? Postmodernity, the Triumph of the Simulacra, and U2." In Mark A. Wrathall, ed., *U2 and Philosophy: How to Decipher an Atomic Band*. Chicago and La Salle: Open Court, 2006.

Heidegger on Ontotheology: Technology and the Politics of Education. Cambridge: Cambridge University Press, 2005.

"Heidegger's Aesthetics." In Edward N. Zalta, ed., *The Stanford Encyclopedia of Philosophy* (2010 edition). <http://plato.stanford.edu/entries/heidegger-aesthetics/>.

"Heidegger's Perfectionist Philosophy of Education in *Being and Time*." *Continental Philosophy Review* 37:4 (2004): 439–67.

"Interpretation as Self-Creation: Nietzsche on the Pre-Platonics." *Ancient Philosophy* 23 (2003): 195–213.

"Ontotheology." In Daniel Dahlstrom, ed., *Interpreting Heidegger: New Essays*. Cambridge: Cambridge University Press, 2011.

"On the Advantages and Disadvantages of Reading Heidegger Backwards: White's *Time and Death*," *Inquiry* 50:1 (2007): 103–20.

"Ontology and Ethics at the Intersection of Phenomenology and Environmental Philosophy." *Inquiry* 47:4 (2004): 380–412.

"Phenomenology and Technology." In S. A. Pedersen, J.-K. B. Olsen, and V. F. Hendricks, eds., *A Companion to Philosophy of Technology*. Oxford: Blackwell, 2009.

"Rethinking Levinas on Heidegger on Death." *The Harvard Review of Philosophy*, Vol. XVI (Fall 2009), 68–87.

"Taylor, Heidegger, Nietzsche: Transcendence and the Problem of Otherworldly Nihilism." *Inquiry* (forthcoming).

"Understanding Technology Ontotheologically, or: The Danger and the Promise of Heidegger, an American Perspective." In J.-K. B. Olsen, E. Selinger, and S. Riis, eds., *New Waves in Philosophy of Technology*. New York: Palgrave Macmillan, 2009.

"The End of Ontotheology: Understanding Heidegger's Turn, Method, and Politics." Ph.D. diss., University of California, San Diego, 1999.

"The Philosophical Fugue: Understanding the Structure and Goal of Heidegger's *Beiträge*." *Journal of the British Society for Phenomenology* 34:1 (2003), 57–73.

"The Silence of the Limbs: Critiquing Culture from a Heideggerian Understanding of the Work of Art." *Enculturation* 2:1 (1998). http://enculturation.gmu.edu/2_1/thomson.html.

Tuan, Yi-Fu, "Time, Space, and Architecture: Some Philosophical Musings." In Xing Ruan and Paul Hogben, eds., *Topophilia and Topophobia: Reflections on Twentieth-Century Human Habitat*. New York: Routledge, 2007.

Tucker, Robert, ed., *The Marx-Engels Reader*. New York: Norton, 1968.

Tuso, Joseph F., ed., *Beowulf*. E. T. Donaldson, trans. New York: Norton, 1975.

Tutu, Desmond, *Believe: The Words and Inspiration of Desmond Tutu*. Boulder, CO: Blue Mountain Press, 2007.

Ungar, Steven, *Scandal and Aftereffect: Blanchot and France since 1930*. Minneapolis: University of Minnesota Press, 1995.

Van Gogh, Vincent, *The Complete Letters of Vincent van Gogh*, 3 vol. R. Harrison, ed., J. van Gogh-Bonger, trans. Boston: Bulfinch, 1991.

Vattimo, Gianni, *Art's Claim to Truth*. S. Zabala, ed., L. D 'Isanto, trans. New York: Columbia University Press, 2008.

Nihilism and Emancipation: Ethics, Politics, and Law. S. Zabala, ed., W. McCuaig, trans. New York: Columbia University Press, 2004.

Vedder, Ben, *Heidegger's Philosophy of Religion: From God to the Gods*. Pittsburgh, PA: Duquesne University Press, 2006.

Von Herrmann. Friedrich-Wilhelm, *Heideggers Philosophie der Kunst*. Frankfurt: Klostermann, 1980.

"Way and Method in Philosophy: Hermeneutic Phenomenology in Thinking the History of Being." P. Emad, trans. In C. Macann, ed., *Critical Heidegger*. London: Routledge, 1996.

Whewell, David, "Aestheticism." In D. Cooper, ed., *A Companion to Aesthetics*. Oxford: Blackwell, 1995.

Williams, Bernard, *Philosophy as a Humanistic Discipline*. Princeton, NJ: Princeton University Press, 2006.

Wittgenstein, Ludwig, *Culture and Value*. G. H. von Wright, ed., P. Winch, trans. Chicago: University of Chicago Press, 1980.

On Certainty. G. E. M. Anscombe and G. H. von Wright, eds., G. E. M. Anscombe, trans. New York: Harper & Row, 1969.

Philosophical Investigations. G. E. M. Anscombe, trans. New York: Macmillan, 1968.

Woessner, Martin, "J. Glenn Gray: Philosopher, Translator (of Heidegger), and Warrior." *Transactions of the Charles S. Peirce Society*, 40:3 (2004).

Wolin, Richard, *The Politics of Being: The Political Thought of Martin Heidegger*. New York: Columbia University Press, 1990.

"Review of Martin Heidegger: Between Good and Evil, by Rüdiger Safranski." *Los Angeles Times Book Review* (12 April 1998).

Wrathall, Mark A., "Between the Earth and the Sky: Heidegger on Life After the Death of God." In Wrathall, ed., *Religion After Metaphysics*. Cambridge: Cambridge University Press, 2005

How to Read Heidegger. New York: Norton, 2006.

ed., *Religion After Metaphysics*. Cambridge: Cambridge University Press, 2003.

Wright, Kathleen, 1998, "Heidegger and Hölderlin." In M. Kelly, ed., *Encyclopedia of Aesthetics*, vol. 2. Oxford: Oxford University Press, 1998.

Young, Julian, *Heidegger, Philosophy, Nazism*. Cambridge: Cambridge University Press, 1997.

Heidegger's Later Philosophy. Cambridge: Cambridge University Press, 2002.

Heidegger's Philosophy of Art. Cambridge: Cambridge University Press, 2001.

Nietzsche's Philosophy of Religion. Cambridge: Cambridge University Press, 2006.

The Death of God and the Meaning of Life. London: Routledge, 2003.

Zabala, Santiago, ed., *The Future of Religion*. New York: Columbia University Press, 2005.

Žižek, Slavoj, *Did Somebody Say Totalitarianism? Five Interventions in the (Mis)use of a Notion*. London: Verso, 2002.

"Disaster Movies as the Last Remnants of Utopia." Interview with Noam Yuran. *Ha'aretz* (English edition), 15 January 2003.

In Defense of Lost Causes. London: Verso, 2008.

Living in the End Times. London: Verso, 2010.

Organs without Bodies: On Deleuze and Consequences. New York: Routledge, 2004.

"Rhetorics of Power." *Diacritics* 31:1 (2001): 98–103.

The Sublime Object of Ideology. London: Verso, 1999.

The Ticklish Subject: The Absent Centre of Political Ontology. London: Verso, 1999.

Index

www.ingramcontent.com/pod-product-compliance
Ingram Content Group UK Ltd.
Pitfield, Milton Keynes, MK11 3LW, UK
UKHW020452010325
455719UK00015B/537